City of Dust

City of Dust

A Cement Company Town in the Land of Tom Sawyer

Gregg Andrews

University of Missouri Press
Columbia and London

Copyright © 1996 by

The Curators of the University of Missouri

University of Missouri Press, Columbia, Missouri 65201

Printed and bound in the United States of America

All rights reserved

5 4 3 2 1   00 99 98 97 96

Library of Congress Cataloging-in-Publication Data

Andrews, Gregg.

   City of dust : a cement company town in the land of Tom

  Sawyer / Gregg Andrews.

     p. cm.

  Includes bibliographical references and index.

  ISBN 0-8262-1074-0 (alk. paper)

   1. Ilasco (Mo.)—History.   2. Ilasco (Mo.)—Social conditions.

3. Portland cement industry—Missouri—Ilasco—History.

4. Working class—Missouri—Ilasco—History.

F474.I23A53   1996

977.8'355—dc20   96-22236

                                                 CIP

Designer: Kristie Lee

Typesetter: BOOKCOMP

Printer and binder: Thomson-Shore, Inc.

Typefaces: Garamond Light, Futura Extra Bold, and Avant Garde

This book was brought to publication with generous assistance
from the Southwest Texas State University Department of History,
and from David and Sally Polc, and Anna Zivicky Polc in memory of John Polc

For Vikki

Make the most of

the sunshine! and

I hope it will last

long—ever so long.

—*Mark Twain*

(CONTENTS)

(ACKNOWLEDGMENTS)

Writing this community history of Ilasco, Missouri, has been a homecoming for me, since I grew up in Monkey Run, a "suburb" of Ilasco. Like many others in the area, I have deep roots in the community on both sides of my family. Except in the book's epilogue, however, I have mostly kept myself out of the narrative. In a few places where I have relied on my own memory for facts and events, I have so indicated in the notes.

One of the great by-products of my Ilasco study has been a personal rediscovery of Mark Twain. As a kid growing up in the Hannibal area, I developed little interest in his writings. Local commercialization of Twain made me apathetic about his literary legacy. For too long, I failed to appreciate the complexities of his thought and writings as a social critic. Fortunately, this study has given me an opportunity to rediscover him.

I have tried to write this book for the public as well as for scholars. I have chosen therefore to avoid historiographical and theoretical discussions, or at least to keep them to a minimum. Above all, history is the study of people, and I have tried to allow the voices of former Ilasco residents to be heard in the narrative. At the same time, I have put the history of Ilasco into a broader context and interpretive framework. This includes a wider treatment of the cement industry, which has scarcely been touched by labor historians.

I hope that I have minimized the misspelling of people's names. Newspapers, court clerks, and census enumerators often butchered the spelling of immigrants' names, and immigrants often changed the spelling of their names at least once. I apologize to those whose names I may have spelled incorrectly.

Working on this book has enriched my life. Ilasco has long been destroyed, but I now better understand how central a sense of community still is to those who grew up there. Research trips home and contacts with former residents around the country have confirmed how tenaciously we still cling to Ilasco. More than ever, I understand that my identity as a historian is rooted in the history of the Atlas Portland Cement Company's labor camp in Ilasco.

I am indebted to many people for sharing photos, family materials, and excitement about this book. Dorothy and Jim Tatman have become accustomed to seeing my car pull into their driveway each summer. They have worked hard to put together an impressive collection of pictures of Ilasco and the cement plant, and they generously provided me with copies of several photos and helped to identify individuals in them. "Ilasco" buttons, hats, videotaped interviews, and license plates are only the most visible manifestations of a deep attachment to the community that they and their families helped to build.

David and Sally Polc also went out of their way to dig up and share family materials and photos. They lavished me with hospitality that included many rich conversations and tasty Slovak sausage washed down with good wine. I am especially indebted to them for much of the information on the Slovak Lutheran community in Ilasco. Without their help, I could never have identified individuals in several of the photos. More importantly, they have become good friends.

Anna Venditti deserves special thanks for opening Al's Tavern on several hot summer days to discuss with me the history of Ilasco. She, too, generously provided me with photos and other materials, as well as her memories. Kenny Lawson joined us on one of those days at Al's Tavern and shared information about his former job at the cement plant and the forced removal of his parents from Ilasco. I hope that Al's Tavern will always be there for Zachary and Alex Andrews, my grandchildren, when they begin to search for their roots.

I also owe special thanks to Armenia Genovese Erlichman for sharing so much of her family's history with me. Getting acquainted with her and her husband, Leonard, has been another pleasant by-product of researching this book. Every family should have someone as dedicated as Armenia to compiling its history.

Perry Jones Jr. has a truly phenomenal memory. Although we have never met, I feel like I know him well as the result of phone conversations and a tape he recorded in response to one of my questionnaires. Fortunately, Jim Tatman videotaped several conversations with him over the last several years and generously provided me with a copy. Perry also furnished many photos.

Numerous others who live or once lived in the area helped me in many ways. Among them are Jane Hemeyer, Stanley D. Sajban, Gloria Vajda Manary, Mildred Kitsock King, Pete Galluzzio, Shirley Lee O'Keefe, Rosa Nemes, John Konko, Melvin Sanders, Rita Mack Beaty, Anna Hustava Sanders, Richard Sanders, Charles Glascock, Dorothy Eichenberger, Angelo Venditti, Juanita Cross Venditti, Virginia Patrick Arthaud, and Henry Sweets, the director of the Mark Twain Boyhood Home and Museum.

I owe a great debt to Hannibal's local historians, J. Hurley Hagood and Roberta Roland Hagood. They generously shared their work and observations on local history and politics. I have benefited from their writings and compilations of local records. They have done a great service to Hannibal. I appreciate their collegiality and value their friendship.

Thomas J. Ferrall and Don Laws, of the USX Corporation, arranged for me to examine selected records of the Atlas Portland Cement Company and its successor, the Universal Atlas Cement Company. They extended many courtesies when I visited USX headquarters in Pittsburgh during the summer of 1992. Although they did not allow me to see payroll records or materials regarding labor, investments, and company practices, they gave me company publications, photos, and public relations materials. Thanks to their authorization, these materials are now in my possession.

Anne Sundermeyer and her staff at the Hannibal Free Public Library made me feel welcome as a regular summer visitor to the Missouri Room. So did Sandra Banghert, the Ralls County Circuit Clerk and Recorder, when I showed up regularly at the courthouse in New London to examine court records. She and her staff cheerfully gave me access to records and a work space in a small, busy office.

Debbi Rhodes, Clerk of the Ralls County Probate Court, also facilitated my access to records. I also appreciate the helpfulness of Carolyn Conners in the Hannibal Court of Common Pleas and other clerks in circuit and county court offices in Pittsfield, Illinois, and Palmyra and Bowling Green, Missouri.

Randy Roberts was especially helpful at the Western Historical Manuscript Collection at the University of Missouri in Columbia. I would also like to thank the staff at the following research centers and archives: Missouri State Archives, State Historical Society of Missouri, Western Historical Manuscript Collection–St. Louis, Mississippi Department of Archives and History, National Archives, Missouri Highway and Transportation Archives, Missouri Historical Society, and the Center for American History at the University of Texas.

Research for this book was funded in part by a Travel to Collections Grant from the National Endowment for the Humanities, and by Faculty Research Enhancement Grants provided by Southwest Texas State University. I wish to thank the State Historical Society of Missouri and the Missouri Historical Society for permission to reprint material from the following articles that were published earlier: "Immigrant Cement Workers: The Strike of 1910 in Ilasco, Missouri," *Missouri Historical Review* 89 (January 1995); "From Robber Caves to Robber Barons: New South Missouri and the Social Construction of Mark Twain, 1910–1935," *Gateway Heritage* 15 (fall 1994); and "Ilasco Cement Workers and the War on Booze in Ralls County, Missouri, 1903–1914," *Gateway Heritage* 17 (spring 1996).

It has been a pleasure to work with Beverly Jarrett, director and editor-in-chief of the University of Missouri Press, and her entire editorial staff, especially Jane Lago, Leanna Hafften, Karen Caplinger, and John Brenner. Beverly enthusiastically supported this book from the beginning. Historians Gary M. Fink and Michael K. Honey provided many helpful suggestions and criticisms of the manuscript while it was under review for publication.

During one of my visits to Hannibal, I was fortunate to walk into Fred's Photos to have some pictures developed. In a conversation with Fred Deters, the owner, I learned that he had many negatives of pictures taken of the cement plant and Ilasco schools. I thank him for allowing me to develop prints from those negatives stored in old boxes that he had kept when he purchased Herring's Studio years ago. Many of the photos in this book come from those negatives.

In a sense, this book has been a family effort. More years ago than I care to remember, my brother, Kevin, and I first discussed why a study of Ilasco would be important to scholars as well as to the people who lived there. We went to the State Historical Society of Missouri and the Ralls County courthouse, where he helped with some of the preliminary research. Some of the notes that he took at that time proved useful as I wrote this book. In addition, Cheryl Genovese, my sister, accompanied me on a trip to the courthouse in Pike County, Illinois, where she, too, took an active part in searching marriage records. Over the years, we have had many conversations about the history of our community.

My father, Maurice Andrews (1917–1965), has been dead for more than thirty years, but many Ilasco residents remember how his guitar playing and singing sometimes made a hard life seem a bit easier. Known for his Depression-era blues, storytelling, and train songs, he left a lot of himself in Atlas's quarries. I hope this book somehow does justice to his life's struggle.

I owe a particular debt of gratitude to my mother, Virginia Sudholt, and her husband, Allan Sudholt. At times, they provided a place to stay and ran errands for me to the Hannibal Public Library and local courthouses. In a few cases, my mother obtained information for me through telephone conversations and visits to people's homes. During pleasant summer evenings, we often discussed Ilasco while feeding ice cream sandwiches to their dog, Big Red. My mother's incredible genealogical bent has been of great value, and her lifelong excitement about the past has obviously been contagious.

I especially want to thank my wife and colleague, Vikki Bynum, who has enriched my life and this book. Being married to a fellow historian has obvious benefits, and I have benefited from her observations, criticisms, and recommendations, as well as her own scholarship and companionship. Summer research trips together have been mutually productive and fun. From her new research on Mississippi to mine on Ilasco, we have shared many conversations, hotels, interstate rest stops, and walks through old cemeteries. She has come to know Ilasco and me. I dedicate this book to her.

City of Dust

(INTRODUCTION)

Human nature cannot be studied in cities except at a disadvantage—a village is the place. There you can know your man inside and out—in a city you but know his crust; and his crust is usually a lie.
—Mark Twain, *Notebook,* 1882

Mark Twain's boyhood home of Hannibal, Missouri, attracts countless tourists eager to see the modern commercial version of the cultural landscape that produced the town's most famous citizen. Commercial exploiters and local guardians of Twain's legacy shuttle visitors from landmark to landmark, gift shop to gift shop, and restaurant to restaurant. The "Twainland Express" hauls tourists to many important sites, including the famous cave hollow just south of town where a mischievous Samuel Clemens and childhood buddies often whiled away Saturdays playing and dreaming of finding riches and adventure.

For those who depart from the standard tour, break from the pack, and drive about a mile further south of the Mark Twain Cave into Ralls County on scenic Highway 79, a sudden break in the steep bluffs along the Mississippi River reveals a huge cement plant that seems out of place in an otherwise rustic setting. Unbeknown to most passersby, a section of the Continental Cement Company's property once known as Pump House Hill, just north of the plant, contains another of Tom Sawyer's caves. Unlike the Mark Twain Cave area, however, the LeBaume Cave did not become a tourist attraction or picnic site. Instead, it became a casualty of the industrial transformation that engulfed Twain's boyhood playground when the Atlas Portland Cement Company built a plant there in 1901. Plant security guards, huge silos, barges, loading docks, quarries, and trucks bringing industrial wastes for incineration in Continental's huge cement kiln now dominate the Saturday land of Tom Sawyer.

A road sign by the cement plant bears the name of Ilasco, at one time a largely immigrant community born of the Industrial Revolution but more recently a casualty of commercial interests. The town's very name, comprised of letters representing cement manufacturing ingredients, suggests that its history and fate have been inextricably linked to the cement plant nearby. As travelers slow down a bit for a better look at the plant and soon negotiate a sharp westward bend

1

in the highway, they see an old concrete bridge across Marble Creek a few hundred feet south of the highway. On the other side of the bridge, which holds only one lane of traffic, the residence of Charlie, Billy, and Rosa Nemes, children of Hungarian immigrants, immediately greets those drawn from the highway by the bridge's rustic appeal. Thanks to a relentless devotion to beauty and hard work, the Nemes family's flower garden and landscaping in the face of periodic floods throughout the years have added a dignified charm to the working-class community of Monkey Run, a "suburb" of Ilasco with modest houses and about one hundred residents.

This section, too, developed in response to the early need for housing among the cement plant's predominantly immigrant workers. Despite the hard work put into beautifying the landscape around the Nemes home since the 1920s, it was not until recently that the foreign-owned Continental Cement Company allowed the family to buy the land on which their home sits. Unlike Ilasco proper, however, most property in Monkey Run was never acquired by the cement plant. Monkey Run, pinched between the Mississippi River and steep hills and bluffs, is still intact despite a record flood in the summer of 1993 that nearly wiped it out.

Travelers through Monkey Run soon discover that they are on a dead-end road and must return to Highway 79. As they turn back onto the highway south, they see other reminders that an industrial community once flourished beneath the very pavement over which their automobiles carry them. The Holy Cross Catholic Church, sandwiched between the highway and the cement plant's old stockhouse number five, still holds services on cement plant property as the result of a long-standing company lease. Next to the church, a house lived in for years by the family of Ruth and Andy Babyak still holds tenants, and part of what used to be a park is nearby.

Almost directly across the highway, a gravel road leads across a rickety iron bridge to Al's Tavern on the banks of Marble Creek. Next to the tavern are an abandoned old concrete jail and the Ilasco Methodist Church. The road comes to an unnaturally abrupt halt at that point, but for those curious enough to get out of their cars and venture into surroundings overgrown with brush, trees, and weeds, the terrain reveals an important secret known mainly to only those who were once part of Ilasco's past. Hidden in the brush are foundations of school buildings, the Church of the Nazarene, a justice of the peace court building, and other homes and stores torn down in the early to mid-1960s when Highway 79 was routed through the middle of the community.

The lights at Al's Tavern are no longer on as much as they once were, but if thirsty or curious tourists, area residents, and historians are lucky, an open front door and perhaps a car or two out front will draw them inside. The proprietor, Anna Sunderlik Venditti, keeps the place open more out of a sense of history than for profit. She has no set hours, but often opens "by appointment" if area residents phone in their requests. She makes change from a change purse and at times treats customers to a beer if she is enjoying the conversation.

Seventy-six years old when I talked to her about this book for the first time in the summer of 1992, "Miss Al," as she is affectionately called by some local residents, took over the operation of the tavern when her husband, Albert Venditti, the son of Italian immigrants, died in 1987. Albert had owned the tavern since 1939, and she decided to keep it open for the sake of tradition and, according to her, to keep her mind sharp. As the daughter of Slovak immigrants, she has maintained a fierce pride in her ethnic roots, working-class identity, and the community of Ilasco that produced her, even though that community was forced to dissolve about thirty years ago. Although Roman Catholic, she often joins other area women who gather at the Methodist church across the road to do quilting, socialize, and keep alive memories of the community.

"Miss Al" urges visitors to sign a register that contains the names of many Mark Twain tourists from places as far away as Japan. A twinkle in her eyes belies a feistiness and zest for life that she gladly shares with patrons as discussions turn to the history of Ilasco. In particular, she likes to share stories about how immigrants from different countries came together, overcame language and cultural barriers, and joined common struggles to carve out a better life for themselves in a rural industrial village. It is here perhaps that some tourists find a slice of American history infinitely richer and more meaningful than that served up by an endless number of Hannibal shops, hotels, restaurants, and other commercial enterprises that bear the name of Mark Twain or his fictional characters.

Not much else is left of Ilasco. On the north side of Highway 79, cement plant equipment has long since flattened the Martin Luther Slovak Church and houses that once surrounded it. To the west, the families of Jack and Mary Rita Zerbonia Brothers and Consetta Fiorella Kellick still cling to their property, but living boxed in between the cement plant's expanded quarries and the highway has at times meant noisy disruptions and inconveniences. Beyond that point, houses along what residents used to call Country Hill still dot the new highway, but they, too, have had problems with company blasting in the quarries that now extend for miles up the valleys on both sides of the highway.

Strangers are surprised to learn that Ilasco, including the sections of Company Row, Monkey Run, and Pump House Hollow, was once a thriving community with perhaps as many as three thousand residents before World War I. Before 1910, it was a hotbed of labor militancy. Following an explosive strike and occupation of the town by the Missouri National Guard in 1910, however, the Atlas company reimposed its power on a community badly scarred by ethnic antagonisms. Not until 1943 did workers overcome these divisions to unionize the cement plant.

For the Atlas Portland Cement Company's junior partners in Hannibal who played a role in the industrial transformation of Mark Twain's boyhood terrain, the introduction of a "foreign colony" with militant workers and full saloons posed a public relations problem in Missouri's Little Dixie. After Twain's death, Atlas's Hannibal attorney, George A. Mahan, and other officials launched a sophisticated campaign designed in part to assure local residents that the eastern corporate newcomers were worthy caretakers of Twain's heritage. This campaign included not only the preservation of Twain landmarks in Hannibal but also a shaping of the public's understanding of Twain's thought and writings. In part, this served to strengthen public support for the very forces responsible for gobbling up Twain's slice of "mossback" Missouri.

Although Ilasco originated as a labor camp, Atlas at first did not control the land site. Company Row and Pump House Hollow belonged to Atlas, but the rest of Ilasco and Monkey Run did not. Atlas extended its efforts to assert greater control over its labor force, however, from the workplace to the community itself. By the 1920s, after complicated will disputes and court-ordered sheriff's sales of land, Atlas had gained control over enough property to convert Ilasco into a company town and play an even greater role in shaping the growth of its schools, churches, and other cultural institutions. This paternalism did not come without strings attached, however, for Atlas and its successor, the Universal Atlas Cement Company, acquired the power to determine the very existence of the unincorporated community.

For about sixty years, native-born and immigrant residents struggled to forge a community identity and build a better life in Ilasco. In the early years, many of Atlas's workers came and left town without staying long enough to sink down roots. Job-related accidents killed or crippled many others. A core of workers and their families stayed long enough, however, to build a community that revolved around cement manufacturing. The struggle for survival bred tough people who fought tooth and nail for dignity and self-respect in an often hostile environment. This was especially true of immigrants and their children from southern and eastern Europe who faced countless insults inside and outside the community. Nearby, a kind of colonial mind-set determined the way Hannibal residents and civic and business leaders viewed Ilasco. They valued Ilasco primarily for its economic worth to Hannibal and reacted to Ilasco with a blend of curiosity, humor, fear, and at times outright contempt.

By 1960, some of the same forces with which the community had long been in conflict determined that Ilasco had become expendable. The U.S. Steel Corporation, parent company of Universal Atlas, working hand in glove with Hannibal commercial interests, the state of Missouri, and the United States government, dissolved Ilasco to make room for a new highway and plant modernization and expansion. This facilitated completion of the Great River Road system extending along both sides of the Mississippi River from Canada to the Gulf of New Mexico, and it promoted the expansion of Missouri tourism. The "City of Dust" became the casualty of forces spearheaded at least in part by Hannibal business leaders who hoped to lure tourists to what was rapidly becoming Hannibal's cottage industry—the commercialization of Mark Twain.

Part I

A Foreign
Colony in
Mossback
Missouri

(1)

From Robber Caves to Robber Barons

Atlas Portland Cement and the Transformation
of Mark Twain's Boyhood Playground

A Robber is more high-toned than what a pirate is—as a general thing. In most countries they're awful high up in the nobility—dukes and such.
—**Mark Twain,** *The Adventures of Tom Sawyer*

In 1882, when Mark Twain returned to the Mississippi River to gather more material for his book *Life on the Mississippi,* it marked the first time in twenty years that he had visited the South. Nostalgia and a romanticized boyhood image of the antebellum South quickly gave way to pessimism and bitterness as he passed southward through his native Missouri. Disturbed by the violence, racism, sluggishness, coarse language, tobacco chewing, and other features of Southern life, he complained of stagnation and lack of economic progress since the Civil War. He found little evidence of the New South transformation championed by those who viewed industrialization, immigration, and urbanization as the keys to dynamic economic and social growth. "There is hardly a celebrated Southern name in any of the departments of human industry," he complained, "except those of war, murder, the duel, repudiation, and massacre."[1]

Twain, of course, grew up on the border of Missouri's agricultural "Little Dixie" region. Ralls, along with other nearby Salt River counties such as Lincoln, Pike, Marion, and Monroe, had constituted the second most significant slave-holding area in Missouri before the Civil War. In 1860, they contained fifteen thousand slaves, or one-eighth of the state's slave population of 114,931. Slaves made up between 15 and 24 percent of the total population of these leading

---

1. Quoted in Edward L. Ayers, *The Promise of the New South: Life after Reconstruction,* 344. For the impact of this trip down the Mississippi River upon Twain's thought, see Arthur G. Pettit, *Mark Twain and the South,* chap. 5.

tobacco-producing counties. During Twain's boyhood years in the area, slaves constituted about 22 percent of Ralls's population.[2]

Ralls County had been a bastion of pro-Confederate sentiment during the Civil War. Shortly after the outbreak of hostilities, in fact, Twain returned to Hannibal, joined the Marion County Rangers, and along with several local associates linked up with Confederate volunteers in Ralls County. When his flirtation with the Confederacy ended after only a few weeks, he left for Nevada, but Absalom Grimes, one of his associates and a fellow river pilot, became a Confederate mail runner. Grimes, who married the daughter of James Glascock, Ralls County's largest slaveholder, delivered mail to Missouri volunteers fighting for the Confederacy in Mississippi and Louisiana.[3]

Although Missouri did not secede from the Union, a bitter guerrilla war unleashed hatreds that offered a preview of race relations that would greet and shape Ilasco's immigrants. By the end of the Civil War, white vigilantes in Missouri had already begun to lynch blacks. For free blacks who refused to leave the region, the threat of lynching loomed on the horizon. In Ralls County, a local German farmer received a threat from a bushwhacker who warned that " 'my garrilis is heard that you have a cople of famallely of negros settle on your plase. . . . If you dont make dam negroes leve there ride away I will hang the last negro on the plase and you will fair wors for we cant stand the dutch [Germans] and negros both.' "[4]

After the Civil War, the area continued to bear the legacy of its pro-slavery, pro-Confederate associations. On the eve of the Atlas Portland Cement Company's arrival, there were still few signs that the New South vision of industrialization and urbanization had even remotely touched Ralls County. The economy and people remained primarily agricultural and wedded to the Democratic party. In 1900, there was an average of only 108 wage earners employed in manufacturing and mechanical industries throughout the county. Seventy-five percent of the county's

2. David D. March, *The History of Missouri,* vol. 1, 810; R. Douglas Hurt, *Agriculture and Slavery in Missouri's Little Dixie,* xii; Goldena Howard, *Ralls County Missouri,* 57–58; 1860 Census Population Schedules, Missouri: Slave Schedules, Ralls County, microfilm roll 146. One of the tracts south of the cement plant that later became a subdivision of Ilasco was once a slave plantation owned by Henry A. Harris. Philip C. Smashey, comp., "History of the Smasheys, 1770–1972," 130.

3. Charles Neider, ed., *The Autobiography of Mark Twain,* 111; J. Hurley Hagood and Roberta Roland Hagood, *The Story of Hannibal,* 53–54; idem, *Hannibal Yesterdays: Historic Stories of Events, People, Landmarks and Happenings in and near Hannibal,* 115–20; 1860 Census Population Schedules, Missouri: Slave Schedules, Saverton township, Ralls County, microfilm roll 146. See Twain's "The Private History of a Campaign That Failed," published in 1885, for an account of his brief experience as a Confederate volunteer.

4. Quoted in Michael Fellman, *Inside War: The Guerrilla Conflict in Missouri during the Civil War,* 70.

490 square miles were devoted to agriculture. Corn was the most significant crop, followed by hay and wheat. Tobacco production no longer took place on a large scale, but horse raising and cattle farming were important enterprises.[5]

The area just west of the future cement plant site consisted of scattered farms that supported a school and a Methodist church with a cemetery on the premises at Marble Creek. Many people in the area depended on produce and orchard farming, gardening, fishing, and woodchopping for their livelihood. The value of land in this timber-bearing area along the Mississippi River bluffs was much below the average price of farms in the county, but the prevalence of limestone soon raised land prices in the county's northeast corner.[6]

The evidence suggests that at least some residents at that time did not view land simply as a commodity to be bought and sold for profit. This does not mean that they were necessarily anticapitalist, but it does indicate that the profit motive was not always at the core of their values. Shortly before Atlas penetrated the area, for example, the owner of a nearby farm had more on his mind than simply financial considerations as he prepared to sell his land. In his own handwriting, he added a stipulation to the sale, requiring the buyer to promise to be a good custodian of the orchard on the land, to clean debris out of it, and to plant new trees if the old ones became damaged.[7]

In 1900, the county's stagnant population of 12,287 had declined by seven since 1890, and its incorporated towns were quite small. New London, the county seat and largest town, had only 881 residents. Next in size were Perry, which had a population of 624, and Center, whose population was 300.[8]

One of the main reasons for Ralls County's stagnant population was the exodus of African Americans between 1890 and 1900. In 1890, there were 1,077 black residents in the county, but ten years later, that figure had dropped by 13.9 percent to 927. In contrast, the native-born white population showed a slight increase during the same period. By 1900, African Americans made up only 7.54 percent of Ralls's people—a far cry from the days when slaves constituted

5. *Census Reports,* vol. 8, Twelfth Census of the United States Taken in the Year 1900. Manufactures, pt. 2: States and Territories, 480; Walter Williams, ed., *The State of Missouri: An Autobiography,* 488.

6. Williams, ed., *State of Missouri,* 488–89. On the Marble Creek Methodist Church, see Church Records Form, July 25, 1941, microfilm roll 573, folder 17459, U.S. Work Projects Administration—Historical Records Survey, Missouri, 1935–1942, Western Historical Manuscript Collection, Columbia, Missouri (hereafter cited as U.S. WPA-HRS, followed by microfilm roll and folder numbers, WHMC–Columbia). On the Marble Creek school, see *Hannibal Courier-Post,* November 21, 1904.

7. A copy of the deed to this land is in the possession of Marvin Sanders. This land is now part of the Continental Cement Company's quarry.

8. *Census Reports,* vol. 1, Twelfth Census of the United States Taken in the Year 1900. Population, pt. 1, 28; Williams, ed., *State of Missouri,* 489.

approximately 22 percent of the county's population. Former slaves had voted with their feet. The Ralls County world that Atlas's immigrants would soon step into was a white one indeed.[9]

A virulent racism at the core of Ralls County's pro-Confederate, slaveholding legacy undoubtedly had helped to drive out many African Americans when they struggled to exercise citizenship rights after emancipation. This racism received expression in the Democratic party, the political instrument used by Southern elites to reestablish white supremacy after the Civil War. So intense was this racial hatred that it became folk wisdom in turn-of-the-century New London that neither blacks nor Republicans were allowed in town after sundown.[10]

Hardening racist attitudes, reinforced by legal segregation, black disfranchisement, and bloodthirsty white lynch mobs, characterized the decade before Ilasco's immigrants arrived. The Missouri Constitution of 1875 prohibited marrying across the color line, but by the turn of the century, Southern whites had become almost obsessed with fears of interracial sex between black men and white women. "Rape and rumors of rape," writes historian Jacquelyn Dowd Hall, "became the folk pornography of the Bible Belt."[11]

Racist ideology emphasized the need to protect white women from black men who allegedly could not restrain their lust since "white women were the forbidden fruit, the untouchable property, the ultimate symbol of white male power."[12] Popular images dehumanized black men as rapists and encouraged a frenzy of grisly lynchings, mutilations, burnings, and other forms of torture by white Southern vigilantes who regarded black men as mere animals. As historian Joel Williamson writes, "Whites began the practice of lynching as a reaction against the presumed threat of the black beast to white womanhood, but it soon became an appalling habit, applicable to a wide range of offenses, real or imagined."[13]

Most lynchings occurred in the Deep South, but they took place in Missouri, too. In 1901, vigilantes near Pierce City lynched three African Americans, burned out five households, and chased thirty families out of their homes in response to the murder of a young white woman. This infuriated Mark Twain, who by now had moved away from his earlier racism. In "The United States of Lyncherdom,"

9. *Census Reports,* vol. 1, Twelfth Census . . . 1900. Population, pt. 1, 28, 510, 547.

10. Jane Hemeyer, telephone interview by author, October 30, 1994.

11. Jacquelyn Dowd Hall, "'The Mind That Burns in Each Body': Women, Rape, and Racial Violence," in Hall, Jacquelyn Dowd, James Leloudis, Robert Korstad, Mary Murphy, Lu Ann Jones, and Christopher P. Daly, *Like a Family: The Making of a Southern Cotton Mill World,* 64; David Thelen, *Paths of Resistance: Tradition and Democracy in Industrializing Missouri,* 139.

12. Hall, "'Mind That Burns,'" 64.

13. Joel Williamson, *The Crucible of Race: Black-White Relations in the American South since Emancipation,* 184; Hall, "'Mind That Burns,'" 64.

written that year but not published until after his death, he criticized the spread of lynch mob violence into his home state and attributed public support for lynchings to moral cowardice.[14]

In this racial context, even the mere sight of a black man at times could throw Ralls County white women into a panic. For example, Ilasco judge John Northcutt bound over John Griggsby, an African American, to a grand jury in July 1906 after Etta Hays accused Griggsby of attempted criminal assault. The trouble reportedly occurred after Hays stepped off a train at Salt River switch and began to walk to her house nearby. She spotted Griggsby, whose "peculiar" behavior frightened her and prompted her to seek refuge in a neighbor's house. Although she admitted that Griggsby never came within fifty yards of her, the judge still held him for the grand jury. The *Hannibal Courier-Post* predicted that the charges would be dismissed, and even complained about the implications of such racial hysteria: "Justices should use some discretion in making decisions as personal liberty at times depends upon their actions."[15]

Although black women were sometimes lynched, too, they more commonly were the victims of sexual exploitation. Slave women had been vulnerable to the sexual demands of their owners, and white men's insistence on sexual access to black women did not end with emancipation. Sexual violence by white men against black women became particularly vicious in the late nineteenth century. Sex with black women was an expression of white men's virility and racial domination. At a time when images of white women as passionless prevailed, notions that black women had more primitive, voracious sexual appetites titillated white men. Samuel Heinbach, a Saverton township woodchopper and one of Ilasco's landlords, insisted that "if a man never had sexual communications with a negro wench, he hadn't lived his full life."[16]

Republicans in the nearby Marion County town of Hannibal criticized Ralls County residents for not shaking off their pro-Confederate feathers and allegiances to the Democratic party. They pointed with pride to Hannibal's economic

---

14. Mark Twain, "The United States of Lyncherdom," in Frederick Anderson, ed., *A Pen Warmed-Up in Hell: Mark Twain in Protest,* 151–59. For a discussion of Twain's views on race, see Philip S. Foner, *Mark Twain: Social Critic,* chap. 6, and Pettit, *Twain and the South,* chaps. 9–12.

15. *Hannibal Courier-Post,* July 12, 1906.

16. *Mary Alice Heinbach v. Jesse Heinbach et al.,* April term, 1918, case no. 20303, trial transcript, 746, Missouri Supreme Court Files, Missouri State Archives, Jefferson City, Mo. (hereafter cited as MSCF-MSA); Hall, " 'Mind That Burns,' " 62–65; Victoria E. Bynum, *Unruly Women: The Politics of Social and Sexual Control in the Old South,* 96–97. Darlene Clark Hine, "Rape and the Inner Lives of Southern Black Women: Thoughts on the Culture of Dissemblance," argues that black women, because of their sexual vulnerability and powerlessness, developed a "culture of dissemblance" that facilitated their survival against rape and fears of rape.

growth around 1900 and tweaked Ralls's leaders for their sluggishness. Republicans took credit for this industrial development. The *Hannibal Courier-Post* chided "Old Ralls" for not breaking the "fetters of burbonism," and urged voters to embrace the Republican party as the instrument of industrial progress.[17]

When Mark Twain visited his boyhood home for the last time in 1902, there were unmistakable signs that Hannibal was in the midst of a transformation. At least a partial uplift was even under way south of town across the county line. Sweeping economic and social changes transformed the cultural landscape that had shaped much of Twain's thought and writing. Industrialization reshaped the image of Hannibal as a sleepy, Southern river town and encroached upon the terrain that had provided a playground for him and boyhood friends.[18]

In part, the transformation was the product of an aggressive campaign by local businessmen, civic leaders, newspaper owners, and lawyers to promote Hannibal as an important manufacturing center in the New South. To woo outside investors, the board of directors of Hannibal's Business Men's Association bought a tract of land close to the Union train station on the south side of town and offered this land as free factory sites. Boosters touted Hannibal's low tax rate, favorable business climate, and excellent shipping facilities by rail or by barge on the Mississippi River. They also praised Hannibal's cultural and religious institutions, schools, and athletic social organizations like the Country Club. This boosterism, coordinated by the Business Men's Association and the Merchants' Association, stimulated the growth of new factories and created rising expectations for even more. Hannibal's leading spokesmen confidently predicted that its population, which had increased from 12,780 in 1900 to 16,529 in June 1903, would reach 40,000 by 1911.[19]

By 1901, eastern capital had invaded the hollow three miles south of Hannibal where the cave popularized by Twain's writings was located. In his *Autobiography,* Twain recalled the importance of this hollow to his childhood, when he and friends had caught "gold fever" from men "streaming through" Hannibal in the frenzied California gold rush of 1849. "On the Saturday holidays in summertime," he wrote, "we used to borrow skiffs whose owners were not present and go down the river three miles to the cave hollow, and there we staked out claims

17. *Hannibal Courier-Post,* October 26, 1906.

18. Robert M. Crisler, "Missouri's 'Little Dixie.'" On the role of slavery in Missouri's Little Dixie, see Hurt, *Agriculture and Slavery.* For a discussion of how Twain's images of Hannibal influenced his writings, see Henry Nash Smith, "Mark Twain's Images of Hannibal: From St. Petersburg to Eseldorf."

19. *Hannibal Courier-Post,* March 18, 1905, and December 21, 1906; Williams, ed., *State of Missouri,* 303–6; Thomas H. Bacon, *A Mirror of Hannibal,* 164–65; *Census Reports,* vol. 1, Twelfth Census . . . 1900. Population, pt. 1, 460. For syntheses of the New South, see C. Vann Woodward, *Origins of the New South, 1877–1913,* and Ayers, *Promise.*

and pretended to dig gold, panning out half a dollar a day at first; two or three times as much, later, and by and by whole fortunes, as our imaginations became inured to the work."[20]

As Twain noted, the cave hollow finally yielded riches not in gold but in the form of portland cement. "That region was all dirt and rocks to us," he remembered, "yet all it needed was to be ground up and scientifically handled and it was gold."[21] To extract the new riches, however, required more than a handful of mischievous boys looking for summertime fun on "borrowed" skiffs. It required extensive quarry and manufacturing operations that could be organized only by a corporation with abundant capital, sophisticated technology, and a large industrial labor force.

It was Yankee capital that financed these operations. Thanks in large part to the pioneering work of David O. Saylor in the 1870s, the Lehigh Valley of Pennsylvania had become the cradle of portland cement manufacturing in the United States. After moving to Allentown, Saylor bought property along the Lehigh Valley Railroad near Coplay station, created the Coplay Cement Company, and began to sell "Saylor's Portland Cement." Other companies popped up around the country, but most soon failed, leaving the United States dependent on foreign cement. In 1881, imports accounted for 221,000 barrels of cement, while domestic output totaled only 60,000 barrels.[22]

The rise of eastern corporations that could harness important technological innovations in cement manufacturing in the late 1880s and 1890s propelled capitalists into an ever-widening search for manufacturing sites and markets. In 1888, Jose F. De Navarro through his son Alfonso had purchased the right to manufacture portland cement under a patent belonging to Frederick Ransome, an Englishman. Under De Navarro, the Keystone Cement Company, incorporated in New York in 1889, also began to produce portland cement in Pennsylvania's Lehigh Valley. It set up a plant at Coplay and introduced the rotary kiln process to burn the raw cement materials. Although the cement was of rather poor quality, production at the Coplay plant soon reached three hundred barrels a day.[23]

De Navarro improved the rotary kiln process but suffered financial problems. He met with John Rogers Maxwell, Wall Street tycoon and president of the Central Railroad of New Jersey, to ask for capital to secure new properties and expand

20. Neider, ed., *Autobiography,* 81.

21. Ibid., 81–82.

22. Robert W. Lesley, John B. Lober, and George S. Bartlett, *History of the Portland Cement Industry in the United States,* 50–55, 67–68.

23. Ibid., 109–10; Earl J. Hadley, *The Magic Powder: History of the Universal Atlas Cement Company and the Cement Industry,* chap. 3. For Jose F. De Navarro's role in the development of the early portland cement industry, I have used a typescript copy of his book, "Sixty-Six Years' Business Record," printed in 1904 (copy in author's possession).

operations in the Lehigh Valley. He asked to borrow sixty thousand dollars, offering no security for the loan other than the properties. He stressed that the main line of Maxwell's railroad, which connected with the Lehigh Valley railroad, passed very close to his cement operations. This, De Navarro emphasized, would sharply increase business and profits for the Central Railroad of New Jersey.[24]

De Navarro received the loan and formed an important business relationship with Maxwell that quickly led to an even bigger deal. When De Navarro incorporated the Standard Portland Cement Company of New Jersey in 1890, Maxwell became president of the new company, while De Navarro and his son Alfonso were elected vice president and second vice president, respectively. Keystone changed its name to the Atlas Cement Company of New York, a subsidiary of the Standard Portland Cement Company, which expanded operations in the mid-1890s at Northampton, Pennsylvania. All of these corporate developments culminated in the formation of the Atlas Portland Cement Company, incorporated in Pennsylvania in 1899. Again, Maxwell became the president, while Jose and Alfonso De Navarro were selected as vice presidents.[25]

High transportation costs encouraged the development of cement manufacturing as primarily a local industry. Markets were often restricted to the territory immediately surrounding the plant. Atlas officials, eager to tap the growing market in the Mississippi River Valley, sent General Superintendent Henry J. Seaman to Hannibal to explore the possibility of building a plant in the area. Hannibal attorney George A. Mahan, a former Democratic state representative with important ties to other corporations, real estate developers, and bankers in St. Louis, showed Seaman a study conducted by a geology professor at the University of Missouri in 1849. The report indicated that the bluffs overlooking the Mississippi River at Hannibal contained rich deposits of limestone and shale. This encouraged Seaman to order extensive topographical surveys in the Mark Twain Cave hollow, where a small brick plant was located. He secured an option to buy the brick plant and the land surrounding it, but not the cave itself.[26]

Guy D. Helmick, a civil engineer from Pennsylvania, arrived in Hannibal on January 1, 1901, to conduct topographical surveys for Atlas. Chemist L. P. Sprout and engineer Frank N. Smith soon joined him. They surveyed the land, drilled for samples of limestone and shale deposits, and shipped samples back east for chemical analysis. Tests performed on these samples revealed that the limestone

24. De Navarro, "Business Record," 4.

25. De Navarro, "Business Record," 5; Lesley, Lober, and Bartlett, *History of the Portland Cement Industry,* 109–10, 284.

26. Bernard H. Topkis, "Labor Requirements in Cement Production," 575; Guy D. Helmick, "The Hannibal Cement Plant Story," Guy D. Helmick Manuscript (January 1952, 1–2), WHMC–Columbia; *Hannibal Courier-Post,* December 31, 1930. A biographical sketch of Mahan is in Floyd Calvin Shoemaker, *Missouri and Missourians: Land of Contrasts and People of Achievements,* vol. 5, 95–96.

and shale were suitable for the manufacture of cement, but the cave hollow, which featured a picnic area for Mark Twain Cave tourists, was too small to accommodate a plant. Atlas officials then hired Hannibal attorneys Mahan and George Clayton to obtain options on farms in a valley about three miles south of Hannibal adjacent to the cave hollow.[27]

Despite efforts by Atlas representatives to keep their activities cloaked in secrecy, the drilling and surveying in the Mark Twain Cave area attracted public attention. On January 12, 1901, the *Hannibal Morning Journal* featured a front-page story trumpeting the expected construction of a large cement plant south of town. The newspaper cautioned that the final decision depended on the results of tests performed on the appropriate raw materials, but added that prospects for securing the plant were good. According to the newspaper, Atlas had already taken options on nearly five hundred acres of land in the area.[28]

Atlas officials also considered locating the plant at Iola, Kansas, or Alton, Illinois, instead of Hannibal. Later that winter Helmick and Sprout traveled to Iola to report on a new plant operated by the Iola Portland Cement Company on a site that included deposits of cheap natural gas used for fuel. They spent a few days there taking samples, and a local promoter finally secured permission to take them on a twenty-minute tour of the plant. Acting on the recommendations of Helmick and Sprout, Atlas authorized the purchase of options at Iola as well as Hannibal, but when Maxwell and other Atlas officials went to Iola, smallpox signs on nearby houses dissuaded them from getting off their private railroad car. They allowed the option to lapse and chose Hannibal as the site for the new plant. Helmick and Sprout had also collected samples of limestone and shale at Alton, but Sprout strongly favored Hannibal, "where he had become active in the social life of the town and disliked the idea of leaving there."[29]

Although the smallpox scare at Iola or Sprout's enchantment with Hannibal's social life may have had an impact on Atlas's decision to build the plant near Hannibal, there were also pragmatic business reasons for selecting the site. Atlas officials could enjoy access to extensive deposits of shale and limestone, and tap the Mississippi River as a convenient source of water power and shipping. A steady stream of steamboat traffic linked Hannibal to St. Louis, just 120 miles to the south, and many key industrial cities in the Mississippi Valley. An impressive network of railroad lines also tied Hannibal to St. Louis, Chicago, and other important markets. Nearby coalfields in Illinois provided reliable access to a fuel supply.[30]

27. Helmick, "Cement Plant Story," 2; *Hannibal Morning Journal,* January 31, 1901; *Hannibal Courier-Post,* December 31, 1930.

28. See also *Hannibal Morning Journal,* January 17 and 31, 1901.

29. Helmick, "Cement Plant Story," 2–3. On the role of natural gas in the early cement industry in Kansas, see Lesley, Lober, and Bartlett, *History of the Portland Cement Industry,* 166–67.

30. *Hannibal Courier-Post,* December 31, 1930.

In June 1901, Atlas publicized its selection of Hannibal. Attorney Mahan informed the local press that he was wrapping up deals to buy the coveted land south of the Mark Twain Cave. "I have been instructed to close up the options on the land, about one thousand acres," he said, "and I shall do that as rapidly as possible."[31]

The local press praised Mahan and Atlas officials for skillfully handling the land deals: "As shrewd business men they moved cautiously and were close-mouthed."[32] Nevertheless, an editorial in the *Hannibal Morning Journal* on June 2, 1901, warned local residents not to become too greedy by asking high prices for land that Atlas wanted. The editorial emphasized that local residents by doing so might cripple Hannibal's bid to compete with other western locations for investments of eastern capital.

By midsummer, Mahan had arranged the purchase of farms situated primarily in sections two and three of Saverton township in the northeast corner of Ralls County. The original Atlas tract, just across the Marion County line south of Hannibal, consisted of more than one thousand acres. It included a farm once owned by David E. Wade, whose earlier attempt to establish a lithographic company on the site had forced him into bankruptcy.[33]

Atlas did not buy the Mark Twain Cave or the picnic area immediately surrounding it, but it did buy the Peter A. LeBaume Cave, once mistakenly thought to have been an old entrance to the same cave used by Samuel Clemens. Heirs of the Wade estate had sold this cave to Edward Medcalf just before he in turn sold it to Atlas. Medcalf told the local newspaper that he wanted the cave "simply as an investment."[34]

Atlas's land appetite drove up real estate values in the area. For example,

---

31. Quoted in *Hannibal Weekly Journal,* June 1, 1901.

32. Ibid.

33. The tract included lands formerly owned by Cato Abbott (120 acres), Madison Turner (100 acres), Willie Edwards (95 acres), Alfred W. Bulkley (15 acres), Alfred W. Bulkley et al. (195 acres), Spencer Tilbe (98 acres), Martin L. Blake (30 acres), Edward Medcalf (171 acres), James C. Tucker (40 acres), Melvina Myers (5 acres), S. P. Balthrope (58 acres), and George Whitecotton (35 acres). Cato Abbott to Henry J. Seaman, May 23, 1901; Madison Turner to Henry J. Seaman, June 3, 1901; Willie Edwards to Henry J. Seaman, May 27, 1901; Alfred W. Bulkley to Henry J. Seaman, June 6, 1901; Edward Medcalf to Henry J. Seaman, June 1, 1901; James C. Tucker to Henry J. Seaman, June 5, 1901; Spencer C. Tilbe to Henry J. Seaman, June 1, 1901; George W. Whitecotton to Henry J. Seaman, June 3, 1901; Martin L. Blake to Henry J. Seaman, June 5, 1901; Melvina Myers to Henry J. Seaman, July 11, 1901; Sarah J. Harding to Henry J. Seaman, August 23, 1901; Alfred W. Bulkley et al. to Henry J. Seaman, June 10, 1901; all in Warranty Deed Record, book 67, 466–74, 478, 519, and book 69, 79–80, Ralls County, Office of the Circuit Clerk and Recorder, New London; *Hannibal Morning Journal,* June 12, 1901. On Wade's lithographic venture, see Bacon, *Mirror,* 16.

34. Quoted in *Hannibal Morning Journal,* April 25, 1901.

Medcalf had purchased 171 acres in section two of Saverton township for twelve hundred dollars on March 1, 1900. He then sold the same land to Atlas just fifteen months later for thirty-three hundred dollars.[35]

Hannibal boosters initiated a campaign to prepare local residents for the profound changes about to transform the agricultural area just south of the cave hollow. Who better to showcase in this campaign to link the old order with the new than Elijah Hawkins, the father of Laura Hawkins Frazier, upon whom Twain based his character Becky Thatcher? W. A. Munger, president of the Business Men's Association, loaned Hawkins several "little books" on cement, and then a Hannibal newspaper featured a story, "Captain Elijah Hawkins Talks for Hannibal." The object of this article was to instill local confidence in the cement plant, by then under construction.[36]

The newspaper reporter did this by recounting a conversation with Hawkins, a local homespun philosopher with the appearance of a commoner but with the intellectual skills of a scholar. In this conversation, Hawkins urged local residents to read the literature on the growing demand for cement, and he trumpeted the construction of the local plant: "This is what Hannibal has drawn in the great lottery of business life."[37]

The article emphasized that residents should rejoice over Atlas's selection of Hannibal as a site for one of its plants. In particular, it used Hawkins to make more palatable the penetration of the area by Yankee capitalists. New South boosters were well aware of prevailing local images of and attitudes toward easterners, and the newspaper reporter touted Hawkins's down-home credentials to lend greater legitimacy to his endorsement of the cement plant:

> He is not a dude in his dress—and really, a stranger casually meeting him on the rock road leading from his country home to the city with his pants in his bootlegs, trudging along through the mud, would not shoot him for a philosopher. But such a wayfarer, clad in broadcloth, boiled shirt, kid gloves, patent leather shoes and a plug hat with an inflated opinion of his scholarly attainments—would feel like a pigmy should he take a day off and rub up against Captain Hawkins, who does not believe (and he is right) that broadcloth, boiled shirts, kid gloves, patent-leather shoes, plug hat and one-eyed glasses are indications of brain—but always infallible signs of lack of "horse sense."[38]

35. Joshua P. Richards to E. B. Medcalf, March 1, 1900, and Edward B. Medcalf to Henry J. Seaman, June 1, 1901, in Warranty Deed Record, book 67, 147, 470, Ralls County, Office of the Circuit Clerk and Recorder, New London.

36. Hagood and Hagood, *Story of Hannibal,* 93; *Hannibal Weekly Journal,* December 7, 1901.

37. Quoted in *Hannibal Weekly Journal,* December 7, 1901.

38. Ibid.

This was an effort to combat cultural biases against easterners and perhaps to overcome public opposition to policies promoting industrialization. "Manufacturers in the east realize that they must get nearer the trade," Hawkins told the newspaper reporter. "They are coming west and God has given Hannibal a freight equalizer whose importance cannot be overestimated—the great Mississippi river . . . Strangers are now teaching us a lesson by coming and developing our rich hidden resources." Since eastern capitalists were doing their part, it only remained for local residents to do their share and support the cement plant. "We have started up grade," Hawkins asserted, "and if we 'old mossbacks' will only do our duty, great things for the city and the people may be confidently looked for within the next few years."[39]

If Hannibal's old mossbacks displayed traditional cultural biases against eastern capitalists, it is also true that images of Missouri at times discouraged outsiders from investing and settling there. Perhaps no one more poignantly expressed the frustration of industrial boosters over prevailing cultural stereotypes of Missouri at that time than Walter Williams, of the University of Missouri's School of Journalism. Writing in 1904, he complained:

> Missouri has been a misunderstood State. Lying in the very pathway of immigration westward, the State has been avoided by immigrants. It has been accused of lawlessness because once a train was robbed within its borders. It has been called mossback, and poor and corrupt, when it has been conservative, rich and honorable . . . To be from Missouri was to provoke a smile. To rejoice therein was regarded as a mild form of lunacy.[40]

Atlas officials in New York and Pennsylvania shared these negative images of Missouri. On one occasion, in response to rumors of smallpox in Hannibal, they fumigated all correspondence from the area. The sensational activities of the legendary bandit Jesse James had earned Missouri a reputation in eastern political and financial circles as the "Robber State." The fact that Missourians had widely regarded James as a cultural folk hero because of his bank and train robberies suggests popular resistance to the symbols of the emerging industrial order. Atlas president and railroad magnate Maxwell must have found this public hostility toward railroad corporations a bit unsettling. He and other Atlas officials, influenced by the "shades" of the James Gang, later decided to pay workers at the Hannibal plant by check instead of cash. They believed it was too risky to haul large amounts of cash over the three-mile stretch between Hannibal and the plant.[41]

---

39. Ibid.

40. Quoted in Lyle Dorsett and Mary Dorsett, "Rhetoric versus Realism: 150 Years of Missouri Boosterism," 82.

41. Helmick, "Cement Plant Story," 4. For a discussion of how traditional values shaped popular opposition to capitalist institutions in industrializing Missouri, and how they

Atlas officials leased office space in the building that housed the Hannibal Bank, whose board of directors included Mahan. This space provided a temporary headquarters from which to direct construction of the plant. On July 10, 1901, engineer Sprout, in conjunction with local railroad officials, selected a site for laying switch track to connect the plant to the main railroad line. He and Helmick located a suitable shale deposit about two miles south of Saverton, a small river community a few miles south of the plant site. They arranged for Atlas to buy property there and put in a railroad siding to allow shipment of shale to the plant.[42]

To build the plant, Atlas contracted the Flynt Construction Company, which brought a large number of African American workers from South Carolina. These workers, who lived in makeshift tents and sheds, dug a trench from the Mississippi River to the plant site and laid a water main to pump water for the plant's boilers and other uses. The construction company hired additional workers from Hannibal who joined crews to build sheds, install a telephone line, and haul sand and gravel from nearby Marble Creek. Henry Templeton, an African American worker from Greenville, South Carolina, became perhaps the first casualty when he drowned on July 15 while trying to bring back sand samples from a sand bar in the Mississippi.[43]

Atlas representatives dispelled rumors that they intended to build a company town around the plant with a company store where workers would have to buy their goods. They assured the public that they were in business to make cement, not to dictate where employees spent their paychecks. The local newspaper reported that with few exceptions all Atlas employees would live in Hannibal, not in housing surrounding the plant. On August 1, 1901, the *Hannibal Morning Journal* emphasized that a reliable source on the "dust question" had suggested, in fact, that it was "impossible for people to reside in close proximity to the mills, and after working the plant for twelve hours each day the employes [*sic*] are only too glad to get as far away as possible."

Atlas officials created the Hannibal Connecting Railroad Company, incorporated under Missouri laws in 1902, to serve the plant's local needs. On the board of directors were Hannibal law partners Mahan and A. R. Smith, whose firm represented Atlas. Company officials prepared to operate a work train that would sweep through Hannibal's west and south sides gathering up workers for the

---

helped to create a view of Jesse James as a social bandit, see Thelen, *Paths of Resistance,* 70–77.

42. *Hannibal Morning Journal,* June 11 and July 28, 1901; J. Hurley Hagood and Roberta Roland Hagood, "History of the Hannibal National Bank, 1888–1988," 49; Helmick, "Cement Plant Story," 4.

43. Helmick, "Cement Plant Story," 4; *Hannibal Morning Journal,* July 16 and 25, 1901.

plant. The Burlington Railroad Company laid an additional track on Collier Street from Main Street west to the Minnow branch bridge just west of Lindell Avenue. This ensured that the cement plant's work train, later dubbed "the Polack," would not interfere with the "Dynamite" train that transported workers to and from a DuPont powder plant at Ashburn, about twenty miles south of Hannibal. The double track would also reduce delays for Atlas's workers.[44]

Plant construction took longer than expected. Engineers predicted that the plant would begin production in the early fall of 1902, but it was not until March 3, 1903, that the Atlas Portland Cement Company was incorporated in Missouri, capitalized at $7.5 million, and produced its first cement in Mill Number Five. Engineer Helmick attributed this delay to the excessively hot summer of 1901 and to the inability of Hannibal's white workers to keep up with the pace set by the Flynt Construction Company's African American workers. Racial stereotypes notwithstanding, there were more tangible reasons for the delay, including a strike by iron workers and a cave-in of two hundred feet of a wall of one of the large kilns. By the summer of 1903, more than fifteen hundred workers were on Atlas's payroll at the Ilasco plant.[45]

On October 19, 1903, Atlas's board of directors authorized the issue of $2.14 million in common stock to be sold for cash at par in order to finance the construction of Mill Number Six at Ilasco and a new plant at Northampton, Pennsylvania. Atlas soon suspended work on number six, but construction resumed after several major Atlas stockholders and officials inspected the Ilasco plant on October 20, 1904. By 1905, both mills were producing cement.[46]

Despite earlier press reports to the contrary, Atlas built barracks and boarding-houses around the plant for trainloads of Rumanian, Slovak, Italian, Hungarian, and other Balkan immigrants who soon arrived to provide the bulk of the cement plant's large labor force. By the time workers produced the first cement in March

44. Hannibal Connecting Railroad, "Directors Elected at Annual Meeting, March 14th, 1911," U.S. Steel Annandale Archives, USX Corporation, Pittsburgh; *Hannibal Weekly Journal,* November 30, 1901; Howard, *Ralls County Missouri,* 219; Hadley, *Magic Powder,* 220–21. Mahan also acted as legal counsel for DuPont and several railroad companies in the Hannibal area. Shoemaker, *Missouri and Missourians,* vol. 5, 95.

45. Atlas Portland Cement Company, Certificate of Incorporation, March 3, 1903, Corporation Division, Office of the Secretary of State, Jefferson City, Mo.; Helmick, "Cement Plant Story," 3; *Stone* 24 (May 1902): 478; *Stone* 25 (March 1903): 470; *Hannibal Courier-Post,* July 3, 1903. According to Williams, ed., *State of Missouri,* 305, Atlas's Ilasco plant employed sixteen hundred workers in 1903.

46. J. R. Maxwell, President, Atlas Portland Cement Company, to Stockholders, November 12, 1903, U.S. Steel Annandale Archives, USX Corporation, Pittsburgh; *Hannibal Courier-Post,* October 20, 22, and 26, 1904, and December 14 and 20, 1904; Fact Sheet, Universal Atlas Cement Division, United States Steel Corporation, Hannibal, Missouri, Plant, enclosed in C. R. Altheide, Plant Manager, Continental Cement Company, Inc., to author, February 26, 1982.

1903, the community of Ilasco had taken shape in the shadow of the sprawling plant, partly on land owned by Atlas and partly on adjacent noncompany land. In an application for a post office filed that same month, Isidore Schwartz reported that Ilasco's population was more than one thousand "and floating much more." Atlas chemist L. P. Sprout gave the community its name—an acronym for some of the mineral ingredients used in making cement (Iron, Lime, Aluminum, Silica, Calcium, and Oxygen). Postmaster Schwartz presided over the opening of the post office on September 18, 1903, and the Ralls County Court created a new voting precinct at Ilasco on October 26, 1904.[47]

Atlas's operations swiftly transformed the local landscape. By 1910, the population of Ralls County had increased to 12,913. More importantly, the population of Saverton township had more than doubled between 1900 and 1910, from 1,460 to 3,075. Nearly 2,000 residents of the township lived in Ilasco, which although unincorporated had become by far the largest town in the county with twice as many residents as New London.[48]

The cement plant's extensive mining, quarrying, and manufacturing operations and the creation of Ilasco put a huge nick in the physical terrain of the area next to the Mark Twain cave hollow. As awareness grew that the Mississippi River bluffs from Keokuk, Iowa, to St. Louis contained rich deposits of limestone, some worried what added manufacturing might do to the future beauty of the bluffs along this stretch. Even the *Hannibal Courier-Post,* one of Atlas's leading boosters, expressed such concerns about the cement industry: "The only regrettable feature in connection with the discoverey [*sic*] and its development is to be found in the fact that the beautiful west bank of the Mississippi river will be ruined if the enterprise goes forward with the same speed at which it has started. Great gashes in the magnificent bluffs that overhang the river have already been made, and the work has only begun."[49]

47. Howard, *Ralls County Missouri,* 197; *Hannibal Morning Journal,* March 18, 1903; "Ilasco," topic no. 260, October 4, 1937, collection no. 3551, microfilm roll 575, folder 17504, U.S. WPA-HRS, WHMC–Columbia; U.S. Post Office Department, Reports of Site Locations, 1837–1950 (Washington: National Archives Microfilm Publications, 1980), target 1: Ralls County, Missouri, microfilm roll 342, and Records of the U.S. Postal Service, Record of Appointment of Postmasters, 1832–September 30, 1971 (Washington: National Archives Microfilm Publications, 1973), vol. 39, microfilm roll 73; both in record group 28, National Archives. The first voting precinct judges were W. W. Davis, John Ryan, Maurice Mulvihill, Fred Hortsmeyer, Sylvester Colburn, and Theodore Johnson. *Hannibal Courier-Post,* October 28, 1904. The *Hannibal Morning Journal,* April 7, 1911, noted in an article on the legal dispute over the will of Ilasco's Samuel Heinbach that Sprout was the Atlas official who named Ilasco.

48. *Census Reports,* vol. 1, Twelfth Census . . . 1900. Population, pt. 1, 246; *Census Reports,* vol. 2, Thirteenth Census of the United States Taken in the Year 1910. Population, 1083; U.S. Federal Manuscript Census, 1910, Saverton township, Ralls County.

49. *Hannibal Courier-Post,* March 15, 1907.

The influx of southern and eastern European immigrants changed the cultural makeup of Ralls County, most of whose early settlers had come from Kentucky, Virginia, and Tennessee. Whereas Germans were by far the largest ethnic group, at 38.5 percent, within Missouri's foreign-born white population in 1910, with Irish immigrants next at 10.2 percent, the immigration pattern in Saverton township was quite different. Most of Ilasco's foreign-born residents in 1910 were Rumanians (44 percent), Slovaks (31 percent), Italians (14 percent), and Hungarians (7 percent), with a sprinkling of Ukrainians, Greeks, Poles, Germans, and others. The foreign-born population of Ralls County had numbered only 297 in 1900, but Ilasco alone had approximately 1,220 immigrants in 1910.[50]

Ilasco would add to the confusion over Missouri's regional identity, a confusion often shared by historians. The town was the product of Yankee industrial capital in a trans-Mississippi western state that contained significant pockets of southern cultural influence, that upheld slavery and produced a bloody civil war but did not secede from the Union. Scholars have recognized Twain as a Southerner, and they have emphasized Missouri's importance in the politics of slavery. Historians of the New South, however, generally have ignored Missouri, which thus rather abruptly loses its classification as a Southern state after 1877.[51]

In Ralls County, the mingling of distinctly Southern and Slavic immigrant influences produced a rich cultural tapestry and important regional variation in Missouri. Old South attitudes greeted Ilasco's Slavic immigrants, the major participants in the county's first and last attempt at a New South transformation. Thus, industrialization almost overnight forced the grafting of new cultural and social arrangements onto the local landscape, bringing sharp class and cultural conflicts to Twain's treasured boyhood playground. Immigrants quickly learned that the intersection of race, region, ethnicity, gender, and class would determine their position in the social pecking order. In the years ahead Ilasco's working-class residents would struggle to build an identity in the face of harsh material conditions, relentless efforts by Atlas to control the community, and often contemptuous attitudes on the part of commercial and civic leaders in Hannibal and New London. This struggle sometimes produced both serious confrontations among Ilasco's residents and at times even more sensational conflicts with the Atlas Portland Cement Company.

50. "Ralls County Historical Sketch," March 23, 1938, collection no. 3551, microfilm roll 574, folder 17494, U.S. WPA-HRS, WHMC–Columbia; *Census Reports,* vol. 2, Thirteenth Census . . . 1910. Population, 1094; U.S. Federal Manuscript Census, 1910, Saverton township, Ralls County; Giovanni Schiavo, *The Italians in Missouri,* 27.
51. See, for example, Woodward, *Origins,* and Ayers, *Promise.*

(2)

Woodchopper Landlords and Cement Mill Tenants

The Social Origins of Ilasco

The human family cannot be described by any one phrase; each individual has to be described by himself. One is brave, another is a coward; one is gentle and kindly, another is ferocious; one is proud and vain, another is modest and humble.

—Mark Twain, *Autobiography*

Ilasco did not originate as a classic company town. Atlas did not pay wages in scrip or set up a company store. It also did not own all of the property, or control housing in the village. A thriving community of houses, grocery stores, dramshops, and other small retail stores quickly took shape just beyond company boardinghouses, three-room cottages rented to workers for eleven dollars per month, and company dining rooms clustered around the cement plant. Most of the noncompany land that formed the town site belonged to either Samuel Heinbach (pronounced HEINBOW by Ilasco residents) or Theodore Johnson, long-standing friends and partners who had settled in the area well before Atlas built the cement plant there.[1]

Since Heinbach's social origins and broken family life later played a major role in the history of property relations in Ilasco, it is important to examine the history of his restless movements from Indiana to the Hannibal area in more detail. A marginalized Union Army veteran of the Civil War, he had first moved his family from Cambridge, Indiana, to the eastern Illinois community of Watseka around 1880. About a year later, he fixed up a wagon with another man and left his wife, Sarah, and their three small children without telling them where he was

---

1. On Atlas rents in 1906, see the *Hannibal Courier-Post*, February 28, 1980.

going. Sarah, left stranded without money for the trip home, wrote her mother for financial help. After the money arrived, Sarah took the kids back to Cambridge and lived with her mother for the next couple of years.[2]

In the meantime, Sam moved to Pike County, Illinois, where he built a cabin and worked as a woodchopper in the Sny bottom along the Mississippi River. After awhile, he sent money for the family to join him. Sarah and the kids came to Hannibal and lived with him across the river until a flood inundated their cabin. Sam told Sarah that she and the kids could either go to Hannibal, or he would take them back to Cambridge.[3]

Sarah apparently had had enough. Sam took her and the kids back to her mother's home in Cambridge, stayed awhile, but again vanished without telling them that he was leaving. This left Sarah and their children—Jesse (age ten), Edith (six), and one-year-old Naomi—in dire straits. As his daughter, Edith Britton, later recalled, "Well we had nothing, [he] just simply took us and left us on our grandmother, and left us with nothing."[4]

Samuel Heinbach's erratic behavior put his family in turmoil, but he attributed his departure from Cambridge to Sarah's infidelity. He later told Ilasco's Fred Jeffers that when he came home from fishing and found another man at the house, he simply "left it with them." Whatever the reason for Sam's departure, his quick exit caught his family by surprise. "Well when he left he just went down the street," his oldest daughter recalled, "just bare-footed, without hat or anything . . . Yes sir. He was in the habit of going bare-footed in the Summer time, and we just supposed he had gone out down in town with some body."[5]

The fate of Sarah and her children illustrates the vulnerability of women and children who lived on the edge of poverty in an era that championed women's subordination, male paternalism, and children's orphanages as solutions to deep social problems. Sam, on a final trip back to Cambridge sometime after 1885, discovered that Sarah had left the children with her mother, who in turn had put them in an orphans home in Richmond, Indiana. Without securing a formal divorce, Sarah remarried in 1896 and moved to Roseland, Indiana, but did not take the kids with her. When Edith left the orphans home, she went to live with

2. "Persons Who Served in the Army, Navy and Marine Corp. of the U.S. During the War of the Rebellion Who Are Survivors, and Widows of Such Persons," Ralls County, Saverton township, Missouri, Special U.S. Census Schedule, June 1890; *Heinbach v. Heinbach et al.*, April term, 1914, case no. 14178, trial transcript, 388–91, MSCF-MSA.

3. *Heinbach v. Heinbach et al.*, April term, 1914, 391–92; *Mary Alice Heinbach, Appellant v. Jesse Heinbach et al.*, November 24, 1914, *Missouri Reports*, vol. 262, 77–78.

4. *Heinbach v. Heinbach et al.*, April term, 1914, 393–96, 406.

5. *Heinbach v. Heinbach et al.*, April term, 1918, 148; *Heinbach v. Heinbach et al.*, April term, 1914, 391–94.

an aunt and then was hired out to a farm family near Roseland. Jesse set out to look for work in Muncie, but none of his family ever heard from him again. Their father had returned to the Illinois Sny bottom, never again to see them.[6]

It is unclear whether Sam had met Theodore Johnson in the Sny bottom or whether Johnson was the man who left Watseka with him, but they chopped wood and "batched" together in the Illinois woods along the Mississippi River. Around 1887 or 1888, Johnson moved across the river to an area three miles south of Hannibal, where he met and married Eliza Jane Smashey, the daughter of Samuel and Maria Smashey, a landowning farm family. Heinbach followed Johnson to Saverton township a year later.[7]

For the next several years Heinbach and Johnson worked as woodchoppers and truck farmers south of Hannibal. Heinbach rented land from David Wade and grew vegetables and produce. On December 1, 1890, through Wade's influence he and Johnson purchased as tenants in common about fifty-two acres of flat land next to where the Atlas plant would later be located. After Wade's death, one of his heirs tried to eject them from the land in 1895, but a jury ruled in favor of Johnson and Heinbach. Theodore and Eliza Jane bought an additional 2.3 acres in 1900, and in 1906, Theodore and Sam divided their tract through mutual conveyances. Until then, they had verbally agreed that the public road would be the dividing line between their holdings, Sam's on the north side of the road and Theodore's on the south. Theodore and Eliza Jane gardened on about twenty-six acres, while Sam built a log cabin and lived alone until late 1908 on his twenty-six-acre tract. Sam grew vegetables and produce for sale, collected "ground rents" from Ilasco residents, and rented out some of his land in small patches of corn and cabbage.[8]

When the Atlas Portland Cement Company built its plant on land next to Heinbach and Johnson, workers and their families looked for places to live nearby. Johnson and Heinbach began leasing building lots for ground rent of about one dollar per month for each lot. Tenants erected houses, or shacks in many cases, and entrepreneurs from Hannibal, Saverton, and New London invested in housing on these rented lots. Although Heinbach had deserted his family, he was sympathetic to poor people and leased lots at cheap rates. According to William Burns, a native of Saverton township, Heinbach told him

6. *Heinbach v. Heinbach et al.,* April term, 1914, 246, 396–407.

7. Ibid., 245–46; Smashey, comp., "History of the Smasheys," 128.

8. *Heinbach v. Heinbach et al.,* April term, 1914, 166, 221, 276–77, 286–87; Estate of Theodore Johnson, January 31, 1914, case no. 4183, Ralls County, Office of the Probate Clerk, New London; *John M. Wade v. Samuel Heinbach et al.,* August 20, 1895, case no. 7053, Circuit Court Record, book N, 67, 325, Ralls County, Office of the Circuit Clerk and Recorder, New London; *Heinbach, Appellant v. Heinbach et al.,* 77–78.

"that gardening would be more money for him, but . . . there was a great many poor people that needed work, and . . . he preferred to give them a show."[9]

Heinbach's paternalism thus contained contradictory elements. He hired agents to handle rent collections, perhaps because he feared that his sympathies for other poor people might ruin him financially. He often loaned money to Ilasco residents, and he allowed Ola Gregory, for example, to live on leased land free. "A woman that was lady enough to take care of herself and three children," he told her, " . . . he was man enough to help her." He explained his dilemma to Max Lomax, who had earlier farmed a piece of his land, cultivating a small cabbage patch on shares. "Well, Lomax, I will tell you," he said, "I have a lot of widow women living on those lots and poor people and not able to pay lot rent . . . I have got too much heart in me . . . to take rent off of them." He added that "he simply had to have some man to look after that business that would attend to it."[10]

Despite or perhaps because of abandoning his own children, Heinbach's paternalism extended especially to the children of Ilasco. Several residents later remembered that he was a soft touch for kids. Josephine Freeman, who operated a boardinghouse in Ilasco between 1903 and 1915, noted that Heinbach at Christmas gave a sack of candy and an orange to each child in the community. Lula Brown recalled how kind he was to her little girl Mildred on other occasions: "The last time I think that he saw her he took her in the drug store and set her on the stool and paid for ice cream for her. He did this lots of times."[11]

At first Thomas Burns, justice of the peace in Ilasco, drew up leases and collected rents for Heinbach. Then Jack Briscoe, a Ralls County attorney, replaced Burns and handled the rent collection from October 1905 to October 1906. Briscoe had worked for the Atlas Portland Cement Company from March 1903 to September 1905, but then had opened a law office in Ilasco. As Heinbach's agent, he drew up a rough plat of the twenty-six-acre tract and took care of the leases, deducting 10 percent of the rents as salary each month. H. F. Fleurdelys, an Atlas employee and naturalized U.S. citizen from France, replaced Briscoe in the fall of 1906 when the latter moved to New London after his election as Ralls County Prosecuting Attorney. Heinbach's rents from 106 lots provided him with a middle-class income—an annual gross of approximately eleven hundred dollars until his death in 1910.[12]

9. *Heinbach, Appellant v. Heinbach et al.,* 77–78; *Heinbach v. Heinbach et al.,* April term, 1914, 287.

10. *Heinbach v. Heinbach et al.,* April term, 1918, 57–58, 64, 440.

11. Ibid., 289, 614–19; *Heinbach v. Heinbach et al.,* April term, 1914, 557–58.

12. *Heinbach v. Heinbach et al.,* April term, 1914, 348–50, 356; *Heinbach, Appellant v. Heinbach et al.,* 77–78; U.S. Federal Manuscript Census, 1910, Saverton township, Ralls County.

Mary Alice Sykes Scott, a longtime resident of Saverton township who lived a few miles south of Ilasco, set her eyes on Heinbach as a potential husband shortly after the death of her fourth husband, John Scott, in January 1907. She inquired about the extent of Heinbach's property and allegedly offered one hundred dollars to William Cutsinger, a neighboring farmer, if he could convince him to marry her. She soon wrote a letter to Heinbach, and according to her, "Then things went."[13]

Before Heinbach had officially divided his tract with Johnson, he secured a divorce from Sarah on March 26, 1906. His health was rapidly deteriorating, largely as the result of alcoholism, but he left his log cabin and married Scott on December 18, 1908, in the home of her brother, H. T. Sykes, in New London. The Heinbachs bought and moved into a comfortable house befitting their status in the community. Their new house, located on a stretch of land that included an orchard tract on a hill overlooking Ilasco, at one time had belonged to T. B. Wilson, and then to Dr. R. M. Winn, a Ralls County physician who had moved to Ilasco in October 1906. Winn had then sold it to Dr. L. H. Tutt, who in turn sold it to Heinbach for six hundred dollars. From the Heinbachs' new residence, the newlyweds prepared to oversee the affairs of their tenants below.[14]

Mary Alice encouraged her husband to draw up a will deeding all of his property to her. She reportedly urged John Hinkson, a former Atlas worker and Ilasco saloon owner, to use his influence to persuade Sam to draw up such a will. According to Hinkson, she promised that "if the will was made that I should not be forgotten . . . if the will was not broken, she would deed me a lot or two . . . as good as she had." On September 27, 1909, Sam drew up a will leaving all of his property to Mary Alice, giving one dollar to each of his children, whom he had not seen in about twenty-five years.[15]

Atlas's demand for a large labor force had spurred the rapid formation of a community at Ilasco. Cassius M. Jeffers, a Saverton township farmer who had known Heinbach for several years, rented a lot from him and opened a butcher shop and ice house with sons William and Fred. Hannibal and Saverton merchants leased land from Heinbach and Johnson and opened branch stores. Cornelius J. Murphy and Clarence J. Lampton opened a produce store in Ilasco,

---

13. Estate of John M. Scott, January 25, 1907, case no. 2244, Ralls County, Office of the Probate Clerk, New London; *Heinbach v. Heinbach et al.*, April term, 1914, 185–88; Statement and Brief on behalf of Defendant Euphemia B. Koller, 6, in *Mary Alice Heinbach v. Euphemia B. Koller et al.*, October 15, 1919, case no. 1219, and Record Book 46, 289, Pike County, Office of the Circuit Clerk and Recorder, Bowling Green, Mo.

14. Marriage of Samuel Heinbach and Mary Alice Scott, December 18, 1908, Marriage License Record, book H, 77, Ralls County, Office of the Circuit Clerk and Recorder, New London; *Ralls County Times*, January 1, 1909; *Heinbach v. Heinbach et al.*, April term, 1914, 181–82, 292, 300–304, and *Heinbach v. Heinbach et al.*, April term, 1918, 15–16.

15. *Heinbach v. Heinbach et al.*, April term, 1914, 3–4, 191–92.

and William Carlile (Carlile Meat Company) operated a meat market there. Herman Lefkovitz and Herman Schwartz established a general merchandise store, and Ilasco's early residents also shopped at Dick Janney's (Jenny) grocery store, William Groth's meat shop, Mitchell T. Smashey's confectionery and grocery store, the general merchandising store of J. T. Fisher and William James, and other stores operated by Hannibal's George Noel, and Gilbert and Staffy. Willis Lawler ran a barber shop, and O. M. Blaney operated a pool hall.[16]

Several dramshops also opened. Dick Janney operated a tavern in addition to a grocery store, and Lefkovitz and Schwartz secured a dramshop license to add to their income from the general store. Joe Blair opened the "Live and Let Live Saloon," and John Hinkson ran "The Last Chance Saloon."[17]

Like a magnet, the cement plant attracted several streams of workers to Ilasco. One of these streams included native-born fishermen and day laborers who traveled up and down the Mississippi River, making homes out of modest cabin boats that they had hoisted ashore. In 1901, for example, the forces set in motion by Atlas's decision to locate a plant just south of Hannibal uprooted many people living in houseboats on Hannibal's southside riverfront. The Burlington Railroad Company had purchased new property in preparation for laying additional track to accommodate Atlas's work train to the plant. This spelled trouble for about forty inhabitants of more than twenty cabin boats that had been pulled up onto the riverbank as makeshift houses. In early January 1901, attorneys for the Burlington Railroad Company notified houseboat squatters between Bear Creek and the yards of the Hannibal Saw Mill that they would have to move within a month.[18]

Most male owners of these cabin boats were fishermen and day laborers, while their counterparts in female-headed houseboats worked as domestic servants or

16. Howard, *Ralls County Missouri*, 252; *Heinbach v. Heinbach et al.*, April term, 1914, 427–33, and *Heinbach v. Heinbach et al.*, October term, 1918, 150, 576; Sublease, Lucien Williams to Lefkovitz and Schwartz, December 24, 1902, and Theodore Johnson and Eliza Johnson to Lefkovitz and Schwartz, December 24, 1902, Deed Record, book 43, 605–7; Leases, Samuel Heinbach to George D. Noel, October 1, 1905, and Samuel Heinbach to C. M. and W. L. Jeffers, September 1, 1905, Deed Record, book 72, 592, 619; Lease, Theodore Johnson to Willis Lawler, June 1, 1906, Miscellaneous Record, book 78, 197; all in Ralls County, Office of the Circuit Clerk and Recorder, New London; *Hannibal Courier-Post*, March 2 and 3, 1906; U.S. Federal Manuscript Census, 1900, Saverton township, Ralls County; and Record F, 177, Ralls County, Office of the County Clerk, New London.

17. At various times before 1914, William Freeman, Charles Churchill, John Hinkson, Andy Moore, John Moore, William Hascall, Arthur Moore, William Moore, George Douglas, Sidney Smart, George A. Poor, Petru Sirbu, Thomas Ball, John Savu, Lewis Basnett, John Ursu, Ewell F. Todd, Louis Geishe, and E. H. Nokes had dramshop licenses in Ilasco. Record F, 30, 74, 128, 179, 252, 299, 303, 306, 309, 313, 449, Ralls County, Office of the County Clerk, New London. See also *Ralls County Times*, March 8, 1907, August 11, August 18, and November 17, 1911, and May 9, 1913; and *Ralls County Record*, August 9 and December 6 and 27, 1912, and January 9, 1914.

18. *Hannibal Morning Journal*, January 9, 1901; U.S. Federal Manuscript Census, 1900, Mason township, Marion County, Mo.

washerwomen. Many of the boats were in terrible shape and required extensive repairs before they could be launched into the icy waters of the Mississippi River. Most owners undertook the needed repairs, but others resisted efforts to force them to move. On April 17, 1901, the *Hannibal Morning Journal* expressed impatience with the levee dwellers and complained that twelve boats still had not moved: "The railroad company notified these people to move some time ago; but some have refused to comply." The newspaper recommended legal action against those who refused to leave, and noted that "yesterday a force of men shoved one of these boat houses owned by a man named [Burt] Huddleston out into the river."[19]

The following profile of a family that was evicted from the levee indicates the social turmoil imposed by poverty upon those who lived in such makeshift accommodations. On April 20, the *Hannibal Morning Journal* further reported that a couple of houseboats had been torn down, including one belonging to Louis Lester, whose eviction was only the latest disruption in a life that had become increasingly fragmented. Born in Kentucky, Lester was a day laborer in his mid to late forties who had recently moved from Griggsville (Pike County), Illinois, to Hannibal amidst marital problems. His wife, Ruth Emeline, had moved to Hannibal in the mid-1890s with their daughters Cinderella, Malissie (Lizzie), and Dora Lyman. He soon followed them to Hannibal, but Ruth Emeline left town temporarily while Lizzie, Dora, and their brother Albert—newly arrived from Illinois—moved in with their father. It is not clear if Louis and Ruth Emeline legally divorced, since both referred to themselves at that time as widowed.[20]

All of the above Lesters, excluding Cinderella, who had perhaps died or left the area, had taken up residence in boats on Hannibal's southside riverfront by 1900. Just a few boats down from Louis's, Ruth Emeline lived with her new husband, Joseph Lamp, a Wisconsin-born fisherman. Fifteen-year-old Albert lived in his father's cabin boat, while Dora Lyman, who was in her mid twenties and divorced, lived in a nearby boat with her twenty-year-old brother, Louis Jr., and thirteen-year-old Lizzie. Nearby but off the levee lived the Lesters' daughter Ella—in her late twenties—and her five- or six-year-old daughter, Blanche Smith. Either divorced or widowed, Ella had recently married Daniel C. Mack (Meck), a Hannibal blacksmith who in 1901 worked in the nearby machine shops of the Burlington Railroad Company.[21]

19. U.S. Federal Manuscript Census, 1900, Mason township, Marion County, Mo.; *Hannibal Morning Journal*, March 6 and April 20, 22, 23, 24, and 26, 1901.

20. U.S. Federal Manuscript Census, 1880, Griggsville township, Pike County, Ill.; Hannibal City Directory, 1895–1896, 1897–1898.

21. U.S. Federal Manuscript Census, 1900, Mason township, Marion County, Mo.; U.S. Federal Manuscript Census, 1880, Griggsville township, Pike County, Ill.; Hannibal City Directory, 1901. On the ages of Louis Jr., Albert, Dora, and Ella, see Birth Record, book 1, #1590, #3567, 122, 274; Marriage Licenses #1096 and #1298, Marriage Record, book 3,

Ilasco provided new opportunities for the Macks, Lesters, and Lamps. After Daniel Mack took a job with Atlas, he and his wife and the Lamps borrowed money in September 1903 to buy 4.75 acres of land just a couple of miles west of Ilasco. The Macks took 2.75 acres, leaving the Lamps with the other 2 acres. By then, the Macks had three sons—Daniel Jr. and Raymond, ages six and four, and Russell, who was less than a year old. Along with Ella's daughter Blanche, Albert Lester, Dora Lyman, and Lizzie Lester, they joined the struggle to carve out a better life and forge a community identity in what would be the most volatile decade in Ilasco's history.[22]

Like the Lesters, many of Ilasco's early native-born residents, including Nelson and Lula Brown, came from Pike County, Illinois. The Browns moved to Ilasco with their baby daughter Agnes in the summer of 1902. Nelson took care of Atlas's "Family" horses at the company barn, and Lula prepared and served meals to Atlas workers in her home. At the time the Browns moved into a company house nearby, Ilasco had barely begun to take shape. "I moved to the plant when there was nothing but the foundations, and few smokestacks," recalled Lula. "No houses there but his [Samuel Heinbach's] log house and the Plant and Mr. [H. F.] Fleurdelys, and that was about all."[23]

Joining the Browns soon thereafter were George and Rosa Douglas, who came from the village of Hull in Pike County, Illinois. With their furniture in a wagon covered with tarpaulin, the Douglases and their four daughters—Maude, age fifteen; Bertha, thirteen; Ruby, six; and Freda, three—ferried across the Mississippi River in the rain. When they looked for a place to live in Ilasco, they found primitive tar-papered shanties. "We come to strike it rich," Ruby Douglas Northcutt later recalled with a smile. "So we wound up in a leaky house; we'd carry our things to another house 'til we found one that didn't leak; then we squatted . . . They were just shacks made out of dynamite boxes." George, a day laborer who four years earlier had been under a manslaughter indictment for shooting a man in a fight on the fourth of July, took a job at the cement plant while Rosa took in laundry. He leased a lot from Samuel Heinbach and

---

211, 223, all in Pike County, Office of the County Clerk, Pittsfield, Ill. Cinderella Lester and C. W. Volkening of Hannibal took out a marriage license on October 4, 1894, but did not file a record of their marriage. Volkening still lived in Hannibal the following year, but Lester did not. Marriage Record, book 9, 368, Marion County, Office of the Circuit Clerk and Recorder, Palmyra, Mo., and Hannibal City Directory, 1895–1896.

22. Daniel Meck and Mary L. Meck, and Joseph D. Lamp and Emeline Lamp, to Thomas C. Wilson and Annie Burns, August 8, 1903, Deed Trust Record, book 70, 249, Ralls County, Office of the Circuit Clerk and Recorder, New London; U.S. Federal Manuscript Census, 1910, Saverton township, Ralls County.

23. U.S. Federal Manuscript Census, 1910, Saverton township, Ralls County; *The Atlas Circle* 3 (June 1918): 14. On the quote from Lula Brown, see *Heinbach v. Heinbach et al.*, April term, 1914, 552–53.

later opened a saloon and served as a constable in Ilasco before he died in an accident at the cement plant on December 2, 1920.[24]

Also from Hull were Mark and Sarah Kinder. In 1900, they had two children—Letha and Ellis. Their household contained three other children from Sarah's earlier marriage—John R., Dora G., and Lucetta McKinney. They moved to Ilasco, where Mark, who had been a day laborer in Hull, now worked at the cement plant along with his stepson. By 1920, Sarah had died, and Mark now lived as a boarder in Ilasco with Nelson and Lula Brown.[25]

Some of the neighborhoods of Hull nearly emptied when Atlas built its plant at Ilasco. Many friends and neighbors of the Douglases and Kinders likewise crossed the Mississippi River in a chain migration in search of new opportunities. Family and neighborhood contacts helped to spread word of jobs at Atlas, and they provided support for those who came from Hull to Ilasco. For example, when Thomas and Marcus Hedges took jobs as riggers at the cement plant, they lived as boarders with Fred and Anna Rupert and their four sons—Dee, David, Harry, and Charles. Both the Ruperts and the Hedges were from Hull.[26]

The families of Elmer and Clara Smith, Rosanna Bradshaw, Amanda Douglas, Cash and Ellen Hornback, Leonard and Hattie Rodgers, Benjamin and Faredy Purcell, Charles and Emma Hedges, and Ewell and Hattie Rogers, also became part of Ilasco's pioneer community. These families had relied primarily on day labor, tenant farming, or sawmill work for their livelihoods in the Hull area, but now embraced more promising opportunities for industrial labor provided by the Atlas Portland Cement Company.[27]

For some Mississippi River Valley residents who came to Ilasco, day labor in agricultural and sawmill work had been one of the few options before the Atlas cement plant attracted them. Perry and Lavina Jones left Cedar Rapids, Iowa, in two covered wagons with their sons Amiel (Jack) and Ollie, crossing the Mississippi River into Illinois, stopping "where they could find work" before crossing the river again and driving their wagons into Ilasco. In 1905, their

24. U.S. Federal Manuscript Census, 1900, Kinderhook township, Hull, Ill.; U.S. Federal Manuscript Census, 1920, Saverton township, Ralls County; Ruby Northcutt, interview by Virginia Sudholt, March 25, 1993; Ruby Northcutt, undated video interview by Jim Tatman, ca. 1990; *Ralls County Record,* December 10, 1920; *Heinbach v. Heinbach et al.,* April term, 1914, 330–38; *Rosa Douglas v. Atlas Portland Cement Company,* February 12, 1921, case no. 11,405, Ralls County, Office of the Circuit Clerk and Recorder, New London; *State of Illinois v. Geo. Douglas,* case no. 8663, November term, 1898, Pike County, Office of the Circuit Clerk, Pittsfield, Ill.

25. U.S. Federal Manuscript Census, 1900, Kinderhook township, Hull, Pike County, Ill.; U.S. Federal Manuscript Census, 1910, 1920, Saverton township, Ralls County.

26. U.S. Federal Manuscript Census, 1900, Kinderhook township, Hull, Pike County, Ill.; U.S. Federal Manuscript Census, 1910, Saverton township, Ralls County, Mo.

27. U.S. Federal Manuscript Census, 1900, Kinderhook township, Hull, Pike County, Ill.

daughter Pansy was born in Ilasco, and Jack and Ollie went to work as teamsters at the cement plant. Perry also worked as a teamster around Ilasco, sometimes at the plant, and Lavina performed unpaid labor in the household and served as a midwife in Ilasco. Their children Perry Jr., Harry, and Mary were born in 1908, 1912, and 1917, respectively.[28]

Missouri ranked twelfth among states that were reported as the final destination of immigrants to the United States between 1899 and 1910. Thanks to the activities of Atlas's labor recruiting agents abroad, advertisements in eastern cities, and a coordinated campaign by Hannibal newspapers, financial interests, and the Missouri Board of Immigration, many immigrants from eastern and southern Europe soon arrived in Ilasco. Some had already been "seasoned" in cement plants in eastern states. In other cases, labor agents, some of whom were early immigrants, went to Europe or eastern cities in the United States to recruit workers for Atlas's Ilasco plant. Kinship and ethnic ties also played an important role in attracting other immigrants to the area.[29]

Rumanians John and Mary Moga were part of Ilasco's largest immigrant group in 1910. Immediately upon immigrating in 1903, John went to work as a blaster in Atlas's quarries. In 1906, Mary immigrated, and in 1909 gave birth to their first son, John, in Ilasco. Mr. Moga became a naturalized U.S. citizen in 1913 and served in the military during World War I. By 1920, the year of his death in a quarry explosion, he and Mary were the parents of three additional children— Pete, Saveta, and Mary.[30]

Petru Sirbu, a Rumanian who had come to the United States in 1905, probably had important connections with the Atlas Portland Cement Company before arriving in Ilasco later that year. He and his wife, Mary, who had immigrated from Rumania in 1908, owned their own home in Ilasco. Petru operated a butcher shop and general store for the Ilasco Supply Company, which he had helped to incorporate. In addition, he operated a tavern and sometimes made trips to eastern industrial cities as a labor agent for Atlas. His connections with Atlas officials, local politicians, and Hannibal attorneys soon paid dividends. The Ralls County Court appointed him to serve as an election judge in the Ilasco voting

28. Perry Jones, tape provided to author, December 5, 1994; U.S. Federal Manuscript Censuses, 1910 and 1920, Saverton township, Ralls County.

29. U.S. Immigration Commission, *Reports of the Immigration Commission, 1907–1910*, vol. 1, 105; Missouri State Board of Immigration, *First Annual Report*. On immigrants as labor agents and the importance of family and ethnic ties in shaping immigration, see John Bodnar, *Immigration and Industrialization: Ethnicity in an American Mill Town, 1870–1940*, 26, and idem, *Workers' World: Kinship, Community, and Protest in an Industrial Society, 1900–1940*, especially 13–62.

30. U.S. Federal Manuscript Census, 1920, Saverton township, Ralls County; *Mary Goucan, Appellant, v. Atlas Portland Cement Company and L. J. Boucher*, July 30, 1927, *Missouri Reports*, vol. 317, 924–25.

precinct, and he began to buy and sell real estate in the area and to accumulate considerable wealth. Some Ilasco residents called him a "big shot."[31]

Living next door to Sirbu in 1910 was a fellow Rumanian, John Savu, who had immigrated in 1902. He worked as a clerk in the store of Fisher and James, married in June 1906, and took out his first naturalization papers in February 1908. He became the first secretary of a Rumanian fraternal society in Ilasco, and by 1910 had become a naturalized citizen. He and his wife, Mary, who had immigrated from Rumania in 1901, had two children, Peter and Sylvia. Savu formed business partnerships with Sirbu and several other investors in Ilasco and soon became a merchant and saloon owner. By 1920, however, he and his family had left Ilasco.[32]

In 1907, there were 338,452 immigrants to the United States from Austria-Hungary, more than from any other nation in any previous year. In Austria-Hungary, older feudal patterns still shaped the system of land tenure and created conditions that encouraged emigration for economic reasons. The average daily wage of emigrants from Austria-Hungary, many of whom came to Ilasco, was about fifty-one cents. The pressures to emigrate were particularly acute in Slovakia as the result of Magyar cultural, economic, and political oppression. Land pressures, limited industrial job opportunities, a population explosion, and Magyar efforts to root out Slovak culture, encouraged a steady exodus of Slovak peasants from their villages in search of jobs elsewhere. In particular, the lure of making money in the United States was so great in the early 1900s that it was common for Slovak newlyweds, after an extended honeymoon, to endure a separation while the husband emigrated to find work overseas before returning with dollars.[33]

31. U.S. Federal Manuscript Census, 1910, Saverton township, Ralls County; *Ralls County Record,* October 23, 1914, and March 28, 1925; *Hannibal Courier-Post,* March 20, 1925; Petru and Mary Sirbu to George W. Myers, January 2, 1918, General Warranty Deed, Deed Record, book 99, 574, Ralls County, Office of the Circuit Clerk and Recorder, New London; Angelo Venditti, interview by author, July 9, 1993; Ruby Northcutt, interview by Virginia Sudholt, March 25, 1993; *Heinbach v. Heinbach et al.,* April term, 1918, 682, 685, 688. On the connections between Sirbu, the Atlas Portland Cement Company, and Hannibal attorney Charles E. Rendlen, see *Euphemia B. Koller v. Mary Alice Heinbach and her guardian John E. Megown, et al.,* January 24, 1923, case no. 11606, Ralls County, Office of the Circuit Clerk and Recorder, New London, and "Suggestions in Opposition to Motion to Reinstate Appeal," March 10, 1921, 3, in *Mary Alice Heinbach v. Euphemia Belle Koller,* case no. 21498, MSCF-MSA.

32. U.S. Federal Manuscript Census, 1910, Saverton township, Ralls County; *Ralls County Times,* June 15, 1906, and February 7, 1908; Circuit Court Record, book Q, 21, Ralls County, Office of the Circuit Clerk and Recorder, New London. Savu secured a saloon license on August 8, 1911. Record F, 295, Ralls County, Office of the County Clerk, New London, and *Ralls County Times,* August 11, 1911. On incorporators of the Ilasco Supply Company, see Jack Briscoe's letter in the *Ralls County Times,* May 8, 1908.

33. U.S. Immigration Commission, *Reports,* vol. 4, 351–52, 361; Marian Mark Stolarik, "Immigration and Urbanization: The Slovak Experience, 1870–1918," 1, 50.

By 1910, Slovaks constituted Ilasco's second largest immigrant group. Among them were Julius and Mary (Roziak) Sunderlik. Julius, who was about twenty-eight years old when he immigrated in 1906, took a job as a miner in Atlas's shale pit. In 1909, he sent for Mary and their two children, Mary and John, who at the time of the 1910 Census were ages six and four, respectively. Julius's wife took in other Slovak and Rumanian boarders, while he continued to work in the shale mine. By 1920, their household no longer included boarders, but additional children Andrew, Joseph, Anna, and Lucy had arrived. Mary, their oldest daughter, was still living at home while working in a Hannibal shoe factory. Mrs. Sunderlik's death in 1922 left Julius with the responsibilities of work and parenting and inflicted loneliness as he confronted demands placed on him by life in a new land.[34]

Like most married immigrant men in Ilasco, Slovak John Sajban came to the United States without his wife, intending to earn money for a specific purpose and then return home. In 1909, he went to Cokesburg, Pennsylvania, to work in the coal mines to save money for a new dwelling on his thirty-five-acre tract of land back home. On June 1, 1911, his fifteen-year-old son George arrived in Cokesburg and began to work in the mines, too. In the meantime, a relative in Ilasco informed them that jobs were plentiful at the cement plant. The Sajbans arrived in Hannibal on November 4, 1912, and quickly took jobs with Atlas, but were disappointed that their pay was considerably less than what they had been earning in the coal mines. Since they had spent their available funds on the trip to Ilasco, however, they decided to stay. John's wife, Mary, joined them in 1916. John worked in the shale mine, and they also operated a rooming house for cement workers in a section of Ilasco known as Pump House Hollow. In 1920, an accident in the shale mine took John's life, but his widow and two children—George and three-year-old Anna—survived to carve out a life in Ilasco. Three of their children remained in Slovakia.[35]

Joining the Sajbans and Sunderliks in Ilasco were Slovaks Josef and Mary (Tushim) Hustava. Josef immigrated in 1908 and took a job in a meatpacking plant in St. Louis. He had to make a couple of trips back to Europe before convincing his wife to bring Irene, their six-year-old daughter, and join him in Missouri. Although afraid to sail across the ocean, Mary finally yielded and brought Irene to St. Louis in 1913. Josef and Mary both worked in the meatpacking plant before moving to Ilasco. There they took positions at the cement plant, Mary as a sack sewer, and Josef in the clinker mill. By 1920, they had added two

34. U.S. Federal Manuscript Censuses, 1910 and 1920, Saverton township, Ralls County; Anna Sunderlik Venditti, interviews by author, June 24 and July 6, 1992.

35. Stanley D. Sajban to Gregg Andrews, July 4, 1994; U.S. Federal Manuscript Census, 1920, Saverton township, Ralls County.

daughters to their family—Anna, age four, and Mary, who was one and one-half years old.[36]

Austria-Hungary also furnished Slovak immigrants John and Susie Viglasky. John immigrated in 1907 and was joined the following year by Susie and their two children—Paul, age six, and Anna, age four. John worked in Atlas's quarry, and Susie performed unpaid labor in the household. They helped to organize a Slovak Lutheran Church in Ilasco and played a role in encouraging the preservation of the Slovak language and culture. They bought a home in the section of Ilasco known as Stillwell's Addition, or Monkey Run. By 1920, they had added six new children to their household—John Jr., Mildred, George, Joe, Mary, and Helen.[37]

The Magyar-speaking population of Austria-Hungary also provided many immigrants to Ilasco. One of them was Gaspar Homolos, a single twenty-five-year-old Hungarian who went first to Painesville, Ohio, in 1902. While there, he learned that Atlas was advertising for workers at the Ilasco plant. Later that year he joined the quarry workforce at the cement plant while construction was still in progress. His brother, Charles K. Homolos, joined him in 1905 and worked as a burner in the kiln building. That same year, Gaspar married Rose Marie Molnar, also a Hungarian, who took in boarders to supplement their income. They settled into life in Ilasco, where they raised two children—Gizella Barbara and James.[38]

Bela Nemes, schoolmate of Gaspar and Charles Homolos in Vesprem, Hungary, immigrated to Ilasco in 1910 at the age of twenty-six and began working as an oiler and fireman at the cement plant. Nemes apparently left behind working in the wheat fields to take up industrial employment with Atlas. On September 5, 1914, he married Mary Borsos, who had immigrated from Austria-Hungary earlier that year before the outbreak of World War I. Borsos, born in 1891, had worked in the wheat fields and a garment factory before coming to Hannibal, where she found work as a maid. She soon met Bela, and after they married went to live in Pump House Hollow. "I think she may have been told by a gypsy fortune teller," mused their daughter Rosa, "that this was a land of riches and she'd have 4 children. She had 11, and we were poor."[39]

For immigrant women in Ilasco, the insecurities of life in a new country became even greater when marriages dissolved, leaving them sole responsibility

36. U.S. Federal Manuscript Census, 1920, Saverton township, Ralls County; Anna Hustava Sanders, interview by author, July 2, 1992.

37. Mildred Viglasky Martinovich to Gregg Andrews, October 30, 1994; U.S. Federal Manuscript Census, 1920, Saverton township, Ralls County.

38. Howard, *Ralls County Missouri,* 247, 385; U.S. Federal Manuscript Census, 1910, Saverton township, Ralls County. See also the obituary of Charles K. Homolos in the *Ralls County Record,* September 6, 1962.

39. Rosa H. Nemes to Gregg Andrews, August 2 and September 25, 1994; U.S. Federal Manuscript Census, 1920, Saverton township, Ralls County.

for raising their children. Such was the case of Susie Betina, a Slovak who had married George Betina in Austria-Hungary in December 1899. She came with her husband to Ilasco in 1901 while the cement plant was under construction. They lived together there until George abandoned her in July 1906.[40]

Shortly after securing a divorce, Susie married James Zugras, a Greek millwright at the cement plant in Ilasco who had immigrated in 1902. In 1910, the Zugras household included Susie's daughters from the previous marriage—Elena, age eight, and Mary, three—and Edna, one, who belonged to James and Susie. Mr. and Mrs. Zugras became naturalized U.S. citizens in 1913, and they had another daughter, Velma, who died at the age of two on November 10, 1917. By 1920, their marriage had produced three new children—Jimmy, Angelina, and Elsie. Mr. Zugras had now become a merchant in Ilasco.[41]

Ilasco attracted a large number of immigrants from southern Italy, which produced 83.4 percent of Italian immigrants to the United States during the eleven-year period prior to June 30, 1909. Whereas a greater proportion of immigrants from northern Italy were skilled workers, most from the southern region were farm laborers. A member of the United States Immigration Commission expressed the biases of the American public when he noted that northern Italians were "a more desirable class of immigrants" and more easily assimilated into American society. Southern Italians, however, "because of their ignorance, low standards of living, and the supposedly great criminal tendencies among them are regarded by many as racially undesirable."[42]

This representative of the U.S. Immigration Commission toured a region in southern Italy in 1907. He noted the high illiteracy rate and marginal existence of many tenant farmers, small landholders, and day laborers who averaged less than fifty cents per day. He reported that tending olive vines required only one-half of a family's time, thus freeing them to work elsewhere for wages part of the year. According to his report, money sent by immigrants back to Italy from the United States had exerted an upward pressure on wages in southern Italy. In some cases, day laborers in the region had earlier earned between twelve and sixteen cents per day.[43]

Thanks to Atlas labor agents and kinship and community ties, many of Ilasco's Italian immigrants came from the southern village of Papanice in the province of Catanzaro. Among them was Joseph "Big Jack" Scampoli. Ilasco's Richard Sanders

---

40. *Susie Bertena v. George Bertena,* February 3, 1908, case no. 9076, Ralls County, Office of the Circuit Clerk and Recorder, New London; U.S. Federal Manuscript, 1910, Saverton township, Ralls County.

41. U.S. Federal Manuscript, 1910, Saverton township, Ralls County; U.S. Federal Manuscript Census, 1920, Saverton township, Ralls County.

42. U.S. Immigration Commission, *Reports,* vol. 4, 177–79.

43. Ibid., 153–55, 177–79, 185–86.

recalled that Scampoli once told him that he was working in his garden one day when Atlas agents came through there seeking workers for the Ilasco plant. Others participating in the chain migration from Papanice included Theodore Polletti, Pantaleone Montefusco, Salvatore Russo, Rosario and Mary L. Galluzzio, and more.[44]

Also from Papanice was Rosa Raimondi, an agricultural laborer on the olive farm of Pasquale Genovese and Josephine Larrata Genovese. On October 16, 1907, at age sixteen, she married twenty-year-old Pantaleone Genovese, a son of the farm owners who employed her. While Rosa was pregnant with "Daisy," the first of thirteen children, Pantaleone and his younger brother Frank left Papanice in 1908 for Ilasco. They took a ship from Naples, docked at Ellis Island, and then traveled by train to Ilasco, where they took jobs in the sack house at the cement plant. They lived in a boardinghouse operated by fellow Italians Joseph and Mary Olive. Joseph worked for Atlas in the rock quarry while Mary cared for the couple's three children, cleaned and cooked, and perhaps did laundry for the seventeen boarders who lived there in 1910. At that time, they were part of an Italian community in Ilasco that numbered 176.[45]

Frank Genovese later left Ilasco for West Virginia, but by 1914 Pantaleone felt comfortable bringing Rosa and Daisy to join him in Ilasco. Within a short time, they opened a grocery store and supplemented their income by renting the upstairs to boarders. They both ran the store, while Pantaleone continued working at the cement plant.[46]

Nicholas ("Mike") and Christina Kitsock were part of a small group of immigrants in Ilasco from the Ukraine, where tiny plots of land, archaic farming methods, and a disproportionately large agricultural population had provided the context for emigration. Although discrepancies in the census materials make it difficult to pinpoint the exact date of their immigration, Nicholas apparently immigrated around 1895 and Christina in 1897 from the western Ukraine. In 1900, they lived in Lehigh County, Pennsylvania, where Nicholas worked at Atlas's Northampton plant and Christina took care of twelve immigrant boarders. While there, they had two children, Mike and Anna.[47]

44. Richard Sanders, interview by author, July 2, 1992; Pete Galluzzio, telephone interview by author, June 14, 1994.

45. Armenia Genovese Erlichman, interview by author, July 9, 1992; U.S. Federal Manuscript Census, 1910, Saverton township, Ralls County; Schiavo, *Italians,* 27.

46. Armenia Genovese Erlichman, comp., "Genovese Family History, 1907–1994," unpaginated; U.S. Federal Manuscript Census, 1920, Saverton township, Ralls County.

47. U.S. Immigration Commission, *Reports,* vol. 4, 265; U.S. Federal Manuscript Census, 1900, Middle District of North Whitehall township, Lehigh County, Pa.; U.S. Federal Manuscript Censuses, 1910 and 1920, Saverton township, Ralls County; Mildred Kitsock King to Gregg Andrews, March 10, 1993; *Hannibal Courier-Post,* December 20, 1984.

Like the Kitsocks who came to Ilasco shortly after the cement plant opened, Ukrainian immigrants Frank and Fannie Yacyla Konko entered Ilasco after living first in the Northampton area. They had immigrated in 1890. Their son John was born in Northampton in 1901, and their daughter Anna in 1904. Around 1905, they came to Ilasco and Frank began working at the cement plant. In the years ahead, many Ukrainian immigrants in Ilasco would go back to Pennsylvania, but the Konkos and the Kitsocks would persist.[48]

When Thomas Randolph went to work for Atlas as a chemist in 1903, he did not fit the typical profile of an immigrant worker in Ilasco. Atlas particularly valued his ability to speak several languages, and often used him as an interpreter at the Ilasco plant. He had changed his name from Renault upon arriving in New York City from his hometown of Nice, France.[49]

Upon arriving in Ilasco, Randolph married twenty-five-year-old Hattie Whitney Rogers, a former resident of Hull, Illinois. Rogers had two surviving children from an earlier marriage, eight-year-old Marion and six-year-old Otto. The Randolphs leased a lot from Samuel Heinbach and built a four-room house. Hattie gave birth to their son Clifford, but in 1905 her husband mysteriously disappeared while she was seven months pregnant. After conducting an unsuccessful search, she concluded that he had gone back to France, leaving her to raise Clifford and Velma, who was born two months after he disappeared.[50]

At the time of the 1910 Census, not a single African American lived in Ilasco. This reflected Atlas's hiring practices and the intense racism among area residents. In 1910, only about sixteen blacks living in Hannibal worked at the cement plant. Not until World War I did Atlas begin to employ significant numbers of African Americans, who as the result of this wartime labor shortage also began to move into Ilasco. By 1920, at least eighty blacks worked at the cement plant and at least eighteen lived in Pump House Hollow: Alice Simon, Mary Davis, Nora Daniels, Lasem Neal, Henry Turner, Ruth Turner, Elmer Herl, Leslie Simon, Luther McCallum, Obie Simon, William Daniels, Georgia Simon, John Davis, Arlie Blackwell, Willie Turner, Herbert Turner, Irene McCallum, and a housekeeper Nora (no last name provided by the census enumerator).[51]

---

48. U.S. Federal Manuscript Censuses, 1910 and 1920, Saverton township, Ralls County; John E. Konko to Gregg Andrews, June 17, 1994; *Hannibal Courier-Post*, December 20, 1984. See also the obituary of Anna Kitsock in the *Hannibal Courier-Post*, January 11, 1993.

49. Velma Youell, "Renault a/k/a Randolph," 14–15.

50. Ibid., 14–16; U.S. Federal Manuscript Census, 1910, Saverton township, Ralls County. In 1900 Hattie was married to Ewell Rogers. Their household included children Marion, Otto, and a baby daughter, Nellie. U.S. Federal Manuscript Census, 1900, Kinderhook township, Pike County, Ill.

51. U.S. Federal Manuscript Censuses, 1910 and 1920, Saverton township, Ralls County, and Mason township, Marion County, Mo. Since the USX Corporation would not let me

These, then, were some of the representative faces of Ilasco's early residents. They came with great expectations. For some, working at the cement plant and living in Ilasco met those expectations. Many others, in what became an impoverished atmosphere of "root, hog, or die," left or lost their lives on the job. As sociologist Ewa Morawska has observed, immigrants quickly viewed America as "a promise, perhaps, but one to be redeemed at the price of terribly hard work, dismal living conditions, recurrent insecurity, and deteriorating health—a price much steeper than they had imagined in Europe."[52]

Whether immigrants or native-born, all found themselves caught up in a cultural drama that shook mossback Missouri and the land of Tom Sawyer. As Ilasco assumed the appearance and character of a rough-and-tumble mining camp, its deep social problems posed a challenge to those who had endorsed Atlas's penetration of the area in hopes that cement manufacturing would shake Ralls County out of its stagnation and dependence on agriculture. Local boosters became alarmed at the industrial "foreign colony" taking shape on the edge of Little Dixie.

---

see payroll records of the Atlas Portland Cement Company, I calculated the approximate number of black workers at the cement plant by examining the federal censuses for the above townships. In no way do I wish to suggest that these numbers are precise. Of Ilasco's eighteen black residents in 1920, eight were born in Missouri, four in Texas, three in Arkansas, and one in Oklahoma.

52. Ewa Morawska, *For Bread with Butter: The Life-Worlds of East Central Europeans in Johnstown, Pennsylvania, 1890–1940,* 112.

(3)

A Labor Camp in the Shadow of Atlas

The saloons were overburdened with custom; so were the police courts, the gambling dens, the brothels, and the jails—unfailing signs of high prosperity in a mining region—in any region for that matter.
—Mark Twain, _Roughing It_

Since Atlas did not own the town site of Ilasco, it lacked the degree of control over workers' lives, leisure activities, and other institutions that corporations had in many company towns at that time.[1] Officials did seek, however, to achieve greater control over their overwhelmingly male immigrant labor force and to extend that control into the community itself. This grew out of a determination to improve labor efficiency and discipline a transient labor force that was the object of much nativist hostility, and out of growing alarm over crime and the heavy use of alcohol in Ilasco. But Ilasco's location on adjacent land owned by other individuals hampered Atlas's efforts to impose cultural restraints on the community.

Ilasco's early residents were tough, hard-bitten people whose reputation for hard drinking was well known in the area. In some cases, their drinking patterns may have grown out of a rural way of life molded by the task-oriented, seasonal rhythms of agricultural work. For Ilasco landlords Samuel Heinbach and Theodore Johnson, heavy drinking had been a regular part of their earlier work culture as woodchoppers. On Saturday afternoons, they had typically sent for one and one-half gallons of whiskey and other hard liquor to have in camp. According to L. T. Smashey, Johnson's brother-in-law, they were constantly under the influence of alcohol while chopping wood. Eliza Jane Johnson, Theodore's wife, admitted that her husband drank a lot but insisted that Heinbach was

---

1. See, for example, David Alan Corbin, _Life, Work, and Rebellion in the Coal Fields: The Southern West Virginia Miners, 1880–1922,_ and David L. Carlton, _Mill and Town in South Carolina, 1880–1920._

the heavier drinker. In the view of W. H. Fisher, an attorney and insurance businessman from Hannibal, Heinbach consumed a lot of alcohol but did not drink "any more than these people that live out in the country." Fisher observed that "nearly all of them take a drink when they come to town and generally go home with a bottle in their pockets and then use it when they get home."[2]

The drinking habits of first-generation factory workers, whether native-born or immigrants, confounded American employers. The customs, festivals, and religious holidays of southern and eastern European immigrants clashed with factory regimentation. The heavy drinking and merrymaking that accompanied wedding festivities, christenings, and holiday celebrations typically lasted several days and cut into the workweek.[3]

In part, however, hard drinking in Ilasco was a by-product of efforts to cope with an extremely harsh life. Long workdays and the dangerous, exhausting nature of cement mill work encouraged the use of alcohol to satisfy the psychological and physical needs of depleted workers. Hungry and thirsty workers at times near dehydration after a long day of work in the heat viewed beer as a cheap source of nutrients, often easier to get than a drink of uncontaminated water. "Yes," noted Andrew Mirtzwa, a Hannibal barber, "that's generally the way with all of them people that work over there [Ilasco]—they work pretty hard and then they load up."[4]

For Atlas immigrants isolated by language and cultural barriers and packed into crowded boardinghouses, drinking offered a temporary escape from cultural isolation, family separation, and loneliness. It also may have temporarily washed away fears of serious injury and possible death due to on-the-job accidents. In addition, it was a vital part of cooperative labor and neighborly traditions in the community. Perry Jones, a former Atlas worker, recalled that "whenever the people had something to do, a lot of people'd just pitch in and get the job done, and then after they got done, especially with the foreign class, why, they'd have a little drinking party."[5]

Lured by the promise of big profits at the expense of Atlas workers, the partnership of Herman Lefkovitz and Herman Schwartz tried to secure a monopoly on the liquor market in Ilasco. On June 21, 1905, they signed a fifteen-year contract with Andrew Christensen, another landowner close to the plant. Christensen agreed not to lease, sell, or assign any part of his premises to anyone engaged in

2. *Heinbach v. Heinbach et al.,* April term, 1914, 160, 255, 319, 323–24.

3. Herbert G. Gutman, "Work, Culture, and Society in Industrializing America, 1815–1919."

4. Corbin, *Life, Work,* 35–38; American Social History Project, *Who Built America? Working People and the Nation's Economy, Politics, Culture, and Society,* vol. 2, *From the Gilded Age to the Present,* 84; *Heinbach v. Heinbach et al.,* April term, 1918, 254, 258.

5. Perry Jones, tape provided to author, December 5, 1994.

the saloon or liquor business in exchange for payment of five dollars per year. Ten days later, Lefkovitz and Schwartz made similar arrangements in a fifteen-year lease of land from Heinbach. They paid him only twenty-five additional dollars for the term of the lease in exchange for a promise to deny leases on his twenty-six-acre tract to anyone involved in the saloon business.[6]

Lefkovitz and Schwartz also signed a contract with John B. Herl Sr., agent for the Dick and Brothers Brewing Company of Quincy, Illinois. They promised to buy at least one-third of their beer from Herl in exchange for the company's agreement not to sell beer to anyone else in Ilasco or to engage directly in the saloon business there. They signed a similar contract with the Hannibal Brewing Company, which agreed in turn not to sell or provide beer to anyone else in Ilasco except to Andy and John Moore and their successors in the building in which the Moores then operated a tavern. The contract was to go into effect when the dramshop license of Joe Blair expired on October 25, 1905, or as soon as Lefkovitz and Schwartz could obtain Blair's interest in the license. Henry Riedel, secretary and treasurer of the Hannibal Brewing Company, agreed not to sell beer to the Moores in anything less than half barrels and bottle beer, and to provide Lefkovitz and Schwartz with as much beer as they wished to buy.[7]

Since Atlas did not hold the leases on lots that housed Ilasco's saloons, it could not simply ban taverns, as was sometimes the case in classic company towns. Unless county voters outlawed saloons in local option elections, the only other way to deny workers access to nearby saloons was for companies to try to block the granting of dramshop licenses. Employers opposed saloons because they feared the impact of drinking on labor efficiency, but they justified their opposition on grounds that workers would probably waste paychecks in saloons on their way to and from the mill. Corporate officials pursued this anti-licensing strategy with only limited success in Ilasco and other industrial towns such as Steelton, Pennsylvania, and Worcester, Massachusetts. In Worcester, for example, the Washburn and Moen Wire Manufacturing Company led frequent campaigns to deny licenses to saloons near the plant, but only on occasions were they successful.[8]

---

6. Contract between Andrew Christensen and Lefkovitz and Schwartz, June 21, 1905; Lease, Samuel Heinbach to Lefkovitz and Schwartz, July 1, 1905; both in Deed Record, book 72, 482–84, Ralls County, Office of the Circuit Clerk and Recorder, New London.

7. Contract between John B. Herl et al. and Lefkovitz and Schwartz, June 26, 1905, and Contract between Lefkovitz and Schwartz and the Hannibal Brewing Company, June 26, 1905; both in Deed Record, book 72, 482–84, Ralls County, Office of the Circuit Clerk and Recorder, New London.

8. Bodnar, *Immigration and Industrialization,* 99; Roy Rosenzweig, *Eight Hours for What We Will: Workers and Leisure in an Industrial City, 1870–1920,* 61, 93–97. Crandall A. Shifflett, *Coal Towns: Life, Work, and Culture in Company Towns of Southern Appalachia, 1880–1960,* 168, finds differences among coal operators over whether to

Atlas officials, in an attempt to control and discipline their transient labor force in Ilasco, spearheaded efforts from the outset to deny licenses to saloon owners "anywhere near the plant." In March 1903, they tried but failed to block the opening of a saloon in Ilasco. They renewed their efforts in 1906, however, reinforced by growing anti-saloon forces in the county. When Lefkovitz and Schwartz, along with Mrs. Andy Moore, petitioned the Ralls County Court to renew their dramshop licenses on April 6, 1906, attorney Albert R. Smith, whose firm represented Atlas, filed a remonstrance against the petition. Testifying in court against licensing were W. A. Smith, superintendent of the cement plant, D. B. Pearson, traffic manager at the plant, and S. W. Burden, an Atlas shipping clerk. Also testifying were Richard Dalton, a big orchard grower and former Democratic state representative from Saverton, and Dr. R. Marvin Winn, an Ilasco physician. The court denied the licenses on grounds that "further legalizing of the liquor traffic at Ilasco where humanity was so conglomerately congested would be a menace to law and order and would to a great extent increase the crime which has already been the result at that point."[9]

Like many corporations in the Progressive Era, Atlas's opposition to saloons grew out of an underlying desire to mold an efficient, disciplined labor force for economic expansion. Corporate officials blamed alcohol for low labor productivity and identified it as the major cause of industrial accidents. They played an important role in the movement to promote alcohol reform. As historian John J. Rumbarger notes, "The concern for the political control of the leisure activity of the masses was not a peripheral academic concern. It was vital to the corporate community which viewed it as a requisite condition of continued economic growth."[10]

Two recent murders "added to the long list at the cement plant" had contributed to the growing public uproar over saloons in Ilasco. Mary Baker, described by Ilasco's Fred Jeffers as "quite a drinking woman," had killed her husband, Joseph, in a domestic dispute on December 15, 1905. She claimed that she shot her husband in self-defense when he charged at her with a fork, threatening to kill her. Other versions of the killing circulated, however, emphasizing that "both

---

campaign against saloons in order to control labor. He cites an operator who reported that one of his managers was trying to convince the county court to reverse itself and grant a saloon license. The operator's firm owned half interest in the tavern. On employer-banned saloons in company towns, see Carlton, *Mill and Town*, 90–91.

9. *Hannibal Morning Journal*, March 22, 1903; *Hannibal Courier-Post*, April 7, 1906; and *Ralls County Times*, April 13, 1906. Bodnar, *Immigration and Industrialization*, 99, shows that company officials in Steelton, Pennsylvania, also tried to block the granting of saloon licenses.

10. John J. Rumbarger, *Profits, Power, and Prohibition: Alcohol Reform and the Industrializing of America, 1800–1930*, 113, 131.

were under the influence of liquor at the time the killing took place." Although authorities arrested Baker, Prosecuting Attorney Ben Hulse concluded that he could not get a conviction, and dismissed the case against her.[11]

On April 6, the same day on which Lefkovitz and Schwartz petitioned to renew their saloon license, the *Ralls County Times* reported the killing of John Honula, a Slavic cement plant worker, in their saloon earlier that week. In what the newspaper described as a "race fight" between Slavs and Poles on one side against Rumanians on the other, an unidentified party hit Honula on the head with a club. Witnesses gave conflicting stories about who did it, one of them claiming that Schwartz, himself, had struck the fatal blow, and the crime went unpunished. "Judging from the reports of a gentleman who was on the ground," the *Ralls County Times* concluded, "this saloon is a regular hell hole and the county court would be justified in refusing a further license when this present one expires."[12]

Atlas's influence over the local court and the growing strength of anti-saloon elements stymied Ilasco saloon operators, some of whom had been earlier prosecuted for selling liquor on Sundays. Lefkovitz and Schwartz prepared another court petition, but Atlas attorney Smith again filed a successful remonstrance against it. Joe Blair's license expired on April 26, 1906, and so did that of Lefkovitz and Schwartz on April 30. They then withdrew their applications and closed their saloons.[13]

"The warfare on saloons and the liquor traffic generally does not stop there," reported the *Hannibal Courier-Post* that summer. "Those opposed to intemperance have become enthused and are now making an attempt to spread over the entire county and do good."[14] The Woman's Christian Temperance Union (WCTU) sent ministers to Ralls County to support a petition circulated by Dr. Winn to put the proposition of local option to voters. Richard Dalton, attorney Jack Briscoe, and Hulse led a meeting at the courthouse on July 16 to organize a county Anti-Saloon League affiliated with the state organization. Dalton and Winn supervised the organization's activities in Ilasco and the rest of Saverton township. These efforts, endorsed by the Ralls County Medical Society, were countywide, but

11. *Ralls County Times,* December 22, 1905, and March 23, 1906. For Jeffers's description of Baker, see *Heinbach v. Heinbach et al.,* April term, 1914, 433–34.

12. *Ralls County Times,* April 6, 1906.

13. *Hannibal Courier-Post,* April 25, May 9, May 11, and June 28, 1906; Record F, 248, 252, Ralls County, Office of the County Clerk, New London. On March 20, 1905, Arthur R. Moore pleaded guilty to charges that he had sold alcohol on Sunday, and the case of Andy Moore on similar charges was continued until the next regular term of the circuit court. Andy Moore died before his case was settled. Circuit Court Record, book P, 135–36, 164–65, Ralls County, Office of the Circuit Clerk and Recorder, New London.

14. *Hannibal Courier-Post,* June 28, 1906.

Ilasco workers were the real target. "The conditions that prevail in Ralls county," noted the *Hannibal Courier-Post,* "are probably much against the establishment of a saloon on account of the characters that are in evidence at the cement plant and the great number of crimes that are undoubtedly the results of the liquor traffic."[15]

Ilasco's immigrants were of particular concern to Ralls County officials and temperance advocates. A state WCTU superintendent emphasized the importance of the campaign against alcohol among immigrants. "These people," she said, "are to help frame our laws, vote in our officials, mingle with our children, marry our sons and daughters; and, unless we educate them in the principles of total abstinence and sobriety—well, figure the result yourself."[16]

After Ralls County temperance supporters filed a petition with 503 signatures, the county court called a special local option election to be held on September 1, 1906, to determine whether voters wanted to ban the sale of liquor. Jack Briscoe, the newly elected county prosecuting attorney, endorsed a ban "because of the worse than dismal conditions prevailing at Ilasco." He complained that most Atlas workers cashed their paychecks in Ilasco's saloons, thus contributing to the poverty and suffering of wives and children.[17]

New London attorney J. O. Allison led the campaign against local option. He had a distinguished background as Ralls County Democratic representative between 1884 and 1892, and he had served as a commissioner to the Louisiana Purchase Exposition at the 1904 World's Fair in St. Louis. He was also a close friend of former Governor David R. Francis and "a good patron" of Sid Smart's saloon in Ilasco. According to the *Hannibal Courier-Post,* Allison had a "certain pledbian [sic] following" in Ralls County, and was regarded as the "political boss" of Ilasco.[18]

The anti-saloon campaign enlisted many speakers, including U. G. Robinson, president of the Missouri Anti-Saloon League. One of the best-known local anti-saloon activists was David Wallace, a New London attorney and former state representative. Many opponents of local option argued that Ralls County badly needed tax revenues from the sale of liquor, but Wallace regarded the liquor traffic as "the most prolific source of shame, poverty and crime the world has

15. *Hannibal Courier-Post,* June 28 and July 18, 1906.

16. Woman's Christian Temperance Union, *Proceedings,* 1906, 96.

17. Record F, 266, Ralls County, Office of the County Clerk, New London; *Hannibal Courier-Post,* August 24, 1906.

18. Roy D. Blunt, *Historical Listing of the Missouri Legislature,* 3; *Hannibal Courier-Post,* August 24, 1906; *Heinbach v. Heinbach et al.,* April term, 1918, 386. On Allison's friendship with Francis, see *Ralls County Record,* August 12, 1910. For his work on the Missouri Commission to the St. Louis World's Fair, see Williams, ed., *State of Missouri,* 583.

never known." The *Ralls County Times* endorsed local option but stressed that the real problem was simply one of lax law enforcement.[19]

Since drugstores were sometimes mere fronts for the sale of liquor, pro-saloon forces accused Dr. Winn of opposing saloons for self-serving reasons. He had a financial interest in an Ilasco drugstore where he could provide a prescription for liquor to anyone who believed that a little nip would make them feel better. These charges prompted Winn to write an angry letter to the public defending his role in the local option campaign. He emphasized that he never left home at night in Ilasco "but that I feared some drunken scoundrel would go there from the saloon and ruin it while I was ministering to some sick patient. There is absolutely no police protection here, and women have been insulted by drunken men, not only in the night, but in broad daylight." He added that a woman had complained to him that "she was out at the back door of her home after coal when a man whose passions were inflamed with the damnable stuff attempted to assault her." When she ran in the house and told her husband, he grabbed a shotgun and chased the assailant into a saloon "where he was protected by the man who got the profit." Winn complained that "the saloons have been the cause of two cold-blooded murders that have gone unpunished . . . to say nothing of the homes ruined and the disgrace, degredation [*sic*] and depravity they have wrought in our midst."[20]

Local option supporters lost the election by only seventy-two votes. Although most Atlas workers—newly arrived immigrants—could not vote, Saverton township voters played an important role in defeating local option. They voted against banning the sale of liquor by a margin of ninety-eight votes. This represented the largest margin against the ban of any township in the county.[21]

19. David Wallace to Rev. U. G. Robinson, Superintendent, Missouri Anti-Saloon League, January 17, 1908, *The Missouri Issue* 6 (January 24, 1908): 2; *Hannibal Courier-Post,* July 16, August 15, and August 22, 1906.

20. *Ralls County Times,* July 6, 1906. Carlton, *Mill and Town,* 108–9, emphasizes how easy it was in some South Carolina mill towns to find so-called drugstores where doctors freely gave out prescriptions for whiskey.

21. *The American Issue* 21 (August 21, 1913): 5; *Hannibal Courier-Post,* September 4, 1906. Thelen, *Paths of Resistance,* 239–40, points out that since the start of local option elections in Missouri in 1888, nearly two-thirds of all such elections occurred between 1904 and 1908 during the gubernatorial tenure of Joseph Folk. Thelen attributes this to the aggressive work of religious evangelicals who endorsed Folk's crusade against saloons and gambling. Certainly such groups played an important role in the Ralls County local option campaign, too, but in the case of Ilasco this interpretation ignores the role of Atlas officials and local politicians with ties to Atlas.

The county court began to reissue dramshop licenses but periodically visited Ilasco to inspect conditions. Missouri lawmakers also tightened regulation of dramshop licensing. *Hannibal Courier-Post,* July 3, 1907; *Ralls County Times,* March 8 and May 10, 1907; Record F, 360, 380, 394, 414, 422, 576, Ralls County, Office of the County Clerk, New London.

The unsuccessful campaign against saloons came on the heels of a fire that ravaged Ilasco's business district. On March 2, 1906, the explosion of a gasoline stove in Janney's store and tavern sparked a fire that quickly destroyed his place along with stores owned by Lefkovitz and Schwartz, Groth, Fisher and James, and the Carlile Meat Company. The merchants immediately made plans to rebuild with more solidly constructed buildings, since Ilasco was now an established town in which they hoped to operate on a long-term basis. "At the time that the other places were put up," reported a Hannibal newspaper, "it was an experiment and the houses were cheap affairs."[22]

In a further expression of hostility toward the community that Ilasco's working people were building, cement plant officials instigated property conflicts in a local display of corporate power. A "spirited controversy" erupted when Atlas disputed the boundary line between company land and the lots leased by merchants from Theodore Johnson. New property surveys by Frank Stout, a former surveyor of Ralls County, and by surveyors representing Atlas and Ralls County supported Atlas officials' claims that the land leased by Johnson to these burned-out businesses belonged to the company. Many older residents of Ralls County sided with Johnson and the merchants, who reportedly announced that they would fight this in court if necessary. A Hannibal newspaper speculated that since the burned stores had been on the north side of the public road, Atlas was trying to force merchants to relocate the business district on the other side of Marble Creek.[23]

The dispute forced a temporary halt to rebuilding the business district. With its overwhelming influence at the county courthouse, however, Atlas soon had its way. By the following month, the affected Ilasco merchants had begun to rebuild despite the fact that Atlas shaved off some of their property.[24]

Despite property conflicts with Atlas, Ilasco quickly experienced a "small sized building boom." Groth bought a small tract of land from Charles Fuhrman for the construction of several tenement houses, and some workers moved southeast along Marble Creek where it emptied into the Mississippi River. Atlas built and donated a concrete bridge to the county to make it easier for workers there to ford the creek. On April 5, 1907, Hannibal businessman Richard H. Stillwell acquired and subdivided a tract of land on the south side of this bridge and began selling lots. Known as Stillwell's First Addition to Ilasco, this tract had once been a slave plantation of more than seventy-eight acres owned by Henry A. Harris. It soon

---

22. *Hannibal Courier-Post,* March 2, 3, and 6, 1906; *William Groth v. The Progressive Town Mutual Fire Insurance Company of Kansas City, Mo.,* February 4, 1907, case no. 8971, Ralls County, Office of the Circuit Clerk and Recorder, New London.
23. *Hannibal Courier-Post,* March 7 and 10, 1906.
24. *Hannibal Courier-Post,* March 3, April 25, May 14, and August 3, 1906.

housed what became known as Monkey Run, which had between one hundred and two hundred residents.[25]

As residents busily built a community, putting up new houses and remodeling old ones, Atlas continued efforts to hamper the formation of a central community. Company officials tried to disperse some of the population away from the plant's southwestern perimeter to a location just north of its pumping station along the river road to Hannibal. By March 1907, grading and construction work was underway in what became known as Pump House (or LeBaume) Hollow. According to officials, Atlas intended to scatter out the "foreign colony" in order to improve sanitary and other living conditions in the community. In addition, as the *Hannibal Courier-Post* reported, "Members of the company say they fear for the safety of their property, through the agency of intoxicated men, with the saloons situated so near the plant."[26]

Atlas officials had a stake in minimizing saloon-based socializing among workers. The company could undercut labor organizing and strikes by housing many workers on company property in Pump House Hollow, further from Ilasco's saloons. In fact, the creation of Pump House Hollow came only a few months after quarry workers confronted Atlas officials in a strike for the first time. Saloons provided important meeting places during strikes and hangouts where workers not only drank but also engaged in cultural exchange, and discussed politics, working conditions, wages, and other job and community issues.[27]

The Pump House Hollow addition would help cement plant officials to shape the behavior of workers on and off the job. At times, the plant's proximity to Ilasco's stores, taverns, and families had interfered with production. Noisy disturbances or confrontations in the community sometimes prompted workers to walk off their jobs temporarily to investigate and resolve these problems. In April 1906, for example, Frank Porter escaped from the state mental asylum and went to Ilasco, where he attacked his wife and children, reportedly intending to murder them. As he tied his child to a tree, the child's screams attracted the

25. *Hannibal Courier-Post,* April 25 and May 9, 1906; Abstract of Title to Fractional Section 1, Township 56, Range 4, in Ralls County, containing 78.41 acres, Stillwell's First Addition to Ilasco, prepared for Michael Karabin on June 10, 1911 (in author's possession). See also the plat filed by Stillwell, April 10, 1907, Ralls County, Office of the Circuit Clerk and Recorder, New London. On this tract as a slave plantation, see Smashey, comp., "History of the Smasheys," 130–33.

The name of Monkey Run probably derived from the fact that some of Atlas's blasting crew, or "powder monkeys," lived there. Members of the plant's blasting crew in the quarries had a tradition of yelling, "Run, monkeys, run," as they ran for safety after setting the explosives. Henry Sweets, Curator, Mark Twain Home Foundation, to Gregg Andrews, August 26, 1991; "Ilasco," topic no. 260, October 4, 1937, collection no. 3551, microfilm roll 575, folder 17504, U.S. WPA-HRS, Missouri, 1935–1942, WHMC–Columbia.

26. *Hannibal Courier-Post,* September 28, 1906, and March 19 and 27, 1907.

27. *Hannibal Courier-Post,* September 11 and 12, 1906. Chapter 5 will examine labor unrest in Ilasco between 1906 and 1910.

attention of cement plant workers who ran to the child's rescue and took Porter into custody.[28]

Relocation would lessen this kind of interference and make saloons less accessible to workers off the job. As the *Hannibal Courier-Post* acknowledged, the company's decision to scatter the community was an attempt to improve job productivity: "It is believed that by getting the settlement farther from the plant and from the saloons of the village, more work will be given the company by its employees."[29]

While Atlas maneuvered to squeeze more work out of its employees, merchants tried to increase their profits in the form of higher food prices to Ilasco's already hard-pressed residents. The three-mile distance to Hannibal made residents particularly dependent on Ilasco merchants, who aroused suspicions that they were taking advantage of their monopoly to prey on customers. In June 1907, just as the nation was feeling the pinch of a serious economic depression, Ilasco merchants "entered into a combine in order to make a standard price on merchandise, especially meat stuffs." This, despite the fact that about six hundred immigrants left Ilasco at the time of the meat hike, thus lowering demand and putting downward market pressure on prices.[30]

In response to the price increase, a group of Slavic residents, probably women, visited Hannibal in June 1907 to buy meat. They complained that the combine in Ilasco made meat unaffordable to workers and their families. The *Hannibal Courier-Post,* in an article entitled " 'Me No Can Buy Meat,' " trivialized their concerns and dismissed the attempted boycott of Ilasco merchants as a "foreigners' union." The newspaper pointed out that the product sold by Ilasco merchants was "most all salt meat and the price has been exceedingly low."[31]

The policies of Ilasco's merchants contributed to the marginalization of residents. Lefkovitz and Schwartz had already partially stifled competition through a lease with Samuel Heinbach providing that Heinbach could not lease any of his property to anyone who would engage in either the liquor or mercantile business. In 1906, at a time when Atlas officials and county authorities were trying to shut down the taverns, Lefkovitz and Schwartz stepped up the collection of debts owed by Ilasco residents. For example, Nick and Vertia Hiriza lost their house and all household goods to Lefkovitz and Schwartz as a result of a debt owed to the store in the sum of $170.10. Lefkovitz and Schwartz also took legal possession of the house and household goods of John Bena and his wife, Sarecta, to collect a debt of $236.06.[32]

28. *Hannibal Courier-Post,* April 18, 1906.

29. *Hannibal Courier-Post,* June 14, 1907.

30. *Hannibal Courier-Post,* June 14, 1907; *Ralls County Times,* June 7, 1907.

31. *Hannibal Courier-Post,* June 14, 1907.

32. *Heinbach v. Heinbach et al.,* April term, 1914, 94–95; Nick Hiriza and wife Vertia to Lefkovitz and Schwartz, June 9, 1906; John Bena and wife Sarecta Lue to Lefkovitz

Residents who could not understand English or who were illiterate were at a particular disadvantage in their dealings with merchants and the law. When Daniel Mack died in debt in the summer of 1905, he left his widow Ella, their three sons, and Ella's daughter Blanche Smith in a tough spot. The Macks, both of whom were illiterate, owed the store of Murphy and Lampton $72.20, and Ella battled to hang onto her property in the face of growing pressure on the Ralls County Probate Court to order a public sale of her real estate to satisfy creditors.[33]

Desperate, Ella tried to persuade Probate Judge W. O. Gardner and Murphy and Lampton to grant her more time to settle the account. At first Murphy and Lampton consented. "It seems that she is waiting upon a third party to furnish her the means of settling her accounts," they told Judge Gardner on August 25, 1905. "We would respectfully request you to delay further action in the matter for a little while to give her ample time to make her arrangements. From the Present outlook, we do not think it would be advisable to make haste in the matter."[34]

Within a few weeks, however, Murphy and Lampton had changed course, heeding the advice of their attorney to request the appointment of a public administrator. Judge Gardner complied with their request and ordered a public sale of the estate. Ella could only watch on May 6, 1907, as Murphy and Lampton scooped up her dead husband's estate, which included two and three-fourths acres of land, for $139. According to family memory, the Macks were "beat out of their land" because illiteracy had made them vulnerable to bill padding by merchants.[35]

High food prices put added pressure on Atlas to raise wages. Further marginalization of Ilasco workers at the hands of gouging merchants, particularly during a period of economic depression, contributed to unrest and perhaps even unionization attempts. This perhaps explains why cement plant officials apparently soon took steps to ensure a greater role for Atlas in the community's day-to-day business life, for a Hannibal newspaper reported that Atlas planned to open a company store to stock all household goods necessary for its workers.[36]

Lefkovitz and Schwartz's plans to set up cheese-making operations in Ilasco, using milk from goats that would be furnished by local farmers, perhaps also

---

and Schwartz, June 4, 1906; both in Miscellaneous Record, book 78, 208–9, Ralls County, Office of the Circuit Clerk and Recorder, New London.

33. Estate of Daniel Meck, case no. 2184, September 18, 1905, Ralls County, Office of the Probate Clerk, New London.

34. Ibid.

35. Ibid.; Administrator's Deed, Daniel Meck (by administrator D. M. Stout) to Murphy and Lampton, May 18, 1907, Miscellaneous Record, book 78, 413–14, Ralls County, Office of the Circuit Clerk and Recorder, New London; Melvin Sanders, interview by author, July 17, 1992.

36. *Hannibal Courier-Post,* April 25 and May 14, 1906.

disturbed Atlas officials. By March 1, 1907, Lefkovitz and Schwartz already had three hundred goats on their farm just south of Ilasco. Their plans to reorient the agricultural economy toward their needs may have posed a challenge to Atlas's bid for control of property use and ownership.[37]

On September 30, 1907, the recently incorporated Ilasco Supply Company, which had close ties to Atlas, bought out the entire interest of Lefkovitz and Schwartz for thirteen thousand dollars. The purchase included 120 sheep, 34 hogs, and a lease on 120 acres of nearby farmland. A local attorney described the new company as a "subsidiary" of Atlas, but the exact connection to Atlas is not entirely clear. The relationship between the new company and Atlas may have been similar to a common type of relationship between company store and parent company in which store owners had no formal connections to the parent company but had a contract allowing direct access to the company payroll to collect workers' debts.[38]

By 1910, the Ilasco Supply Company operated two general stores, two butcher shops, and a drugstore. J. T. Fisher, formerly of Fisher and James, purchased the interests of his partners J. W. James and William Foster and became a member of the Ilasco Supply Company. He operated one of its general stores, and Foster, too, soon accepted a position with the company. William F. True, a justice of the peace and drugstore operator in Ilasco who had organized the new company, ran one of its general stores. Other incorporators included the well-connected Atlas labor agent Petru Sirbu, as well as John Savu, Hannibal's Dr. L. H. Tutt, and H. A. Adkisson, the sheriff of Ralls County. The corporation's valuation for tax purposes was seven thousand dollars in 1911.[39]

When the Ilasco Supply Company bought out Lefkovitz and Schwartz, the conditions of sale contained a stipulation that neither Lefkovitz nor Schwartz could ever again engage in any business in Ilasco that would compete with True's. Lefkovitz, who managed the saloon part of the business and who only a

37. *Ralls County Times,* March 1, 1907.

38. The purchase transferred control over forty-six lot leases to the Ilasco Supply Company. *Heinbach v. Heinbach et al.,* April term, 1918, 224–25. On the Ilasco Supply Company as an Atlas subsidiary, see "Suggestions in Opposition to Motion to Reinstate Appeal," March 10, 1921, 3, in *Mary Alice Heinbach v. Euphemia Belle Koller.* For a description of this type of company store, see Charles B. Fowler, Daniel Bloomfield, and Henry P. Dutton, "The Economic and Social Implications of the Company Store and Scrip System: A Report Made Pursuant to Article IX, Section 4 of the Code of Fair Competition for the Retail Trade," rev. ed., November 16, 1934, box no. 5, entry 31, 79, Records of the National Recovery Administration, RG 9, National Archives.

39. *Heinbach v. Heinbach et al.,* April term, 1918, 18–21, 220; *Heinbach v. Heinbach et al.,* April term, 1914, 86–94; Angelo Venditti, interview by author, July 9, 1993. See also book G, 317, Ralls County, Office of the County Clerk, New London; *Ralls County Times,* May 8, June 26, and December 11, 1908, and April 23, 1909. On Fisher's links to the Ilasco Supply Company, see the report of his death in *Ralls County Record,* October 20, 1916.

few weeks earlier had renewed his dramshop license, left for New York City on October 1, 1907. He allegedly left written authority with Sirbu to continue running the saloon during his absence from Ilasco. Sirbu had managed the saloon for Lefkovitz before the sale. According to their version of events, Lefkovitz merely intended to take a European vacation.[40]

Rumors circulated that the Ilasco Supply Company in fact had bought the saloon license from Lefkovitz, a transaction that would have been illegal since the law prohibited the transfer of saloon licenses. The editor of the *Center Herald* accused prosecuting attorney Jack Briscoe of having his hands in a crooked saloon deal and of giving official protection to the Ilasco Supply Company. Briscoe, who defended himself in public letters, claimed that he investigated the deal but could find no evidence that the Ilasco Supply Company had in fact purchased the saloon license. J. T. Fisher went to New London and discussed the case with Judge Reuben Roy. Fisher and other members of the Ilasco Supply Company insisted that Sirbu, with written authority, was simply running the saloon until Lefkovitz returned.[41]

Judges of the Ralls County Court discussed the case but concluded that there was no evidence to warrant prosecution. They served a citation on Lefkovitz, however, requiring him to appear at a special court session on December 14, 1907, to show why his license should not be revoked. Lefkovitz did not return to Ilasco but sent a written explanation that his temporary absence was the result of poor health. He claimed that illness kept him from returning for the special court session. He denied having transferred the license to the Ilasco Supply Company. Sirbu, he stressed, was merely managing the saloon as his agent during his absence.[42]

In an election year, this was a hot issue in county politics. What made it particularly controversial was the fact that one of the members of the Ilasco Supply Company was Sheriff Adkisson, who did not seek reelection that fall. Instead, he left the county for Hannibal, where he bought a livery barn and lived while he tended to business interests in Ilasco, including the Adkisson-Brown Meat Company. The court revoked Lefkovitz's license and notified Sirbu but insisted that no law had been broken. A grand jury investigation confirmed prosecuting attorney Briscoe's conclusions. In a letter that appeared on the front page of the *Ralls County Times,* the grand jury expressed confidence in Briscoe and Adkisson, assuring the public that "the proceeds from the saloon were accounted for and were found to be satisfactory."[43]

40. *Ralls County Times,* May 8, 1908.
41. *Ralls County Times,* March 6 and May 8, 1908.
42. *Ralls County Times,* May 8, 1908.
43. *Ralls County Times,* May 8, October 30, and December 11, 1908, and January 8, 1909. On the Adkisson-Brown Meat Company, see *William F. True v. Joe Bernstein,* January 12, 1912, case no. 10,088, Hannibal Court of Common Pleas, Hannibal.

For some reason, business squabbling prevented consummation of the deal that would have required Schwartz never to engage in business in Ilasco again. Sirbu operated the saloon for the Ilasco Supply Company for several months, but after the court revoked Lefkovitz's license, True sold the saloon back to Schwartz. The latter not only bought the saloon but also an exclusive liquor privilege that he and Lefkovitz had negotiated in the original lease of the lot from Heinbach. This privilege prohibited Heinbach from leasing other lots that would be used for purposes of selling liquor. Schwartz soon sold his 120 acres in Ilasco, however, and left for Kansas City without honoring the contract.[44]

The Ilasco Supply Company quickly tried to expand its financial interests in the community. When True's brother-in-law, Charles Perkins, applied for a saloon license in April 1909, Richard Janney, Sid Smart, John Hinkson, and other saloon owners remonstrated against granting Perkins a license. They protested that "the saloon was to be run in the interest of the Ilasco Supply Co." The Ralls County Court denied the license on grounds that Perkins would not be "the sole owner of said Dram shop."[45]

Because of Samuel Heinbach's opposition, Ilasco did not become incorporated. According to Fred Jeffers, several people tried to persuade Heinbach to sell some of his lots so they could incorporate a town. William True, George Douglas, Cassius Jeffers, and several others tried without success to buy land from Heinbach, who refused on grounds that incorporation would mean higher taxes for him.[46]

Nevertheless, residents took steps to lend greater organization to the community. In early 1909, Heinbach and Hannibal's W. H. Fisher spread a rough pencil plat of Ilasco across a showcase in True's drugstore, and at Fisher's suggestion named those streets running north and south. In addition, residents circulated a petition requesting the construction of a train depot at Ilasco. They presented the petition to state representative–elect W. B. Fahy in December 1908. After a meeting in Ilasco with the railroad commissioners and after four months of wrangling, Fahy announced that Ilasco would get a depot and freight agent. "I feel proud of this victory," he told New London's Joe Burnett, "and I think I may justifiably feel so, because at every meeting I have been opposed by all the

44. The Ilasco Supply Company sued to recover full payment from Schwartz. *Heinbach v. Heinbach et al.,* April term, 1918, 20–21, 35, 220, 225, 687–88; *William F. True v. Herman Schwartz,* March 16, 1908, case no. 9093, Ralls County, Office of the Circuit Clerk and Recorder, New London.

45. Record F, 590, 601, Ralls County, Office of the County Clerk, New London; *Ralls County Times,* April 9 and 16, 1909. On the relationship of True and Perkins, see U.S. Federal Manuscript Census, 1920, Mason township, Marion County, Mo.

46. *Heinbach v. Heinbach et al.,* April term, 1914, 91–92, 331–32, 431; and *Heinbach v. Heinbach et al.,* April term, 1918, 150.

railroad people, and never a very friendly ear from the majority of the Railroad Commissioners."[47]

The struggle by Ilasco's early residents to build a community under the watchful eye of Atlas and Little Dixie onlookers took place under difficult circumstances. Impatient critics cut the town little slack in regard to its deep social problems. As a labor camp on Missouri's industrial frontier, Ilasco was plagued by violence and crime, especially during the first decade of its existence. Constables John Wiggs and T. B. (Barney) Wilson and justices of the peace John Northcutt, Alex Leaf, William F. True, Thomas E. Burns, and William Ragland had their hands full dispensing justice. Atlas furnished the cement for the construction of Ilasco's jail—a dark, smelly concrete structure approximately 10 feet by 14 feet with a small barred window. The jail often housed intoxicated residents on weekends or served as a holding pen for perpetrators of more serious crimes until they could be transferred to the county jail in New London. "We want to say to all who get unruly," warned the Ralls County Record, "that they better look out for it is sure a sweat box. It has four cells and is as dark as any night."[48]

Much of the constables' work consisted of breaking up fights that grew out of excessive drinking. "They had a fight every night," remembered Ruby Douglas Northcutt. "The jail was full down here."[49] Perhaps typical was a brawl that broke out in early August 1908, when "knives, pistols and rocks were brandished in a lively fracas" that led to the wounding of Dan Sirbu and subsequent arrest of six men. Sirbu's gunshot wound in the left arm was not serious. The *Hannibal Courier-Post* blamed the fracas on "a crowd of carousing Roumanians mixed with a liberal sprinkling of 'red eye.' "[50]

Less than two weeks later, William Davis shot August Dexheimer with a double-barreled shotgun following an argument. Afterward, Davis summoned a doctor and took Dexheimer to his house for treatment. According to a newspaper reporter who investigated the incident, the shooting was in retaliation for Dexheimer's having reportedly thrown a brick that struck Davis in the head. Davis then went home and returned with a shotgun. The confrontation apparently grew out of financial differences: "It appears that they have been farming a certain

47. *Heinbach v. Heinbach et al.*, April term, 1914, 145, 161–62; *Ralls County Times*, December 18, 1908, and February 19, 1909. Fahy's letter to Burnett is reprinted in the *Ralls County Record*, May 14, 1909.
48. "Ethnic Identity and Bilingual Community—Ilasco, Ralls County," October 4, 1937, collection no. 3551, microfilm roll 575, folder 17506, U.S. WPA-HRS, Missouri, 1935–1942, WHMC-Columbia; *Ralls County Times*, November 5, 1909; *Ralls County Record*, November 12, 1909.
49. Ruby Douglas Northcutt, undated video interview by Jim Tatman, ca. 1990.
50. *Hannibal Courier-Post*, August 7, 1908. Reports of such fights in Ilasco are scattered throughout local newspapers. For the flavor of such reports, see, for example, *Hannibal Courier-Post*, November 7 and 17, and December 2 and 21, 1904.

piece of land on shares and difficulties arose over the selling of some of the products."[51]

Petty theft was so common that it became woven into the culture of Ilasco. Joseph Lamp, while working for the Ilasco Supply Company, carried a slingshot when he delivered groceries in order to keep young boys from raiding his wagon. Chicken theft was so widespread that Harrison Decker at times hurriedly sold his chickens at lower prices than the market would bring. "Either do that," he complained, "or have them stolen from me, I just let them have them."[52]

As a peddler discovered in July 1906, even giving a home demonstration of wares in Ilasco required a watchful eye. He caught Ethel Rose trying to steal a couple of shirts while he was displaying items in her home. "From all accounts obtainable," reported the *Hannibal Courier-Post,* "the peddler had spread his stuffs upon the floor for the inspection of his prospective purchasers. Mrs. Rose also spread out upon the floor, and during the process made an unsuccessful attempt to secrete a couple of shirts that she thought would be about the proper fit for her husband, beneath her."[53]

For outsiders, such experiences confirmed images of Ilasco as a dangerous place. As Hannibal Baptist minister J. C. Trower discovered in April 1907, even church services in Ilasco were not immune to alcohol-related pranks and disruptions. While he was preaching in Ilasco one Sunday evening, several intoxicated young men barged into the church and "conducted themselves very badly." They left after Trower reprimanded them, but two other intoxicated young men soon interrupted the service. They, too, left after he rebuked them, but later as Trower was leaving for Hannibal, an unidentified attacker hit him in the shoulder with a rock, stunning him momentarily in the darkness.[54]

On June 23, 1906, Jack Scott disrupted religious services at the Salvation Army hall in Ilasco and asked to speak to a "Mrs. Huddleston," with whom he had once lived for about eighteen months after convincing her to leave her husband. Huddleston had reunited with her husband earlier in 1906, but Scott tried to persuade her to run away with him again. When she refused, he grabbed her, forced her to the side of the building, and beat her until her eyes were swollen shut and her body badly bruised.[55]

51. *Hannibal Courier-Post,* August 19, 1908.

52. Melvin Sanders, interview by author, July 17, 1992. On the quote from Decker, see *Heinbach v. Heinbach et al.,* April term, 1914, 218–19.

53. *Hannibal Courier-Post,* July 21, 1906.

54. *Ralls County Times,* April 19, 1907.

55. *Hannibal Courier-Post,* June 27, 1906. See also the assault case against Fred Jeffers and Marshall Woods, accused of assaulting Anna Schwartz on May 27, 1906. *Hannibal Courier-Post,* May 31, June 1, and July 6, 1906.

For financial or other reasons, Ilasco's residents sometimes failed to legalize relationships through marriage and divorce. A good illustration is the relationship of Lulu and Louis Luther Lester, who had married on April 3, 1901. The marriage may have given Louis a place to land after he was evicted along with other houseboat dwellers from Hannibal's southside levee in early April 1901, but he and Lulu split up on April 11, 1905. They did not get a divorce until March 22, 1907. In the meantime, Louis and Sallie Truitt lived together in Ilasco, but were arrested in August 1906 for "rooming."[56]

Such arrests often grew out of legal complaints filed by the spouse of one of the parties, and this may have been so in the case of Louis and Sally. About three weeks after their arrest, Sally's husband, Ben P. Truitt, a railroad worker who lived on the southern edge of Hannibal, went to Ilasco, perhaps to try to persuade Sally to leave Louis. When he finished his business in Ilasco that night, he decided not to wait for the train but to walk to Hannibal on the public road. Along the way, he encountered someone with whom he exchanged angry words. "After a few words they came together," reported a local newspaper, "and in the tussel the unknown man pulled his revolver and fired." The shot wounded Truitt in the leg, but he made it home and was treated by a doctor. Perhaps fearing further retaliation, he refused to reveal the identity of his assailant.[57]

Ralls County authorities also hounded Albert Lester, Louis's brother. Although Albert had married Mary Baker after she killed her husband, their involvement in a subculture that included perhaps the illegal sale of alcohol, gambling, and prostitution made them the target of authorities. On August 30, 1909, Ralls County Prosecuting Attorney Jack Briscoe went to Ilasco to prosecute them for "keeping an immoral house," only to find that they had already fled.[58]

Briscoe published Ralls County's 1907 crime statistics, which if anything were probably conservative, since much of Ilasco had emptied during the national depression that year. According to those statistics, however, of 275 arrests, 122 were immigrants from Ilasco. Briscoe attributed 240 of these arrests directly or indirectly to alcohol. He concluded that "the liquor traffic is the greatest menace we have," and he stressed that "Saverton township has the greatest number of crimes to her credit, more because of the vast amount of money paid out every

56. *Luther L. Lester v. Lulu Lester,* February 6 and March 22, 1907, Circuit Court Record, book P, 456, 487, Ralls County, Office of the Circuit Clerk and Recorder, New London; *Hannibal Courier-Post,* August 30, 1906.

57. *Hannibal Courier-Post,* September 22, 1906. By 1910, Sallie and Ben Truitt were again living in the same household. U.S. Federal Manuscript Census, 1910, Mason township, Marion County, Mo. On August 18, 1909, a fast-moving passenger train killed Louis Lester Jr. near Orchard's Farm, Missouri. Lester, who boarded at Hannibal's Central Hotel, was working on the bridge gang of the Burlington Railroad at the time of the accident. *Hannibal Courier-Post,* August 19, 1909.

58. *Ralls County Record,* September 3, 1909.

two weeks to the employees of the Atlas Portland Cement Company than for any other reason." He pointed out, however, that "the dens in the other parts of the county sailing under the Christian name of drug store are just as prolific [of crime] and a great deal more subtle in their procedure."[59]

Law enforcement agents had trouble convicting those accused of committing murder or attempted murder in Ilasco. At the trial of Sam Russo, who confessed to shooting and killing fellow Italian Carmelo Maidi inside the clinker mill of Plant Number 5 in the early morning of December 17, 1910, several witnesses provided evidence strongly suggesting that Russo was guilty of premeditated murder. Both men were recent immigrants from Papanice in southern Italy and reportedly had a history of quarreling. Senta Merenda (Mirande), who kept a boardinghouse where Russo lived, testified that he told her that Maidi "had been saying bad things about him for a long time and he had a revolver to use on him sometime." She further testified that she saw Russo take the gun with him to work that morning, and Patsy Tallarico, who operated a grocery business in Ilasco, testified that Russo confessed to him that he had killed Maidi.[60]

The killing ignited passions in the community. After Russo had been arrested, Tallarico urged Constable Wilson to take him "where he could be protected from the mob." An angry mob threatened to storm the jail, thus compelling Wilson to remove Russo to the county jail in New London.[61]

A jury in the Ralls County Circuit Court acquitted Russo, who claimed that he shot Maidi in self-defense. Upon acquittal, however, Russo refused to return to Ilasco despite efforts by several Italians to persuade him to do so. The *Ralls County Record* attributed Russo's determination to leave the area to fear that feuding between rival Italian "clans" might cost him his life.[62]

As the following case illustrates, even judges were unwilling to be too harsh on immigrants who used violence against other immigrants. Late on the night of March 13, 1907, workers summoned Constable Wilson and Dr. C. A. Mackey to Company House Number 24, where John Ciavica had stabbed George Dragomir several times, having mistaken Dragomir for Agricola Nicoli. Dragomir's wounds were serious, including one in the back that penetrated the right lung. Constable Wilson hunted for Ciavica while Dr. Mackey attended Dragomir, arranging to have him taken to Levering Hospital early the next morning. After searching several Rumanian "shanties" in Ilasco and several saloons in Hannibal, Wilson found

59. Briscoe published these statistics in a letter to the public in the *Ralls County Times* on January 10, 1908.

60. *State of Missouri v. Sam Russo,* February 21, 1911, case no. 9422, Ralls County, Office of the Circuit Clerk and Recorder, New London; *Ralls County Record,* December 23, 1910.

61. Ibid.

62. Ibid.; *Ralls County Record,* November 17, 1911.

Ciavica the following afternoon "hiding under a bed, covered up with boxes and bedclothes." He then delivered Ciavica to county authorities in New London.[63]

A reporter who investigated the story for the *Hannibal Courier-Post* attributed the attempted murder to a grudge emanating from a quarrel over a woman that had occurred in Rumania more than a year earlier between Ciavica and Nicoli, one of Dragomir's roommates in Ilasco. According to the reporter, Ciavica shortly after this quarrel came to work at the cement plant, but had then moved to Ashburn to work at the DuPont powder plant. In the meantime, Nicoli also immigrated to Ilasco and found employment at the cement plant. Upon learning that his old nemesis had come to Ilasco, Ciavica awaited an opportunity to return to Ilasco and get revenge.

On the evening of March 13, Ciavica allegedly went to Company House Number 24 and pretended to have put aside his differences with Nicoli. He joined Nicoli, Dragomir, and other Rumanian workers in drinking and socializing until an opportunity for revenge presented itself. When several workers stepped outside, Ciavica whipped out a knife and stabbed Dragomir repeatedly, mistaking him in the darkness for Nicoli. Although Dragomir's wounds were serious, he recovered and pressed charges against Ciavica for assault with intent to kill. Ciavicia threw himself upon the mercy of the court and received a sentence of only three months in the county jail and a fine of one hundred dollars.[64]

The rather lenient treatment of such crimes perhaps grew out of public attitudes that put a low premium on life in general among the lower classes, or that regarded the perpetrators of capital crimes as stealthy survivors of Old World feuds who simply acted in self-defense. Whatever the case, in the three months after Russo's acquittal, jurors also refused to convict Nick Bucur, accused of murdering John Miga, and Frank Varga, charged with assault with intent to kill. The case against Varga, who had attacked Andrew Pavalenda with a knife, resulted in a hung jury, and Bucur was acquitted. Both men confessed to their deeds but claimed self-defense. Before Bucur's case ever went to court, the *Ralls County Times* editorialized that "the killing was justifiable," since Miga had earlier given Bucur an "awful beating."[65]

The following incident perhaps best illustrates the tumultuousness of life in Ilasco during this era. Constable T. B. Wilson, while returning home late at night on June 7, 1909, encountered two men stealing beer from a saloon. One of

63. *State of Missouri v. John Ciavica*, June 10, 1907, case No. 9006, Ralls County, Office of the Circuit Clerk and Recorder, New London; *Hannibal Courier-Post,* March 14, 1907.

64. *Hannibal Courier-Post,* March 14, 1907; *State of Missouri v. John Civicia,* common assault, November 4, 1907, Circuit Court Record, book Q, 21–22, Ralls County, Office of the Circuit Clerk and Recorder, New London.

65. *State of Missouri v. Frank Varga,* March 4, 1911, case no. 9440, Ralls County, Office of the Circuit Clerk and Recorder, New London; *Ralls County Record,* April 7 and 21, 1911; *Ralls County Times,* March 24, 1911.

the men was inside handing beer bottles to his partner outside when Constable Wilson discovered them. The outside burglar, identified as Andrew Mojzis, hit Constable Wilson with a beer bottle and tried to run away. Before he could escape, however, Wilson shot him in the back and killed him. According to a local newspaper, the dead man's wife was en route at the time from Europe to Ilasco.[66]

The disdain for Ilasco's working people that was shown by company officials, local judges and authorities, newspaper editors, and the native-born middle class was overwhelming. For some who battled personal and social despair in Ilasco, suicide seemed the only option. For example, William Layland tried to kill himself by drinking carbolic acid on May 28, 1907, and just after supper on April 2, 1906, Paul Dendish, a thirty-year-old Slovak worker at the cement plant, emptied a shotgun into his jaw in front of his boardinghouse. Dendish survived, but his was apparently only one of several such suicide attempts around that time. As the *Hannibal Courier-Post* noted, "There seems to be an epidemic of suicides in this vicinity."[67]

Local newspapers at times portrayed Ilasco's workers as little more than animals. In an article entitled "Wild Man at Large," the *Hannibal Courier-Post* reported on June 7, 1906, that a beastlike man had been sighted in "the dense forests and the dark, deep and gloomy hollows" near the cement plant. Comparing him to other species of wild animals known to have inhabited this area, the newspaper described the recluse as "a man with disheveled hair, furtive, uneasy eyes, stealthy, panther-like tread and a long, gaunt hungry form." The subject, armed with a knife in his right hand, reportedly lived off stolen chickens and other domestic fowl. "It is thought," concluded the newspaper, "that from the general appearance the man is an insane foreigner who has become unbalanced from over-work or other such unnecessary endeavor."[68]

Perhaps the images conjured up in the above article best expressed the uneasiness of many Hannibal observers over the social and cultural transformation that was yet in its infant stages. The "Wild Man" embodied the chaos that loomed if Ilasco's already marginalized immigrants and "poor white trash" completely lost their grip in this Darwinian social environment. He also perhaps served as a reminder of the pitfalls of "over-work," whether "unnecessary" or otherwise for industrial workers. Overwork might drive others to insanity and lead them to

66. *Ralls County Record,* June 11, 1909; Record F, June 8, 1909, 636, and Record G, July 5, 1909, 6, both in Ralls County, Office of the County Clerk, New London. The *Hannibal Courier-Post,* June 7, 1909, claims that the dead man was Paul Krudy, but the Ralls County sources above are probably more accurate.

67. *Hannibal Courier-Post,* May 29, 1907, and April 3, 4, and 7, 1906.

68. *Hannibal Courier-Post,* June 7, 1906. For a good discussion of similar anxieties and fears of townspeople in regard to crime and disorderliness in the cotton mill villages of South Carolina, see Carlton, *Mill and Town,* especially chap. 4.

revert back to a more primitive species roaming the hills and hollows around the cement plant.

For many middle- and upper-class observers, Ilasco represented social instability and cultural disorder. The industrial taming of the frontier south of Hannibal brought economic benefits but raised fears that earlier species of wild animals near Ilasco had merely been replaced by a subspecies of humans with equally primitive, animal-like instincts. In effect, many middle-class townspeople had merely grafted their fear of immigrants onto the nightmarish images of "white trash"—degenerate rural native-born people who were the subject of many eugenic family studies around the turn of the century. Animal imagery, so pervasive in the language of eugenics researchers at that time, not only degraded poor rural whites but also sent a clear signal that their degeneracy grew out of genetic deficiencies, not environmental conditions. In other words, poverty, alcoholism, crime, and other social problems had genetic roots.[69]

Exotic images of Ilasco's residents may have provided fascinating material for area readers, but Hannibal authorities at times took a dim view of immigrant visitors from the village. Just a few weeks before the "Wild Man at Large" article appeared, Hannibal police arrested a Slav spotted in town "dressed in a peculiar manner." Reportedly hungry and in bad need of clothing, the immigrant was apparently lost and unable to communicate effectively. The newspaper concluded that he was a cement plant worker and that "on account of his appearance and being unable to speak English he was thought to be crazy and was placed in jail" until the sheriff could find out his identity.[70]

Area newspapers also complained of mean barking dogs that roamed the streets and hollows in and around Ilasco. Amid reports that hydrophobic dogs were being killed in Ilasco during the spring of 1906, a reporter complained that "a trip through Ilasco would be the means of seeing more dogs in a given length of time than in the same territory on any other portion of the globe . . . all have a bad way of barking at visitors." The reporter, noting with approval that some dogs were being killed simply as a precaution, added that "it is to be hoped that the last dog requires killing before the right one is got."[71]

Newspapers at times dehumanized Ilasco's immigrants in references to them as "exports of Europe" whose names were "unspellable and unpronounceable in an English tone of voice." In some cases, reporters never bothered to learn the names of immigrants who appeared in their newspaper accounts "because of the fact that it makes no particular difference." On one occasion, even when a local

69. On eugenics studies, see Nicole Hahn Rafter, ed., *White Trash: The Eugenic Family Studies, 1877–1919,* 1–31.
70. *Hannibal Courier-Post,* May 21 and July 10, 1906.
71. *Hannibal Courier-Post,* May 18, 1906. Employers sometimes banned dogs in mill towns. See Carlton, *Town and Mill,* 90–91.

newspaper called attention to the growing volume of souvenir postal cards that immigrants were sending to their families in Europe at Christmas, it trivialized the "scribbling" on the postal cards as "a puzzle in itself."[72]

As Hannibal residents reacted to the transformation of the cultural landscape just south of town, menacing images of immigrants gripped many of them. On December 4, 1908, a large audience listened to a Chautauqua speech by Dr. Thomas E. Green, who was praised by the *Courier-Post* as a "clear and deep thinker and student of modern affairs," and as "one of the greatest Chautauqua orators now on the platform." In a speech, "Civic Bacteriology," Green warned of the evils of unrestricted immigration, complaining that it posed the greatest internal threat to the United States. He attacked intemperance and called for national constitutional prohibition. Finally, he compared the problem of immigration to a bacteriological disease and challenged the audience to remove the problem completely: "So God just took great chunks of heathenism that you neglected and dropped down in your back yards and said, 'Now, what are you going to do about it?' "[73]

Ilasco's critics attacked the symptoms but not the underlying causes of its social distress, pain, and volatility. Atlas officials and local elites valued the community primarily for the profits that its residents could produce with their labor, no matter how dangerous the working conditions, how filthy or overcrowded the living conditions, or how unfulfilling the hours after work. Exploitative relationships encouraged predatory attitudes on the part of merchants and others who regarded Atlas's labor camp inhabitants as easy pickings. "The Atlas Portland Cement Company is a paying institution to the county financially," observed the *Ralls County Times,* "but it is likely to be quite an 'elephant' from a moral and criminal standpoint. However, as in the economy of creation it was destined for one man to prey upon another, perhaps it is all right."[74]

That living conditions in Ilasco were deplorable is undeniable. These conditions, along with job exposure to dusty conditions that produced coughing and spitting in hot, poorly ventilated areas, often contributed to a high rate of sickness, including several deaths from tuberculosis in 1909. On December 17, 1909, a reporter for the *Ralls County Record* called attention to the links between squalid living conditions and extensive illness among residents that winter. "The Board of Health ought to take it in hand and have some of the filth cleaned up," urged the reporter, "and it is a fright, some of the places around Ilasco."[75]

72. *Hannibal Courier-Post,* September 27, 1904, July 12 and October 6, 1906, and December 26, 1908.

73. Quoted in *Hannibal Courier-Post,* December 5, 1908.

74. *Ralls County Times,* June 2, 1905.

75. *Ralls County Record,* December 17, 1909. Roberta Hagood and J. Hurley Hagood, comp., "A List of Deaths in Hannibal, Missouri, 1880–1910," 40, 73, 75. In 1909, Missouri had a tuberculosis death rate of 160.8 per 100,000 people. *Thirty-Second Annual Report*

County, state, and company officials at times became frustrated over the lack of cooperation by Ilasco residents to halt the spread of disease. Residents, perhaps afraid of losing work time, resisted a quarantine imposed by Atlas when smallpox broke out in the spring of 1914. Doctors from the State Board of Health accompanied Ralls County Judge Henry J. Priest and a local doctor to Ilasco, where they found at least seven cases. Prosecuting Attorney Joe Barry arrived, and the county sheriff put guards around the quarantined section.[76]

Concerns over unsanitary conditions, however, reflected more than just public health concerns. They were part of a growing middle-class preoccupation with personal cleanliness and orderliness in turn-of-the-century industrial America. As greater numbers of African Americans, poor whites from the countryside, and immigrants from southern and eastern Europe became industrial workers, cleanliness became a moral and patriotic issue for middle-class Americans, who associated dirt and disorder with immigrants in particular. To attain American citizenship required, in effect, that Ilasco's immigrants adopt personal standards of hygienic cleanliness.[77]

Ilasco's critics did not acknowledge the connections between squalid living conditions, poverty, and the workers' relationship with Atlas. They ignored dangerous working conditions at the plant and the harsh material context in which workers struggled to eke out a living. Ilasco was often a dangerous place, but so, too, was the work environment at the cement plant. When workers dared to protest such conditions, Atlas officials and local elites condemned them. When victims of frequent job-related accidents or their families sued to recover damages, Atlas's lawyers tried to block them, often arguing that the victims themselves were responsible. Local newspapers, ministers, alcohol reformers, and elites condemned the fractured family life in Ilasco, but ignored the devastating toll of poverty and work-related deaths upon the family structure. In short, they blamed the victims for their own degradation and poverty.

---

of the State Board of Health and Bureau of Vital Statistics of Missouri, 1914, 65. On the public health campaign against tuberculosis during this period, see Michael E. Teller, *The Tuberculosis Movement: A Public Health Campaign in the Progressive Era,* chap. 8.

76. *Ralls County Record,* April 24, 1914; *Thirty-Second Annual Report of the State Board of Health,* 22. Carlton, *Mill and Town,* 153–55, points out that during a smallpox outbreak in 1897, mill workers in South Carolina feared that vaccination would increase the risk of infection to the vaccinated arm and force them to lose work time or perhaps even their jobs.

77. Suellen Hoy, *Chasing Dirt: The American Pursuit of Cleanliness,* chap. 4. See also Mary Douglas, *Purity and Danger: An Analysis of Concepts of Pollution and Taboos.*

(4)

The Wages of Cement

Who are the oppressors? The few: the king, the capitalist, and a handful of other overseers and superintendents. Who are the oppressed? The many: The nations of the earth; the valuable personages; the workers; they that *make* the bread that the softhanded and idle eat.
—Mark Twain, speech, "Knights of Labor—The New Dynasty," March 22, 1886

So the Monkey Nest's mouth is stopped with dust, but in its time it had its pound of flesh. Yes, I figure it had its tons of flesh, all told, if laid side by side in Sugar Creek graveyard.
—Jack Conroy, *The Disinherited*

In 1910, the plant at Ilasco was one of four producing cement in Missouri—two others were in St. Louis County and one was outside Kansas City in Jackson County. These four plants employed 2,548 persons and produced 4,465,135 barrels of cement, making Missouri the fifth largest cement-producing state. Within the state, Ralls County was by far the leading producer, having manufactured 2,013,137 barrels in 1909; in contrast, St. Louis County produced 1,105,863 barrels, and Jackson County only 335,247.[1]

Such production figures meant obvious economic benefits, but the profits that accrued to eastern capitalists and stockholders, and to Hannibal merchants, bankers, and lawyers, came on the backs of workers subjected to dangerous working conditions. Local newspapers often graphically described accidents at the cement plant in which victims were suffocated, burned, mutilated, and

---

1. Missouri Bureau of Labor Statistics, *Annual Report* 32 (1910), 41–42, 214, and Missouri Bureau of Labor Statistics, *Annual Report* 33 (1911), 504–5; Ernest F. Burchard, "Cement Industry in the United States in 1910," in U.S. Geological Survey, *Mineral Resources of the United States, Calendar Year 1910*. Pt. 2—Nonmetals, 509.

mangled by machinery, crushed by rock slides in the shale mines, blown up by premature dynamite explosions, or injured in a variety of ways. The crushing and grinding so vital to the cement manufacturing process took a heavy toll not only on machinery but on workers as well.[2]

Atlas officials generally clustered their predominantly male labor force according to race, ethnicity, and gender. Although this pattern was not absolutely rigid, hiring practices encouraged clustering along these lines. This grew partly out of prevailing employer stereotypes about the alleged suitability of certain racial and ethnic groups for certain jobs, and partly out of employees' efforts to get jobs for relatives and fellow ethnic boarders. Since white foremen played a key role in hiring, native-born racist stereotypes of African Americans as inefficient, unstable, and unsuitable for industrial employment sharply limited the hiring of blacks. Employers generally preferred Slavs for their alleged deference to authority and willingness to work long hours without grumbling.[3]

In Ilasco's early quarries, where the especially labor-intensive stage of the manufacturing process began, Rumanians and Slovaks constituted the bulk of Atlas's labor force. Quarry workers, who averaged between $9.50 and $10.50 per week in 1906, used dynamite and operated air and electric drills and steam shovels to loosen limestone. Martin Polc, Gaspar Homolos, Dan Sirbu, and others used sledgehammers to break the rocks into smaller pieces after "powder monkeys" had blasted the limestone. They then shoveled the rocks into dump cars attached to teams of mules and horses.[4]

In 1906, the average weekly pay of teamsters—usually native-born workers like brothers Amiel (Jack) and Ollie Jones, and Bruce Peterson—was $9.67. Teamsters hauled the cars of rock to a railroad loading ramp where shovelers loaded the raw materials into hopper cars that were taken by steam locomotives to the mills. "It was a never-to-be-forgotten sight," Atlas engineer Guy D.

---

2. The accident rate among Missouri's manufacturing workers increased from 4 percent in 1905 to 14.1 percent in 1913. Thelen, *Paths of Resistance*, 49.

3. Daniel Nelson, *Managers and Workers: Origins of the New Factory System in the United States, 1880–1920,* 79–86; John Bodnar, Michael Weber, and Roger Simon, "Migration, Kinship, and Urban Adjustment: Blacks and Poles in Pittsburgh, 1900–1930," 553–54; Morawska, *Bread with Butter,* 117–18. U.S. Federal Manuscript Census, 1910, Saverton township, Ralls County.

4. To describe cement manufacturing, I have relied primarily on H. J. Seaman, "Cement and Its Manufacture," enclosed in Seaman to Stuart Dudley, January 19, 1912 (in author's possession); Edward D. Boyer, "The Famous Lehigh Valley," *The Atlas Circle* 4 (July 1918): 1–6; Henry Andrew Buehler, *The Lime and Cement Resources of Missouri,* 192–94; Lesley, Lober, and Bartlett, *History of the Portland Cement Industry,* 104–29; and Percy C. H. West, *The Modern Manufacture of Portland Cement: A Handbook for Manufacturers, Users, and All Interested in Portland Cement,* vol. 1, *Machinery and Kilns.* U.S. Federal Manuscript Census, 1910, Saverton township, Ralls County; Howard, *Ralls County Missouri,* 385; Missouri Bureau of Labor Statistics, *Annual Report* 28 (1906), 448.

Helmick later recalled, "to see the stampede of horses and carts at the noon and evening hours."[5]

Julius Sunderlik, George Muntean, Paul Babyak, and other shale miners loaded shale on cars that were pulled by mules to the mouth of the mines and then were hauled by cable up an incline to waiting hopper cars. Once the shale had been automatically dumped into the cars, a steam engine hauled it to the mills. At the mine south of Saverton, steam shovels loaded the shale from an open cut.[6]

Locomotive operators transported the limestone and shale to the rock crusher. Here Mike Kitsock and others dumped the raw materials into bins that opened into gates crushers. These crushers with corrugated crushing rolls reduced the raw materials to about the size of a chestnut. Workers put these materials into large storage bins, from which they then entered fifteen-feet rotary driers. A stream of heated air and gas eliminated moisture from the materials.

Once the materials dropped from the lower end of the cylinder dry and warm, workers took them to the raw mill, where chemists attended automatic machine mixers that weighed out and mixed the proper proportions of limestone and shale. Mill workers then conveyed the crushed and dried mixed materials to pulverizing machines that ground them into particles of fine sand. Tube mills, which were horizontal cylinders about twenty-two feet long and six feet in diameter, pulverized the materials further into a fine powder.

At the kiln house, workers put the raw pulverized material into steel tanks at the head of large rotary kilns. These kilns at the Ilasco plant in the early 1900s were about 108 feet long and between five and twelve feet in diameter. Small screen conveyors fed the material into these revolving cylinders lined with fire brick. Into the lower end of the cylinders kiln firemen fed a steady stream of pulverized coal, which ignited to produce intense heat. This eliminated any remaining moisture, encouraged the material to sinter together, and produced red-hot globular hard masses known as clinkers. Workers dropped these clinkers into double rotary coolers about thirty-five feet high and eight feet in diameter that lowered the temperature enough to allow clinkers to be crushed through a set of corrugated crushing rolls. Kiln workers took these clinkers, slightly damp as they emerged from the cooling cylinders, and stored them in large bins. In 1906, kiln workers earned between $9 and $12.50 per week.[7]

Henry Ryan and other switch engineers operated transfer engines that hauled the clinkers over elevated tracks from the kiln building to the clinker grinding

5. Missouri Bureau of Labor Statistics, *Annual Report* 28, 448; Helmick quoted in Hadley, *Magic Powder,* 40. On the Joneses and Peterson, see the U.S. Federal Manuscript Census, 1910, Saverton township, Ralls County, and Perry Jones, tape provided to author, December 5, 1994.

6. U.S. Federal Manuscript Census, 1910, Saverton township, Ralls County.

7. Missouri Bureau of Labor Statistics, *Annual Report* 28, 448.

mills, where Martin Balko, George Kelemetz, and George Polc were among those employed in 1910 as clinker grinders, mixers, and other laborers. Clinker mill workers averaged between $6 and $8 per week in 1906. They dumped clinkers into large storage tanks, and mixers added mineral gypsum to the clinkers to extend the setting time of portland cement. Grinders operated tube mills, similar to those used for grinding the raw materials, which pulverized the clinkers. The product was portland cement ready for use.[8]

From the clinker mill, the final product of Atlas's dry process of manufacturing went to the packing house or the stockhouse where workers put it in bins to await weighing and packing. Skin color shaped Atlas's hiring practices here, where cement dust heavily filled the air, as well as in the coal mill, where darker-skinned workers had particularly dirty, low-paying jobs. Large numbers of Italian workers such as Tony Vecoli, Joseph Trapagni, Alfonso DeMarco, and Joe Cherdo worked here. So did several of the tiny number of African Americans employed at the plant in 1910, including Oscar Henderson, William Hunt, and John Thomas, all of whom lived in Hannibal.[9]

In the early, more labor-intensive years of cement manufacturing, a worker stood in front of bins in the packing house with a shovel and filled the sack, adjusting the levels with hand scoops until the sack weighed ninety-four pounds. He then tied the sack and loaded and trucked it to a freight car. Machines soon revolutionized this process, however. An automatic conveyer belt now brought cement from the bin and dumped it into the hopper of a packing machine with a small spout at the bottom. Here sat a sack filler who slipped an opening in the sack over the spout and turned on the cement. A mechanism automatically shut off when the sack contained ninety-four pounds. The filler then simply pushed the sack until it fell onto another conveyor belt that dropped it at the door of a freight car. Ilasco workers also loaded wooden barrels that contained four sacks, or 376 pounds, of cement onto barges for shipment on the Mississippi River.[10]

During the summer, Atlas often hired teenage schoolboys, both white and black, to tie empty sacks and clean returned cotton sacks for reuse. There was a wire cage in the sack house that tumbled the sacks to shake out the dust. Among those hired as summer sack cleaners was Marion Powers, a black student from Hannibal. Atlas did not allow the boys to fill the sacks, only to clean them. As

8. Ibid., 448; U.S. Federal Manuscript Census, 1910, Saverton township, Ralls County. On Ryan, see *State of Missouri v. Sam Russo,* trial transcript, 1, Ralls County, Office of the Circuit Clerk and Recorder, New London.

9. U.S. Federal Manuscript Census, 1910, Saverton township, Ralls County, and Mason township, Marion County, Mo.

10. On technological changes in filling cement sacks, see *New York Times,* March 18, 1923.

Powers later recalled, "Cement came hot from the tank and a sack might burst during filling, spewing hot cement."[11]

Since cement companies provided customer rebates on empty sacks shipped back to the plant, this part of the business created slots that were increasingly filled during and after the First World War by women who cleaned, repaired, and classified returned sacks. The wages of sack house women workers averaged much less than men's. Perry Jones, who began working at Atlas's Ilasco plant as a sack tier in 1922, recalled the role played by women in this phase of the operation. First, men unloaded bundles of returned sacks from freight cars and sent them up a conveyor belt and down a chute, where several men grabbed the bundles, put them on a table, and cut the wires. They put the sacks into a machine similar to a Laundromat drier, which tumbled the sacks and shook out the cement. Mildred Viglasky and other classifiers worked in stalls sorting out sacks that had small chunks of dried cement left in them, that were not reusable, or that needed repairs. Sacks that needed to be patched went to Mary Hustava, who turned them inside out before six or eight other women sewed on the patches. Others then turned the sacks outside in before they sent them to Jones, Sammy Venditti, Manuel Craven, and nine or ten other teenagers who tied the empty sacks.[12]

According to the Missouri Bureau of Labor Statistics, Missouri's five cement plants in 1916 employed only twenty-two wage-earning women, of whom sixteen worked in bag departments. These numbers increased after the United States declared war against Germany in 1917. Ilasco's Hattie Randolph operated a machine that stamped numbers on the sacks, and later her stepdaughter, Amanda Seal, worked there as a teenager, along with Clifford Randolph, Hattie's fifteen-year-old son. By 1920, sack house workers at the Ilasco plant included at least ten black women from Hannibal—Anna Parson, Margaret Lane, Lottie Moore, Katherine Boisher, Ersie Rubin, Jennie Smith, Eliza McCleary, Lucy Lueden, Flossie Hall, and Clara England.[13]

Cement manufacturing raised concerns about the long-range harmful effects of working in such a dusty atmosphere. Jane Hemeyer recalled that her mother, Ruby Sykes, went to work in the sack house but soon quit after choking constantly on the dust. Machinists at the plant complained in 1910 that "owing to the thick dust and smoke, this work is very unhealthy and wages paid are low." Tuberculosis and lung-related diseases were of particular concern. A reporter

11. Marion D. Powers, "Today Is Better," 20.

12. Perry Jones, tape provided to author, December 5, 1994; Mildred Viglasky, interview by Sally Polc, October 30, 1994.

13. *Missouri Red Book,* 1918–1920, 120; Youell, "Renault a/k/a Randolph," 16; U.S. Federal Manuscript Census, 1920, Saverton township, Ralls County, and Mason township, Marion County, Mo.

for the *St. Louis Labor* who described Ilasco's workers as "the hardest working and poorest paid men," noted that "several years work for the Atlas Portland Cement Co. will mean consumption for any laborer who is not provided with an exceptionally strong constitution."[14]

Many industry specialists regarded dust as a "nuisance," but for other reasons. One specialist, calling for dust collectors in cement plants, did not even mention the harmful effects of dust on workers. Instead, he complained that "dust works its way into the bearings, adheres to gearing and causes considerable wear upon the moving parts of the machinery: for this reason its existence is most objectionable."[15]

In addition to the possible long-term effects of dust and smoke, danger existed for workers at every stage of the production process. Local newspapers were often filled with accounts of industrial accidents that maimed or killed workers at the Ilasco plant. In this sense, Ilasco was not unique, for the entire industrial land-scape in the United States was treacherous for workers. As a report noted in 1904, "It is an undeniable fact that several millions of men and women in the United States are to-day engaged in occupations that yearly take their toll of human life and health as inevitably, as inexorably as the seasons roll in their grooves."[16]

Cement manufacturing was a notoriously dangerous process. Even Earl J. Hadley admits in his otherwise worshipful study of the Atlas Portland and the Universal Portland Cement companies that the cement industry before 1924 ranked "close to the bottom of the industrial list in safety." Thus, accidents took a staggering toll on workers at the Ilasco plant. In February 1905 a "peculiar" accident caused the death of Raphael Diadario, an unmarried, twenty-four-year-old Italian immigrant. Workers discovered his body completely covered by pulverized rock in a tank into which this rock flowed from the crusher. The *Hannibal Courier-Post* speculated that Diadario had entered the tank to get warm, having climbed a ladder inside to avoid the crushed rock, but then had fallen asleep and was overcome by dust. This reportedly caused him to fall from the ladder into the tank, where the falling rock crushed him.[17]

14. Jane Hemeyer, telephone interview by author, October 30, 1994; *St. Louis Labor,* May 21, 1910. On machinists' complaints, see Mark Twain Machinists' Lodge Number 537 at Hannibal to Organized Labor Everywhere, reprinted in *St. Louis Labor,* May 28, 1910. David Rosner and Gerald Markowitz, *Deadly Dust: Silicosis and the Politics of Occupational Disease in Twentieth-Century America,* 16–31, provides a good discussion of Progressive-era debates among labor leaders, settlement workers, social planners, and medical and public health authorities over the links between occupational dusts and tuberculosis. On the interrelationship of heredity, environment, and tuberculosis, see Teller, *Tuberculosis Movement,* chap. 8.

15. West, *Modern Manufacture of Portland Cement,* 141.

16. Quoted in Philip S. Foner, *History of the Labor Movement in the United States,* vol. 3, *The Policies and Practices of the American Federation of Labor, 1900–1909,* 22.

17. Hadley, *Magic Powder,* 244; *Hannibal Courier-Post,* February 3, 1905.

Whether the newspaper's account of Diadario's death, which it blamed on human error, was accurate or not, it is clear that slides of material constituted a leading cause of accidents in the cement industry. Dangers lurked everywhere in storage tanks and bins. On June 7, 1907, a tank of pulverized rock claimed the life of Alex Rorala, a twenty-three-year-old Rumanian. He was using a long-handled rake to keep crushed rock moving into a tank when he somehow fell into the hopper. About thirty minutes later, a worker discovered his body suffocated under five feet of crushed rock with a mangled left foot caught in the conveyer. Rorala had been in the United States for about three years, and he left behind a brother who had recently joined him to work at the cement plant.[18]

Poor lighting and dusty conditions aggravated safety problems for those who worked around dangerous machinery. A few weeks after Rorala's death, four workers narrowly escaped death by suffocation in the kiln building. After one of them fell into the shale tank, another went to the rescue only to be overcome by dust. The other two shortly suffered the same fate as they tried to haul their coworkers from the tank. Finally, someone lowered a rope and rescued all four of them, although one of the victims had swallowed a lot of dust and took awhile to recover.[19]

A worker in the kiln building likened the heavy cloud of dust that sometimes gathered to a "terrible fog," which nearly obscured the incandescent lights and contributed to accidents. On October 12, 1911, George E. Yost, a shift foreman from Hannibal, fell through an open trapdoor, or conveyor box, situated atop a coal bin above one of the kilns. Yost, who could not see that the trapdoor was open, suffered broken ribs.[20]

Vasilie Joszisu, a twenty-eight-year-old Rumanian box tender in the kiln build-ing for two years, suffered a fatal accident on July 7, 1908, at around eleven o'clock at night. He lost his footing while working on a platform above the kilns and fell more than seventy feet to instant death on the concrete floor below. The only struggle of death as he hit the floor was "just a forced breath and a stiffening of the muscles." Hannibal residents looked on as wagon loads of Rumanians came to town to attend the young man's funeral and burial services at St. Mary's Cemetery.[21]

Moving belts, pulleys, and flywheels constituted a serious threat to workers, who had to fight through fatigue on shifts that lasted between ten and thirteen hours to avoid a single careless slip lest they find themselves pulled into the

18. *Monthly Labor Review* 17 (August 1923): 165–66; *Hannibal Courier-Post,* June 8, 1907.

19. *George E. Yost, Respondent, v. Atlas Portland Cement Company, Appellant,* St. Louis Court of Appeals, June 8, 1915, 430; *Hannibal Courier-Post,* June 29, 1907.

20. *Yost v. Atlas Portland Cement Company,* 422–34; *Hannibal Courier-Post,* February 27, 1913.

21. *Hannibal Courier-Post,* July 8 and 9, 1908.

machinery. When the clothing of Hannibal's Henry Hollenbeck snagged in the machinery while he was oiling a large flywheel in Mill Number Six in November 1907, the wheel spun Hollenbeck around until it crushed him to death.[22] Just before Christmas in 1910 a similar fate befell Robert W. Watkins in the clinker mill. Watkins, a former Democratic nominee for city attorney in Hannibal, was putting on a belt when his clothing caught in the chain of a power shaft. The chain swirled him around to his death. By the time general foreman Dunkirk Richards and foreman Fred Todd discovered the accident, Watkins's legs had been "mashed to a pulp with every vestige of flesh torn from the bone."[23]

Construction and scaffold work also resulted in many injuries to those working on the ground as well as up high. An immigrant worker identified as Krajes Macra lost his life in January 1907 when a huge beam that was being used in forms for making concrete pillars for Mill Number Six fell on him. He left behind a brother-in-law who worked at the cement plant and a wife and four children in Europe. John Williams, a member of the rigging gang, broke a thigh when he fell from one of the buildings on April 6, 1906, and Hannibal's John Keith narrowly escaped death on May 21, 1909, when a piece of iron ribbon fell from the top of the smokestack of the kiln building and hit him on the forehead and arm. He received a serious scalp wound and a broken arm.[24]

Heat and steam posed special hazards for those in the kiln building and clinker mill. As an industry chemist acknowledged, working around coal dust was particularly dangerous: "Several disastrous fires and explosions have occurred at cement works owing to the accidental ignition of the coal dust." He blamed most of these accidents, however, on "the carelessness or ignorance of the workmen."[25]

On July 9, 1906, a mechanical engineer named Hansen (no first name given) suffered serious facial burns when flames shot about ten feet out of the door where coal dust was blown into a rotary kiln. Escaping steam scalded the face and upper body of Hannibal's Boone Griffin as he was removing a cap from a boiler on June 29, 1905. In the case of Martin Konopa, handling burnt clinkers proved to be fatal. On May 9, 1910, he died after being stricken and overcome with heat.[26]

Hazards also abounded for those handling explosives in the quarry or shale mine. On May 23, 1907, Avram Tecau, who had been recruited by Atlas labor

22. *Hannibal Courier-Post,* November 12, 1907.

23. *Ralls County Record,* December 23, 1910; *Hannibal Courier-Post,* December 20, 1910.

24. *Hannibal Courier-Post,* January 22, 1907, April 7, 1906, and May 21, 1909.

25. West, *Modern Manufacture of Portland Cement,* 228.

26. *Hannibal Courier-Post,* July 10, 1906, and June 30, 1905; *John S. Wood, Administrator, Estate of Martin Konopa, v. The National Casualty Company,* September 20, 1910, case no. 9355, Ralls County, Office of the Circuit Clerk and Recorder, New London.

agents in Rumania, was killed in a rock quarry explosion, and on March 6, 1908, doctors amputated four fingers on the right hand of Vasilie Mihu after a stick of dynamite exploded in his hand. A similar accident in the rock quarry on February 6, 1905, left an Italian worker with a mangled right arm and robbed him of sight in his right eye. While blasting at the shale pit near Saverton on June 26, 1906, Rumanian Andrew Constantine "suffered untold agonies" when lime blew into one of his eyes.[27]

Work in the shale mine was especially hazardous. In December 1909, while shoveling and loading shale into a car, Paul Babyak, a Slovak immigrant, suffered a crippling injury when rock and shale from the roof of the mine fell on him. The falling rock crushed and severed one of his feet and inflicted severe bruises and wounds on his back and shoulders. A couple of months later in the shale mine, Paul Sluvka suffered a similar accident that shattered his nervous system, leaving him permanently crippled. On October 6, 1910, falling rock and shale struck Paul Vintan, who sustained permanent damage to his left leg and ankle.[28]

Many mining accidents ended in death. Such was the case of a Rumanian identified by the *Hannibal Courier-Post* as Inatu Gligau, who died on July 25, 1906, when falling rock crushed his skull. Four other workers suffered less severe injuries in the same accident. On November 2, 1910, Martin Tretiak suffered a fatal accident when a large quantity of rock and shale fell on him inside the shale mine. Like many immigrants killed in such accidents, he left behind a widow, Anna, in Europe.[29]

On June 21, 1912, more than two hundred pounds of shale fell on and killed Vasilie Popa, and about six months later a cave-in killed Ernest Lawson and Mihail Josen in the shale pit. Until Popa's death, Atlas relied on Jack Jones and a fast team of horses to transport injured workers to the hospital in Hannibal. Shortly after Popa's death, however, the *Ralls County Times* noted that "the many accidents at Ilasco have caused the cement company to install a fine ambulance. The vehicle will be stationed at the plant, ready for any and all calls."[30]

27. Hagood and Hagood, comp., "List of Deaths," 79; *Hannibal Courier-Post,* March 6, 1908, February 6, 1905, and June 27, 1906. On Tecau's recruitment by Atlas labor agents, see Joe Welschmeyer's special article, "Cement Plant at Ilasco Attracted East European population," in the *Hannibal Courier-Post,* December 20, 1984.

28. *Paul Babyek v. Atlas Portland Cement Company,* March 1, 1911, case no. 9427; *Paul Sluvka v. Atlas Portland Cement Company,* September 13, 1910, case no. 9350; *Joseph Vintan v. Atlas Portland Cement Company,* March 1, 1911, case no. 9428; all in Ralls County, Office of the Circuit Clerk and Recorder, New London.

29. *Hannibal Courier-Post,* July 24 and 26, 1906, and November 3, 1910; *Anna Tretyak v. Atlas Portland Cement Company,* March 1, 1911, case no. 9430, Ralls County, Office of the Circuit Clerk and Recorder, New London.

30. *Ralls County Times,* April 19 and June 21, 1912; *Ralls County Record,* January 17, 1913; Perry Jones, tape provided to author, December 5, 1994.

Hannibal resident Bryan Sigler later recalled the dangerous conditions inside the shale mine. Sigler, who drove the mules that hauled carts of shale from the mine, remembered that when a big blast was about to go off in the rock quarry above the shale mine, someone would yell, "Big shot on the hill—three five." This meant that the blast was set for five minutes after three. Shale miners then had about five minutes to seek shelter in the big room of the mine where it was safer and wider. Sigler remembered an accident in 1920 that stemmed from efforts to pry a threatening big rock that had been loosened by such blasts. "One day I was working with a man named [Solomon] Snodgrass," he recounted, "and he had both legs mashed off . . . I hauled him out on a cart."[31]

The nearby Mississippi River added to the constant danger posed by falls, falling objects, and flying pieces of rock from drilling. Since the shale mine was below the riverbed, water constantly seeped into it. This was hazardous, for there was a switchboard at the bottom of the mine for lights. Electric pumps kept out the water. Sigler remembered wearing rubber boots to avoid electrocution. He also recalled the danger posed by a lack of oxygen in the mine: "You could tell when the air was getting bad, because you could see the rats. The rats and mice would be getting out of the mine. They knew the air was bad, and you had better be getting out, too."[32]

The attitudes of Atlas officials suggested only a casual regard for dangerous working conditions. A good illustration is the case of Thomas Randolph (Renault), a French immigrant who worked as a chemist at the Ilasco plant from 1903 until his mysterious disappearance on October 19, 1905. He never showed up again dead or alive, and although evidence later convinced his wife, Hattie, that he had simply abandoned his family for France, his daughter Velma remembered that some of the cement plant bosses at first concluded that he probably "got ground up in one of the big machines."[33]

Atlas officials, local politicians, and newspaper editors blamed alcohol for the violence and disruption of family life in Ilasco, but they refused to acknowledge links between the workplace environment and social organization. They did not admit that dangerous working conditions contributed to social disruptions or encouraged attitudes that put a low premium on workers' lives. Angelo Venditti, a retired quarry worker and former resident of Ilasco, complained that Atlas in fact regarded its mules more highly than it did its workers.[34]

31. Bryan Sigler, interview by Roberta and Hurley Hagood, January 24, 1983. I would like to thank the Hagoods for providing me with a transcript of this interview. On the accident involving Snodgrass, see also *Hannibal Courier-Post,* November 16, 1921.

32. Sigler, interview by Hagood and Hagood, January 24, 1983. On mining hazards, see, for example, Ronald C. Brown, *Hard-Rock Miners: The Intermountain Years, 1860–1920,* 75–98.

33. Youell, "Renault a/k/a Randolph," 14–15.

34. Angelo Venditti, interview by author, July 9, 1993.

Newspaper coverage of accidents reinforced this view at times, routinely describing the loss of human life with amazing detachment. By contrast, when an accident claimed the life of one of Atlas's big gray horses in the summer of 1903, the *Hannibal Courier-Post* mourned, "It was a fine animal."[35]

Ilasco did not have its own newspaper to offer workers' views on the causes of such accidents. Hannibal and New London newspapers desensitized the public to the conditions of work that contributed to job-related injuries and deaths. They often described victims of on-the-job accidents as "unfortunate," suggesting that their fate was simply a matter of bad luck. In many cases, reporters routinely put a good spin on accidents. Consider, for example, the following two accounts by the *Courier-Post* of accidents at the cement plant. On March 27, 1907, the newspaper reported that the two foreigners (unnamed) from Ilasco "who had the misfortune last week to suffer severe injuries" were "reported as getting along very nicely." Less than two weeks later, the newspaper reported that a foreigner (again unnamed) in Ilasco nearly lost his life when another worker accidentally kicked a large brick off a high scaffold. The brick hit the "unfortunate" worker on the head, knocking him unconscious for several hours. The newspaper noted that for awhile the injured man was expected to die, but that after getting medical attention he, too, was "getting along very nicely."[36]

By shifting public attention away from working conditions at the Atlas plant, local newspapers fulfilled their role as instruments of boosterism, refusing to antagonize Atlas officials or Hannibal's elites who had ties to Atlas. Connected through local civic and business organizations, the Country Club, and common class interests, newspaper editors and town elites interpreted industrialization for the public in a way that robbed Ilasco workers of their very humanness.

The *Hannibal Courier-Post* at times conjured up vivid, romantic images of immigrants as workers too industrious and frugal for their own good. Take, for example, the case of a Rumanian identified as Wessel Bricklie, who was found dead in his Ilasco rooming house in June 1909. He was perhaps a victim of tuberculosis, but the newspaper concluded that he "literally worked himself to death in an effort to secure funds with which to bring his wife and family here from their home in the old country." He reportedly had refused to see a doctor or "take any steps that would lead to a lessening of the little sum of savings to which he was adding daily in the hopes of bringing his family to him." The newspaper noted that Bricklie's heroic dedication to work and his subsequent fate were not altogether uncommon for Ilasco workers. "No more pathetic case of vain effort and heroism has ever been called to the attention of the authorities at Ilasco or Ralls County," the newspaper remarked, "although

---

35. *Hannibal Courier-Post,* July 21, 1903.
36. *Hannibal Courier-Post,* March 27 and April 9, 1907.

similar cases have been known among the foreigners employed at the great cement plant."[37]

To help cope with medical care expenses incurred as the result of industrial accidents, workers turned to fraternal associations. On November 4, 1907, Rumanians in Ilasco formed the Ardeleana Rumanian Beneficial Union, which provided burial insurance and other forms of collective support, and promoted the preservation of their cultural heritage. The National Slovak Society and the Slovak Evangelical Union also provided such benefits.[38]

Shortly before the formation of the Ardeleana fraternal society, J. Leonard Rodgers, a foreman at the Ilasco plant, took advantage of his power to hire and fire by selling insurance to immigrants whom he supervised. He exploited their fear of on-the-job accidents and put money in his own pocket at the same time. As an agent for a Chicago insurance company, he put together "quite an insurance business among the foreign workmen" before he abruptly disappeared from Ilasco. As a local newspaper noted, immigrant workers under his supervision "felt it almost their duty to take out insurance on account of Rogers [sic] being their foreman."[39]

Atlas also sponsored a Hospital Association fund to ensure that victims of on-the-job accidents would have access to medical care at Levering Hospital in Hannibal. Workers contributed a day's salary per year to the fund, which covered only job-related accidents, not ordinary cases of illness. Company doctors were in charge of such patients. Employer-sponsored schemes provided badly needed help, but historian Robert Asher points out that "business largesse all too frequently came with many strings attached, strings that reflected the tension between humane impulses and the drive to pursue instrumental, self-serving objectives."[40]

Organized labor in Missouri lobbied for state intervention to ensure a safer work environment, but the growing tendency of corporations to build factories

37. *Hannibal Courier-Post,* June 17, 1909. Paul Andre Jakovis, a forty-year-old immigrant, also died of tuberculosis just a few days earlier in Ilasco. For other cases of tuberculosis that same year, see Hagood and Hagood, comp., "List of Deaths," 40.

38. On the Ardeleana Society, see Circuit Court Record, book Q, 21, Ralls County, Office of the Circuit Clerk and Recorder, New London, and the *Hannibal Courier-Post,* September 15 and 22, 1908. For Assembly 139 of the Slovak Evangelical Union, see "50th Anniversary of Lutheran Church at Ilasco to Be Observed on Sunday," *Hannibal Courier-Post,* August 10, 1961.

39. *Ralls County Times,* January 11, 1907.

40. Robert Asher, "The Limits of Big Business Paternalism: Relief for Injured Workers in the Years before Workmen's Compensation," in *Life and Labor: Dimensions of American Working-Class History,* 19–20. Contributions to the Hospital Association fund reached $1,730 within the first year of its formation. *Hannibal Courier-Post,* November 17, 1904; *Ralls County Times,* June 10, 1904.

in small towns like Ilasco exposed the limits of Missouri's factory inspection laws. J. W. Sikes, Missouri's factory inspector, called attention to this in his report for 1907–1908. Such laws were inadequate, he stressed, since they covered only factories in towns whose populations exceeded ten thousand. After receiving many complaints from areas not covered by these laws, he recommended extending legal jurisdiction to all factories, regardless of their location.[41]

Missouri's trade union movement played a leading role in the campaign to secure legislation to compensate injured workers and their families, but this was a lengthy, expensive effort that did not pay off until the state finally passed its first workmen's compensation law in 1926.[42] In the meantime, injured workers and their families had only limited options. Laws passed by the Missouri legislature in 1907 widened the scope of employers' liability and allowed recovery of ten thousand dollars in damages in cases of death that were the result of contributory negligence. To sue Atlas for damages, however, was expensive and slow. Even if such suits were successful, workers often did not reap the lion's share of awarded damages. A business agent for Machinists' lodges in the district complained that "most of the money paid for damages goes to Lawyers and Doctors and when a final settlement [is reached] the workmen have very little left."[43]

The absence of a workmen's compensation law, coupled with frequent accidents at the cement plant in Ilasco, created a climate conducive to litigation. This meant a bonanza for attorneys, and by 1926 perhaps even Atlas officials had become worn down trying to contain workers' use of the legal system to obtain compensation for job-related injuries. In September 1925 a Hannibal grand jury indicted two St. Louis lawyers for allegedly splitting fees with Hannibal's Henry Hicklin for his referral of damages suits involving workers at the cement plant. Hicklin, a former Atlas worker himself hurt in an accident at the plant, had reached a favorable settlement with Atlas through these attorneys. He then referred several cases to them, including that of Roy Uplinger, who was

41. Gary M. Fink, *Labor's Search for Political Order: The Political Behavior of the Missouri Labor Movement, 1880–1940,* 48–49; "Official Report of J. W. Sikes, State Factory Inspector, from May 11, 1907, to December 31, 1908," in *Journal of the House of Representatives* (Missouri), 1909, 4.

42. On the struggle for a workmen's compensation law in Missouri, see Ruth W. Towne, "The Movement for Workmen's Compensation Legislation in Missouri, 1910–1925," and Fink, *Labor's Search,* 48–53, 82–93.

43. Fink, *Labor's Search,* 49; "Report of Business Agent Lamb," October 8, 1914, Meeting of Joint Executive Board, vol. 4, International Association of Machinists and Aerospace Workers, District 9, Records, 1901–1965, Western Historical Manuscript Collection, University of Missouri, St. Louis (hereafter cited as IAMAW Records, WHMC–St. Louis). In 1922, only Arkansas, Mississippi, North Carolina, South Carolina, Florida, and Missouri still relied on liability and damages suits to achieve compensation for on-the-job accidents. *Monthly Labor Review* 16 (January 1923): 175.

killed when a switch engine ran over him in the quarry. He also referred four cement plant workers hurt when the Hannibal shift train to Ilasco collided with a locomotive engine south of the Burlington railroad yards on August 17, 1925. Although the indicted lawyers were charged with splitting fees with Hicklin, the case was thrown out of court due to lack of evidence that money had passed between them.[44]

Appellate and federal district courts often upheld companies like Atlas in damages suits, invoking the doctrine of assumed risk and arguing that employers and workers have equal rights under freedom of contract. As the argument ran, workers had the freedom to quit if they did not like the conditions laid down by employers. If they chose not to quit, they assumed the legal risks connected with the job. When possible, Atlas's attorneys removed suits from local juries and took them into courts dominated by more conservative judges. Attorney George A. Mahan, who represented not only Atlas but also several other corporations in such suits, concluded in 1919 that "the greatest danger to the country comes from dishonest jury verdicts." If Atlas lost, it appealed the decision, no matter how small the judgment, to courts where the doctrine of assumed risk was more popular with judges.[45]

Emmanuel M. Grossman, a Progressive attorney who was elected treasurer of the Missouri Bar Association in 1910, pointed out the limits of the so-called freedom of contract. "Courts lay this doctrine down in all solemnity," he complained, "while everyone knows that the laborer in the mills and in the mines and the women and the children in the factories must accept employment under whatever conditions the employer may choose to impose, or join the army of the unemployed and throw those dependent upon them on the mercy of public charity."[46]

In part, Grossman linked the public's low regard for lawyers to the public's lack of respect for court rulings against workers in damages suits. In his view, lawyers "must demonstrate that, above employment to private interests for mere pecuniary gain, they also value and cherish the ideal of serviceableness to mankind." Urging fellow lawyers not to "serve the greed and tyranny of a favored few," he summed up the dilemma faced by injured workers seeking compensation in the courts: "A poor man wronged by a wealthy individual or corporation who undertakes to obtain relief through the courts of the land is in not much better position than was Tantalus doomed by the gods eternally to

44. *Ralls County Record,* September 25, 1925, and February 19, 1926.
45. On Mahan's criticism of the jury system, see *Ralls County Record,* September 26, 1919.
46. Emmanuel M. Grossman, "Some Reasons for the Growing Disrespect for the Law," in *Proceedings of the Twenty-Eighth Annual Meeting of the Missouri Bar Association,* 1910, 139.

stand up to his neck in water which fled from him when he tried to drink of it, and over whose head hung fruits which the winds wafted away whenever he tried to grasp them."[47]

Accident victims might simply fend for themselves as best they could or rely on the goodwill of company officials for some kind of settlement or agreement. Thomas Johnson, a black resident of Hannibal who worked in Mill Number Six, suffered an accident after "he had crawled under a coal car to adjust the door on the bottom." The accident almost scalped him, but he survived, and the company promoted him to foreman. This gave him prestige and authority not commonly enjoyed by most of Atlas's few black workers. "It seemed that in a sense," recalled Hiawatha Crow, Johnson's granddaughter, "the promotion was to make up for the accident."[48]

Atlas officials, backed by local newspapers, encouraged injured workers to rely on company paternalism instead of lawsuits. When Harry King returned to work in the summer of 1903 after a three-month absence due to a plant accident, the *Courier-Post* praised Atlas officials for their generous treatment of him. The newspaper noted that Atlas officials "certainly did the right thing by him. They allowed him half time for the number of days he was sick and guaranteed him a lifetime position."[49]

Atlas sometimes persuaded, or coerced, injured workers to sign agreements surrendering all rights to future legal action against the company in exchange for a relatively small sum of money. They sometimes sweetened the agreements with promises of lifetime employment at acceptable wage levels and duties that the injured could perform in their limited capacity.

As the case of James H. Burge indicates, these "agreements" did not always eliminate conflict. Burge, a millwright whose left arm and hand were permanently crippled in an accident on July 23, 1906, while he was repairing machinery in the rock mill, claimed that Atlas reneged on its promises to him. Atlas officials had convinced him at first that a permanent job with them would be worth much more than a suit for damages. In a signed agreement on September 4, 1906, Atlas agreed to pay him seventy dollars to make up for thirty-five lost days of work at his normal salary of two dollars per day; in return, he waived future rights of legal action against the company.

According to Burge, however, Atlas officials soon violated their verbal assurances that he would have a guaranteed lifetime position with light duties that he could perform with his crippled arm. After they forced Burge to engage in heavy lifting and reduced his wages to $1.80 per day, he quit and filed a lawsuit

47. Ibid., 150, 153.
48. Hiawatha Crow, "I Remember," 41.
49. *Hannibal Courier-Post,* July 29, 1903.

for breach of contract. In a separate case, he asked for damages in the amount of $1,975, but later dropped the suit, perhaps as the result of an out-of-court settlement.[50]

Sensitive to public concerns over workers' safety, Atlas officials often invited prominent guests to tour the Ilasco plant. Physicians from the Ralls County Medical Association inspected the plant in October 1906, escorted by Atlas officials who "took great pains to explain points of interest to them." A few days later, company officials took Governor Joseph Folk for a brief tour of the plant. "I have been down to Ilasco," Folk told a local reporter. "That's a great industry and is a credit to the state."[51]

On November 15, 1917, Atlas officials rolled out the red carpet for delegates attending the Northeast Missouri and Western Illinois Lumbermen's convention in Hannibal. Atlas sent a special train to Hannibal for the delegates and their wives and treated them to an informational tour of the plant. Atlas General Superintendent A. G. Croll was on hand for the occasion.[52]

Had this tour taken place a day later, delegates would have witnessed a fire that raged in the power house. The fire probably broke out when an oil transformer blew up. George Piper, a power operator, was killed; Wesley Riley received serious burns on his neck, face, and hands; and Ora Fessenden suffered minor burns on his face.[53]

In the era of the First World War, Missouri was one of only two states that did not publish statistics on work-related accidents. Based on a report issued by the Portland Cement Association, however, it is clear that accident rates in the cement industry increased between 1918 and 1920. Data compiled from seventy-two cement plants in the United States reveal that the frequency and severity rates of such accidents went up steadily during this period. In 1920 there were 2,668 accidents, including 53 deaths and 82 permanent disabilities.[54]

As Ilasco's fifty-four-year-old Joseph Thomas discovered, some of these accidents were the result of unsafe work orders by supervisors. On January 17, 1919, he was working as a carpenter, using tin sheets to put a new metal roof on an Atlas building. These sheets overlapped at the edges, and he and a coworker were seated on a swinging scaffold squeezed just underneath the roof, riveting sheets together with metal rivets. "Bucking rivets" required Thomas to press up against the tin sheets with an iron bar that was flattened at one end and held a

50. *James H. Burge v. Atlas Portland Cement Company,* November 15, 1910, case no. 9383, and *Burge v. Atlas,* August 15, 1911, case no. 94721; both in Ralls County, Office of the Circuit Clerk and Recorder, New London.

51. *Hannibal Courier-Post,* October 12 and 16, 1906.

52. *Hannibal Morning Journal,* November 16, 1917.

53. *Hannibal Morning Journal,* November 17, 1917.

54. *Monthly Labor Review* 12 (March 1921): 170–71; *Monthly Labor Review* 13 (October 1921): 177.

metal rivet sharp end up. A worker on top of the roof would then hammer a spot where he estimated the rivet to be. This would drive the rivet through and allow the worker on the roof to flatten it in order to secure the new roof.[55]

On that particular day, wet paint on the tin sheets increased the risk of injury from flying rivets. When sheets were wet, reportedly about one of every three or four rivets would slip and fly through the air, whereas about one rivet in eight or ten would do so when dry roofing was used. Thomas had complained many times about the danger of doing this work while the sheets were still wet. In his view, it was "just like holding up a 22 rifle and letting them shoot at you." His foreman agreed that it was dangerous but emphasized that he had orders to finish the job immediately. Thomas could either do the work or quit.[56]

Shortly after Thomas began working on that day, one of the rivets that he was holding in place slipped when his coworker struck a hammer blow from the roof. The rivet flew through the air and hit Thomas in the mouth, knocking out two of his teeth. He took a short break to spit blood and look after his injury, but then got back on the scaffold and resumed work. A little later, a rivet slipped again and shot through the air when his coworker struck another hammer blow from the roof. This time, the flying rivet hit Thomas in one of his eyes, resulting in the loss of sight in that eye.[57]

Thomas sued Atlas for damages and won a judgment of twenty-five hundred dollars in the Hannibal Court of Common Pleas, but the St. Louis Court of Appeals reversed the decision on grounds that Thomas was fully aware of the dangerous nature of his job and thus assumed all risks involved in the performance of duties. The appellate court expressed its "sympathy" to Thomas and scolded Atlas for directing him to perform dangerous work, but gave the twenty-five hundred dollars back to Atlas. "Could it be said that a reasonably prudent man," one of the judges wrote, "working under such conditions . . . after having two teeth knocked out as a warning and demonstration of the danger of the work in which he was engaged, and with a full and complete realization that he was in the position of a man being shot at with a 22 rifle, would have continued in such employment because the master had directed him to do so? We think not."[58]

For Atlas workers John Moga and Sam Giunta, the question of whether to follow unsafe work orders or risk getting fired was a matter of life and death. A premature dynamite explosion in the rock quarry on the morning of October 12, 1920, killed both of them and injured Joe Giunta, Sam's brother. All three were

55. *Joseph C. Thomas, Respondent v. Atlas Portland Cement Company, Appellant,* December 5, 1922, 141–44.
56. Ibid., 144–45.
57. Ibid.
58. Ibid., 148.

immigrants who survived military service during World War I only to lose their lives, or in the case of Joe, to sustain injuries, in service to Atlas.[59]

As the Portland Cement Association noted, accident victims were often experienced workers such as Moga and the Giuntas. Moga was a thirty-eight-year-old Rumanian immigrant and naturalized American citizen who had worked for Atlas as a blaster for more than twenty years. Industry officials attributed accidents involving experienced workers to the fact that veteran workers typically became more lax and routine in the performance of their tasks.[60]

The circumstances in this case, however, challenge the assumptions of industry officials in regard to the alleged links between seniority, carelessness, and accidents. On the morning of October 12, Moga, along with the Giuntas and other blasters, began loading dynamite into three holes that were about fifty-three feet deep. Customarily, the drilling team would have removed the machinery that had dug these holes before blasters began to load the dynamite, but due to an earlier delay, drillers Mike Bayjohn and Eli Hickerson continued to operate a Star well drill nearby. Abram Adams, a Rumanian immigrant and blaster who witnessed the accident, later explained that the continued operation of drilling machinery while blasters filled the holes with dynamite posed a serious danger:

> I had never known in my experience . . . a drill to work or to be going and operating within fifteen, twenty or twenty-five feet when the holes were being loaded with dynamite. The drill makes a noise and we men drop a piece of dynamite into the hole. You listen and hear whether or not it goes down and when the drill makes noise we cannot hear it. When a drill is operating close by and making one of these holes, it jars the earth and makes a vibration of the ground around the holes.[61]

Safron Lupu loaded hole number one, while John Patrick and foreman Pete Limbean took care of hole number three. At hole number two, however, Moga had problems with the one hundred pounds of dynamite that he had loaded. After Moga checked to ensure that all of the dynamite had reached the bottom of the hole, Limbean told him to lower another twenty-five pounds. While Moga was preparing to carry out his foreman's order, the Star well drill started up again nearby. Moga protested to Limbean that the drilling equipment should be turned off first. "Then I said to the driller," Limbean recalled, "you should stop that drill, we could not let the dynamite go down into the hole." The driller refused to stop

59. *Hannibal Courier-Post,* October 12, 1920.
60. *Monthly Labor Review* 9 (November 1919): 261–62; U.S. Federal Manuscript Census, 1920, Saverton township, Ralls County; *Mary Goucan, Appellant v. Atlas Portland Cement Company and L. J. Boucher,* July 30, 1927, 925.
61. *Goucan v. Atlas,* April term, 1927, case no. 27836, trial transcript, 15–19, MSCF-MSA.

drilling a new hole nearby and replied, "I got orders to get the hole down as quick as I can."[62]

Limbean then told Moga to keep loading the hole. When Moga checked to see if the additional dynamite had reached the bottom of the hole, he discovered that it had become stuck on a ledge. "Oh boy," he exclaimed, "dynamite stopped, lodged up here about twelve feet below the surface." Limbean urged him to use a wooden tamping stick to dislodge it. Moga had been working with the stick for about three minutes when the explosion occurred. "I was loading dirt when I heard the explosion," recounted Abram Adams. "I turned my head back. I saw a big fire and the explosion made a light and a big smoke in the air. It blew him to pieces, and for several days we found pieces of his body scattered around."[63]

Efforts by the families of these victims to obtain compensation from Atlas illustrate how expensive and time-consuming the process of recovering damages for industrial accidents could be. Joe Giunta recovered from the accident, became the administrator of Sam's estate, and filed a suit requesting three thousand dollars for his brother's death. He and Atlas soon reached an out-of-court settlement, but Mary Moga's suit dragged on for nearly nine years. As a widow with four children, she sued in the Ralls County Circuit Court to recover damages in the amount of ten thousand dollars, but on November 16, 1923, Judge C. T. Hays sustained Atlas's demurrer to prevent the case from going to a jury. Atlas's attorneys argued that there was no proof that the Star well drill had caused the accident. They insisted that Moga's carelessness was probably to blame, and that he understood clearly and assumed the risk of injury as the result of his contract for employment. They convinced Judge Hays to sustain Atlas's demurrer in the interest of "the due protection of property rights."[64]

On appeal, the Missouri Supreme Court remanded the case on July 30, 1927. At a trial in the Hannibal Court of Common Pleas, a jury awarded Moga's widow, Mary Goucan, nine thousand dollars plus costs, but Atlas appealed to Jefferson City. Before the state supreme court could rule again on the case in 1929, however, she reached an out-of-court compromise settlement with Atlas.[65]

In 1920, accidents at the Ilasco plant contributed to a particularly high percentage of nationwide work-related injuries in the cement industry. For example, a

62. *Goucan v. Atlas,* July 30, 1927, 923–28; *Goucan v. Atlas,* April term, 1927, 24.

63. *Goucan v. Atlas,* July 30, 1927, 926–27; *Goucan v. Atlas,* April term, 1927, 16.

64. *Joseph Giunta, Administrator of the estate of Samuel Giunta, deceased v. Atlas Portland Cement Company,* January 24, 1921, case no. 11393, and *Mary Moga v. Atlas Portland Cement Company,* April 12, 1921, case no. 11422; both in Ralls County, Office of the Circuit Clerk and Recorder, New London. See also *Goucan v. Atlas,* July 30, 1927, 922–25.

65. *Goucan v. Atlas,* July 30, 1927, 919–33; *Goucan v. Atlas,* case no. 29556, April term, 1929, MSCF-MSA.

shale mine accident also killed John Sajban, whose grandson, Stanley, remembered that "workers had to go to the Rock Quarry to obtain a team of horses and a wagon to haul him to the Hannibal hospital." Sajban died later that day at the age of fifty-one, leaving behind his widow and two children—George and Anna—in Ilasco, and three children in Slovakia.[66]

In 1920, an accident also killed George Douglas, one of Ilasco's earliest residents. An unguarded sprocket wheel caught his clothing while he was repairing a chain belt in the weigh house. The wheel whirled him around at least one hundred times. He lived for a couple of painful hours after the accident.[67]

As more states passed workmen's compensation laws and employers tried to undercut the appeal of unions after World War I, the cement industry gradually paid greater attention to safety. In 1924, the Portland Cement Association began presenting safety awards to plants that operated through a calendar year without a lost-time accident. The association urged greater supervision and more effective use of safety ropes and belts, but still stressed "the human element" as "the important connecting link between safety and death."[68]

The fact that long hours were the rule in the cement industry undermined the association's emphasis on safety. In 1916, those in Missouri's five cement plants who worked between seventy and ninety-one hours per week included brakemen, head burners in the clinker mill, chemists and chemists' assistants, electricians and electricians' assistants, switch engineers, switchboard operators, yardmen, and those classified as "miscellaneous." Laborers, millers, and motor tenders worked between fifty-six and ninety-one hours per week, while males in the bag department, drillers' helpers, engineers, and trackmen worked seventy hours. Only air-compressor operators and bricklayers worked as few as forty-eight hours per week.[69]

A comprehensive study of workers, wages, and hours in the cement industry, based on the payroll data of 102 portland cement plants covering the last four months of 1929, indicates that in many departments around the country, work was continuous around the clock. For example, the burning and grinding of rock was usually done on a continuous basis by either two or three shifts of workers. So, too, was grinding work in the raw mill. Since pulverized coal was needed to fire the kilns, the coal mill departments usually operated continuously with two or three shifts. The quarries and the cement department, where packing, storing, and shipping were done, generally operated on only one shift during the day.

66. Stanley Sajban to Gregg Andrews, July 4, 1994.

67. *Rosa Douglas v. Atlas Portland Cement Company,* February 12, 1921, case no. 11,405, Ralls County, Office of the Circuit Clerk and Recorder, New London; *Ralls County Record,* December 10, 1920.

68. Hadley, *Magic Powder,* 244; *Monthly Labor Review* 17 (August 1923): 165–66.

69. *Missouri Red Book, 1918–1920,* 120.

Where two shifts operated, wage earners often worked both shifts, or twenty-four hours, on one day of the week. They then alternated every week or two so that they had twenty-four hours of continuous work followed by twenty-four hours off duty every other week. In other words, they would work ninety-six hours one week and seventy-two the next.[70]

Men worked an average of 60.8 full-time hours per week and earned an average of 51.8 cents per hour. In eastern Missouri and Iowa, the district that included the Ilasco plant, the average number of full-time hours worked by men was 61.6, and the average hourly wage for men was 47.9 cents. The average hourly earnings of male cement workers ranged from a high of 60.9 cents in Oregon and Washington to a low of 37.3 cents in Texas. Male cement workers in Oregon and Washington enjoyed the shortest number of full-time hours worked each week—53.9—while their counterparts in Texas worked the most full-time hours, an average of 67.9 per week.[71]

For males, "laborers" in the coal-mill department averaged 36.3 cents per hour, the lowest earnings in the industry, while "packers," or "sackers," earned an average of 87 cents per hour, the highest in the industry. "Elevator tenders" in the coal mill worked an average of 80 full-time hours per week, an industry high, while "sack cleaners" worked the lowest average number of full-time hours per week—54.5.[72]

Women in the industry averaged 38.9 cents per hour and 52 full-time hours per week. The average weekly earnings for women in all job classifications was $20.23, compared to $31.49 for men. The lowest average number of weekly hours worked by women was 48.8 by "sack tiers" in the bag house, while the highest was 52.2 by "other employees" in the same department.[73]

Only four of the 102 plants included in this 1929 study paid extra for overtime or work on Sundays and holidays. Bonus systems were used in nineteen of these plants to reward safety and production. For example, in three of these plants packers were paid a bonus based on a specified number of barrels of cement to be packed. In another couple of plants, quarry workers earned bonuses based on the number of cars of rock loaded. According to Perry Jones, sack tiers at the Ilasco plant in the 1920s were paid fifty-five cents per one thousand sacks, and received bonus wages after they tied more than five thousand per day. Jones made only fifty-five cents on his first day of work but later increased his speed so that he could tie about one thousand sacks per hour.[74]

70. "Wages and Hours of Labor in the Portland Cement Industry, 1929," *Monthly Labor Review* 31 (August 1930): 165–70.

71. Ibid., 157–60.

72. Ibid.

73. Ibid.

74. Ibid., 168–70; Perry Jones, tape provided to author, December 5, 1994.

Despite management's growing attention to safety, the cement industry posed great dangers for workers throughout the 1920s. In 1929, there were 503 accidents in Missouri's cement plants. This figure did not include quarry accidents, which totaled 1,011.[75] For a small community like Ilasco, the deaths and crippling injuries sustained by Atlas workers as the result of what historian Robert Asher has called "technological aggression" were especially devastating. As Ilasco's workers looked to the future, they no doubt shared the concerns expressed on the following labor wish list:

> [That] the workman shall enjoy the fruit of his labor;
> That his mother shall have the comfort of his arm in her old age;
> That his wife shall not be untimely a widow;
> That his children shall have a father, and
> That cripples and hopeless wrecks who were once strong men
> Shall no longer be a by-product of industry.[76]

In many respects, dangerous working conditions made Atlas's workplace as violent as certain aspects of Ilasco's social life. Perhaps nothing better serves as an important symbolic illustration of this than two tragedies at the plant just before Christmas in 1910. On December 17, Henry Ryan, while operating a transfer engine on elevated tracks between the kiln building and the clinker mill, discovered the murdered body of Carmen Maidi at the clinker mill. Two days later, a job-related accident killed W. R. Watkins in the clinker mill when a power shaft chain ground his legs "in such a manner as to deprive them of all integuments from the knee to the ankles." These two tragedies, although unrelated, seemed to convey a strange symbolism in regard to violence in the community and the workplace. Since the clinker mill had perhaps the most notorious reputation as a killer and maimer of workers, Maidi's murderer perhaps thought it only fitting that his crime be carried out there.[77]

---

75. "Third Annual Report of the Missouri Workmen's Compensation Commission for the Period from January 1, 1929, Through December 31, 1929," 13.

76. Quoted in Foner, *History of the Labor Movement,* vol. 3, 24. On "technological aggression," see Robert Asher, "Industrial Safety and Labor Relations in the United States, 1865–1917," in *Life and Labor: Dimensions of American Working-Class History,* 115–30.

77. *State of Missouri v. Sam Russo,* case no. 9422, filed February 21, 1911, Ralls County, Office of the Circuit Clerk and Recorder, New London; *Ralls County Record,* December 23, 1910. Asher, "Industrial Safety," 115–30, stresses the psychological impact of job accidents on the worker's outlook and behavior. According to him, workers directly exposed to such accidents were more prone to violence and aggressive behavior.

(5)

The Militia Comes to Town
Labor Unrest and the Strike of 1910

I am a revolutionist by birth, reading and principle. I am always on the side of the revolutionists because there never was a revolution unless there were some oppressive and intolerable conditions against which to revolute.
—**Mark Twain,** *New York Tribune,* 1906

At the time Atlas built its Ilasco plant, Missouri trade unions had only about forty thousand members, more than half of whom lived in the St. Louis area. Although the labor movement in Missouri grew at a rapid clip during the next decade, only 8 percent of the state's 1.5 million workers belonged to unions in 1914. Most were in the skilled crafts and building trades in St. Louis and Kansas City, but "outstate" towns like Hannibal, St. Joseph, Sedalia, and Springfield also featured a growing number of craft unions affiliated with the Missouri State Federation of Labor (MSFL). In Hannibal, the Trades and Labor Assembly was the coordinating body for about twenty local unions, including the Teamsters and Machinists. Like other central labor bodies, it lobbied the state government for reform legislation, including convict labor reform and workmen's compensation.[1]

Such lobbying paid only modest dividends. Sympathetic Progressive politicians such as Governors Joseph Folk (1904–1908) and Herbert S. Hadley (1908–1912) endorsed some of labor's objectives. During Folk's Democratic gubernatorial tenure, he and Hadley, his Republican attorney general at that time, vigorously challenged monopolistic practices of corporations and discriminatory railroad rates. They used their power to persuade the 1907 Missouri legislature to pass consumer protection laws and curb the power of corporations. Antitrust legislation, attacks on corporate corruption, measures to widen employers' liability for

---

1. Fink, *Labor's Search,* 1–5; Thelen, *Paths of Resistance,* 189–200; Hagood and Hagood, *Story of Hannibal,* 107.

on-the-job accidents, and other labor reforms were hallmarks of the "Missouri Idea." When Hadley became governor, he worked closely with MSFL leaders to devise a workmen's compensation system, although these efforts did not produce a state workmen's compensation law until 1926.[2]

Despite such Progressive efforts, Ilasco workers had little protection against company policies and practices. With a few exceptions, Atlas's Ilasco workforce was nonunion. Plant officials, wedded to the open shop, at first hired a few Hannibal Teamsters to help with plant construction, but replaced them with nonunion drivers and company horses shortly after manufacturing began in 1903. They also tolerated an uneasy relationship with about thirty members of Hannibal's Mark Twain Lodge 537 of the International Association of Machinists (IAM) who worked in Atlas shops. If Atlas's predominantly unskilled, nonunion production workers dared to try to unionize or protest wages, hours, and dangerous working conditions, plant officials exploited ethnic and racial divisions among workers to maintain control. They could also count on local newspapers to spew out anti-immigrant venom during strikes in order to whip up public support for the company.[3]

Despite the rapid growth of Missouri's cement industry in the early 1900s, mill workers remained unorganized. In part, the fact that many immigrants did not intend to remain in the United States permanently may have discouraged them from becoming dues-paying union members. On the other hand, the MSFL's failure to organize Atlas workers may have reflected an underlying disregard for the cement plant's unskilled labor force. Important, too, were contemptuous ethnic biases of skilled trade unionists against immigrants from southern and eastern Europe. Unions affiliated with the American Federation of Labor (AFL) often dismissed immigrants as hopelessly unorganizable, and AFL President Samuel Gompers worked feverishly for immigration restriction. When a business agent representing the IAM's ninth district visited a cement plant in the St. Louis area, he complained that 80 percent of its workers were Hungarians and "Pollocks," and that "it is impossible to do anything with them." Missouri union leaders much preferred to denounce immigrants rather than to commit resources to organize them. In 1909, the MSFL's legislative committee endorsed a bill to force employers to limit the number of immigrants on their payrolls to no more than 10 percent of their labor force.[4]

2. Fink, *Labor's Search,* 19, 42–57; Thelen, *Paths of Resistance,* 238–65.

3. On the Teamsters' ouster, see *Hannibal Morning Journal,* July 1, August 15, and November 4, 1903.

4. Philip S. Foner, *History of the Labor Movement in the United States,* vol. 2, *From the Founding of the A.F. of L. to the Emergence of American Imperialism,* 361–64; Executive Board Minutes, July 14, 1904, International Association of Machinists and Aerospace

Without a union, some Atlas workers fought back in individualistic ways, such as altering payroll checks to squeeze a few dollars or in some cases a few cents out of the company.[5] Others, in response to dangerous working conditions, unsatisfactory wages, the ten-hour day, and the sixty-hour workweek, became increasingly militant before 1910. This militancy, expressed in the strikes of 1906, 1908, and 1909, set the stage in 1910 for the most spectacular labor-capital confrontation in Ilasco's history. By the time the dust had settled on the strike of 1910, Atlas had used the Missouri National Guard to squash this militancy, deepen ethnic antagonisms, and scar the community.

Labor transiency at the Ilasco plant alarmed Atlas officials. Local newspapers reported the frequent comings and goings of immigrants at the Union train station in Hannibal, attributing this transiency to a desire to visit families in Europe before returning to the cement plant. "It appears that when a Pollock gets quite a large amount of money saved that he returns to the Old Country," explained the *Hannibal Courier-Post*, " . . . to show what he has been doing in this country."[6] When hundreds of immigrants left Ilasco in the spring of 1906, the *Ralls County Times* observed that "the cement plant stands in serious prospect of losing all their European employees if the number that have been shipped from that point in the last few months is any indication."[7]

To impose greater labor discipline, Atlas officials took steps to raise productivity. In September 1906 they put quarry workers on piece wages, commonly used by mill owners in that era to shift the burden of an inefficient factory system onto workers themselves. In the quarries, where the most inefficient, labor-intensive steps in cement manufacturing took place, workers earned $1.40 per day, but Atlas put them on piece rates at 14 cents per cart.[8]

Quarry workers went on strike to protest the imposition of piece wages. For men who handled explosives and heavy rocks, Atlas's attempt to increase productivity by speeding up work in the quarries only increased the likelihood of accidental explosions and mangled and mashed limbs. On September 7 the

---

Workers, District 9, Records, vol. 2, WHMC–St. Louis; Fink, *Labor's Search*, 55; Senate Bill #1, *Missouri Journal of the Senate*, 1909, 785–86.

5. On such complaints, see, for example, *Hannibal Courier-Post*, September 21, 1904, and *Ralls County Times*, July 5, 1907.

6. *Hannibal Courier-Post*, November 2, 1906. For additional coverage of immigrant labor turnover, see, for example, *Hannibal Courier-Post*, July 18, 1903, December 17, 1904, November 27, 1906, April 9, 1907, and April 2, 1908.

7. *Ralls County Times*, June 8, 1906.

8. *Hannibal Courier-Post*, September 11, 1906. For a broader discussion of immigrant workers and employers' use of piece wages, see David Montgomery, *Workers' Control in America: Studies in the History of Work, Technology, and Labor Struggles*, 37–40. On the social organization of nineteenth-century factories, see Nelson, *Managers and Workers*, chap. 3.

quarry gang at Mill Number Six initiated the strike, which by September 10 had spread to all quarry workers, most of whom were Slovaks and Rumanians. Although unorganized, they briefly overcame ethnic differences to attract other immigrants and native-born workers to the strike. "The trouble is not confined to any nationality of people represented at the plant," wrote a local reporter, "but embraces men of all colors and creeds."[9]

Unable to drive a wedge between striking immigrant groups in the quarry, Atlas officials then tried to exploit white racism against blacks to break the strike. A few weeks earlier, Atlas had arranged through an employment agency to bring about sixty-five African American workers from St. Louis to the Ilasco plant. The *Hannibal Courier-Post* attributed this to a labor shortage in the area, but it was also probably a move by Atlas to have strikebreakers on hand in case quarry workers protested the implementation of piece rates. On September 10, when black workers discovered that they had been brought to Ilasco as scabs, they turned away from striking immigrants who confronted them as they tried to report for work. The *Courier-Post* noted that "nothing serious transpired, as the colored people involved are said to have considered discretion the better part of valor, and retreated."[10]

The strike nearly forced a plant shutdown, but a settlement was quickly reached. Atlas had its way. The agreement called for the payment of piece rates on a tonnage basis. Atlas officials touted the new scale. They emphasized that under favorable conditions quarry workers could now earn as much as three dollars per day.[11]

The national panic of 1907 had a devastating impact on Ilasco and increased labor transiency. In March 1907, Atlas had purchased new properties along the Salt River near New London for anticipated expansion of quarrying operations, but by July 1 the deepening recession had shut down Ilasco's Mill Number Five. Hundreds of immigrants waved good-bye at Hannibal's Union depot as they waited for incoming trains to take them east. Only a few remained as part of a reduced force in Mill Number Six, and even they suffered a 10 percent wage cut in January 1908.[12]

According to a Hannibal reporter, more than one thousand residents had left Ilasco by January 1908 as the result of the depression. Most who left were immigrants and former workers at the cement plant. To at least one prominent

---

9. *Hannibal Courier-Post,* September 11, 1906.

10. Ibid. On the alleged labor shortage, see also *Hannibal Courier-Post,* July 20, 1906.

11. *Hannibal Courier-Post,* September 12, 1906.

12. *Hannibal Courier-Post,* June 6 and 28, 1907, and July 16, 1907; Executive Board Minutes, June 10, 1909, IAMAW Records, District 9, vol. 3, WHMC–St. Louis. On Atlas's purchase of farms along Salt River, see *Hannibal Courier-Post,* March 15, 18, 21, and 26, 1907.

native-born resident of Ilasco, this was cause for celebration. He told a newspaper that within a year "there will be very few of the old residents of the little town left. However as soon as they leave their positions are given to Americans, who do the work equally as well if not better than the foreigners, and besides gives all the residents of this city and locality a better chance to secure employment and put a better and higher class of people in Ilasco." He predicted that "the foreigners' day at the plant is at an end."[13]

Mahan, Atlas's attorney, blamed the recession and glutted stockhouses on depressed world demand. He attributed this in part to state and national Progressive legislation, which he regarded as "drastic and injurious to business enterprises and more or less confiscatory of popular rights."[14] The *Hannibal Courier-Post* agreed, speculating that legislative efforts to set railroad rates in Missouri had forced railroad companies to postpone construction improvements and cancel large cement orders.[15]

By late summer in 1908, business conditions had improved. Mahan credited courts for overturning what he regarded as harmful legislation and thereby "giving business men more nerve." More importantly for Ilasco and Hannibal, Atlas secured a contract with the federal government in August to provide 4.5 million barrels of cement for the Panama Canal. The new contract for $5.5 million enabled only Mill Number Six to resume operations in September. "Our output will be materially enlarged in the next few months," noted plant superintendent W. A. Smith, "but we will not put the now-idle plant No. 5 in operation . . . We can increase our output sufficiently, I think, without employing more men or starting the other plant. The big order will simply insure additional activity here for the next three years at least."[16]

Labor unrest greeted Atlas when Mill Number Six reopened. Many immigrants walked off their jobs on September 15, 1908, only a week after George Habric was killed in a shale mine accident. Atlas quickly fired them. The evidence does not reveal the nature and source of this unrest, but given the timing it probably grew out of new conditions imposed by Atlas upon restarting operations. To downplay the conflict, the *Hannibal Courier-Post* refused to call it a strike: "A large majority of those who quit are returning to the old country, so it is supposed that they naturally wanted to return across the waters and took this time as a golden opportunity."[17]

13. Quoted in *Hannibal Morning Journal,* January 24, 1908.
14. Quoted in *Hannibal Courier-Post,* September 16, 1908.
15. *Hannibal Courier-Post,* June 28, 1907.
16. Mahan and Smith quoted in *Hannibal Courier-Post,* September 16 and August 25, 1908, respectively.
17. *Hannibal Courier-Post,* September 19, 1906. On Habric's death, see Hagood and Hagood, comp., "List of Deaths," 32.

By that very evening, however, Atlas had closed the entire plant, notifying employees that the lockout would be indefinite. Plant officials claimed that a minority of workers had cowed the rest into refusing to work. Ilasco's saloon owners, hoping to avoid further confrontations with Atlas officials and county politicians in their bid to renew licenses, voluntarily closed their establishments to avoid trouble.

Plant superintendent Smith concluded after two days of shutdown that he had scared enough workers into returning. He reopened the plant, noting that enough men were on hand to resume work. He claimed that no representatives of the disgruntled workers had ever called on him with a list of demands for higher wages and better working conditions.[18]

While the strike, or lockout, was in progress, delegates to the annual Missouri State Federation of Labor convention gathered in Hannibal. They listened to welcoming speeches by attorney Eugene Nelson and L. Morris Anderson on behalf of Hannibal's mayor and Commercial Club. Nelson urged them to continue organizing, and Anderson stressed the common interests of unions and civic organizations like the Commercial Club. Surprisingly, the labor dispute at Ilasco did not receive attention at the convention, nor did the broader question of how to organize Atlas workers. Delegates took a steamboat ride down the river, stopping to visit the Mark Twain Cave, but took no notice of what was going on at the plant on the riverbank less than one-half mile to the south.[19]

Although Ilasco's workers had suffered defeats in 1906 and 1908, these set-backs did not dampen their growing militancy. At a time of growing militancy and Socialist popularity among rank-and-file machinists in midwestern manufacturing towns on the Mississippi River, machinists at the Ilasco plant struck on May 17, 1909. They tried to reclaim the 10 percent wage cut imposed in January 1908. Benjamin F. Lamb, their business agent from district headquarters in St. Louis, negotiated an acceptable settlement, but later that summer unskilled workers led by Italians in the packinghouse confronted Atlas officials over wages. At the change of shifts on the night of July 29, Italians in the packinghouse walked out. Fellow workers in the sack house joined them the next morning, and the strike soon included several hundred workers.[20]

The confrontation became explosive when a group of strikers seized Atlas's powder magazine and two carloads of dynamite on the night of August 2. A striker apparently dynamited one of Atlas's small buildings but did not do much damage. In addition, "the strikers paraded the streets and warned the company

18. *Hannibal Courier-Post,* September 19, 21, and 22, 1908.
19. Ibid.
20. Montgomery, *Workers' Control,* 67–74; Executive Board Minutes, June 10, 1909, IAMAW Records, vol. 3, WHMC–St. Louis; *Hannibal Courier-Post,* July 30 and 31, 1909.

they would not permit others to take their places." A Slavic organizer from St. Louis arrived the following morning to help Ilasco workers adopt a more disciplined, coherent strategy as Ralls County Sheriff J. O. Roland and twenty-five deputies guarded Atlas property. Strikers formed a committee to present demands to plant officials, and they appointed several men to ensure that no workers damaged Atlas property. A bugler summoned strikers from their homes in Ilasco to attend open-air meetings and discuss strategies and aims.[21]

On the morning of August 3, several hundred strikers armed with clubs and other weapons greeted Atlas's work train from Hannibal. On board were "American employees" and strikebreakers. Strikers, according to a local newspaper, were "inflamed by the speeches of a professional strike leader." They warned scabs from Hannibal "that if one of them alighted he would be killed." The train returned to Hannibal after a man named Hedges tried to enter the plant and was beaten but not seriously hurt.[22]

Until now, the *Hannibal Courier-Post* had been somewhat restrained in its expression of ethnic hatred of Ilasco's immigrant workers. The strike of 1909, however, prompted a shocking outpouring of editorial venom as the newspaper shed all self-restraint: "Ilasco, the city of dust, is a seething, boiling pot of beer-demented, striking foreigners . . . Law and order has been supplanted by drinking and revelry." The newspaper expressed scorn for Ilasco's "garlic-smelling . . . maddened mass of non-citizen employees." Denouncing strikers as a "foreign mob," a reporter registered his disgust at the community's paradelike resistance to Atlas: "A martial bugle call sounds the taps and assembly and from every door and shanty appears a 'hunk' ready to do the unreasonable beckoning of an overwrought leader."[23]

A reporter on the scene for the *Perry Enterprise* noted that "angry demands were heard that the foreigners be driven from Ilasco," but he pointed out that the cement plant's operations "depended upon the rough work done by the foreigners." Atlas officials contacted Governor Hadley's office about sending the National Guard, but withdrew their request when they reached a settlement with workers on August 3. Atlas granted a pay increase of twenty-nine cents per day.[24]

---

21. *Ralls County Record,* August 6, 1909; *Perry Enterprise,* August 5, 1909; *Hannibal Courier-Post,* August 3, 1909. The local newspapers did not mention this dynamiting at the time, but on May 17, 1910, the *Hannibal Courier-Post* noted that a dynamiting of one of Atlas's buildings had taken place during an earlier strike. I assume that this incident occurred in 1909.

22. *Ralls County Record,* August 6, 1909; *Hannibal Courier-Post,* August 3, 1909; *Perry Enterprise,* August 5, 1909.

23. *Hannibal Courier-Post,* August 3, 1909.

24. Ibid.; *Perry Enterprise,* August 5, 1909; *Ralls County Record,* August 6, 1909. On Atlas's request for the National Guard, see also the *Hannibal Courier-Post,* May 17, 1910.

At this time, Atlas was particularly eager to avoid lengthy disruptions in production. In addition to producing cement for the Panama Canal, Atlas had a contract to provide cement for a new power station and dam at Keokuk, Iowa, about sixty miles north of Hannibal on the Mississippi. Construction, which began on January 10, 1910, required 650,000 barrels of cement. Atlas officials reopened Mill Number Five during the first week of February 1910. This marked the first time in two and one-half years that Number Five had been running. During the shutdown, Atlas had installed two of the largest kilns in the world, each of which was approximately 240 feet in length.[25]

The reopening of Mill Number Five prompted the hiring of 250 new workers to meet the increased demand for cement, but by April 1910 labor unrest again threatened production. Twenty-eight members of Machinists Lodge 537 presented plant officials with a proposed agreement on March 28, calling for a nine-hour day and a wage increase from 34½ to 38 cents per hour. Atlas officials refused even to meet with a union committee and business agent. Following a meeting in Hannibal's Trades and Labor Assembly Hall with district representative and business agent Lamb, the machinists struck on April 20.[26]

Tensions smoldered for nearly a month. Lamb expected an early settlement and went back to Hannibal from his headquarters in St. Louis on May 3 to arrange a conference to resolve the strike, but Atlas had planned well for the confrontation. Since the IAM had targeted railroads as part of a broader campaign to win the nine-hour day, and since a coal strike was brewing, Atlas had carloads of coal on hand in case coal shipments were disrupted. With large stocks of cement on hand, and low prices and squeezed profit margins in the East, Atlas officials fired the strikers in an attempt to bust the union. They announced plans to move the machine shops to their plant at Northampton, Pennsylvania. Prepared to resist workers' demands, they dug their heels in deeper when steamfitters struck in support of the machinists on May 4, and when blacksmiths did the same on May 14. Carpenters, millers, and workers in the packinghouses and quarries joined the picket line on May 16.[27]

---

25. Universal Atlas Cement Company, "Data on Keokuk Power Station and Dam," February 12, 1941 (in author's possession); *Ralls County Record,* February 11, 1910; and "News Siftings from the Mills," *Cement Record* 3 (January 1910): 31.

26. "News Siftings," 31; *Hannibal Morning Journal,* April 21, 1910; Missouri Bureau of Labor Statistics, *Annual Report* 32 (1910), 275–77. See also a letter from the Mark Twain Lodge No. 537 to Organized Labor Everywhere, read before a meeting of the Central Trades and Labor Union in St. Louis and reprinted in *St. Louis Labor,* May 28, 1910. Local 537, founded on December 15, 1901, consisted mainly of employees of the cement plant and Burlington Railroad. See *Hannibal Courier-Post,* December 17, 1906.

27. *Hannibal Courier-Post,* May 16, 1910; *Ralls County Record,* March 25, 1910; Mark Twain Lodge No. 537 to Organized Labor Everywhere; Meeting of the Joint Executive Board, May 12, June 9, and July 14, 1910, IAMAW Records, vol. 4, WHMC–St. Louis;

Once again, Italians in the packinghouses mobilized unskilled workers in the strike. They left the packinghouses and went to the quarries and mines to prevail upon fellow workers. Quarry workers quickly joined them, but a fight almost erupted at first with some shale miners who opposed the strike. At the depot, strikers intercepted the afternoon work train from Hannibal. Since it was payday, however, they allowed them to visit the paymaster provided they left their dinner pails on the train and agreed to return to Hannibal as soon as they picked up their checks. Most workers from Hannibal complied, but one insisted on going to work. When strikers grabbed him, friends had to rescue him. He then put his dinner pail back on the train and went with others to get their paychecks. Atlas paymasters, after distributing the checks, told Hannibal workers to go home until further notice.[28]

Atlas officials shut down the plant and adopted a hard line against strikers. "When they marched through the various departments, armed with sticks and rocks, intimidating the men," a plant official said, "we at once determined to shut down the entire works to avert trouble. . . . We are paying better wages than any cement plant of which I have knowledge, and we could not accede to the demands made previously by the machinists and others."[29]

This time, Atlas officials wasted no time in contacting the authorities. Ralls County Sheriff Roland sent deputies to guard the plant. At the behest of plant superintendent Smith, he also contacted Governor Hadley and Adjutant General F. M. Rumbold to request the dispatch of National Guardsmen. According to Atlas officials, they feared that strikers would dynamite the plant. At about 11:30 in the morning, Ralls County Prosecuting Attorney Jack Briscoe notified Hadley that rioting was in progress. He complained that armed strikers were using violence and threats to keep other workers off the job.[30]

Governor Hadley at first refused the request, urging Briscoe and Roland to monitor the situation and contact him again later that day. In the meantime, Hadley ordered two members of his staff to investigate. They did not go to Ilasco but concluded after consulting with "reputable parties" that troops were necessary. Later that day, Briscoe and Roland sent the following telegram to the governor's office: "Send 300 militia at once to Ilasco, Ralls county, to suppress insurrection and lawlessness. A state of lawlessness, tumult, mob riot and resistance to the laws of the State by a body of men acting together by force with

Missouri Bureau of Labor Statistics, *Annual Report* 32, 275–77; *Wall Street Journal,* April 22 and 29, 1910.
    28. *Hannibal Morning Journal,* May 17, 1910.
    29. Quoted in ibid.
    30. Governor Herbert S. Hadley to R. B. Leeds, Secretary, Hannibal Trades and Labor Assembly, June 3, 1910, Herbert S. Hadley Papers, WHMC–Columbia; *St. Louis Republic,* May 17, 1910.

intent to resist laws and offer violence to persons and property exists at Ilasco. Fifteen hundred men are striking at Atlas Cement Works."[31]

Atlas officials switched all freight cars out of the railroad yards to make room for the militia. At about 10:30 P.M., Company C from Kirksville arrived in Hannibal, where it joined local Company E under the command of Captain J. Fred Meyer. These companies took a train past the plant to Saverton to meet and pick up two cars of National Guard companies from St. Louis, and then proceeded back to the plant. Assistant Superintendent F. S. Rucker greeted and quartered them. The Hannibal and Kirksville militia unloaded at the packinghouse in Mill Number Six, while St. Louis guardsmen occupied the packinghouse in Number Five. Major H. Chouteau Dyer, the senior officer from St. Louis, posted sentries around the plant. By 5:15 in the morning, Colonel Clay MacDonald, a former Confederate soldier, had arrived from St. Joseph to command the operation, which then consisted of 17 officers and 141 enlisted men. Shortly thereafter, a detachment from Company L in Jefferson City arrived, beefing up the force to 18 officers and 158 enlisted men.[32]

Ilasco workers struggled to maintain unity, but the crisis strained relationships in the community. Amid reported heavy drinking on the night of May 16, heated arguments broke out in the saloons. The stabbing of Jacob Catoni prompted the issuance of warrants the following day for the arrest of Almaine and Nicola Spostu. In addition to a couple of other stabbings that night, Nick Scalise allegedly shot himself accidentally in the left shoulder while playing with a loaded revolver.[33]

Ilasco's residents were agitated when they awoke on May 17 to find their village under military occupation. The eerie silence that engulfed the cement plant provided a veneer of calm over a community in turmoil. "Over the deserted plant silence hangs like a pall," observed a local reporter. "The quiet is only broken by the sharp command of an officer or the challenge of a sentry. The

31. *Hannibal Courier-Post,* May 16, 1910; Governor Hadley to R. B. Leeds, June 3, 1910. Copies of the telegram are reproduced in *Hannibal Morning Journal,* May 17, 1910, and Missouri State Federation of Labor, *Proceedings of the Nineteenth Annual Convention,* 1910, 89, Missouri State Labor Council, AFL-CIO Records, 1891–1975, collection no. 216, folder 5, WHMC–Columbia. One of these "reputable parties" was probably J. Fred Meyers, captain of Hannibal's National Guard unit, Company E. Given his position and social contacts with cement plant manager W. A. Smith and other Hannibal elites with ties to Atlas, he would have been a likely source for the governor's office to contact for information. On Captain Meyers's social contacts with Atlas officials, see Hagood and Hagood, *Hannibal Yesterdays,* 187–88.

32. *Hannibal Courier-Post,* May 16, 1910; *Hannibal Morning Journal,* May 17, 1910; *St. Louis Republic,* May 17, 1910; Governor Hadley to R. B. Leeds, June 3, 1910; "Report of Colonel C. C. MacDonald," May 21, 1910, Appendix M, in *Biennial Report of the Adjutant General of the State of Missouri for the Years 1909–10,* 421.

33. *Hannibal Morning Journal,* May 17 and 19, 1910.

village of Ilasco, however, seethes with sullen men and women who greet every appearance of the soldiers with hisses and cat-calls."[34]

The military occupation of Ilasco attracted considerable newspaper attention. Much of that coverage emphasized alcohol as the primary explanation for the behavior of Ilasco's workers. A headline on the front page of the *Hannibal Morning Journal* on May 17, 1910, declared: "FOREIGNERS CARVE EACH OTHER IN DRUNKEN BROILS AT ILASCO LAST NIGHT." Whereas this newspaper attributed violence to alcohol, the *St. Louis Republic* on the same date explained, on the other hand, that there had yet been no violent clash between strikers and the militia because the troops had "discovered nearly everybody in a drunken stupor."

In an attempt to prevent tensions from escalating, Governor Hadley sent a telegram to Colonel MacDonald at 6 A.M., ordering him to close all saloons at once. In part, this reflected an underlying tendency to blame labor strife on alcohol, but by closing the saloons, MacDonald could also deprive strikers of important cultural meeting places where they could plan strategy and mobilize collective support. Ilasco's saloon owners complied with the order after MacDonald and Captain Leroy Robbins of Company A from St. Louis notified them in person, "though there were some murmurs of dissatisfaction at its promulgation."[35]

On May 17, under protection of the National Guard, Atlas officials tried to restart the plant with workers from Hannibal, but strikers again intercepted the work train. Shortly after MacDonald had closed the saloons, a bugler summoned several hundred strikers to form a marching column, and along the river they walked two abreast to the unloading station to stop the train from reaching the plant. A reporter described the procession: "A bugler at their head blew strenuously, making the hills ring with his crude music."[36]

In response, MacDonald deployed nearly all of his troops to the train station. A local reporter on the scene captured the drama as he described the confrontation between strikers and troops:

> As the men neared the company's property a file of soldiers moved down towards the depot, the two lines gradually approaching each other until only a narrow strip of roadway separated them. When almost opposite the depot, the strikers stopped. The soldiers, still moving in single file, then swung directly across the road and, at a command, slowly stepped towards the strikers, who moved back a few paces. It was an intensely dramatic scene.[37]

MacDonald warned strikers against violence and lawlessness. A striker replied that there would be no violence, but insisted that workers had a right to demand

34. *Hannibal Courier-Post,* May 17, 1910.
35. "Report of Colonel MacDonald," May 21, 1910, 421–22.
36. Ibid., 422; *St. Louis Republic,* May 18, 1910.
37. *Hannibal Morning Journal,* May 18, 1910.

and receive higher wages. When the work train arrived, the militia escorted workers from the train without any disturbances, and the crowd went back to the village.[38]

Tensions escalated later that morning when three snipers fired shotgun blasts at sentries guarding Atlas's dynamite magazine. MacDonald quickly led a squad to investigate and reinforce the magazine. There were no casualties, but the buckshot had left marks on the platform in front of the magazine. The unidentified snipers had retreated into the hills.[39]

In the afternoon, a report reached MacDonald that saloon owners had illegally opened back doors to their establishments. He sent Captain Robbins to investigate with orders to arrest any owner who violated the decree. When Robbins reached the saloon of Richard Janney, he discovered a crowd of approximately thirty-five men drinking inside. The back door to the tavern was open. Robbins arrested Janney and his Rumanian bartender, John Blagu. He escorted them at gunpoint past what a reporter described as "a seething mass of foreigners at the bar."[40]

The arrests triggered a "wild demonstration" by strikers and supporters in the street who taunted, hissed, and sneered at the men in uniform. As Robbins escorted the prisoners past the jail to temporary military headquarters on Atlas property, Janney and Blagu must have wondered whether they were prisoners of the state or of Atlas. Robbins released Janney the next morning in exchange for a promise to keep his saloon closed, but turned Blagu over to Ralls County civil authorities, who had earlier issued a warrant for Blagu's arrest on criminal charges of rioting.[41]

The growing turbulence convinced Colonel MacDonald that he needed reinforcements. He asked Governor Hadley for an additional 120 men, but received only two more officers and twenty-five enlisted men the following morning. After five men were recalled to Jefferson City on the morning of May 19, MacDonald's troops numbered 21 officers and 180 enlisted men. Atlas officials did all they could to make the troops feel comfortable, including arranging for officers to eat at the company boardinghouse.[42]

Apparently not enough workers showed up when Atlas tried to reopen the plant under militia protection. Nevertheless, ethnic divisions began to weaken the strikers' united front. A local reporter claimed that most Slovaks and Rumanians

38. *St. Louis Republic,* May 18, 1910.
39. Ibid.; "Report of Colonel MacDonald," 422; *Hannibal Courier-Post,* May 17, 1910; *St. Joseph Gazette,* May 18, 1910.
40. "Report of Colonel MacDonald," 422; *Hannibal Courier-Post,* May 17, 1910; *St. Louis Republic,* May 18, 1910.
41. *St. Louis Republic,* May 18, 1910.
42. "Report of Colonel MacDonald," 423; *St. Louis Republic,* May 18, 1910.

did not support the strike energetically and were willing to return to work if they received protection. A group of Poles and Hungarians met with Atlas officials to complain that Italians were the ringleaders. Atlas officials claimed that about seventy-five Italians were bullying fifteen hundred workers into staying off the job.[43]

On May 18, a strike committee headed by Italian Tony Mirande asked plant Superintendent Smith to address workers on a plain between the plant and village. Smith consented. During this meeting Mirande complained that receiving between $1.65 and $2 per day for a ten-hour workday was unacceptable. He apparently insisted on union representation and the removal of Assistant Superintendent Rucker, who insisted that "we run an open shop, and will continue to do so." Smith told strikers that their wages were as high as those paid by any cement company. Atlas wanted to treat them right, he assured, emphasizing his desire for a speedy resolution of differences. He agreed then to discuss grievances with the strike committee, but expressed doubts that strikers would honor Mirande's promise that they would accept an agreement negotiated by this committee.[44]

For Ilasco's residents, military occupation had turned their world upside down. Much to the surprise of newspaper reporters on the scene, the atmosphere was festive, almost carnivalesque. This may have shocked Hannibal elites, but a similar atmosphere was often present among workers during such conflicts. As radical journalist, poet, and songwriter Ralph Chaplin observed of the famous Paint Creek–Cabin Creek strike among West Virginia coal miners in 1912, "The fact that many of the strikers seem to rather enjoy the situation makes some of the local respectables furious with rage. It isn't just what one would expect of a striker to see him holding his head high and walking around as if he owned the whole valley."[45]

Just before the meeting between Smith and the strikers' committee, the community's bugler sounded the now-familiar call for assembly, and in response residents poured from their homes. Two men wearing bright blue trousers and red sashes took positions on each side of a donkey mounted by a Rumanian. Demonstration organizers tied bright-colored ribbons around the donkey's head and covered him with cloth. The rider, with his two colorful companions on each side of the donkey, and seven hundred or eight hundred Rumanians and Slovaks behind them, marched through the streets and village commons area. The procession did not stop until it reached the plain between the plant and community. After putting on what a newspaper reporter described as a fancy

43. *Hannibal Morning Journal,* May 17, 1910; *St. Louis Republic,* May 18, 1910.
44. *St. Louis Post-Dispatch,* May 18, 1910; *Hannibal Morning Journal,* May 17, 1910; *Hannibal Courier-Post,* May 18, 1910.
45. Quoted in Corbin, *Life, Work,* 93. For a fuller discussion, see Jeremy Brecher, *Strike.*

drill, the paraders broke up into separate groups based on nationality and continued the festivities. Strikers, as a reporter observed, watched "with great glee the antics of some of their comrades on the plain . . . In the bright sunshine one of the leaders rode a stick-horse back and forth, amid the cheers of his comrades."[46]

Such ritualistic expressions of community solidarity "gave a decidedly peaceful aspect to the strike situation." Angelo Venditti recalled that militiamen played with him and other curious children who visited the packinghouses where troops were quartered. Strikers even circulated among troops without confrontations. In fact, National Guardsmen took time out to play baseball in the community's park. The game featured officers versus enlisted men, and Ilasco workers in the grandstands cheered according to the way they chose sides during the strike. Colonel MacDonald did the pitching for the commissioned officers, who were cheered by nonstrikers, while strikers cheered for the enlisted men. All in all, the strikers, "instead of being in an ugly mood, were as happy and as jolly as a lot of school boys on a frolic."[47]

Smith, after meeting with the strike committee, announced that they would hold other conferences as needed to resolve the dispute. Newspapers concluded that a settlement was at hand, and later that afternoon Colonel MacDonald telephoned Governor Hadley that "the danger of mob violence and lawlessness had passed." The governor's office notified MacDonald that barring any new threatening developments, all troops could be withdrawn by the morning of May 19. By 5:40 P.M. on the nineteenth, all troops had left Ilasco.[48]

The departure of the National Guard left Deputy Sheriff Charles T. Weaver and twenty-five deputies in charge. Sheriff Roland, who was in hot water with state officials, had apparently been yanked from the Atlas assignment. When Colonel MacDonald had first arrived in Ilasco on the morning of May 17, he tried to contact Roland but was told that the sheriff was indisposed. Atlas officials told MacDonald that Roland "was not fit for duty, on account of intoxication." MacDonald did not meet Roland until the evening of May 18, when he handed prisoner John Blagu over to Prosecuting Attorney Briscoe. "At this time," reported MacDonald, "he [Roland] was so intoxicated that he could not get into his buggy without assistance, and I realized that it was useless to attempt to hold any communication with him."[49]

46. *St. Louis Post-Dispatch,* May 18, 1910; *Hannibal Morning Journal,* May 19, 1910; and *Hannibal Courier-Post,* May 18, 1910.

47. Angelo Venditti, interview by author, July 9, 1993; *Hannibal Courier-Post,* May 18, 1910; *Hannibal Morning Journal,* May 17 and 19, 1910.

48. *Hannibal Courier-Post,* May 18, 1910; "Report of Colonel MacDonald," 423.

49. *Hannibal Courier-Post,* May 20, 1910; "Report of Colonel MacDonald," 423–24.

On the morning of May 20, Atlas officials abruptly suspended negotiations with the strike committee and announced that the plant would be closed indefinitely. Plant superintendent Smith rejected the committee's demands as unreasonable and informed them that all of the men would get paid off in the morning and that most employees would be laid off indefinitely. Only engineers, foremen, and watchmen would be employed to ensure fire and safety inspection of plant buildings.[50]

Atlas's strategy to turn up the heat on strikers and strain ethnic divisions to the breaking point in Ilasco was successful. On the night of May 20, Italian workers requested protection from their consulates in Chicago and St. Louis. They complained that other ethnic workers in Ilasco had threatened their lives and property. In response, Italian consuls in St. Louis and Chicago wired Governor Hadley for troops to protect the Italian colony in Ilasco from violence. Hadley contacted Briscoe in New London, urging him to use local law enforcement personnel to protect the Italians. A couple of days later, however, Hadley complained to Briscoe that he had since learned from MacDonald that the Italians were the "principle disturbers."[51]

Despite the plant officials' threat to close the plant indefinitely, they discussed plans with county officials to resume operations on the morning of May 21 in order to drive a deeper wedge between the militants and those who favored ending the strike. Between 5 and 6 A.M., workers assembled to discuss the issue. Most favored ending the strike and communicated this to Superintendent Smith.[52]

Meanwhile, a special representative of the Italian consul in St. Louis arrived. Michael Deelo, a prominent Italian businessman from St. Louis, met with Italian workers in Ilasco and talked to Smith in an effort to resolve the crisis. A Hannibal reporter noted that Deelo was well cast in the role of peacemaker: "He is a pleasant talker, a shrewd wide awake businessman, and has had a great many years' experience in dealing with matters of this kind."[53]

After Deelo failed to broker an agreement, a large number of workers prepared to report for work. In response, forty or fifty strikers, most of whom were Italians, threatened violence to anyone who broke ranks and returned to work. This prompted a "small sized riot." The rest of the workers, including the more "peaceable" of the Italians, attacked the militants, who retreated to their homes. The angry crowd, after smashing windows with rocks and knocking down doors,

---

50. *Hannibal Courier-Post,* May 20, 1910.
51. Hadley to Briscoe, May 23, 1910, Hadley Papers, WHMC–Columbia. The telegrams from the Italian consulates in Chicago and St. Louis are in *Hannibal Courier-Post,* May 21, 1910.
52. *Hannibal Courier-Post,* May 21, 1910.
53. *Hannibal Morning Journal,* May 22, 1910.

dragged the strike ringleaders out of their homes. Deputy Sheriff Weaver hurried over with several deputies to prevent more damage and violence, but stood by while the crowd dragged several strike leaders to the plant to pick up their paychecks and then chased them out of town.

When Prosecuting Attorney Briscoe learned of the conflict, he asked Governor Hadley to put Hannibal's National Guard unit back on alert in case troops were again needed. Local law enforcement officials handled the situation, however. To explain why the Guard was not dispatched again to Ilasco, the *Hannibal Courier-Post* emphasized that no threats were made against Atlas officials or property, and that the violence was confined to Ilasco workers. Apparently the lives of Ilasco workers and strike leaders were regarded as less important than the lives of Atlas officials or the protection of company property.[54]

Governor Hadley's use of the militia to cripple the strike, besides putting Ilasco on the front page of the *New York Times,* drew fire from organized labor in Missouri. The Central Trades and Labor Union in St. Louis condemned the dispatch of troops "before all of the strikers had even left the plant, during which time there was not a semblance of violence and not the least pretext for calling out the troops." A resolution introduced by Benjamin F. Lamb of Machinists' District Council Number 9 in St. Louis demanded the removal of Sheriff Roland. The Socialist *St. Louis Labor* blasted Hadley as a "miserable peanut politician" and ridiculed him for posing as "the great friend of labor." The newspaper noted that Hadley "complied with the request as promptly as any capitalist politician ever did within the last 25 years of labor troubles." It also mocked Hadley and the hysteria promoted by Atlas officials in order to secure troops against the strikers: "The 'foreigners' failed to dynamite the dynamite storage building; the 'rioters' failed to throw rocks at the manager of the cement company; the strikers acted like men and by their excellent discipline morally compelled Governor Hadley to order his Sunday soldiers back home to mamma."[55]

Hadley received letters of protest from several labor organizations, including the Hannibal Typographical Union, the Hannibal Trades and Labor Assembly, Lodge Number 41 of the Machinists' Union in St. Louis, and the Central Labor Union in Marceline. He defended his actions by emphasizing that Sheriff Roland had lost control of the situation, and he insisted that the militia carefully avoided taking sides during the dispute. He blamed Roland's intoxication for the trouble and pointed out that he had encouraged Briscoe to initiate proceedings to remove him from office. "It is as much to the benefit of the labor classes as it is to the benefit of the employers of labor," Hadley told R. B. Leeds, Secretary of the

54. *Hannibal Courier-Post,* May 21, 1910; *Hannibal Morning Journal,* May 22, 1910.
55. *St. Louis Labor,* May 21 and 28, 1910; *New York Times,* May 17, 1910.

Hannibal Trades and Labor Assembly, "that acts of violence, resulting in the destruction of lives and property, be avoided."[56]

Governor Hadley went out of his way so that the introduction of troops into Little Dixie did not rekindle lingering Civil War resentments in the area. This can be seen in his selection of MacDonald, reportedly a former Confederate soldier, to command the National Guard's expedition to Ilasco. In communications with Hannibal labor leaders after the strike, Hadley stressed MacDonald's Confederate credentials.[57]

Despite Hadley's contention that his actions were fair, restrained, justified, and equally beneficial to labor's interests, it is clear that he regarded Ilasco workers as a serious ongoing threat. This emerges from his communications with Briscoe over Sheriff Roland's future. Hadley suggested that Briscoe have Roland submit his resignation to the county court, which would then not accept it unless Roland started drinking again. If Roland refused, Briscoe should then begin proceedings to remove him under the derelict officials act. The stakes were too high to let Roland keep his job if he could not curb his drinking. "In view of the apparently flagrant disregard of his official obligations on the part of the sheriff," Hadley told Briscoe, "it seems to me that it is inadvisable to permit him to continue to perform the duties of this important position with the constant danger from violence and disturbance from the class of laborers employed at Ilasco."[58]

Hannibal's newspapers portrayed the strike as a foreign uprising, generally ignoring the cooperation, even if short-lived, between immigrant and native-born strikers. According to such accounts, strikers were foreigners whereas workers who opposed the strike were Americans, and strikers were from Ilasco whereas opponents of the strike lived in Hannibal. This interpretation may have served the public relations needs of Atlas, but as the *St. Louis Star*'s coverage indicated, it slighted the role of native-born machinists and other skilled workers in the strike. Many of them lived in Hannibal. Most of the pro-Atlas newspaper coverage also ignored the role of native-born workers in what Superintendent Smith regarded as primarily a sympathy strike on the part of unskilled workers. The *St. Louis Star* noted, however, that although immigrants had led earlier strikes at the cement

---

56. Hadley to R. B. Leeds, June 3, 1910, 89–90, in MSFL, *Proceedings of the Nineteenth Annual Convention*. See also Hadley to George Nein, Recording Secretary, Lodge No. 41, International Association of Machinists, St. Louis, May 23, 1910; Hadley to C. A. Hill, Secretary, Hannibal Typographical Union, June 8, 1910; Hadley to Geo. R. McGregor, Secretary, Central Labor Union, Marceline, June 28, 1910; all in Hadley Papers, WHMC–Columbia.
57. Hadley to R. B. Leeds, Secretary, Hannibal Trades and Labor Assembly, June 3, 1910, in MSFL, *Proceedings*, 89–90.
58. Hadley to Briscoe, May 23 and 27, 1910, Hadley Papers, WHMC–Columbia. The *Perry Enterprise*, June 2, 1910, urged Sheriff Roland to account for his behavior during the strike.

plant, "this time it is said the Americans at the plant have led the strike movement and the foreigners have followed as a matter of accommodation."[59]

When Ilasco's Justice of the Peace John Northcutt, acting on behalf of Prosecuting Attorney Briscoe, tried to decapitate the strike early by issuing arrest warrants for fourteen Ilasco residents on charges of rioting, he targeted several native-born residents. Those for whom Northcutt issued arrest warrants included Tony Mirande (strike committee spokesman), Antone Vecoli, Leonard Talanka, Thomas Bennett, C. Boyd, Clay Scott, Roy Scott, George Schwartz, John Blagu, Fred Zimmerman, Frank Montgomery, Tony Benito, and Tony Jacquinto. The fact that authorities were able to arrest only Blagu, Boyd, and Bennett probably suggests community cooperation to prevent the apprehension of those marked for arrest.[60]

As indicated by the large ritualistic demonstrations by Ilasco residents during the military occupation, this was more than a labor strike. It was a community on strike, a community under siege. When Richard Janney defied martial law by opening the back door of his saloon, much more was at stake than simply profits and alcohol. As evidenced by the angry, hissing crowd and demonstrations against his arrest, he represented a broader defiance against Atlas's use of outside authorities to impose its will on the community. A native-born resident who took in boarders and whose tavern was frequented by native-born and immigrants alike, Janney was perhaps a good example of Ilasco's early efforts to forge a multi-ethnic class identity.[61]

The scarcity of evidence makes it difficult to ascertain the role of Ilasco's women in the strike, but they participated in the demonstrations and perhaps marched behind the bugler to intercept the shift train bringing workers from Hannibal. They may have formed ethnic brigades to enforce support for the strike. When Ilasco postmaster Joseph Bernstein allegedly criticized Rumanian strikers for being too lazy to work, four Rumanian women decided to get revenge. They waited for him on the morning of May 21 and "proceeded to straighten matters to their own satisfaction and to the discomfort of the gentleman."[62]

When the *Hannibal Courier-Post* reported on May 23, 1910, that Atlas had resumed operations, it noted that "the faces of the foreign element were wreathed in smiles at the prospect of resuming work." What the newspaper did not report, however, was that the machinists' strike against the local Atlas plant was still in

---

59. *St. Louis Star,* May 17, 1910.

60. The *Hannibal Courier-Post,* May 18, 1910, contains the names of those targeted for arrest.

61. For a list of Janney's boarders, see U.S. Federal Manuscript Census, 1910, Saverton township, Ralls County.

62. *Hannibal Morning Journal,* May 22, 1910; U.S. Federal Manuscript Census, 1910, Saverton township, Ralls County.

progress. The *Ralls County Record* pointed out on May 27 that although many had returned to work in Ilasco, the machinists, steam pipefitters, and blacksmiths were still on strike and had been "paid off" by Atlas. In July, Hannibal's Machinists' Lodge 537 appealed to the Central Trades and Labor Union in St. Louis for financial help on behalf of its striking members at the cement plant. It complained that the National Guard had intimidated the vast majority of strikers into returning to work.[63]

Governor Hadley's role in breaking the strike damaged his reputation with organized labor. Trade unionists in Kansas City opposed inviting him to speak there on Labor Day. Hadley, proud of his reputation as a Progressive, was stung by this criticism. "No fair-minded and intelligent man," he asserted, "could know the facts and entertain the opinion that I was not fully justified in sending the militia to Ilasco."[64]

At the annual convention of the Missouri State Federation of Labor in September 1910, Hannibal Trades and Labor Assembly President B. F. Brown introduced two resolutions relative to the Ilasco strike. The first was a statement of protest by Machinists Lodge 537 urging the MSFL to denounce Governor Hadley and Ralls County authorities for "assisting a corporation in defeating working men from improving their conditions." The Committee on Strikes approved the resolution, which was then adopted by the convention.[65]

The second resolution condemned the "most deplorable" working conditions at the Ilasco cement plant, attributing this to the fact that most of the workers were foreign and therefore "unacquainted with our movement." It also pointed out that even most skilled workers there did not belong to unions, and it called attention to the machinists who were still on strike against Atlas in an effort to win the nine-hour day and a wage increase. The resolution urged the MSFL to lend the "widest publicity and moral support" to the ongoing machinists' strike at Ilasco. More importantly, it called on the state federation to request all affiliated unions to send organizers to Ilasco "so that the toilers of that city may be formed into local unions for their mutual protection and benefit."[66]

This was an important call for a major organizing campaign at Ilasco, but the Committee on Resolutions passed a mere watered-down substitute of this resolution. After the committee read a letter from Governor Hadley to the Hannibal Trades and Labor Assembly defending his actions, they offered a much more tepid resolution that simply condemned the dispatch of the National Guard "during labor disputes under any pretext whatsoever." The convention adopted

---

63. *St. Louis Labor,* July 16, 1910.
64. Hadley to Col. C. V. Dahlgren, August 6, 1910, Hadley Papers, WHMC–Columbia.
65. MSFL, *Proceedings,* 1910, 23, 67, MSLC Records, folder 5, WHMC–Columbia.
66. Ibid., 23.

the substitute resolution, which ignored the call for unions to send organizers to Ilasco.[67]

MSFL leaders were perhaps reluctant to antagonize Hadley too much because of efforts to work with him and employers on proposals for workmen's compensation legislation. Hadley had appointed MSFL President Owen Miller as a delegate to a conference on Uniform State Legislation sponsored by the National Civic Federation, and to the National Conference on Workmen's Compensation for Industrial Accidents. At the annual convention of the American Federation of Labor in St. Louis later that year, Hadley gave a speech that centered around the need for a workmen's compensation law. He did not mention the Ilasco strike.[68]

The *St. Louis Labor* pointed out the contradictions between Governor Hadley's progressive remarks to AFL convention delegates and his use of the militia in Ilasco. It also criticized the formation of a branch of the National Civic Federation (NCF) in St. Louis shortly after the Ilasco strike. The NCF, which sought ways to avoid the outbreak of serious labor-capital conflicts like the one in Ilasco, included local capitalists and prominent politicians like David R. Francis. It also included MSFL President Miller and Eugene Sarber, a business agent of the International Association of Machinists in St. Louis. Upon invitation, Hadley gave a speech at the founding meeting of this NCF branch in June 1910, for which he was later blasted by the *St. Louis Labor*. The newspaper challenged his efforts to paint himself as a friend of labor and reminded readers that he "enjoys the questionable honor of being the first Missouri Governor for many years who called out the State militia for strike-breaking purposes."[69]

Despite the MSFL's failure to endorse an organizing campaign at Ilasco, Machinists' business agent Lamb discussed the situation with union president James O'Connell at the AFL convention in St. Louis in November 1910. He urged O'Connell to persuade AFL President Gompers to send an organizer to the Atlas plant. In February 1911 an AFL organizer arrived, but Atlas shortly thereafter reached a settlement with Lodge 537 to end the strike on terms originally demanded by the machinists. The AFL did undertake efforts that year to organize cement mill workers into Federal Unions, but as a result of the settlement between Lodge 537 and Atlas officials, the AFL apparently called off plans to organize Ilasco workers, who remained ethnically divided, unorganized, and collectively

67. Ibid., 89–90.
68. MSFL, *Proceedings,* 1910, 7–10, 89–90, in MSLC Records, folder 5, WHMC–Columbia; American Federation of Labor, *Proceedings,* 1910, 128–35.
69. *St. Louis Labor,* June 25, October 29, and November 26, 1910. On the general relationship between the NCF and the labor movement, see Marguerite Green, *The National Civic Federation and the American Labor Movement, 1900–1925.*

powerless until the 1940s. The National Guard had helped to squash the militancy of Ilasco's earliest working class.[70]

The strike strained ethnic tensions in Ilasco, perhaps beyond repair in some cases. According to Guy D. Helmick, an Atlas civil engineer who helped to found the plant at Ilasco, the company segregated the nationalities in Ilasco following this "little Balkan war," which he described as "a forerunner of the Balkan wars which began a few years later." Absent in the federal census taken in Ilasco the month after the strike was Tony Mirande, spokesman for the strike committee. He was probably one of the casualties in the roundup of strike leaders who were forced by others to pick up their paychecks and leave Ilasco.[71]

Given the important strike role of Italian militants with syndicalist traditions from their homeland, it is safe to assume that many homes smashed by angry mobs in the community belonged to Italians. They may also have been influenced by the radicalism of the Industrial Workers of the World (IWW), although there is no evidence that the IWW played a formal role in the strike. Certainly Michael Deelo, who came from St. Louis in an unsuccessful effort to broker a settlement of the strike, felt compelled to assure Hannibal residents that there was no need to link Italians to labor militancy. In a newspaper interview, he tried to smooth over the troubles at Ilasco: "Your cement plant is a wonderful institution. It has done and is doing a great deal to build up your city. . . . I think it was the result of a misunderstanding for I am certain that many of my countrymen had the wrong idea about things. The Italians are good people and they want to do right at all times."[72]

"Everytime poor wage workers go on strike the 'foreigners' make their appearance," noted the *St. Louis Labor* in reference to headlines that blasted immigrant strikers in Ilasco, "but so long as the 'foreigners' submit quietly to starvation wages and long hours they are praised as the angels of mankind."[73] This editorial exposed the class basis of public attitudes toward Ilasco's predominantly foreign labor force. Romanticized images of sturdy, hardworking immigrants saving every

70. Meeting of the Joint Executive Board, January 12, January 18, February 9, and March 9, 1911, IAMAW Records, vol. 4, WHMC–St. Louis; AFL, *Proceedings,* 1911, 202.

71. Helmick, "Cement Plant Story," 3; U.S. Federal Manuscript Census, 1910, Saverton township, Ralls County.

72. Deelo quoted in *Hannibal Morning Journal,* May 24, 1910. On the transfer of labor radicalism from southern Italy to the United States, see Donna Gabaccia, *Militants and Migrants: Rural Sicilians Become American Workers.* See also Paul Buhle, "Italian-American Radicals and Labor in Rhode Island, 1905–1930"; Rudolph J. Vecoli, ed., *Italian American Radicalism: Old World Origins and New World Developments*; and Samuel L. Baily, "The Italians and the Development of Organized Labor in Argentina, Brazil, and the United States, 1880–1914."

73. *St. Louis Labor,* May 21, 1910.

penny, even if it meant death, to bring their families to the United States gave way to bitter denunciations of "garlic-smelling foreigners" when Ilasco's workers struck against Atlas for higher wages and better working conditions.

Local newspaper reporters were not the only ones to paint the strike of 1910 as a foreign uprising. National Guardsmen organized a new military society to commemorate their self-styled valor in Ilasco. Members of this society called themselves the "Organized Veterans of the Insurrection," elected officers, and adopted colors. To celebrate their combat mission "abroad," they adopted a motto that had special significance for Ilasco: "The ties of friendship cement us."[74]

74. *Hannibal Courier-Post,* May 20, 1910.

Part II

Whose
Community?

(6)

Extending the Control of Old Man Atlas, 1910–1930

They all laid their heads together like as many lawyers when they are gettin'
ready to prove that a man's heirs ain't got any right to his property.
—Mark Twain, quoted in Fred W. Lorch, "Mark Twain in Iowa"

The strike of 1910 exposed Atlas's inability to contain escalating class conflict
in Ilasco without the aid of troops. This prompted a new approach toward
controlling the community. Although Atlas embarked on a campaign after 1910
to stabilize labor and community relations through a paternalistic strategy that
included fostering schools and churches, it was hampered by the fact that it
did not own the tracts on which the town was located. By the 1920s, however,
through sheriff's sales that grew out of lengthy, complicated will disputes over the
estates of Samuel Heinbach and Theodore Johnson, Atlas had acquired clear legal
title to most of Ilasco proper. This squeezed out competing landlords, converted
Ilasco into a company town, and gave Atlas a free hand in regulating community
affairs and determining future land use.

Between 1910 and 1930, Atlas also consolidated its power on the national, state,
and local levels. Like many corporations, Atlas cooperated with the Woodrow
Wilson administration on behalf of the Allied war effort and emerged from the
war enjoying a greater position of monopoly in the cement industry. Company
officials also took advantage of the conservative postwar atmosphere and pro-
business policies of Republican administrations in the 1920s to strengthen their
position as one of the nation's top two cement producers. They survived attacks
by Missouri proponents of state-owned cement plants in the early 1920s and
consolidated their power in Ralls County. Through marriage and extensive social contacts, Atlas widened its influence among county judges and prominent
political families in the area. This enabled the company to beat back attempts by
disgruntled Ralls County citizens in the mid-1920s to force the county to abandon
what many regarded as an unfair tax policy that favored Atlas at the expense of
farmers and other landowners.

In 1910, Ilasco not only was rocked by strike-related conflicts but also was in the middle of an important property rights struggle that further unsettled residents. The death of Samuel Heinbach on January 3, 1910, sparked a bitter legal battle over his property, even though he left a will specifying that his widow, Mary Alice, should inherit his entire estate. This included the twenty-six-acre tract on which many of Ilasco's businesses, saloons, and homes were located. New London attorney J. O. Allison, a former Democratic state representative, provoked a dispute between Mary Alice and Samuel's estranged adult children from a previous marriage. He located Sam's children and persuaded them to deed six-tenths of their interest in the estate to him if he could break the will.[1]

Judge T. E. Allison, J. O.'s brother and law partner, rejected the will in probate court and appointed William F. True, manager of the Ilasco Supply Company, as administrator of the estate. Mary Alice hired Hannibal attorneys Charles E. Rendlen and Frederick W. Neeper to initiate a suit against Sam's children. In addition, she and her sister Euphemia B. Koller established a joint deed of tenancy to make it more difficult for others to carve up the estate. In a trial in the Ralls County Circuit Court, J. O. Allison charged that Samuel Heinbach's alcoholism had destroyed the soundness of his mind and made him vulnerable to Mary Alice's "undue influence." This, he argued, invalidated the will. After a jury ruled in Allison's favor, Mary Alice appealed to the Missouri Supreme Court, which reversed the decision on November 24, 1914, and remanded the case to be retried.[2]

In a new trial in the Pike County Circuit Court at Bowling Green, Mary Alice won, but the case again went to the Missouri Supreme Court on appeal. "I say," emphasized one of her attorneys, "during all the years that this man [Heinbach] was doing business there, his making leases and in selling garden seed, and all the business that he was in with them, not one of them up until the time of his death thought that his acts were those of a man of unsound mind."[3]

On April 26, 1918, the Supreme Court upheld Mary Alice's victory, but she then tried to sell the entire tract to Petru Sirbu, who had close connections to Atlas and attorney Rendlen. She left the state and hid out for two years while Sirbu and Rendlen tried unsuccessfully to break the joint deed, alleging that Koller had coerced her into signing it. By the time the hotly contested matter was

1. *Heinbach v. Heinbach et al.,* November 24, 1914, 69–91.

2. Ibid., 91; *Heinbach v. Heinbach et al.,* April term, 1914, 1–14; *Mary Alice Heinbach et al. v. Euphemia B. Koller et al.,* October term, 1919, film no. 72, box 222, nos. 21, 19, Pike County, Office of the Circuit Clerk and Recorder, Bowling Green, Mo.

3. Attorney Gene Pearson quoted in "Motion for a New Trial," in *Heinbach v. Heinbach et al.,* April term, 1916, film no. 70, box 200, no. 8, Pike County, Office of the Circuit Clerk and Recorder, Bowling Green.

settled, Probate Judge B. B. Megown determined that Mary Alice was mentally incompetent. He appointed his brother, J. E. Megown, as her guardian. The latter was assistant cashier of the Ralls County Bank. The Ralls County Circuit Court then ordered a sheriff's sale of the Heinbach tract. Atlas bought it for only ten thousand dollars in December 1921 over fierce protests by Koller, who charged that her sister's sanity was "'Bargained away' for the sole purpose of money graft." As the *Ralls County Record* observed, "The price paid was cheap enough and the Atlas Company has a bargain."[4]

The other major tract on which much of Ilasco was located suffered a similar fate. Theodore and Eliza Jane Johnson owned this tract. Eliza Jane died first on September 11, 1911, and Theodore continued to collect ground rents until his death on January 28, 1914. In Eliza Jane's will, she left all of her personal property and one-half of her real estate to Theodore. Since she had no children, she provided that her nephew, Seymour Tranum, was to inherit the other half of her real estate with the stipulation that he contribute five dollars per year to the Marble Creek Methodist Church as long as he owned the property. She appointed J. O. Allison as executor of the will.[5]

Shortly after Eliza Jane's death, her niece, Florence Thompson, filed a suit contending that Eliza Jane's sister, Ary L. Clark, and brothers David, Littleton, and Thomas Smashey were each entitled to one-fourteenth of the fifteen acres that Eliza Jane had originally brought to her marriage with Theodore. Thompson's suit also contended that she, Tranum, William Porter, and Mary Richardson should each get a one-twenty-eighth share of the land, with yet lesser shares going to Grace Prosser and William, Charles, Peter, and Albert Davis. Thompson also charged that the choicest part of Theodore Johnson's tract—the section of 2.23 acres that housed the business district—had been bought in 1899 with the

---

4. *Ralls County Record,* December 23, 1921; E. S. Holt, Sheriff's Deed in Partition, December 16, 1921, Miscellaneous Record, book 106, 505–6, Ralls County, Office of the Circuit Clerk and Recorder, New London; "Statement and Brief on behalf of Defendant Euphemia B. Koller," in *Heinbach et al. v. Koller et al.,* October term, 1919. Koller's allegations against Atlas and county officials are outlined in a petition that she prepared and filed on January 24, 1923, and amended on January 14, 1924. See *Koller v. Heinbach et al.,* January 24, 1923, Ralls County.

This fascinating legal battle in which Koller continued to challenge the sheriff's sale until the county committed her to the State Hospital for the Insane in Fulton is the subject of a book-length manuscript that I have in progress, titled "Insane Sisters: The Gendered Politics of Property Rights in the Making of a Missouri Company Town, 1910–1930."

5. *Ralls County Times,* September 15, 1911; Estate of Eliza Jane Johnson, February 28, 1916, case no. 4273; Estate of Theodore Johnson, January 31, 1914, case no. 4183; both in Ralls County, Office of the Probate Clerk, New London; *Florence Thompson et al. v. Theodore Johnson et al.,* September 15, 1911, case no. 9484, Ralls County, Office of the Circuit Clerk and Recorder, New London.

separate money of Eliza Jane. According to Thompson, Theodore had furnished none of the money and secured the deed without his wife's written consent.[6]

Thompson's suit requested the circuit court to sell the lands in question and divide the proceeds among all of the heirs. She argued that Theodore should continue to hold the business tract section in trust for his dead wife's estate. Her case languished, however, until after Theodore's death. In fact, Judge Megown did not admit Eliza Jane's will until February 28, 1916, five years after her death. When Theodore died, Probate Judge T. E. Allison appointed C. T. Lamb as the administrator. Lamb, the mayor of New London, had been in the real estate business for several years, specializing in bottomlands. J. O. Allison, Eliza Jane's executor, was listed as one of the securities when his brother appointed Lamb.[7]

After Lamb's appointment, all of Eliza Jane's heirs joined Thompson in a suit against Theodore's estate. On May 23, 1916, the Ralls County Circuit Court, on grounds that the estate could not be divided due to the large number of contending parties, ordered a cash-only sheriff's sale of the Johnsons' property. At the sale on November 8, 1916, J. O. Allison bought a tract of fifteen acres for $685. This had belonged to Eliza Jane, whose estate he had administered. He then sold the tract four months later to Severino Fiorella for $1,000. Hannibal merchant Theodore Rendlen, the brother of attorney Charles Rendlen, bought the other two tracts, one of which consisted of the 2.23-acre business section. Rendlen paid $2,010 for this strip and $7,700 for another twenty-six acres that included numerous lots with houses on them.[8]

Theodore Rendlen quickly turned both strips over to the Atlas Portland Cement Company for the same amount of money, according to court records. Given his close connections to the Hannibal National Bank, Atlas's attorney George A. Mahan, and other Hannibal businessmen, Rendlen no doubt had reached an agreement with Atlas beforehand to hide his profit from the transaction. This was consistent with Atlas's general policy of purchasing land through intermediaries. Rendlen soon joined Mahan on the Hannibal National Bank's board of directors.[9]

The period between 1910 and 1930 witnessed the growing control of finance capital over the top cement companies. Shortly after the strike of 1910 in Ilasco, rumors swept Wall Street of financial instability and power struggles in the

6. *Thompson et al. v. Johnson et al.*

7. Ibid.; Estate of Eliza Jane Johnson; Estate of Theodore Johnson; *Hannibal Courier-Post,* August 3, 1917.

8. *Ralls County Record,* November 3 and 10, 1916; *Hannibal Courier-Post,* August 3, 1917; J. O. Allison to Severino Fiorella, March 12, 1917, Deed Record, book 99, 432; Quit Claim Deed Record, book 100, 135–36; Sheriff's Deed in Partition, Miscellaneous Record, book 97, 630–32; Sheriff's Deed in Partition, Miscellaneous Record, book 101, 7–8; all in Ralls County, Office of the Circuit Clerk and Recorder, New London.

9. Quitclaim Deed Record, book 100, 135–36; Hagood and Hagood, "History of the Hannibal National Bank," 49–50.

corporate boardrooms of Atlas, the nation's largest cement producer at the time. In 1909, a year in which the industry operated at only 60 percent of capacity, Atlas had invested heavily in a plant at Hudson, New York. The project proved much more costly than anticipated. This, along with expenses related to the expansion of production facilities at Northampton and Hannibal, required extensive bank loans. To make matters worse, record surpluses and steadily falling prices plagued the industry at the time. The average price per barrel of portland cement in the United States had fallen from $1.09 in 1900 to $.81 in 1909. Prices in the East were even lower. By the spring of 1910, the price per barrel in Pennsylvania's Lehigh Valley ranged from $.45 to $.80. "The price of the product is so low," complained an industry analyst, "that one cannot scrape the free sand from the gutters at much less cost per barrel than the present price of cement."[10]

Cement prices were much higher in the West. The reason for this was quite clear, according to a representative of an Eastern cement company. "There has been no controversy among Western mills regarding prices for some time," he pointed out, "as this question was settled by a gentlemen's agreement not to undersell each other." He complained that "in the middle West and East the same antagonism as to prices that has caused such a demorilization [sic] during the past year or two continues to prevail and there is no prospect of an improvement unless consumption increases."[11]

These conditions created serious problems for Atlas, which had been engaged in particularly bitter competition with the Universal Portland Cement Company. Universal, a subsidiary of the United States Steel Corporation, was the nation's second largest cement producer. Borrowing money became more difficult for Atlas as its profits dropped. In the summer of 1910 the company suspended payment of its dividend to stockholders. Atlas President J. Rogers Maxwell, reputedly one of the largest individual holders of railroad stocks in the anthracite region of the Northeast, publicly denied that he had lost control of the company. He tried to squelch rumors that financial problems had forced him to sell large chunks of his stock in Atlas and several railroad corporations.[12]

By October 1910, despite Maxwell's denial that his power was slipping, J. P. Morgan and Company had acquired a sizable interest in Atlas, sizable enough to replace Maxwell with John R. Morron of Chicago as president. Morgan's actions

10. Hadley, *Magic Powder,* 86–87; "Cement Production Breaks Record," *Cement Record* 6 (December 1911): 487; "The Cement Industry in 1910," *Cement Record* 6 (July 1911): 307; Lesley, Lober, and Bartlett, *History of the Portland Cement Industry,* 172–73; *Wall Street Journal,* April 21, April 29, and July 30, 1910. The quote is in Hadley, *Magic Powder,* 72.

11. Quoted in *Wall Street Journal,* April 22, 1910.

12. *New York Times,* July 30 and 31, 1910; *Wall Street Journal,* July 30 and October 28, 1910.

indicated the New York banking community's growing recognition that cement had become one of the top three extractive industries in the nation, alongside iron and coal. Maxwell became chairman of Atlas's board of directors, while Morgan put F. W. Stevens, an attaché of the Morgan banking house, on the board to replace F. L. Hine, president of the First National Bank. The financial community regarded these moves as evidence of U.S. Steel's growing interest in the cement industry. Morron had no experience in the cement business, but he had close ties to the house of Morgan. Many financial experts regarded Morron as Morgan's direct representative in the management of Atlas. The *Wall Street Journal* concluded that Morgan's growing role in the industry would eliminate some of the bitter competition between Atlas and Universal and lead to higher prices.[13]

The elevation of Morron, a native of Peoria, Illinois, and president of the Peter Cooper Glue Company in Chicago, signaled the growing importance of Atlas's Midwest operations. By 1910, Missouri had become the fifth largest cement-producing state. Whereas in 1897 the Lehigh Valley had produced 74.8 percent of the nation's total output of cement, by 1905 that figure had dropped to 49.3 percent, by 1910 to 34.3 percent, and by 1918 to 27.7 percent. The average price per barrel of cement in Missouri and other parts of the Midwest in 1910 was ninety-one cents, compared to seventy-five cents in the East. This led Atlas's directorate to promote officials like Morron and others who were more in tune with production, transportation, and marketing in the Mississippi River Valley.[14]

As another indication of the growing importance of cement manufacturing in the Midwest and West, the Association of American Portland Cement Manufacturers held its semi-annual meeting in Kansas City, Missouri, in June 1911. Never before had the association held a convention this far west. Due to the growing volume of business in the area, the Cement Products Exhibition Company also scheduled a cement exhibit to be held in Kansas City in March 1912. This marked the first time that exhibits were held outside of New York and Chicago.[15]

In a move that perhaps reflected the fallout from the Ilasco strike of 1910, W. H. Baker replaced W. A. Smith as superintendent of the Ilasco plant on April 1, 1911. During Smith's final days as superintendent, Mill Number Five was temporarily shut down, but he finally settled the machinists' strike, which had lasted nearly one year. According to the agreement reached with Machinists' Lodge 537, Atlas

13. Lesley, Lober, and Bartlett, *History of the Portland Cement Industry,* 273; Hadley, *Magic Powder,* 87; *New York Times,* October 21, 1910; *Wall Street Journal,* October 28, 1910.

14. Burchard, "Cement Industry," 473; "The Cement Industry in 1910," 307–8; "Cement Production Breaks Record," 489; Boyer, "Famous Lehigh Valley," 1–6; Lesley, Lober, and Bartlett, *History of the Portland Cement Industry,* 68; U.S. Geological Survey, *Mineral Resources of the United States, 1918.* Pt. 2, 574.

15. *Cement Record* 6 (July 1911): 309–11.

would now pay thirty-eight cents per hour for a nine-hour day, and time and one-half for all overtime work. In effect, Atlas had conceded to the provisions of a contract demanded by Machinists before the strike.[16]

Just a few weeks after the roundup and forced exodus of the ringleaders of the 1910 strike, a booster edition of the *Hannibal Courier-Post* touted Hannibal as a "working man's paradise." This was partly in response to Atlas's need for additional workers to produce cement for construction of the Keokuk Dam. It also indicated Atlas's determination to avoid rehiring strikers. Atlas was willing to grant pay increases in line with what machinists had requested before the strike, but only after the strike had been defeated. To impress workers that they would be better served by corporate paternalism than by strikes, Atlas also granted a 10 percent raise to workers paid by the day, and a 12.5 percent raise to those on piecework.[17]

Bitterness over the strike of 1910 did not go away overnight, however. In January 1916 a Slovak worker attacked fellow worker Oscar Steers while Steers was putting on his overalls in one of Atlas's kiln buildings. The assailant, who continued beating Steers after he had knocked him unconscious with a coupling pin, had reportedly been planning the attack for quite some time. A local newspaper suggested that the assault was connected to the strike nearly six years earlier. Steers at that time served as one of the sheriff's deputies who had helped to quell the strike.[18]

Soon after the Ilasco strike the AFL launched a campaign to organize cement mill workers, but the campaign did not have much lasting success. There were jurisdictional disputes and jealousies among AFL craft unions over where to put cement mill workers, most of whom were unskilled. The AFL's solution was to form federal labor unions not based on craft, but some craft unions complained that their turf was being violated. What little success the AFL enjoyed after 1911 in organizing about twenty federal labor unions in the industry was wiped out in the pro-business climate of the 1920s.[19]

16. Minutes, Meeting of Joint Executive Board, March 9, 1911, IAMAW Records, vol. 4, WHMC–St. Louis. On Baker's replacement of Smith at the Ilasco plant, see *Wm. O. Gardner v. Atlas Portland Cement Company*, December 19, 1913, case no. 9743, trial transcript, 24, Ralls County, Office of the Circuit Clerk and Recorder, New London. On the shutdown of Mill Number Five in the late winter and early spring of 1911, see *Heinbach v. Heinbach et al.*, April term, 1914, 277.

17. *Hannibal Courier-Post*, June 8, 1910; *Ralls County Record*, June 3, 1910.

18. There was some confusion among newspaper reports over the identity of the assailant, identified as either John Huska, John Plavecy, or John Fusco. See *Ralls County Record*, January 7, January 14, and March 10, 1916. On Steers as a sheriff's deputy during the strike of 1910, see County Court Record, book G, 127, June 7, 1910, Ralls County, Office of the County Clerk, New London.

19. AFL, *Proceedings*, 1911, 202, 342; AFL, *Proceedings*, 1913, 165, 168, 324, 344; Gary M. Fink, ed., *Labor Unions*, 51–52.

Organized labor also promoted a boycott of nonunion cement. Julius H. Cronin, a machinist at the Ilasco plant and a representative of the Hannibal Trades and Labor Assembly, attended the Arkansas State Federation of Labor convention as a fraternal delegate in 1911, and upon his return praised the state labor body for its efforts along those lines. He reported that on one occasion the governor of Arkansas had banned the use of nonunion cement in the construction of a new state capitol building. The governor had singled out Atlas cement, noting that the building trades had issued a ban against it.[20]

These efforts failed, too, and cement mill workers around the nation remained overwhelmingly unorganized until the 1930s. This left them primarily dependent on company-sponsored services and benefits, or welfare capitalism. By the mid-1920s, approximately 80 percent of the employees of large companies had access to company housing, doctors, gardens, recreation, churches, schools, pensions, recreational activities, employee representation plans, or other corporate-sponsored activities. These welfare practices were designed to strengthen workers' loyalty to the company and to discourage trade unionism.[21]

Atlas's paternalism at times had other tangible benefits. For example, when seventeen-year-old Anna Rell reached Ellis Island in 1922 en route from Czechoslovakia to Ilasco, she hit a bureaucratic snag with immigration personnel who detained her. She was on her way to marry George Sajban, who worked at the cement plant. Sajban told Atlas plant Superintendent Ray E. Hoffman about Rell's detention. Hoffman contacted Atlas's New York office, which sent someone to Ellis Island to arrange for her release.[22]

If workers challenged Atlas's control, however, they soon learned the limits of corporate paternalism. On September 7, 1912, Atlas hired William Outside Gardner, a former Ralls County probate judge, as a night watchman to guard a site where two new shale mines were under construction just north of the plant. Gardner, formerly of Center and once described by the *Ralls County Times* as "one of Center's most honest, most honorable, most highminded, most conscientious, most truthful and most popular citizens," apparently had a physical condition that limited the manual labor that he could do. C. T. Hays, Hannibal mayor and next-door neighbor of plant superintendent W. H. Baker, had urged Baker to hire Gardner, who now lived in Hannibal, too. According to Baker, Hays presented Gardner as "a man who had served his country well . . . [who] was in sore circumstances." Baker believed that Gardner "on account of some infirmity could not be given a position requiring any manual labor,

20. MSFL, *Proceedings,* 1911, 67–68, folder 6, MSLC Records, WHMC–Columbia; U.S. Federal Manuscript Census, 1910, Mason township, Hannibal, Marion County.
    21. Stuart D. Brandes, *American Welfare Capitalism, 1880–1940,* 28–29.
    22. Stanley D. Sajban to Gregg Andrews, July 4, 1994.

but [that] he could serve in some positions, clerkship, watch, something of that nature."[23]

A dispute soon soured the relationship between Gardner and Atlas. After Gardner had been on the job as night watchman for about three months, supervisors shifted him to the machine shop, but he quit, perhaps because of the physical demands of the new job. "It was just as fine a place for him," insisted Baker, "I was trying to take care of Mr. Gardner."[24]

Gardner complained that Atlas had cheated him out of wages in the amount of $25.12 while he was working as night watchman. Instead of earning about $2.25 per night as Baker allegedly promised, he received $2.04 for thirteen and one-half hours per night. After trying unsuccessfully to resolve the matter with Atlas officials, Gardner on July 29, 1913, filed a claim for $25.12 in Justice of the Peace Bruce Peterson's court in Ilasco. Atlas lost the judgment but won an appeal to the Ralls County Circuit Court. A jury awarded Gardner the judgment, but Atlas then took an appeal to St. Louis. In March 1917, nearly four years after the dispute, the St. Louis appellate court reversed the judgment in favor of Atlas.[25]

Given the size of the judgment, it is clear that it was not the money per se but control that was at issue for Atlas. It undoubtedly cost Atlas much more than $25.12 to contest Gardner's victories in Judge Peterson's office and the circuit court before taking the case to St. Louis. Workers had to accept paternalism on Atlas's terms.

Once Atlas officials regained the upper hand after the strike of 1910, they looked for new ways to improve the profitability of the Ilasco plant and to consolidate their power locally. They sought to make more extensive use of the Mississippi River for shipping at a time when they were disturbed by discriminatory rates charged by railroads against competitors of the Universal Portland Cement Company. In April 1912 they formed the Atlas Transportation Company with a capital stock of one hundred thousand dollars and purchased a river fleet consisting of the Josh Cook steamer and several other barges. Until early 1918 this fleet hauled cement, raw materials, and other freight between St. Paul, Minnesota, and New Orleans, Louisiana.[26]

The Upper Mississippi River Association, organized in 1901, represented the interests of business groups in river towns from Minneapolis/St. Paul to St. Louis.

23. *Gardner v. Atlas,* trial transcript, 25, 30; *Ralls County Times,* September 6, 1907.

24. *Gardner v. Atlas,* trial transcript, 26.

25. Ibid.; Circuit Court Record, book R, 554, Ralls County, Office of the Circuit Clerk and Recorder, New London; *Ralls County Record,* March 16, 1917.

26. *New York Times,* February 27 and April 24, 1912; Hadley, *Magic Powder,* 221. For the Atlas Transportation Company's Articles of Association, April 16, 1912, and Certificate of Incorporation, May 9, 1912, see Miscellaneous Deed Record, book 218, 324–25, 359, Marion County, Office of the Circuit Clerk and Recorder, Palymra, Mo.

The chief aim was to harness the increasingly polluted river to promote industrial development through an integrated rail and water transportation network. The association had lobbied Congress to authorize the creation of a permanent six-foot river channel in 1907, and it encouraged the construction of municipal terminals. Atlas officials and the Hannibal Commercial Club played an important role in the association, which held its convention in Hannibal a couple of months after the formation of the Atlas Transportation Company. The major item of business on the convention agenda was a call for river terminals.[27]

More than 120 officers of the Upper Mississippi River Improvement Association listened in October 1913 as officials from Atlas's Ilasco plant pleaded for better municipal wharves and terminal facilities in river towns to facilitate hauling cement on barges. "In taking up river transportation," said plant manager Baker, "we are not working against the railroads for we believe that the rail lines make short hauls cheaper. It was in order to extend that we conceived the idea of using the river." J. J. Collister, traffic manager at the Ilasco plant, added that it would be up to the Association to maintain harmony and understanding with "your railway friends."[28]

Atlas's call for municipal terminals fit into a broader campaign by regional commercial interests to tame the Mississippi River. Central to this vision was the construction of a massive hydroelectric dam sixty miles north of Hannibal at Keokuk, Iowa, where the Des Moines rapids had impeded low-water navigation for nearly one hundred years. River towns like Hannibal, whose earlier lumber-based economy once depended on rafts of white pine sent down the river from Wisconsin mill towns, now cheered the economic opportunities created by the Keokuk power dam. The Keokuk and Hamilton Water Power Company, later replaced by the Mississippi River Power Company, awarded Atlas the contract for cement to be used in the construction project. Ilasco workers produced the cement, and Atlas in turn purchased ten thousand horsepower from a power company substation at Hull, Illinois. Dedication services for the new lock and dam took place in late August 1913.[29]

From the outset, local Atlas officials had established close family and social contacts with Hannibal's elites. For example, engineer Guy D. Helmick had married the sister of Robert E. Coontz, who received an appointment to the

27. Philip V. Scarpino, *Great River: An Environmental History of the Upper Mississippi, 1890–1950,* 37–39.

28. Baker and Collister quoted in *Hannibal Courier-Post,* October 6, 1913.

29. See Scarpino, *Great River,* chap. 1, for a discussion of the development of and support for the hydroelectric dam, and for a discussion of the energy context in which the project was conceived. Construction of the dam was completed on May 31, 1913. Universal Atlas Cement Company, "Data on Keokuk Power Station and Dam," February 12, 1941 (in author's possession).

U.S. Naval Academy and was promoted to rear admiral in 1917. Atlas officials continued to forge such important alliances with local elites in the 1910s and 1920s. A. G. Croll, a graduate of Cornell University who had risen from engineer to mill superintendent at the Northampton plant and then to Atlas's general superintendent, married New London's Ann Conn in December 1913. This marriage directly linked Atlas to a prominent family with important connections to Ralls County banking and politics. Although the Crolls took up residence in East Orange, New Jersey, they owned a farm west of New London and on occasions used the farm for family reunions. These reunions solidified Atlas's influence with the Conn, Hays, and Megown families, all of whom featured prominent Ralls County and Hannibal politicians. Among those who socialized with Croll at these family gatherings were Circuit Judge C. T. Hays, and B. B. Megown and his brother J. E. Megown.[30]

At the time of Croll's marriage to Conn, Atlas had just enjoyed a banner year. The construction of concrete roads and the growing practice of building farm silos with cement helped to boost the average factory price per barrel of cement from approximately $.813 in 1912 to $1.005 in 1913. Cement production leaped forward nationwide in 1913, increasing in the Missouri district while production in Pennsylvania's Lehigh district dropped to 30 percent of the total national output. As a reflection of this success and to help ensure uninterrupted production, Atlas granted a 25 percent wage increase and hired an additional five hundred workers at Ilasco in the spring of 1913. In fact, a labor shortage forced Plant Number Five at Ilasco to shut down temporarily in June 1913. A local newspaper attributed this temporary shutdown to "the general prosperity of the country and the unprecedented demand for laborers in every line of industry."[31]

By the fall of 1913, electricity generated by the new dam at Keokuk enabled Atlas to convert its Ilasco plant from steam to electric power. It also encouraged formation of the North Missouri Light and Power Company to bring power to Ralls County towns, including Ilasco, whose small electric light plant had been destroyed by a fire only two weeks before the Keokuk Dam was completed. Capitalizing on Atlas's underwriting of the project to bring power to the plant on favorable terms, Ralls County lawyers, judges, and other investors bought shares in the North Missouri Light and Power Company to extend the current from Ilasco

---

30. Hagood and Hagood, *Story of Hannibal,* 101; George A. Mahan, "Missourians Abroad: Rear Admiral Robert E. Coontz, U.S.N.," *Missouri Historical Review* 13 (July 1919): 372–76; *Ralls County Record,* October 13, October 17, October 31, and December 26, 1913, and September 1, 1922; *Portrait and Biographical Record of Marion, Ralls, Pike Counties Missouri 1895,* 439–40, 453–54; Shoemaker, *Missouri and Missourians,* vol. 5, 266–68. Croll's obituary is in the *Hannibal Courier-Post,* January 13, 1943.

31. Lesley, Lober, and Bartlett, *History of the Portland Cement Industry,* 275–76; *Hannibal Courier-Post,* February 28, 1913; *Ralls County Times,* June 20, 1913.

to New London, Center, Perry, and the Pike County town of Frankford. By late 1914, these towns were receiving power as the result of such efforts.[32]

The cozy relationship between Atlas officials and local lawyers and politicians, many of whom were tied to banking and commercial interests, encouraged those with entrepreneurial appetites to speculate in real estate near Ilasco. Atlas had granted a right-of-way to the North Missouri Light and Power Company for construction of power lines and poles. Lawyers aware of Atlas's plans to bring electricity from Keokuk to its plant bought adjacent land and granted easements for these purposes. Ben E. Hulse and Jack Briscoe bought 120 acres from Herman Schwartz on June 3, 1911, and then executed an easement to the North Missouri Light and Power Company, in which they held shares. Andrew Christensen, an earlier owner of this land, had also granted Atlas the right-of-way for possible construction of an overhead cable system for hauling rock. Although Atlas never constructed such a tramway carrier, the fact that it purchased right-of-way concessions from several landowners around Ilasco further encouraged land speculation.[33]

When the United States declared war on Germany in April 1917, Atlas took steps to mobilize industrial resources and promote support for the Allied war effort. On the national level, Atlas and other companies sent "dollar-a-year men" to Washington to help the Woodrow Wilson administration coordinate production strategies. Drawing only a token government salary while still receiving salaries from their companies, they staffed government agencies set up to foster government-business cooperation and planning by allocating raw materials and contracts and prioritizing production goals. The Wilson administration suspended antitrust laws to strengthen this wartime partnership between business and government.

Atlas President John R. Morron chaired the cement committee, which worked with Bernard Baruch's War Industries Board, the agency entrusted with overseeing wartime industrial production. Willard A. Holman, who was assistant to the

---

32. *Hannibal Courier-Post,* October 15, 1913; *Ralls County Record,* September 26 and October 31, 1913, January 30 and July 10, 1914. The largest individual shareholders in the North Missouri Light and Power Company were J. O. Allison, T. E. Allison, and Judge Reuben F. Roy. For a list of shareholders, see *Ralls County Record,* September 26, 1913. On the fire in Ilasco, see *Ralls County Times,* May 16, 1913.

33. Herman Schwartz to Ben E. Hulse, June 3, 1911, Warranty Deed Record, book 92, 122; Ben E. Hulse and Ella S. Hulse to Jack Briscoe, September 14, 1911, Warranty Deed Record, book 94, 508; Ben E. Hulse and Ella S. Hulse, and Jack Briscoe and Sadie Briscoe to Nick Rukvena and Mary Rukvena, May 5, 1923, Miscellaneous Deed Record, book 112, 499–500; all in Ralls County, Office of the Circuit Clerk and Recorder, New London. On Atlas's aborted plans to build an overhead cable system, see, for example, Lulu McNulty and Mary E. Elzea to Atlas Portland Cement Company, August 9, 1910, Deed Record, book 86, 411, and numerous similar concessions granted to Atlas, 410–22, Ralls County, Office of the Circuit Clerk and Recorder, New London. See also Howard, *Ralls County Missouri,* 265.

president at Atlas, and William A. McIntyre, also of Atlas, assisted Morron, government officials, and other cement executives on the committee. E. K. Borchard, editor of the *Contractor's Atlas,* was also among those loaned to the government by "Old Man Atlas." Officials used him as a consultant on the construction of concrete ships.[34]

Since portland cement was one of the most vital war building materials, the War Service Committee on Portland Cement cooperated with the Price Fixing Committee of the War Industries Board to set prices for cement sold to the government. In addition, cement executives agreed to hold down prices to the general public through voluntary cooperation, but with the understanding that the government committee might set those prices if necessary. To ensure adequate supplies of cement for the war, the Wilson administration tried to curtail construction in the private sector since it was deemed nonessential to the war effort. Although only 54 percent of the industry's capacity was used in 1918, supplies of cement were so abundant that by April, the Fuel Administration reduced the supply of fuel to cement mills to 75 percent of normal requirements on grounds that the fuel should be diverted to other war industries more in need of it.[35]

According to a study published by the War Trade Board in 1920, the government's price-fixing was designed to allow cement firms a 6 percent return on their investments and to force marginal plants to shut down. Critics of the cement industry complained about the 73 percent increase in the average price of cement between 1913 and the end of 1918, but industry executives emphasized that this compared favorably to the increase of 102 percent for all commodities during the same period. Production in 1918 fell to the lowest level since 1909, but the average factory price per barrel had risen to $1.60, the highest price in twenty years.[36]

Public criticisms of the cement industry surfaced during the war. On May 4, 1917, Missouri Congressman L. C. Dyer introduced a resolution in the U.S.

34. Hadley, *Magic Powder,* 168–71; Universal Atlas Cement Company, "Universal Atlas Golden Anniversary: Fifty Years of Progress in the Manufacture and Uses of Cement," November 8, 1939 (in author's possession); "Uncle Sam Adopts Borchard," *The Atlas Circle* 4 (July 1918): 12; Robert D. Cuff, *The War Industries Board: Business-Government Relations during World War I,* 158.

35. Defendants' Answer, *United States of America v. Cement Manufacturers Protective Association et al.,* in the District Court of the United States, Southern District of New York, April 4–May 26, 1922, 50–54 (copy in author's possession); Lesley, Lober, and Bartlett, *History of the Portland Cement Industry,* 278–79.

36. *U.S. v. Cement Manufacturers Protective Association et al.,* 52–54; Lesley, Lober, and Bartlett, *History of the Portland Cement Industry,* 278–79; U.S. Geological Survey, *Mineral Resources of the United States, 1918.* Pt. 2, 565; "Meeting of the Industrial Board with Representatives of the Cement Manufacturing Industry," March 24, 1919, George N. Peek Papers, collection no. 2270, folder 1585, WHMC–Columbia. Of 114 cement mills in the nation, six were idle in 1918.

House of Representatives requesting the attorney general to inform Congress what steps were being taken to investigate the cement industry for alleged violations of antitrust laws. Earlier that year, Representative Dyer had written a letter to the attorney general's office accusing cement companies of price-fixing. He enclosed a copy of a resolution adopted by the Iowa General Assembly urging an investigation.[37]

On May 17, 1917, an editorial in the *Fort Wayne Daily News* alleged that a cement trust, "a hard and fast union of conspirators," was holding up new construction projects because of its monopolistic practices. This trust, according to the Indiana newspaper, was responsible for cement companies' submitting identical inflated bids for construction projects. The newspaper complained that the trust "simply laughs the law to scorn and makes little or no attempt to conceal the fact that it regards piracy as its privilege and extortion as its God-given right."[38]

In response to a letter from President Wilson inquiring about high cement prices, the War Industries Board supported the industry's opposition to setting a maximum price for the public. When cement officials proposed to charge the government twenty cents per barrel below the base price established for the public at large, the board urged them to devise a new proposal that would avoid a fixed base price for government purchases and rely instead on a specific net price at shipping points. By late 1917, the board had approved a proposition by industry officials to establish fixed prices for government purchases over the next four months. These prices ranged from $1.90 per barrel in El Paso, Texas, to $1.30 in Pennsylvania's Lehigh Valley. The schedule fixed the price of cement in the Ilasco area at $1.50 per barrel.[39]

The wartime cooperation between business and government accelerated a trend toward heavier concentration of capital. Larger firms in each industry benefited the most from price-fixing and other practices sanctioned by government committees and agencies. In 1908 there had been ten centralized corporate groupings in the cement industry, but by the end of the war only five such groupings remained. Those that survived, including Atlas, consolidated their position within the industry and emerged with enlarged holdings.[40]

This strengthened the power of big companies to defeat a workers' militancy that had grown feverishly since around 1910. Wartime conditions intensified this

37. "Extension of Remarks of Hon. L. C. Dyer, of Missouri, in the House of Representatives," June 19, 1917, *Congressional Record,* vol. 55, pt. 8, 65th Cong., 1st sess., Appendix, 346–47. A copy of the resolution passed by the Iowa General Assembly is in *Congressional Record,* vol. 54, pt. 3, 64th Cong., 2d sess., February 12, 1917, 3054.

38. A copy of this editorial is in "Extension of Remarks of Hon. L. C. Dyer," 347.

39. Meeting of the War Industries Board, October 3, December 7, and December 12, 1917, and February 6, 1918, microfilm rolls 1, 2, Minutes of War Industries Board Meetings, 1917–1918, RG 61, National Archives.

40. Lesley, Lober, and Bartlett, *History of the Portland Cement Industry,* 175–76, 186.

militancy. After war broke out in Europe in 1914, munitions and armaments orders had increased American jobs and prosperity. Prices also shot up, however, and American workers engaged in an unprecedented number of strikes. This continued after the United States entered the war in 1917. In response to inflation, workers displayed a boldness that posed a serious challenge to corporate and government leaders. Reuben Wood, president of the Missouri State Federation of Labor, attributed this strike fever to the shameful activities of "industrial pirates and commercial vampires" who took advantage of the war crisis to line their own pockets through "unprecedented food speculation."[41]

Public complaints against the cement industry, coupled with wartime inflation that ravaged the earnings of American workers, fueled resentments by Missourians against corporations and monopolies in general. Skyrocketing food costs led even the conservative editors of the *Ralls County Record* to urge Congressional action to ensure a fair price for farmers and consumers. In their view, speculators, "robber food barons," and "other grasping hogs" were the problem. The editors also complained that farmers were shouldering the heaviest tax burden while huge corporations had received extremely lenient treatment by U.S. officials. "If there is one truth that stands out more plainly than any other in this county," the editors emphasized, "it is that capital and capitalists have been more favored than in any other country on the globe."[42]

These complaints against profiteering intensified after the war when high meat prices prompted the U.S. Justice Department to prosecute the largest meatpacking companies. The *Ralls County Record*'s editors urged swift prosecution of guilty meatpacking firms, attacking "the wholesale and deliberate robbery of a helpless public." They even cautiously suggested a government takeover of the industry, although they acknowledged that high meat prices might in fact be the result of higher labor and transportation costs, the latter attributable in their opinion to government control of the railroads. The editors expressed frustration that many Americans felt after the war: "Already many people, men and women of sound and patriotic principles, are predicting revolution as the only means of checking this wholesale and lawless thievery . . . Public endurance is at the breaking point. Revolution is hovering dangerously near."[43]

Union membership shot up dramatically during this period, but the Bolshevik Revolution provided employers with a powerful club against American workers. The lifting of wartime controls sparked an unprecedented strike wave in 1919, but

41. Fink, *Labor's Search*, chap. 4, contains a good discussion of this militancy in Missouri. The quote by Wood is on p. 63. See also Montgomery, *Workers' Control*, chap. 4., and James R. Green, *The World of the Worker: Labor in Twentieth-Century America*, chap. 3.
42. *Ralls County Record*, July 6 and December 21, 1917.
43. *Ralls County Record*, August 8, 1919.

by 1920, that wave had crested. Employers and government officials successfully encouraged a public hysteria over the possible spread of Bolshevism among workers in the United States, and this Red Scare in turn contributed to the defeat of important strikes and fueled mean-spirited attacks on immigrants. In the public's view, radicalism and immigrants were organically linked. Employers also mounted a powerful Open Shop campaign to defeat labor's demands for an eight-hour day, union recognition, and other improvements in wages and working conditions. In Missouri, staunch anti-union employers' associations had initiated this Open Shop offensive earlier during the war itself to beat back union militancy.[44]

As the Wilson administration grappled with postwar economic, social, and political problems, cement firms came under fire again for high prices. In an effort to stabilize postwar prices, the Industrial Board of the United States Department of Commerce held discussions with fourteen representatives of the cement industry, including Atlas's W. A. Holman and W. E. Miner, on March 24, 1919. The cement executives, led by Universal Portland Cement's B. F. Affleck, who was also president of the Portland Cement Association, listened as the Industrial Board's George N. Peek assured them that the board did not intend or even have the authority to fix prices. "Our purpose," explained Peek, "is to let industry come in the room with us and agree upon prices which they think are fair to offer to the Government bureaus and to the country at large, and if we can concur in the conclusions, why we are willing to advocate those as fair prices and urge that the Government departments make their purchases at the prices."[45]

Peek noted that his board had received more complaints about cement prices than about any other industry. He stressed that he had received numerous telegrams from governors, mayors, and public commissions around the country inquiring as to whether existing cement prices were fair. State and local officials, eager to undertake road-building and public work projects, were reluctant to initiate those projects until cement prices dropped. Peek emphasized that the cement industry, in fact, could expand its capacity only if companies established fair prices that the government could publicly endorse.[46]

Holman insisted that cement companies were entitled to a "fair" return on their investments, a profit of at least 10 percent in his view. Although the industry as a

---

44. Fink, *Labor's Search,* 63, 71, 98–99.

45. Meeting of the Industrial Board with Representatives of the Cement Manufacturing Industry, 2. On the scope and significance of the Industrial Board's activities, see Robert F. Himmelberg, "Business, Antitrust Policy, and the Industrial Board of the Department of Commerce, 1919," and E. Jay Howenstine Jr., "The Industrial Board, Precursor of the N.R.A.: The Price-Reduction Movement after World War I."

46. Meeting of the Industrial Board with Representatives of the Cement Manufacturing Industry, 2, 12.

whole was operating at only 50 percent of capacity, the cement representatives refused to lower their prices, except for a reduction in charges for returnable sacks. Instead, Holman complained that the industry was the victim of public ignorance and unfair press attacks. "There has been a very marked effort on the part of people throughout the country, we feel," he noted, "that is based entirely upon a lack of knowledge of our situation, to the effect that the prices of cement are exorbitantly high. The governors of several of the Western states have almost taken the position that until a very material reduction is made in the price of cement, no road building will be carried on, and the press, particularly of the middle West, within the last week or two, carried some very venomous articles regarding what they term 'the cement trust.' "[47]

Frustrated by the insistence of cement executives that they could not lower prices and still maintain adequate profits, members of the Industrial Board warned about the dangers of social unrest posed by postwar unemployment and economic problems, especially in light of the triumph of Bolshevism in Russia. Against a backdrop of unemployment and growing public fears of radicalism, labor unrest, and immigrants, Peek urged industry leaders to take a broader, patriotic view by making concessions on prices in order to stimulate the economy and alleviate conditions that bred demands for radical solutions. "We believe this is the opportunity for business men to prove their leadership and do the constructive thing for the country," he asserted. "We believe it is absolutely essential for the best interests of the country that industry be started up actively, and that men be employed, and that unless business takes advantage of this opportunity to be constructive and do the thing which should be done, why I think they may confidently expect that some other element will assume leadership before we get through with the upset conditions which exist throughout the world today."[48]

Several companies lowered the price by fifteen cents per barrel in early April 1919, but cement executives blamed rising labor and fuel costs for the industry's high prices. The wartime disruption of immigration and the siphoning of manpower by the military had increased the bargaining power of workers. This prompted complaints by cement executives that wages represented more than one-third of the price of cement. They noted that the labor situation in their industry was especially bad.[49]

Local Atlas officials prepared to reduce labor costs, reimpose control over discipline, and resist demands that contributed to the labor militancy of 1919.

47. Ibid., 8–10.
48. Ibid., 2.
49. Ibid., 11; Defendants' Answer, *U.S. v. Cement Manufacturers Protective Association et al.*, in Equity, no. 22/25, in the District Court of the United States, Southern District of New York, February 1923, 56–57 (in author's possession); Lesley, Lober, and Bartlett, *History of the Portland Cement Industry*, 235, 279.

Mahan, Atlas's Hannibal attorney, was named by "acclamation" on July 7, 1919, to head Hannibal's new Law and Order League. Baker, the superintendent of the Ilasco plant, announced a wage increase in late July and then resigned a few days later. Ray E. Hoffman, a graduate of the Missouri School of Mines at Rolla, replaced him. Hoffman, widely disliked by workers for his authoritarian methods, had joined Atlas's Ilasco plant as a mining engineer on November 6, 1906, and then advanced to mine and quarry engineer and assistant plant manager before becoming plant manager in 1919. Atlas officials were confident that his authoritarianism was what was needed to ensure control and enforce Open Shop policies in the 1920s.[50]

Unlike four million American workers who were on strike in 1919, Ilasco's workers did not challenge Atlas's policies by striking that year, but Atlas and other cement firms soon came under fire for high prices, monopolistic practices, and low taxes paid to local government. As Missouri initiated a comprehensive road-building program under the direction of the newly created State Highway Commission, state officials had to overcome public skepticism and opposition, particularly among farmers. Highway construction and improvements consumed nearly half of the state's expenditures, and the high price of cement angered lawmakers. The Missouri House of Representatives appointed a committee to investigate the feasibility of manufacturing cement under state ownership for use on state roads and highways. The committee, hoping to follow the lead of South Dakota, which had created a state-owned plant, denounced the "gormandizing and capricious interests of certain corporations . . . who respect no law, but become a law unto themselves to combine and exact from the State Highway Commission their own price."[51]

Some lawmakers proposed the construction of state cement plants that would be under the control of the prison board, but the committee recommended against using convict labor in state-sponsored cement manufacturing. The committee concluded that the state of Missouri, using wage labor, could manufacture

50. *Hannibal Courier-Post,* July 7 and August 1, 1919; Universal Atlas Cement Company, "Cement Plant News," Hannibal, December 1946 (in author's possession); Angelo Venditti, interview by author, July 9, 1993. Under the leadership of A. G. Croll, the Atlas Portland Cement Company leased land in Ralls County for oil exploration in 1919 and 1920. This led to the formation of oil and gas companies by Ralls County investors, but Atlas's drilling of test wells in the summer of 1920 ended in failure. Howard, *Ralls County Missouri,* 285; *Ralls County Record,* September 19, November 7, and November 14, 1919, and June 11, 1920.

51. Richard S. Kirkendall, *A History of Missouri, Volume V: 1919 to 1953,* 36–37, 75; Missouri General Assembly, House of Representatives, "Report of the Committee to Investigate the Feasibility and Practicability of the State Acquiring Raw Materials for the Purpose of Manufacturing Portland Cement," to the Fifty-First General Assembly, Jefferson City, Mo., 1921, 6–8.

cement and sell it profitably at a price of not more than $1.50 per barrel. The average price of cement nationwide in 1920 had been $2.02 per barrel. The committee even endorsed the takeover of existing plants if cement companies "refuse to meet the state on a fair basis." Their report praised the road construction program then under consideration and emphasized that the legislature "owes to itself and to the taxpayers of this great commonwealth the further duty that the material used in the construction of the roads and bridges should not be exploited for unfair and unrighteous profits by any concern whatsoever."[52]

Missouri did not set up state cement plants, but Atlas and other cement companies at the time faced an even more serious challenge from the federal government regarding their pricing and production practices. Between 1919 and 1925, the U.S. Justice Department initiated a series of criminal and civil suits against Atlas and nearly all other cement corporations for engaging in a conspiracy in restraint of trade. According to the government's allegations, cement companies limited production between 1915 and 1919 to keep prices high. The suits charged that trade associations like the Cement Manufacturers' Protective Association and the Mid-West Cement Credit and Statistical Bureau had facilitated monopolistic marketing and selling practices. Jesse Barrett, Missouri's attorney general, cooperated with the government and predicted that these suits would benefit Missouri's road-building program.[53]

The government failed to get a conviction in the criminal suits, but in 1924 the Federal Trade Commission outlawed the Pittsburgh plus system of pricing as monopolistic. Under this pricing system, used widely in the steel industry, companies quoted delivered prices to customers based on the price at Pittsburgh plus standardized freight rates from Pittsburgh, regardless of the plant's location. A leading company usually published its base price, and then others would peg their prices to this figure. This restrained competition. What's more, customers could not avoid the all-rail freight costs built into their quoted delivered price, even if they could make their own arrangements to pick up the product at the mill

52. *Ralls County Record,* February 18, 1921; Missouri House of Representatives, "Report of the Committee," 8–9; Lesley, Lober, and Bartlett, *History of the Portland Cement Industry,* 281.

53. *New York Times,* August 14, 1919; *Hannibal Courier-Post,* November 1, 1921; Hadley, *Magic Powder,* 186–88; Robert F. Himmelberg, *The Origins of the National Recovery Administration: Business, Government, and the Trade Association Issue, 1921–1933,* 13, 34–35; H. P. Ingels, Acting Secretary, War Industries Board, to G. Carroll Todd, Assistant to the Attorney General, March 4, 1918, Meeting of the War Industries Board, March 4, 1918, Minutes of War Industries Board Meetings, microfilm roll 2, RG 65, NA; Frank K. Hebeker, Assistant to the Attorney General, to Interstate Commerce Commission, February 24, 1921, microfilm roll 910, case no. 89, 289–371, Records of the Federal Bureau of Investigation, Bureau of Investigative Case Files, 1908–1922, RG 65, NA.

and haul it more cheaply. Thus, the more companies could lower transportation costs through water or truck shipments, the bigger the profit.[54]

When the Atlas Portland Cement Company built the Ilasco plant, it implemented a similar pricing system based on freight rates charged from Pennsylvania's Lehigh Valley. This "Valley plus" system evolved gradually, coordinated by the Association of American Portland Cement Manufacturers, which was renamed the Portland Cement Association in 1916. Although price wars at times broke out, pricing became more systematic after 1910 as more companies adopted this formula of "imperfect collusion" to restrain bitter competition and increase profits.[55]

In early 1923, Judge John C. Knox of the United States District Court of New York, Southern District, also ruled against the cement companies in a civil case, but they appealed to the Supreme Court of the United States. On June 1, 1925, the Supreme Court reversed the decision. The government soon dropped other suits against the cement industry.[56]

The Supreme Court's decision reflected the pro-business orientation of the Republican administrations of the 1920s. It was consistent with the policies of Secretary of Commerce Herbert Hoover, who promoted cooperation between government agencies and trade associations such as the Cement Manufacturers' Protective Association. Hoover's Commerce Department disseminated important information on prices and costs to members of the Association in order to keep cutthroat competition in check and promote economic growth. "The system worked so well," write business historians Mansel G. Blackford and K. Austin Kerr, "that when other agencies requested sealed bids for construction projects, the supposedly competing cement manufacturers submitted bids that were nearly identical."[57]

While the federal government was pressing suits against the cement companies, farmers and other taxpayers in Ralls County mounted growing protests

---

54. David Lynch, *The Concentration of Economic Power*, 185–86. Soon after abolition of the Pittsburgh plus system, companies in many industries, including cement and steel, adopted the multiple basing-point price system, which will be discussed in chapter 10.

55. Samuel M. Loescher, *Imperfect Collusion in the Cement Industry*, chap. 4, discusses the evolution of the basing-point system of pricing in the cement industry.

56. Hadley, *Magic Powder*, 188–93. When the U.S. Congress debated the Fordney-McCumber Tariff in 1922, opponents of higher protectionist schedules for the cement industry called attention to the government's lawsuits against Atlas and other cement companies. For the flavor of arguments in the tariff debate in the Senate, see *Congressional Record*, vol. 62, pts. 7 and 8, 67th Cong., 2d sess., 1922, 7323–31, 8104–11.

57. *Business Enterprise in American History*, 315–16. On the implications of the Supreme Court's ruling for other trade associations, see Louis Galambos, *Competition and Cooperation: The Emergence of a National Trade Association*, 99–101. Colin Gordon, *New Deals: Business, Labor, and Politics in America, 1920–1935*, chap. 4, stresses that business associationalism failed to control competition in the 1920s and early 1930s.

against low tax assessments of Atlas's Ilasco plant. Drake Watson, a Ralls County attorney, landowner, and former Democratic Speaker of the Missouri House of Representatives, led the attack on behalf of county farmers who were already unhappy over Republican Governor Arthur Hyde's tax policies. On March 30, 1923, the *Ralls County Record* published a letter from Watson complaining that Atlas was escaping payment of $37,500.20 per year in county taxes. "They are not only escaping paying that sum now," he said, "but they have been for many years so doing."[58]

Watson, who had obtained from the Missouri attorney general's office the sworn testimony of Atlas's general auditor at Jefferson City on June 2, 1921, complained that although Atlas acknowledged that it had $5 million invested in the Ilasco plant, the company was only being assessed for $1.5 million invested there. This meant an undue tax burden on other landowners. Watson urged the Ralls County Board of Equalization to remedy this at its upcoming meeting in early April 1923.[59]

The Board of Equalization raised Atlas's valuation to $3 million, but local plant officials protested. They appeared before the board in late April to appeal the decision and request a reduction in Atlas's tax assessment. The board then ordered them to file with the county clerk an itemized statement of Atlas's investments in the local plant.[60]

Watson soon wrote another public letter urging a reduction of farmers' taxes by 10 percent that year and another 10 percent the following year. He stressed that Atlas officials had not complied with the board's request for an itemized statement of investments, and he charged that they had even refused to allow a tax expert to enter the Ilasco plant. "It appears to me," he asserted, "that they are trying to ride roughshod over the people of the county."[61]

By the end of the summer of 1923, Watson's frustration with the County Board of Equalization had grown considerably. Officers from the State Tax Commission and expert examiners hired by the state had conducted a valuation of the Ilasco plant and assessed its value at $4,155,802, but the board delayed, instead fixing the assessment at only $3 million. In another public letter, Watson attacked local Atlas officials and attorneys for avoiding a public meeting with the board: "Why were the cement plant officials in private conference with members of this board?"[62]

---

58. On Watson's popularity with farmers and his opposition to Governor Hyde's tax policies, see *Hannibal Courier-Post,* December 14 and 22, 1921.

59. *Ralls County Record,* March 30, 1923.

60. *Ralls County Record,* June 15, 1923.

61. Watson's letter is in ibid.

62. *Ralls County Record,* August 24, 1923.

The Board of Appeals published a notice inviting taxpayers to attend a meeting on September 4 to discuss Atlas's assessed valuation. A few weeks after that meeting, at which attorneys George A. Mahan and Elgin T. Fuller argued on behalf of Atlas, the board rolled back the tax assessment to an increase of only $176,320. This put Atlas's assessed valuation at around $1,750,000, far lower than the valuation of $4,155,802 offered by expert engineers.[63]

County farmers, unhappy over the board's preferential treatment of Atlas, obtained several hundred signatures on a petition protesting the board's discriminatory tax assessments. The petition called on the board to increase Atlas's property assessment to $4 million and thus ease the tax bite on other property owners. On September 8, 1924, the board modestly raised Atlas's property valuation to $2 million after discovering that Atlas had failed to file a manufacturing return with the county assessor, as required by law. A week later, the board met again to discuss how much valuation to put on Atlas's manufacturing property. Members, in consultation with state tax experts, placed a valuation of $500,000 on Atlas's finished manufactured product.[64]

In December 1924, Atlas paid a manufacturing tax of $6,750. "This is the first year they have ever paid any manufacturer's tax," noted the *Ralls County Record,* "although they have been operating here for more than twenty years." Although the total assessed value of Atlas's investments in the Ilasco plant was still around $2 million—only one-half of what experts had recommended—editors of the *Record* chose to be optimistic: "The entering wedge has been driven and we now look for the time when the other two and a quarter million will be reached, for if two million dollars is not paying taxes then the public is failing to get $27,000 per year in tax from them that should pay. We desire to compliment those who have driven the 'entering wedge,' for it is difficult to cope with big corporate wealth."[65]

The newspaper's optimism was premature. Several hundred taxpayers packed a meeting a few months later to discuss Atlas's valuation again. They, along with representatives of the State Tax Commission, urged the Board of Equalization to raise the assessment to $4.5 million in order to tax Atlas on the same basis as the county taxed real estate. "There are many people in the county," complained B. H. Finley, president of the Ralls County Farm Bureau, "who believe this company is escaping payment of their just part of the taxes while we farmers are paying excessively." On September 7, 1925, however, the board knuckled under to Atlas's demands and ruled that the valuation was high enough and fair.[66]

63. *Ralls County Record,* August 31, September 14, and October 5, 1923.
64. *Ralls County Record,* April 11 and September 19, 1924.
65. *Ralls County Record,* December 19, 1924.
66. *Ralls County Record,* April 10, August 28, and September 18, 1925.

The reluctance, or refusal, of county officials to increase Atlas's tax assessment illustrated the power of a company that was by far the largest industry in the county. In 1925, Atlas employed eleven hundred at the Ilasco plant, and on the eve of the Great Depression, the local plant still had 891 employees.[67] Some politicians clearly had strong ties to Atlas, but others perhaps believed that they could get more for the county through Atlas's paternalism than through actions that would antagonize plant officials.

Between the strike of 1910 and the Wall Street crash in 1929, Atlas had consolidated its power on every level. New plants at Leeds, Alabama, and Waco, Texas, were symbols of Atlas's expanded territorial markets, and acquisition of the estates of Samuel Heinbach and Theodore Johnson through sheriffs' sales had strengthened its control in Ilasco. By 1925, the only real estate in Ilasco proper that was not owned by Atlas was the Lendak subdivision, created from lots purchased from Nick and Mary Rukavena on May 18, 1925. The Rukavenas had bought 120 acres from Ben E. Hulse and Jack Briscoe on May 5, 1923, and then sold lots to John and Mary Lendak. Hulse and Briscoe had bought the 120 acres from Herman Schwartz on June 3, 1911. The Lendaks subdivided their tract and immediately began to sell lots to John Polc, Michael Rajt, Stefan Stimel, and others. This section of Ilasco was dubbed "Hunktown" by native-born residents, an indication of the deep-seated ethnic tensions that still plagued the community.[68]

Atlas's consolidation of power enabled it to demonstrate that its brand of paternalism had much more to offer Ilasco residents than did that of their previous landlord, Samuel Heinbach. The switch from woodchopper to corporate landlord, however, brought with it important differences and implications for the community. Atlas continued to charge Ilasco residents ground rent of only one dollar per month, but its corporate resources enabled it to do much more than simply treat kids to ice cream downtown, allow widows to escape payment of ground rent, and distribute buckets of candy and oranges at Christmas.

Atlas's paternalism, moreover, grew out of different underlying motives, including the need to assure middle-class onlookers in the area that they had nothing to fear from the cement plant's workers in Ilasco. Paternalism would

---

67. *Hannibal Courier-Post*, Special "New Home Edition—Mark Twain Section," March 28, 1925; Missouri Labor and Industrial Inspection Department, *Annual Report* 50 (1929): 80.

68. Herman Schwartz to Ben E. Hulse, June 3, 1911, Warranty Deed Record, book 92, 122; Ben E. Hulse and Ella S. Hulse to Jack Briscoe, September 14, 1911, Warranty Deed Record, book 94, 508; Ben E. Hulse and Ella S. Hulse, and Jack Briscoe and Sadie Briscoe to Nick Rukvena and Mary Rukvena, May 5, 1923, Miscellaneous Deed Record, book 112, 499–500; Nick Rukvena and Mary Rukvena to John and Mary Lendak, May 18, 1925, Miscellaneous Record, book 113, 432; all in Ralls County, Office of the Circuit Clerk and Recorder, New London. On the sale of lots by Lendak, see "Real Estate Transfers" in the *Ralls County Record*, December 11 and 25, 1925.

uplift workers and provide an antidote to crime, violence, and labor unrest.[69] Atlas could now demonstrate its largesse by subsidizing schools and churches and enforcing cleanliness standards for its tenants. However, this did not come without a price tag. By purchasing the town site, Atlas had acquired tremendous power to shape Ilasco's social and cultural institutions, indeed, to determine the future fate of the community itself.

69. Carlton, *Mill and Town,* 89–90, 145–46, emphasizes that cotton mill paternalism in South Carolina grew out of an underlying effort to calm townspeople's fears of a dangerous, unstable white industrial working class. In the case of Ilasco, it was primarily a southern and eastern European immigrant working class that was the object of public fears.

(7)

Schools and Churches

Don't talk about it, Tom. I've tried it, and it don't work; it don't work, Tom. It ain't for me; I ain't used to it. The widder's good to me, and friendly; but I can't stand them ways. She makes me git up just at the same time every morning . . . I hate them ornery sermons . . . I can't chaw. I got to wear shoes all Sunday. The widder eats by a bell; she goes to bed by a bell; she gits up by a bell—everything's so awful reg'lar a body can't stand it.
—Mark Twain, *The Adventures of Tom Sawyer*

After the strike of 1910, Atlas launched a campaign to stabilize Ilasco by encouraging the growth of cultural institutions such as schools and churches. This would nurture a sense of permanency in the community, reform the labor-camp atmosphere a bit, and check unrest among Atlas's transient workers. It would also facilitate efforts to instill greater discipline and industrial values in the children of workers. All in all, this paternalism was designed to bind workers more closely to the company and head off possible efforts to unionize the plant.

At the same time, Atlas's strategy helped to satisfy the desire of those in the community who sought to make it a more lasting and attractive place to live. Many worked to build permanent churches and schools out of their own desire for a more stable community. Their efforts created a distinctive cultural landscape in rural Missouri. By the time this process of community building was over, the hills and flatland around Ilasco became the home of not only a Nazarene, a Roman Catholic, and a Methodist church but also a Slovak Lutheran and a Greek Catholic church. In addition, new schools became the pride and center of the community.

As the result of Ilasco's almost overnight appearance in 1903, the Marble Creek School District's educational facilities were ill-equipped to accommodate the children of workers in Atlas's labor camp. The fact that so many immigrant men had left their families in Europe relieved the strain on county resources, but in the early years teachers and school officials used makeshift facilities until they could devise a more comprehensive educational plan for the community. After Atlas acquired the Heinbach and Johnson estates and converted Ilasco into a company town, cement plant officials worked closely with county officials to nurture the growth of schools and shape the children of their labor force.

On November 21, 1904, a newly reconstructed school opened at Marble Creek, about a mile west of Ilasco, after construction problems had delayed its opening. The new school, better equipped to accommodate at least some of the growing student population around Ilasco, consisted of two rooms and could hold up to one hundred students. A local newspaper described it as an "ideal country school house."[1]

In Ilasco proper, a public school opened but did not have a permanent building at first. Elmer Stewart, the teacher, conducted classes in the Rumanian Hall. Velma Randolph Youell remembered the makeshift facilities that she and other students endured inside the hall: "They laid boards across the little wooden kegs that dynamite had come in, and the kids sat on the boards and got their lessons."[2]

In addition to a tuition school, a grade school operated in 1914 by Addie Penn and Ruby Engle was held in what had once been a Baptist mission. This relieved some of the crowding, but the county also took steps that year to secure a future site for a new school, aided by a recent law empowering local school boards to condemn land for such purposes with compensation to the owner. On November 16, 1914, Marble Creek School District Number One, represented by board members Nelson Brown, Frank Moore, and Frank Loomis, initiated condemnation proceedings against part of the Heinbach tract for a school site. At that time, Samuel Heinbach's will was still in litigation. Shortly after the Missouri Supreme Court had remanded the case to the circuit court, the school district peeled off several lots appraised at $550. This sum was to be turned over to the Ralls County Clerk until the courts determined the validity of Heinbach's will, which had left his estate to his widow, Mary Alice.[3]

Once Atlas acquired title to the Heinbach estate, however, ownership of the condemned property did not remain in the county's hands. Instead, Atlas assumed title to the land and established deeds of gift allowing the school district to use the land exclusively for school purposes. The deeds contained

---

1. *Hannibal Courier-Post,* September 12, October 15 and 16, and November 3, 17, and 21, 1904; Thelma Herska, "Ilasco School Reunion," May 23, 1987, copy in author's possession.

2. *Heinbach v. Heinbach et al.,* April term, 1918, 344; Youell, "Renault a/k/a Randolph," 17.

3. *Ralls County Times,* April 11, 1913; *Ralls County Record,* September 25, 1914; Herska, "Ilasco School Reunion"; *School District Number One, Ralls County, Missouri v. Mary Alice Heinbach et al.,* November 16, 1914, Miscellaneous Record, book 97, 207–9, Ralls County, Office of the Circuit Clerk and Recorder, New London.

an important stipulation that the land would revert to Atlas in the event that it was no longer used for such purposes.[4]

Under Atlas's supervision, the district built a new grade school. Atlas also donated land and equipment for a playground next to the grade school. Plant officials maintained the equipment and supervised the playground jointly with the school board. School officials and employees staged a celebration in April 1921 to honor Atlas's bestowing of the playground on Ilasco children.[5]

Overcrowding still posed a problem. Maude Couch, superintendent of Ilasco schools, made a pitch in 1921 for public support for building expansion. She emphasized that Ilasco's facilities—three rooms for 246 students—were still "entirely inadequate."[6]

In response, citizens approved school bonds in the amount of sixty-five hundred dollars to support building additions. Under the leadership of board members Nelson Brown and John McKinney and with the cooperation of Atlas, the school district undertook this expansion. The grade school in Ilasco proper soon featured new rooms and an auditorium, and in 1926 the district built a new grade school in Monkey Run. Mildred Kitsock, Perry Jones, and Anna Hustava were among those who in the early 1920s had attended grade school taught by Katherine Howard and others in the basement of the St. Peters Ukrainian Church in Monkey Run. The new school, under the direction of Ida Davis, was held in what later became the home of John and Juanita Malone. Edna Sudsberry, Ethel Lewis, Anna Tompkins, and Melvenah Cattle taught grades one through eight at the other grade school, and Laura Riggs presided over the Marble Creek School. In addition, a newly constructed high school opened during the 1926–1927 school year. Students helped high school teachers Maude Couch, Mary Bell Hart, and Evelyn Fay Cox move books and materials to the new one-story stucco building on Atlas property in the middle of the year.[7]

During the 1925–1926 school year, the Ilasco schools had 292 students enrolled and ten teachers (Fanny Tompkins and the nine listed above). The high school

4. Atlas Portland Cement Company to Marble Creek School District No. 1 of Ralls County, Deeds of Gift, July 26, 1926, July 7, 1927, Miscellaneous Deed Record, book 116, 125, 385, Ralls County, Office of the Circuit Clerk and Recorder, New London.

5. Herska, "Ilasco School Reunion"; *Hannibal Courier-Post,* April 19, 1921. Universal Atlas Cement Company, "Company Houses—Hannibal Plant," June 16, 1933 (in author's possession).

6. Quoted in *Hannibal Courier-Post,* April 6, 1921.

7. Herska, "Ilasco School Reunion"; *Hannibal Courier-Post,* May 18, 1926; Atlas Portland Cement Company to Marble Creek School District No. 1 of Ralls County, Deed of Gift, July 26, 1926, Miscellaneous Deed Record, book 116, 125, Ralls County, Office of the Circuit Clerk and Recorder, New London; Anna Hustava Sanders, interview by author, July 2, 1992; Mildred King to Gregg Andrews, March 10, 1993; Perry Jones Jr., tape provided to author, December 5, 1994.

enrollment was just fourteen female and fourteen male students. C. E. Miller, secretary of the school board, justice of the peace, and merchant, awarded high school diplomas to his daughter Nedra Miller, Louise Gould, and Anna Rhodes, but not a single male graduated from high school that year or the previous year.[8]

It is difficult to determine how much influence cement plant officials had over the school system, but the evidence suggests that it was substantial. Nelson Brown, superintendent of the school board and loyal manager of the cement plant's company barn, was probably Atlas's point man in shaping school district policies. In fact, as we shall see in chapter 8, Atlas officials and their supporters in Hannibal used the schools to instill company loyalty and patriotism and to Americanize the children of Ilasco immigrants.[9]

What Atlas tried to accomplish in regard to Ilasco students was consistent with what had been the broader aims of Missouri public school reformers since the end of the Civil War. Rather than concentrate on expanding the intellectual horizons of students, state officials concentrated on molding the habits and attitudes necessary for an efficient industrial labor force. Punctuality, obedience, sobriety, respect for authority, and self-discipline were among the values preached by those who trumpeted the growing corporate domination of American life. In the eyes of public school reformers, a full-scale cultural offensive to instill these values in students was critical to continued industrial expansion. They viewed this as particularly necessary among children of rural Americans and immigrants from preindustrial societies whose work rhythms, habits, and culture often collided with factory discipline. In their view, schools must above all inculcate popular respect for the corporations running American economic life.[10]

Efforts to instill discipline and punctuality among Ilasco students may not have been as successful as some would have liked. Perry Jones, after going home from grade school for lunch one day in 1919 or 1920, returned late to school, fearing that he would get into trouble with Maude Couch, his teacher. Upon returning to school, he discovered that every boy in the class had skipped school in the afternoon to go ice skating on the Mississippi River. Couch whipped all of them one at a time the next day.[11]

---

8. "Report of High School Inspector," March 24, 1926, Missouri Reports to North Central Association of Colleges and Secondary Schools, 1892–1962, vol. 35, WHMC–Columbia; *Hannibal Courier-Post,* May 18, 1926; *Ralls County Record,* July 24, 1925.

9. Bodnar, *Immigration and Industrialization,* 12, notes the extensive influence of Pennsylvania Steel upon the school system in Steelton, where the company also put one of its officials on the school board and paid part of the superintendent's salary. In many coal company towns, too, operators often had this added control. See Corbin, *Life, Work,* especially 127–30.

10. For a good discussion of this campaign by public school reformers in Missouri, see Thelen, *Paths of Resistance,* 108–16. On the collision of immigrant cultures and industrial discipline, see Gutman, "Work, Culture, and Society in Industrializing America."

11. Perry Jones Jr., tape provided to author, December 5, 1994.

Atlas's paternalistic role in the school system undoubtedly yielded public relations benefits and contributed to the molding of future workers, but it would be misleading to view schools as something merely imposed from above. The dreams that Ilasco's working-class parents had for their children through education may have differed sharply from what plant officials or state educational authorities hoped to achieve through public education. Teachers did more than simply carry out instructions from Atlas officials to discourage unionization and produce obedient future workers for the cement plant. They, too, had their own goals and values, which at times may not have overlapped with those of Atlas officials.

Ilasco teachers worked under adverse conditions, especially in the 1910s and 1920s. Plagued by overcrowded classrooms and low salaries averaging slightly more than one hundred dollars per month in 1920, they sometimes had to deal with students who were several years apart in age but in the same classroom. In addition, they lacked training with respect to pupils who could not speak English. Ponto "Pete" Galluzzio, the son of immigrants Rosario and Mary Galluzzio from Papanice, Italy, could not speak English when he entered school at Ilasco in the late 1920s. Pete, later a graduate of the University of Missouri, recalled that it was his first-grade teacher, Laura Riggs, who after calling roll on the first day of school gave him the name of Pete as he smiled and nodded.[12]

Teachers at times had to contend with parents who insisted that they, not the teachers, should resolve problems that arose at school between their children. Perry Jones Jr. recalled that he intervened on one occasion at school when Frank Scalise had Jones's younger and much smaller brother Harry down on the ground beating him up. Perry jumped on Scalise and chased him home, but when he returned to school after lunch and saw Scalise's mother at the school with a butcher knife, he decided to hide in the creek instead of return to school. According to Jones, Mrs. Scalise stayed until the bell rang, although Maude Couch, the teacher, implored her to go home and leave the discipline to her. Couch whipped Jones the next day.[13]

On another occasion, when Jones was apparently acting up while lining up at the door for the first bell, Mrs. Henderson, his teacher, somehow bloodied his nose by pushing or striking him. He hid the incident from his parents, but someone informed them. His mother complained to Henderson about the incident and pulled him out of school. As a result, he did not pass that year, but when he returned the following year, Henderson was gone.[14]

---

12. Pete Galluzzio, interview by author, June 14, 1994. The *Ralls County Record,* September 3, 1920, lists the salaries of Ilasco teachers Melvenah Cattle, Maude Couch, and Ethel Coontz.

13. Perry Jones Jr., tape provided to author, December 5, 1994.

14. Ibid.

Like Pete Galluzzio, Rosa H. Nemes also tackled school and the English language at the same time. The daughter of Hungarian immigrants Bela and Mary Nemes, she later graduated as a valedictorian, and Charles, one of her brothers, was a salutatorian. Their mother spoke little or no English at the time, and Rosa's father relied on her to teach him the questions and answers for the test to become a naturalized U.S. citizen. "I don't remember how we ever managed at school," she noted. "We spoke Hungarian before we learned English so we had to learn English at school."[15]

The climate of ethnic and racial bigotry that was so widespread in the 1920s also challenged teachers as they tried to encourage harmony among students and respect for Ilasco's diverse population. The children of immigrants were often the targets of insults and name-calling that reflected the deeply ingrained prejudice against immigrants in the community and nation. Gloria Vajda Manary, the daughter of Slovak immigrants John Vajda and Susan Valach Vajda, remembered being called a "garlic snapper" and numerous other derogatory names, but such insults only strengthened her determination to "show the world I was not a dummy."[16]

In Manary's case, if Atlas officials hoped to use the schools to instill their attitudes in the children of immigrants, they certainly failed. Her father, who worked as a hammer driller in the quarry but acquired welding skills in trade school, "hated the cement plant" because he felt that they treated him "like a dummy." She complained that in the eyes of plant officials, "He was just a 'dumb Hunk.' "[17]

Likewise, if Atlas officials hoped that Ilasco's public schools would discourage trade unionism, the Vajda family demonstrates that such hopes were not always realized. The Vajdas, tired of being "poorly paid" and "not respected for their work," left Ilasco for Detroit in 1943. Gloria's mother, Susan, who had worked as a sewing machine operator in the sack house at the cement plant, found more rewarding opportunities in Detroit, as did her husband. She took a job with TRW, became an "avid UAW member and retired with excellent benefits and pension," while her husband found an opportunity to use his skills as a welder and sheet metal fabricator. He, too, became a devoted trade unionist.

Gloria graduated from the University of Michigan and became a speech and English teacher in Bay City, Michigan. As she reflected upon her roots and family experiences in Ilasco, she recalled the importance of Ilasco teachers as role models who encouraged the expansion of students' intellectual horizons. "I loved school," she emphasized, "my parents encouraged me to *learn*. I told Miss Riggs (grade 1) I was going to college and be a teacher just like her . . . I think

15. Rosa H. Nemes to Gregg Andrews, August 2, 1994.
16. Gloria Vajda Manary to Gregg Andrews, June 29, 1994.
17. Ibid.

we were so blessed with excellent teachers. I went home with them often and they showed me the 'other world.'"[18]

Even long after the dissolution of Ilasco, former teachers continued to provide various forms of intellectual and artistic encouragement. For example, Melvenah Cattle Davis sometimes purchased library cards for former Ilasco students who at the time lived outside Hannibal's city limits and thus were not entitled to free borrowing privileges at the Hannibal Public Library. She also sometimes gave free piano lessons to former students who could not afford them otherwise.[19]

On October 20, 1949, voters in Ilasco and five other Ralls County school districts agreed to consolidate, creating the Ralls County R-1 district. Ilasco became the center of this reorganized district, which had 291 students during its first year of operation. A new gymnasium soon became a prominent feature of the new school system and a center of social life in Ilasco. Student enrollment remained constant at slightly more than three hundred throughout the 1950s.[20]

Like schools, permanent churches were somewhat slow to develop during the early years, but soon after the cement plant opened, Hannibal religious leaders promoted missions in Ilasco. The Fifth Street Baptist Church supervised construction of a short-lived mission after a successful revival in Ilasco by evangelist Jim Ledford in February 1906. The revival netted fifty-five converts, and twenty-one baptisms in the cold waters of the Mississippi River.

Trustees of the Salvation Army in Hannibal also expanded their work to Ilasco. On March 24, 1904, Ensign Addie T. Briscoe leased from Samuel Heinbach a lot on which Salvation Army services were held. The mission did not last, however, and the lease was later transferred to the Holiness Mission.[21]

The Holiness movement within Methodism that produced the Ilasco mission had gained increasing popularity in southern and midwestern states since the Civil War. Holiness advocates condemned the swing toward more educated, trained ministers and what they regarded as more lax practices and services. They urged a return to old-time religion with an emphasis on simple dress, camp meetings, revivals, and altar calls. They condemned leisure activities such as dancing, playing cards, and gambling. After the General Conference of the Methodist Episcopal Church, South, officially criticized the movement in 1894, some Holiness supporters continued to support the Methodist church while others joined breakaway groups from the Holiness movement.[22]

---

18. Ibid.
19. My brother Kevin and I were recipients of this generosity.
20. Howard, *Ralls County Missouri,* 127; *Hannibal Courier-Post,* May 7, 1959.
21. Deed Record, book 79, 436–37, and Quit Claim Deed Record, book 100, 571; both in Ralls County, Office of the Circuit Clerk and Recorder, New London.
22. See Vinson Synan, *The Holiness-Pentecostal Movement in the United States,* chap. 2, for a discussion of the rise of the Holiness movement.

C. M. Jeffers, an Ilasco merchant and farmer, spearheaded the campaign to establish a Holiness Mission in 1910. Formerly a Sunday school superintendent of the Saverton Methodist Church, he worked with Atlas's Ludwig Anderson to plan the mission. Anderson was paymaster at the cement plant, secretary-treasurer of Atlas's Hannibal Connecting Railroad, and superintendent of the Holiness Mission in Hannibal. After Jeffers secured the lease formerly held by the Salvation Army, he launched a highly publicized fund-raising campaign to construct a suitable building so that Anderson could continue the mission after his death. In the meantime, he held religious services at a temporary location.[23]

Intense emotionalism characterized services at the Holiness Mission. On July 4, 1910, a friend asked Al Stewart, "How did you like them great talkers down at the church Sunday night? About as good as the one the other night." Velma Randolph Youell recalled that when she attended the Holiness Mission with "Grandpa" [James] and "Grandma" [Elizabeth] Smashey, "They would set me on the seat between them and kneel on the floor to pray. They could pray so you felt the Lord right in there."[24]

After Jeffers's death in February 1911, Anderson and other Holiness trustees took control of the mission, but in 1926 the Church of the Nazarene replaced it with the full backing of Anderson and Atlas. The Holiness trustees transferred the lease back to Atlas, which then granted a month-to-month lease to the Nazarene church. By the end of a two-week revival in March 1927, Sunday school attendance had reached a record-breaking high of 148. Pastor Harlow Reed, who headed the new church until I. G. Young succeeded him in 1933, presided over the dedication of a new building in 1928. After brief stints by Reverends F. R. Wasson and Lee Wolverton, Charles Rache, a Hungarian immigrant who also worked at the cement plant, became pastor in 1936. He occupied that position for nearly thirty years. Lay pastors Raymond Sanders and Samuel Smashey succeeded him briefly until the church was dismantled when Ilasco was torn down in the mid-1960s.[25]

23. *Ralls County Record,* March 11, September 9, and November 25, 1910; "Church Records Form," July 21, 1941, U.S. WPA-HRS, 1935–1942, microfilm reel 573, folder 17457; U.S. Federal Manuscript Census, 1910, Saverton township, Ralls County. On Anderson's election as an officer of the Hannibal Connecting Railroad, see *Hannibal Courier-Post,* March 10, 1908.

24. ? to Al Stewart, July 4, 1910, Robert Stewart Collection of Letters, private possession of Debbie Hendricks; U.S. Federal Manuscript Census, 1910, Saverton township, Ralls County; Velma Youell, "Renault a/k/a Randolph," 17. I would like to thank Debbie Stewart Hendricks for sharing the Stewart Collection with me.

25. Ludwig Anderson et al. to Atlas Portland Cement Company, May 17, 1929, Quit Claim Deed Record, book 100, 571, Ralls County, Office of the Circuit Clerk and Recorder, New London; "Church of the Nazarene," Church Records Form, July 21, 1941, microfilm reel 573, folder 17457, U.S. WPA-HRS, 1935–1942, WHMC–Columbia; *Hannibal Courier-*

At the time of the founding of the Holiness Mission in Ilasco, many American Protestant churches had been transformed by the Social Gospel movement, which in the late nineteenth and early twentieth century called on people to apply Christian ethics and principles to solve social problems created by the Industrial Revolution. Social Gospel ministers regarded it as Christian duty to work on behalf of the poor in a variety of ways. They challenged others to combat poverty, oppression, and exploitation of industrial workers. This often meant working in urban slums and calling on corporations to share a bigger slice of the economic pie with their labor force. Those awakened by the Social Gospel urged employers to raise wages and benefits, improve working conditions, and in some cases to recognize labor unions. By applying the golden rule to industrial society, Social Gospel ministers hoped to invigorate churches and promote social justice.[26]

The Holiness movement did not endorse the Social Gospel. Although Holiness sects pitched their appeal to the lower classes, they emphasized the need to get rid of personal sin rather than poverty. The conservative spiritual approach advocated by leaders of the Ilasco Holiness Church encouraged worshippers to look to the Lord and not to trade unions or the government for solutions to their problems. It was not that leaders were unconcerned with poverty and degradation, but that they believed social betterment would come through personal redemption and strict adherence to old-time religion.[27]

This philosophy discouraged links between religion and labor reform ideas, and thus proved useful to Atlas as paymaster Anderson helped to set up the Ilasco Holiness Mission shortly after the strike of 1910. As historian Charles Edwin Jones has written, "Holiness believers who often made a mental association between unions and secret societies (which they opposed), may have been regarded as natural allies by company management."[28] However, Anderson's work in Ilasco was not merely a cynical attempt by Atlas to foist the Holiness doctrine on militant workers. Anderson was a genuine Holiness believer; in fact, he also supervised the Holiness church in Hannibal. Nevertheless, his religious activities must be put in the context of his broader social outlook. In his view, what was good for

---

Post, March 5 and 9, 1927. On Jeffers's death, see his obituary in the *Ralls County Record,* February 24, 1911. As a former member of the Ilasco Church of the Nazarene, I have relied on my own memory for the tenure of pastors Rache and Smashey during the final years of the church.

26. For a discussion of the Social Gospel movement, see Ronald C. White Jr. and C. Howard Hopkins, with an essay by John C. Bennett, *The Social Gospel: Religion and Reform in Changing America.*

27. Synan, *Holiness-Pentecostal Movement,* 56–59; Timothy L. Smith, *Called Unto Holiness. The Story of the Nazarenes: The Formative Years,* 199–204.

28. Charles Edwin Jones, "Disinherited or Rural? A Historical Case Study in Urban Holiness Religion," 405*n32.*

Atlas was good for Atlas workers, social stability, and Holiness worshippers. He represented a more urban-based, middle-class leadership within the movement that tried to promote order and stability among lower-class followers.[29]

For Ilasco's Protestant native-born women, in particular, the church may have served another important function. Historian Dolores E. Janiewski has emphasized that religious strictures against drinking, gambling, and extramarital sex benefited women who hoped to curb the destructive behavior of men upon whom they were dependent. In this sense, women's interests dovetailed with those of Atlas officials in their campaign to stabilize the community, but for different reasons. As Janiewski explains, "Men who were 'saved' were more faithful husbands, better providers, and more diligent employees, which was more desirable for women, employers, and churches alike."[30]

The Holiness Mission's biggest rival for native-born worshippers in Ilasco was the Methodist church. Methodism was somewhat slow to embrace the message of the Social Gospel, but in 1908 the Northern General Conference adopted the Social Creed of Methodism. The creed urged several labor reforms, including higher wages, worker protection from unsafe occupational conditions and diseases, regulation of working conditions for women, and the abolition of child labor. It also endorsed arbitration to resolve strikes.[31]

This creed laid the basis for an even broader church program that called for social insurance, the eight-hour day, and collective bargaining rights for trade unions. By the early 1930s, when the nation was in the grip of the Great Depression, Methodist bishops had become sharply critical of the plight of industrial workers. "Industry has as a rule given labor a grudging, insufficient wage," they complained, "keeping it down by child exploitation, by suppression of legitimate organizations, and by other expedients, while at the same time huge fortunes have been amassed for the favored owners of the resources of production. To-day the burden is without conscience shifted to the worker, after giving his labor for miserable financial results, is turned off to starve or beg."[32]

Before 1917, a small church at Marble Creek accommodated Methodists in the Ilasco area. The Marble Creek Methodist Church, South, organized around 1881 under supervision of the Hope Street M. E. Church in Hannibal, dedicated its

---

29. See ibid., 395–412, for a discussion of the urban component of the holiness movement in Kansas City. For a view of the movement as an effort by "certain groups experiencing acute social maladjustment to recapture their sense of security through religious revival and reform," see John B. Holt, "Holiness Religion: Cultural Shock and Social Reorganization."

30. *Sisterhood Denied: Race, Gender, and Class in a New South Community*, 139.

31. Emory Stevens Bucke, ed., *The History of American Methodism*, vol. 3, 379–81.

32. Quoted in ibid., 382.

new building on July 11, 1883. Previously, Andrew Hillhouse had presided over a Sunday school which met in the old Marble Creek schoolhouse.[33]

Ilasco Methodists soon sought their own church. Mary Perkins and others solicited public support for the campaign, and on September 9, 1917, they held their first Sunday school services in a store building owned by Curd Fisher. Attendees sat on powder boxes, nail kegs, and six benches donated by the Broadway M. E. Church in Hannibal. By June 1919 the average attendance had reached 187, and members had purchased a large building for a permanent site.[34]

C. E. Miller, a merchant and justice of the peace, played a leading role in the drive to organize a new Methodist church. So did Clarence F. Nerlich, an employment manager at one of Hannibal's shoe factories. He and his wife, Katherine, often stopped on their way from Hannibal to the Ilasco Methodist mission to pick up children such as Velma Randolph, who later fondly remembered that Mrs. Nerlich used to pick her up in "her surrey with the fringe on top pulled by a black horse."[35]

At one time, men from the First M. E. Church in Hannibal furnished cars to bring teachers from Hannibal to the Ilasco Sunday school. In January 1927 the congregation bought a bell for the Sunday school, and Atlas built the belfry and installed the bell free of charge. Atlas also wired the building and furnished the electricity.[36]

Seventy-seven charter members belonged to the Ilasco Methodist Church when it was formally organized on July 31, 1927. By then, the Marble Creek Church had become defunct. Rev. T. E. Sisson presided over the new church's dedication ceremonies, but Rev. Eugene Wood replaced him in September 1928. Rev. Wood moved into a new parsonage built at the edge of Ilasco on a lot donated by C. E. Miller. Significantly, the Atlas Portland Cement Company relinquished title to the church site on August 19, 1928, in exchange for five dollars and "other considerations." The deed transferring ownership provided that "neither Atlas nor its successors can claim any right to this land."[37]

The Loyal Ladies Aid played a dynamic role in the Ilasco Methodist Church and community. Much of the financial support for the parsonage and church came

---

33. "Marble Creek Methodist Church," Church Records Form, July 25, 1941, U.S. WPA-HRS, 1935–1942, microfilm reel 573, folder 17459, WHMC–Columbia.

34. "Ilasco Methodist Church," U.S. WPA-HRS, 1935–1942, microfilm reel 573, folder 17457, WHMC–Columbia. For the fund-raising campaign and activities of Perkins, see *Ralls County Record,* January 24, 1913, and May 18, 1917.

35. Youell, "Renault a/k/a Randolph," 17. See also Juanita Venditti's article, "Ilasco UMC Recalled," which appeared in the *Hannibal Courier-Post,* November 11, 1987.

36. "Ilasco Methodist Church."

37. Ibid.; "Marble Creek Methodist Church"; Atlas Portland Cement Company to Ilasco Methodist Episcopal Church, "Deed," August 19, 1928, Miscellaneous Deed Record, book 118, 550, Ralls County, Office of the Circuit Clerk and Recorder, New London.

from this organization's fund-raising activities. Bessie Tatman, Ruby Northcutt, Catherine Dryden, Maude Lee, Bertha McKinney, and many others prepared and carried hot meals to workers at the cement plant. They made quilts, prepared food for chili and turkey suppers, held ice cream socials, and at times served hot lunches to Ilasco school children.[38]

The Methodist Loyal Ladies Aid strengthened religious and social bonds and community institutions, and later passed on such traditions to the United Methodist Women. These women felt (and still feel) a deep attachment to the community. At times this has meant tensions between them and cement plant officials. The feistiness that Juanita Cross Venditti once displayed to plant manager Ray Hoffman, for example, perhaps grew out of evolving social attitudes within Methodism as the church developed a more critical view of corporations. She complained to Hoffman that he was handing over money for charities that was deducted from the paychecks of Atlas workers to Hannibal instead of Ralls County community agencies. She reminded him that the plant was in Ralls County, not Hannibal. Despite the fears of her husband, Angelo, that he might lose his job at the cement plant if she kept hounding Hoffman, she persisted. When Hoffman finally relented, she quickly pressed him, "When can I pick up the check?"[39]

Perhaps in part because of Ilasco's early instability, missionaries at times roamed through the community, passing out religious tracts that targeted specific immigrant groups. A Polish missionary arrived in March 1905, but found only three Polish families alongside a large population of Rumanians and other nationalities. After distributing tracts, he announced to a meeting of Hannibal's Ministerial Union held at the Presbyterian church that he would send another missionary who could speak Rumanian.[40]

Ilasco's immigrants at first had to cobble together religious arrangements until they could create their own churches. Since there was no Eastern Orthodox church in the Hannibal area, the St. Thomas Rumanian Orthodox Church in St. Louis furnished priests who sometimes traveled to Ilasco to officiate weddings and conduct baptisms. For the site of children's christenings, Rumanian residents chose a spot where a large spring emptied at the bottom of a hill. They inscribed a cross in the rock above the spring. Celebrations that included dancing and big feasts typically followed baptisms. Such celebrations often lasted a couple of days.[41]

---

38. Juanita Venditti, "Ilasco UMC Recalled"; Juanita Cross Venditti, interview by author, July 9, 1993.

39. Juanita Cross Venditti, interview by author, July 9, 1993.

40. *Hannibal Courier-Post,* March 13, 1905.

41. Joe Welschmeyer, "Cement Plant at Ilasco Attracted East European Population," in *Hannibal Courier-Post,* December 20, 1984. See also *Hannibal Courier-Post,* August 24, 1908.

Early Ukrainians also relied on priests from St. Louis to minister to them in the Byzantine or Greek Catholic (Uniate) tradition. Priests came by train for divine liturgies, marriages, funerals, and baptisms. Although Ilasco's Ukrainians acknowledged the Roman papacy's authority, they maintained Greek liturgies, rituals, and practices, including the use of married clergy.[42]

At other times, Mike and Christina Kitsock, Frank and Fannie Konko (Chomka), and other Ukrainian families held religious services in each other's homes, singing hymns and sharing Scripture readings. Not until 1919 did they have their own place of worship—the St. Peters Ukrainian Church, which was built with funds provided by the Greek Catholic Union, a Ukrainian fraternal society in Philadelphia. The Kitsocks, who had bought a farm in Monkey Run, leased hillside land to the church. Atop the steeple and bronze cupola, a Greek cross with three horizontal bars stood out above the "Onion Bulb" dome overlooking the Mississippi River with its message of rebirth and eternal life.[43]

As Atlas's demand for labor declined in the 1920s, Ilasco's Ukrainians could no longer support their church. Many returned to Pennsylvania. Those who stayed were hard-pressed to pay the traveling expenses of priests from St. Louis. As a result, visits by priests to say mass, give the sacraments, and provide other services dropped off until the church closed in 1924. After that, the county temporarily used the stone basement of the building for a public grade school. Before the church was torn down in 1938, the Nazarene congregation bought the bell for its new church.[44]

Eventually, members of the St. Peters Ukrainian Church joined the Holy Cross Catholic Church in Ilasco, but for awhile continued to gather in each other's homes for Scripture readings and hymns. As a young girl, Mary Kitsock learned Greek liturgical chants for such services. Her sister Mildred Kitsock King later recalled: "My fondest memory of my mother is of her telling us Bible stories and kneeling . . . praying in the Ukranian language."[45]

Until the Ilasco Holy Cross Catholic Church was built in 1915, Slovak, Polish, Italian, Austrian, and other Roman Catholics relied on outside priests or attended the Immaculate Conception Church in Hannibal. In 1915, the Atlas Portland Cement Company furnished the site, most of the building materials, and a ninety-nine-year lease, and paid carpenters to build a mission belonging to Hannibal's Immaculate Conception Church. Father Daniel Sullivan came from Hannibal once a month to conduct services for about sixty families who became founding members. First communions, baptisms, confirmations, marriages, and funerals

42. Howard, *Ralls County Missouri,* 170; Welschmeyer, "Cement Plant at Ilasco."
43. Welschmeyer, "Cement Plant at Ilasco."
44. Ibid.
45. Ibid.; Mildred Kitsock King to Gregg Andrews, March 20, 1993.

were still held in the Hannibal church due to a lack of space and materials. Between 1915 and World War II, the Ilasco church was the scene of only one marriage ceremony, that of Steve Milkucik and Anna Kitsock in 1917.[46]

Father Carlisle B. Green took charge of the mission in 1935 and soon expanded services. The mission now featured mass each Sunday and on all Holy Days of Obligation. In 1936 it held the first Holy Communion for children, and in 1939 C. H. LeBlond, D.D., Bishop of St. Joseph Diocese, presided over the first mass ever conducted by a bishop in the mission. At that time, he also ministered the first Sacrament of Confirmation in Ilasco.[47]

Around the turn of the century, about 13 percent of the population in Hungary's Slovak counties were Lutherans. Those who came to Ilasco quickly began to set up their own church. They contacted Pastor C. F. Drewes, of the St. John's Lutheran Church in Hannibal, about how to bring services to Ilasco. Drewes in turn got in touch with faculty at the Missouri Synod's Concordia Seminary in Springfield, Illinois, where several Slovak students were preparing for the ministry. John Hudry became the first of many students to conduct Slovak services at the St. John's Lutheran Church in Hannibal and in the homes of Slovaks in Ilasco.[48]

When J. H. Witte became pastor of the St. John's Church on January 5, 1906, he organized a Slovak congregation in Ilasco made up of forty-two members. With the strong backing of Assembly 139 of the Slovak Evangelical Union formed in 1905, the congregation launched a campaign on February 3, 1911, to raise money to build a chapel. This campaign was so successful that on February 26, aided by student pastor George Majoros, supporters held a meeting and services in the home of Stefan Stimel to organize their own church. At that meeting, the congregation established the Dr. Martin Luther Church of Ilasco and elected the following officers: president, Stefan Pozel; secretary, Stefan Kristof;

46. Church Records Form, September 18, 1941, microfilm reel 573, folder 17465, U.S. WPA-HRS, 1935–1942, WHMC–Columbia; Howard, *Ralls County Missouri*, 171–72. Among the founding members of the Holy Cross Catholic Church were the families of Andre Baliak, Mikolay Kitsock, Josef Musansky, Andre Golian, Fecko Konka, Simon Mihu, Duro Podolec, Stefan Monia, Matus Zatko, Paul Melaga, Stefan Urkop, Paul Mozzis, Joe Hustyeva, Julius Sunderlik, Jan F. Furdak, Jacob Oresick, Yomas Konicky, and Pavel Babiak.

47. Church Records Form, September 18, 1941. On the blend of Old World and New World religious practices and traditions in Slovak Catholic churches, see June Granatir Alexander, *The Immigrant Church and Community: Pittsburgh's Slovak Catholics and Lutherans, 1880–1915*, chap. 4.

48. *Hannibal Courier-Post*, August 10, 1961; Howard, *Ralls County Missouri*, 169. See M. Mark Stolarik, *Growing Up on the South Side: Three Generations of Slovaks in Bethlehem, Pennsylvania, 1880–1976*, 55–58, for the building of religious institutions by Slovak Lutherans in Bethlehem, Pennsylvania.

treasurer, John Viglasky; and trustees, Stephen Kucera, George Selecky, and John Krudy Sr.[49]

Benjamin E. and Ella S. Hulse donated recently acquired land for the church site. They stipulated that it be used only for religious and educational purposes and that in twenty-five years it would become the sole property of the Dr. Martin Luther Church. There were 163 members who contributed to the building fund, as well as many contributors from other denominations, especially Catholics. Construction of the chapel began in August 1911 under the guidance of St. John's Pastor Witte, who held dedication services on November 5, 1911. He gave a brief speech in English, but John Marcis, a student from Concordia Seminary in Springfield, Illinois, delivered the main sermon in Slovak.[50]

Under Rev. Witte's supervision, seminary students continued to come to Ilasco once a month to conduct services in Slovak until the Slovak Lutheran Synod took over the work. In 1914 the congregation placed the church under the administration of Pastor George Majoros and the St. Lucas Church in St. Louis. As in other Slovak Lutheran churches, Ilasco's Lutheran laity enjoyed considerable power in governing their church without excessive interference from ecclesiastical authorities. A church council elected by the congregation supervised administrative affairs and set the pastor's salary. Each Sunday, the president and vice president of the church council read sermons, and a minister came from St. Louis periodically to conduct Holy Communion and other festival services.[51]

The congregation added a vestibule in 1916, and in the summer of 1917 summoned Andrew Ontko, a seminary student, to provide religious instruction and teach the Slovak language to children between the ages of five and fourteen. Assembly 139 of the Slovak Evangelical Union paid for one-half of the costs to construct a one-room brick school for such purposes. In exchange for this financial support, the congregation allowed the Slovak fraternal society to use the new building for its meetings. Ontko and other student ministers came to Ilasco to provide summer instruction until 1942.[52]

Student pastor Stephen M. Tuhy also founded an English Sunday school in the summer of 1932 under the supervision of Pastor W. G. Schwehn of the St. John's Lutheran Church in Hannibal, which provided the necessary visiting staff. Frank

49. *Hannibal Courier-Post,* August 10, 1961; Rev. W. G. Schwehn, "A Brief Historical Sketch of Saint John's Evangelical Lutheran Church, Hannibal, Missouri," 29, 32–33; Church Records Form, Dr. Martin Luther Church, August 8, 1941, microfilm reel 573, folder 17459, U.S. WPA-HRS, 1935–1942, WHMC–Columbia.

50. Ibid. Marcis soon became pastor of the Holy Emmanuel Slovak Evangelical Lutheran Church in Pittsburgh. Alexander, *Immigrant Church,* 80–82.

51. Schwehn, "Brief Historical Sketch," 29, 32–33; Alexander, *Immigrant Church,* 74.

52. Schwehn, "Brief Historical Sketch," 29, 32–33; Gloria Vajda Manary to Gregg Andrews, June 29, 1994.

Heitman was the Sunday school superintendent, and Katherine Hoffman, Louise Wichern, Virginia Cheek, and Bill Roesler were teachers. Pastor Schwehn also began to conduct services in English twice a month on Sunday afternoons, and electric lights were installed in 1932. Student pastor Franklin Maoina helped to organize the Ladies Aid, the Men's Club, and Young People's Club in the summer of 1934 to support both the church and the school.[53]

According to figures provided by George Tretiak, president of the church council for twenty-five years, the Dr. Martin Luther Church, without a resident pastor, still had 119 members in 1941 despite Ilasco's declining population. Pastor Majoros served as administrator until he died in 1949. Dr. George Dolak, a professor at the Concordia Seminary in St. Louis, succeeded him until 1956. At the time of the church's fiftieth anniversary in 1961, Pastor John Kovac of St. Louis was handling all special services in Ilasco. At that time, the church had conducted a total of fifty baptisms, ninety-six confirmands, twenty-one marriages, and thirty-five funerals. Tretiak died the year before, but Steve Valach, who had served on the board of trustees since 1931, still held office in the church.[54]

Student ministers from Concordia Seminary stayed with members of the congregation and customarily visited with each member after Sunday services. For student pastors, the generosity of Ilasco parishioners became legendary. Gloria Vajda Manary recalled that in 1968 she attended a church in Garfield, New Jersey, whose pastor had once been her teacher in Ilasco's "Slovak School." After the service, she introduced herself to him, and they shared memories of Ilasco. "He said he was warned by previous teachers," she recounted, "to watch out or he would be drunk every Sunday evening because every family insisted he taste their wine and they served it in water glasses. He said anyone that ever served in Ilasco never forgot the generous spirit of the people. He said it was a 'coup' to get assigned to do Summer School at Ilasco."[55]

Although bitter religious squabbles often broke out in Ilasco, including intraethnic disputes between Catholic and Lutheran Slovaks, it was not uncommon for residents to attend other churches on occasions. This was especially true in the case of immigrant children attracted by the lay exhorting, joyous singing, and "hallelujahs" that broke the village stillness during revival services at the Church of the Nazarene. Immigrants at times sent their children elsewhere if services at their own church were not yet available on a regular basis. For example, sisters Rosa and Mary Nemes attended the Holy Cross Catholic Church when it was still a mission with services only once a month. Rather than stay home, they attended the Methodist church three Sundays each month. "Mom couldn't see us staying

---

53. Schwehn, "Brief Historical Sketch."
54. Ibid.
55. Gloria Vajda Manary to Gregg Andrews, June 29, 1994.

home the other three," Rosa remembered, "so she sent us to Methodist Sunday School, and when we finally had mass every Sunday, the Methodist preacher pleaded with Mom to let us go back, but to no avail."[56]

From basketball games to school-related chili suppers to church-sponsored ice cream socials, Ilasco's schools and churches featured programs and events that promoted a sense of community among residents long divided by racial and ethnic tensions. When saloons disappeared in Ilasco between World War I and the 1930s, schools and churches were about the only local institutions that residents had. Even before national prohibition, Atlas and county officials hoped to use religion as an effective tool in the ongoing campaign to eliminate saloons. The battle against alcohol during prohibition became synonymous in Ilasco with the campaign to Americanize Atlas's labor force. In addition, the propaganda machine unleashed by the United States during World War I put patriotic pressures on immigrants. Officials used schools and churches to apply such pressures.

---

56. Rosa H. Nemes to Gregg Andrews, August 2, 1994.

ATLAS PORTLAND CEMENT CO.'S PLANT, AT HANNIBAL. L

Ilasco Plant of the Atlas Portland Cement Company, 1904.
Courtesy Roberta and J. Hurley Hagood.

ENT PLANT IN THE WORLD. EMPLOYS 2000 PEOPLE.

Elmo Mack, c. 1930. Courtesy Virginia Patrick Arthaud.

John and Lilly Stringer, Company Row. The Stringers earlier lived in sawmill camps. Courtesy Perry Jones Jr.

Atlas teamster Jack Jones outside house in Ilasco. Courtesy Perry Jones Jr.

Mary Roziak Sunderlik with son John and daughter Mary, about to leave Slovakia and join husband Julius in Ilasco, 1909. Courtesy, Anna Sunderlik Venditti.

L-R, Rosa Raimondi Genovese, Pasquale Genovese, Josephine Genovese; in front, Daisy Genovese. Rosa and daughter Daisy about to leave Papanice, Italy, to join Pantaleone Genovese in Ilasco, 1914. Courtesy Armenia Genovese Erlichman.

Ilasco, c. 1910. Courtesy Jim and Dorothy Tatman.

Company row houses 309–312, built by the Atlas Portland Cement Company in 1902. The houses had no sewage disposal or sanitary or lighting facilities, and tenants furnished their own stoves. Courtesy USX Corporation.

Company houses in Pump House Hollow, built c. 1907. Courtesy Perry Jones Jr.

Perry and Beatrice Stringer Jones and children Betty Lou, Dora Sue, and Ida Lee at their house in Monkey Run, c. 1937. Courtesy Perry Jones Jr.

Postcard of cement plant with view overlooking Monkey Run. Courtesy David Polc.

Ilasco jail, 1992. Built in 1909. Courtesy author.

Hannibal funeral procession for Ilasco workers Sam Giunta and John Moga, killed in a dynamite explosion in Atlas's quarry, 1920. Courtesy Roberta and J. Hurley Hagood.

Immigrant quarry workers: In front, Tony Nicosia; L-R, John Sunderlik, Paul Mazola, John Patrick, unidentified man, Tom Zupan, and Steve Kisel, c. 1922: Courtesy Virginia Patrick Arthaud.

Quarry workers, c. 1950. Courtesy Fred's Photos.

Universal Atlas shale miners, 1940. Courtesy Fred's Photos.

Nellie Young Ragland, repairing and sewing cement sacks. Courtesy Fred's Photos.

Workers in the packing and sack house, September 6, 1935. Courtesy USX Corporation.

Operating department, September 6, 1935. Courtesy USX Corporation.

Mary Alice Heinbach, one of
Ilasco's landlords, 1910–1921.
Courtesy Jane Hemeyer.

Charlie Haynes (catching) and Elmo Mack (batting). The Atlas Portland Cement Company sponsored baseball in Ilasco's park. Courtesy Virginia Patrick Arthaud.

Teacher Elmer Stewart and pupils attending school in Rumanish Hall, 1913. Velma Randolph pictured in back row, fourth from right. Courtesy Jim and Dorothy Tatman.

Ilasco grade school, June 16, 1933. Courtesy USX Corporation.

Ilasco high school, c. 1929. Courtesy Charles Glascock.

Students outside grade school, April 5, 1917. Front row, L-R: Virgil Stewart, Sammy Venditti, Mike Kelemetz, John Moga Jr., Nick Kitsock, Nick Avamootz, Willie Fiorella, Mike Karabin, John Sirbu. Middle row: Anna Debonar, Victoria Kobalotsky, Anna Avamootz, Janie Seal, Goldie Seal, Minnie Lawson, Mary Bozalka, Louell Boss, Lucille Douglas, Thelma Morgan, Ruth Tucker, Ethel Northcutt. Back row: Mabel Yates, Mary Kelemetz, Gladys Taylor, Vivian Murray, Nedra Miller, Nell Henderson (teacher), Jimmy Homolos, unidentified, Arthur Yates, Edward Beavers. Nedra Miller later returned to teach the fifth and sixth grades in Ilasco. Courtesy Jim and Dorothy Tatman.

Ilasco students, c. early 1920s. Front row, L-R: Louise Andrews, unidentified, unidentified, Opal Northcutt, Margaret McKinney, Harry Jones, Trion Tanase, John Mojzis. Row two: Thelma McKinney (face turned with white dress), Margaret Karabin, Naomi Hurst, Armenta Arthur, Hilda Lease, unidentified, Nick Kitsock, John Bozalka, George Lee, Joe Sunderlik. Back row: Minnie Thompson, Cleo Boss, Helen Karabin, Ruby McGlaughlin, Lula (Billie) Tatman, Hallie Lane, John Malone, Elmo Doyle (Mack), Claude Dixon, Frank Scalise. Courtesy Jim and Dorothy Tatman.

Courtesy Fred's Photos.

Children of Magyar immigrants Bela and Mary Nemes. L-R, Anna, Rosa, James, Mary. Courtesy Rosa Nemes.

Shirley Lee leading grade-school students through lunch line. Lunches served by Anna Zivicky Polc and Anna Hustava Sanders, 1959. Courtesy Fred's Photos.

Ilasco Church of the Nazarene, June 16, 1933. Courtesy USX Corporation.

Ilasco Methodist Episcopal Church, South, 1992. Courtesy author.

Albert Venditti getting spring water at former site of Rumanian christenings. Courtesy Anna Sunderlik Venditti.

St. Peter's Ukrainian Catholic Church. Under jurisdiction of the Byzantine-Ukrainian Rite Catholic Bishop of Philadelphia, Pennsylvania. Courtesy State Historical Society of Missouri.

Ilasco Holy Cross Catholic Church, June 16, 1933. Courtesy
USX Corporation.

Ilasco's Dr. Martin Luther Slovak Lutheran Church, c. 1912. Courtesy David Polc.

Ilasco's post office, c. 1917. Courtesy Virginia Patrick Arthaud.

Ilasco's Sylvester Bird in one of Universal Atlas's kilns. Courtesy Fred's Photos.

Funeral of John Bosani Viglasky, Ilasco's Slovak Lutheran Church, February 20, 1920. Children sitting on ground, L-R: Anna Luptak, Susan Luptak, John Mojzis, Mildred Viglasky. Women seated next to casket: Susan Viglasky (left), Maria Zivicky (right). Standing in doorway, L-R: Steve Valach, John Slancik, Mary Slancik, John Slancik Jr., George Besina. Standing, L-R: Mary Herska, John Luptak, Anna Konopova, Mary Slezak, Mary Babyak Mazola, Maria Polc, Mary Mojzis, Mary Hustava, Anna Viglasky, Paul Viglasky, John Viglasky Sr., Stefan Polc, Matus Gasko, John Gazur, Anna Luptak, unidentified man, Mary Sunderlik, Steve Viglasky, George Zivicky, John Kuzma, Rev. George Majoros, unidentified minister, Eva Valach, John Bozalka, Mary Chmelko, Steve Valentik, Steve Tkacik, Anna Valentik, Ilonka Karabin. Courtesy David Polc.

Wedding of Stefan Simko and Anna Krudy at Ilasco's Slovak Lutheran Church, November 1918. First row, L-R: Mary Babyak, Mildred Viglasky, Anna Zivicky. Second row, L-R: Andy Babyak, Anna Stimel, George Sajban, Ilka Betina, Stefan Simko (groom), Anna Krudy (bride), John Krudy, Anna Viglasky, unidentified man, Anna Hlasnik, Anna Lendak. Third row, L-R: Andy Mikula, Paul Viglasky, unidentified man, George Ukrop, John Kucera, Susan Hlasnik, unidentified woman, unidentified woman, unidentified woman. Back row, L-R: John Slancik, John Sajban, John Viglasky Jr., John Viglasky Sr. Courtesy David Polc.

Slovak dance and festivities. Courtesy Virginia Patrick Arthaud.

Young Folks Circle of the National Slovak Society in Ilasco, 1917. Front row, L-R: Andy Balko, Andy Gasko, George Viglasky, Mike Karabin. Second row, L-R: Mary Mikula, Anna Zivicky, Mary Milcik, Mildred Viglasky, Helen Karabin, Mary Babyak, Steve Valentik. Third row, L-R: Steve Mikula, Mary Bozalka, Herska, Anna Betina, unidentified girl, Anna Valentik, Anna Viglasky, Paul Viglasky, Steve Milcik. Back row, L-R: Andy Mikula, Anna Besina, Andy Babyak, Joe Herska, John Mojzis, Paul Gasko, John Karabin, John Viglasky, unidentified boy, John Polc, Ilka Betina, John Viglasky Sr. Courtesy David Polc.

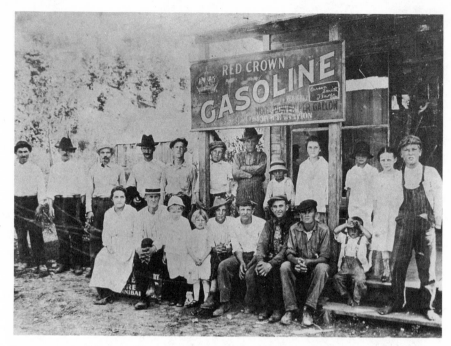

Grocery store of Steve and Anna Milkucik in Monkey Run, 1920. Seated in front, L-R: Anna Kitsock Milkucik, Steve Milkucik, Alex Koblizik, Mildred Kitsock, Andy Golian, Andy Mikula, Charley Rache, Paul Viglasky, Joe Viglasky. Standing in back, L-R: Mike Kitsock, Tony Wojcik, Mikula, Kitsock, Alex Lester, John Kitsock, Carson Smith, Nick Kitsock, Katie Kitsock, Mary Koblizik, Katie Konko, Guy Smith. Courtesy David Polc.

Walter Tatman and Jimmy Homolos, c. late 1920s. Courtesy Jim and Dorothy Tatman.

Velma Northcutt and Sammy Venditti. Courtesy Charles
Glascock.

Three generations of Atlas cement workers, May 1946. L-R, Delbert, George, Merle, Leon, Gerald, and Richard Lee. Courtesy Shirley Lee O'Keefe.

Maurice and Virginia Sanders Andrews with daughter Cheryl in Ilasco, 1948. Courtesy Virginia Sudholt.

Cement company picnic at Hannibal's Clemens Field, c. 1959. Courtesy Fred's Photos.

Depression-era family of Pantaleone and Rosa Genovese on farm near Ilasco. Courtesy Armenia Genovese Erlichman.

Universal Atlas workers and families during safety celebration festivities, June 24, 1936.
Courtesy USX Corporation.

Ilasco immigrants and children during safety celebration festivities, June 24, 1936. L-R, Anna Sirbu, Judy Kristoff, Margaret Valach, Mary Mojzis, Anna Sajban, Elsie Sajban, Anna Sajban. Courtesy USX Corporation.

Universal Atlas quarry workers during safety campaign, September 6, 1935. Courtesy USX Corporation.

Flint pickers and new members of Local 205, United Cement, Lime and Gypsum Workers Union, August 1943. Standing, L-R: Steve Malaga, Paul Gasko, George Sajban, Anna Sajban, John Arthur, unidentified man, Jim Ragan. Seated, L-R: Anna Polc, Ruth Babyak, Omie Tatman, Nettie Viglasky, Fern Stimel, Betty Albert. Courtesy David Polc.

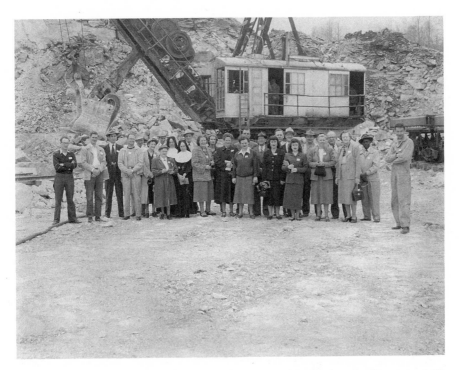

Area teachers touring cement plant during Business-Industry-Education Days, April 27, 1951. Courtesy Fred's Photos.

Workers enjoying beer picnic. Courtesy Fred's Photos.

Universal Atlas laying claim to the heritage of Mark Twain to sell cement. From the *Hannibal Courier-Post,* March 6, 1935. Courtesy USX Corporation.

George Mahan and Governor Guy Park reenacting famous whitewashing scene from Tom Sawyer. From Mark Twain Centennial Program, 1935. Courtesy author.

Superintendent Cleo White and Ilasco's last graduating class. Courtesy Fred's Photos.

Al's Tavern, 1992. Courtesy author.

Remains of Ilasco gymnasium floor buried in thickets, 1992. Courtesy author.

Immigrant tombstones, Marble Creek Cemetery, 1992. Courtesy Kevin Andrews.

Armenia Genovese Erlichman hanging onto her past. Courtesy
Armenia Genovese Erlichman.

(8)

Company Patriotism and the War on Booze, Blacks, and Immigrants, 1910–1930

A round man cannot be expected to fit in a square hole right away. He must have time to modify his shape.

—Mark Twain, *More Tramps Abroad*

Before 1910, efforts by Atlas officials and temperance advocates to rid Ilasco of saloons had failed. However, amid the turmoil created that year by the Missouri militia's occupation of Ilasco, state and county alcohol reformers renewed their campaign for local option. By 1914, aided by a few sympathetic elements in the community, they had succeeded in closing the saloons.

When the United States declared war on Germany in 1917, Atlas officials manipulated patriotic sentiment by emphasizing to workers that loyalty to country also meant loyalty to company. They and many corporate officials supported national prohibition and after the war supported law enforcement's crackdown against violators. Thus, attempts to Americanize Ilasco during and after the war included a concerted campaign to wipe out the widespread illegal manufacture of moonshine. In the eyes of disapproving observers in New London and Hannibal, Ilasco's immigrants and home brew went hand in hand.

It was the explosive strike of 1910 that lent an added sense of urgency to the ongoing countywide war against alcohol. Ilasco's C. M. Jeffers and Atlas official Ludwig Anderson stepped up efforts to establish a Holiness Gospel Mission in the community. Jeffers, who was in the middle of a fund-raising campaign for the mission when he died on February 20, 1911, emphasized the urgency of his efforts in a letter requesting public donations: "We are asking the prayers of all Christians and the aid of all who would like to see a good work prosper where it is greatly needed."[1]

---

1. *Ralls County Record,* March 11 and November 25, 1910. The quote is in a letter from Jeffers to Joe Burnett, September 7, 1910, reproduced on the front page of the *Ralls County Record,* September 9, 1910.

Jeffers also worked with the Woman's Christian Temperance Union (WCTU). During the early stages of the strike of 1910, Alice Scott Abbot, a state WCTU lecturer and organizer, helped to form a local chapter in Ilasco. She and New London's Jennie Alexander, district president and sister of former state representative David Wallace, addressed the opening meeting held at the Holiness Gospel Mission. Elected as officers of the Ilasco chapter were Mrs. James [Rebecca] Tucker, R. Clara Peterson, Mrs. [Nora] Jorgenson, and Mrs. [Alice] West.[2]

The role of these Ilasco women in the WCTU indicates that the local campaign against alcohol was more than simply an external attack on the community or a mere cynical, self-serving effort by Atlas officials to discipline its labor force and increase productivity. Some in the community shared a desire to reduce the destructive impact of alcohol upon family life and community stability. For many women whose husbands abused alcohol, temperance offered at least a partial check against domestic violence and the squandering of household resources in saloons. With the exception of Alice West, whose husband Volney worked as a house carpenter, all of the Ilasco officers of the WCTU were married to men who worked at the cement plant—Milton Jorgenson as a foreman, Bruce Peterson as a teamster, and James Tucker as a repairer of storage cars.[3]

The formation of Law and Order Leagues in Ralls County underscored the growing public hostility toward the abuse of alcohol. Jack Briscoe, T. E. Allison, Joe Burnett, and other prominent citizens of New London created a Law and Order League at a meeting in the courthouse on May 6, 1910. Elected chairman was David Wallace. Also among the founders was Rev. Thomas Wallace, a prohibition lecturer who lived in Tipton, Missouri. He was the brother of Jennie Alexander and David Wallace. Rev. Wallace, who spoke several languages and sometimes served as an interpreter for Ilasco immigrants in the Ralls County Circuit Court, also helped to establish a league in Ilasco. The purpose of these leagues was to pressure law enforcement officers to arrest those guilty of intoxication and the indiscriminate sale of alcohol.[4]

Rev. Wallace noted that of all the places he had visited in the United States and abroad, Ilasco was the one most badly in need of reform. He complained that numerous children were sent to saloons in Ilasco every hour of the day. Atlas,

2. *Hannibal Courier-Post,* May 2, 1910; WCTU, *Proceedings,* 1910, 79, 134. U.S. Federal Manuscript Census, 1910, Saverton township, Ralls County.

3. U.S. Federal Manuscript Census, 1910, Saverton township, Ralls County. On Volney West's drinking, see *Heinbach v. Heinbach et al.,* April term, 1914, 178–79. For a view of temperance as a feminist issue, see Ruth Bordin, *Women and Temperance: The Quest for Power and Liberty, 1873–1900.* See also Barbara Leslie Epstein, *The Politics of Domesticity: Women, Evangelism and Temperance in Nineteenth-Century America.*

4. *Ralls County Record,* May 13 and August 26, 1910. On Wallace's language skills and interpreting for the court, see *Ralls County Record,* September 22 and November 10, 1911.

he acknowledged, "keeps all clean and orderly within its limits, but beyond this lawlessness, profanity, drunkenness and fighting are common." He described the business section that housed Ilasco's five saloons as "a veritable Sodom and Gomorrah—hell's half-acre with the devils turned loose."[5]

The lucrative, exploitative nature of the saloon business, combined with the social problems to which it contributed, disturbed many in the area. Dr. Andrew J. Detweiler of Hannibal regarded Ilasco as "the worst place I ever saw when it comes to liquor."[6] A reputable source informed local newspaper editors that each Ilasco saloon took in more than one hundred dollars per day. "This is quite a sum to take from the workmen at the cement plant," complained the *Ralls County Times*. "Is the booze worth it?"[7]

Rev. Wallace did not always find a receptive audience in Ilasco. In August 1910, attacks on him at a public meeting led to the arrests of John Hinkson, A. J. Meyer, and Charles Churchill for disturbing Wallace's peace. Meyer and Churchill allegedly threw rocks at Wallace "from the rear." Hinkson owned The Last Chance saloon in Ilasco, and Churchill, too, operated a saloon. Meyer worked as an oiler at the cement plant. A local newspaper cheered their arrests and convictions: "Lawlessness is on the wane in this county and it will not be long before it will be dangerous for any one to assault a man when he is engaged in trying to better the conditions of those who are in the habit of guzzling whiskey and beer."[8]

The *Ralls County Record,* which supported statewide prohibition, reported favorably on the coordinated drive against alcohol in Ilasco. It urged the public to support C. M. Jeffers's fund-raising campaign for a permanent Holiness Mission building. It also reported on attendance at the mission, noting especially the number of immigrant children in the congregation.[9]

Ilasco's saloons were under attack in a variety of ways, but perhaps most interesting was an attempt by an Ilasco woman to prosecute owners and merchants for selling liquor to her husband. In the fall of 1910, Maude Lee sued Arthur R. Moore, Herman Schwartz, and William Moore for allegedly selling liquor to her husband, Delbert, an Atlas worker who, she said, was well known as a heavy drinker. According to her, these saloon owners had sold liquor to Delbert on several occasions in spite of her repeated warnings. She charged that they had violated Missouri's dramshop laws by providing her husband with alcohol against her announced wishes, even though they were aware of his drinking problems.

5. Quoted in *Ralls County Record,* August 26, 1910.
6. *Heinbach v. Heinbach et al.,* April term, 1918, 863.
7. *Ralls County Times,* August 19, 1910.
8. *Ralls County Record,* August 26, 1910; *Ralls County Times,* September 16, 1910; U.S. Federal Manuscript Census, 1910, Saverton township, Ralls County.
9. *Ralls County Record,* September 23 and November 25, 1910. On November 20, 1910, forty-five people attended services, including twenty or twenty-five immigrant children.

Ralls County authorities granted her the right to sue as a poor person entitled to free legal representation.

The trial began in the circuit court on November 3, 1910, but the jury ruled against her, assessing her court costs. Undaunted, she filed another case on March 3, 1911. She sued for five hundred dollars in statutory damages and requested that the defendants' dramshop bond of two thousand dollars also be awarded her. The case was dismissed, however, after the defendants complained that she was no longer a resident of Missouri, but had moved to Illinois. They also countered that she, herself, had bought liquor for her husband and even drank with him on many occasions.[10]

Ilasco saloon owners apparently complained about the conduct of law enforcement officers in the campaign against alcohol. They were forced by authorities to contribute to a special fund for police protection. The Ralls County Court, in response to charges of official corruption, extortion, and discriminatory treatment of Ilasco residents, authorized a grand jury investigation. In a report presented at the end of the court's November term, 1913, the jury assured the public that Ilasco officers were enforcing the law "without favor or discrimination toward any persons or classes . . . under circumstances and conditions presenting greater difficulty than elsewhere in Ralls County." The report recommended, however, that "any special funds collected, by agreement, from dramshop keepers at Ilasco, for police protection, shall be paid to the County Clerk or other official to be designated by said court, and that the practice of payment by the dramshop keepers direct to the officer be forthwith discontinued."[11]

Although the new WCTU branch in Ilasco soon folded, county temperance reformers organized another local option campaign at the end of December 1913. Rev. W. G. Hooper, district president of the Missouri Anti-Saloon League, lent organizational and financial backing to the petition drive to put local option on the ballot. The campaign was coordinated by several ministers, former Prosecuting Attorney Jack Briscoe, and former State Representative David Wallace. Organizers

10. U.S. Federal Manuscript Census, 1910, Saverton township, Ralls County; *Maud Lee v. William Moore,* September 24, 1910, case no. 9365; *Maud Lee v. Arthur R. Moore,* September 24, 1910, case no. 9366; *Maud Lee v. Herman Schwartz,* September 24, 1910, case no. 9367; *Maud Lee, State Ex Rel v. Arthur Moore et al.,* October 6, 1910, case no. 9371; *Maud Lee, State Ex Rel v. Arthur Moore et al.,* October 7, 1910, case no. 9372; *Maud Lee, State Ex Rel v. Herman Schwartz,* October 7, 1910, case no. 9373; *Maud Lee, Ralls County Ex Rel v. William Moore,* March 3, 1911, case no. 9431; all in Ralls County, Office of the Circuit Clerk and Recorder. See also *Hannibal Courier-Post,* November 3, 1910; *Ralls County Record,* November 11, 1910, and March 24, 1911. At the time the case was dismissed in March 1911, Mill Number Five at the cement plant was shut down. This perhaps explains why Maude was no longer in Missouri. Some Atlas employees from the area around Hull and Kinderhook, Illinois, returned there during slack times at the plant.
11. A copy of this report is in *Ralls County Record,* November 28, 1913.

presented a petition to the county court with 823 signatures calling for a special election to determine the fate of saloons. By a majority of 320, voters on February 14, 1914, outlawed saloons in Ralls County, the last county in northeast Missouri to become dry.[12]

This, of course, did not mean the end of drinking in Ilasco. John B. Herl, a Hannibal agent of the Dick and Brothers Brewing Company, sent a driver there to take orders for beer and then deliver the goods. Soon after local option went into effect, however, George Foehringer, Herl's driver, was arrested and convicted in Justice of the Peace Bruce Peterson's court in Ilasco for violating the local option law. The case was appealed to the Ralls County Circuit Court, where Foehringer's conviction was upheld. He paid a three-hundred-dollar fine, but Andrew Pavalenda, an interpreter who worked with him, was acquitted by the jury.[13]

A few months after Foehringer's conviction, about 150 citizens of Perry, Center, and New London publicly offered a twenty-five-dollar reward to anyone furnishing evidence leading to the conviction of violators of the local option law. They announced that Ilasco Constable T. B. Wilson would receive a reward for Foehringer's arrest and conviction. They praised him for working on other similar cases whose outcomes had not yet been determined.[14]

Ilasco typically was the major object of concern in regard to alcohol, but county authorities may not have been so diligent and evenhanded in their treatment of New London liquor law violators, especially drugstore owners with better class, family, and political connections. By the summer of 1915, Prosecuting Attorney T. E. Allison was forced to respond to public charges that leaders of the local option movement had lost confidence in his commitment to prosecuting liquor law violators. At least in part, these accusations grew out of a case against William A. Conn, a drugstore owner in New London who was charged with the illegal sale of alcohol. When officials agreed not to prosecute in exchange for a mere promise that no more liquor would be sold there, editors of the *Ralls County Times* cheered: "We are glad that the matter is settled . . . We do not believe that any of the druggists are now violating the law and everybody is feeling good over the matter. Let everybody pull for the town and put away your hammers."[15]

Local option had an important impact on Ilasco's economic and social life. Many small businesses soon closed, leaving residents more dependent on the

12. *Ralls County Record,* December 26, 1913, January 2 and 9, 1914, and February 20, 1914; WCTU, *Proceedings,* 1913, 138; *The American Issue,* January 8, 1914, 4; *The American Issue,* March 5, 1914, 4. On local option and the coming of prohibition to Missouri, see G. K. Renner, "Prohibition Comes to Missouri, 1910–1919."

13. *Ralls County Times,* August 28, 1914; *Ralls County Record,* November 20, 1914.

14. *Ralls County Record,* January 29, 1915.

15. *Ralls County Times,* August 20 and September 3, 1915.

Ilasco Supply Company. The closing of saloons also deprived residents of important meeting places where residents could engage in cultural exchange and discuss politics, work, and family and community affairs. Saloon keepers had often provided a banking function, too. They cashed workers' paychecks and sometimes made short-term loans to patrons. In addition, brewery agents in Hannibal sometimes provided such services to Ilasco workers. This was true in the case of Herl, whose Dick and Brothers Brewing Company once operated a distributing house in Ilasco. "Well, I went down," he recalled, "I went for about two years twice a month or once a month and took some money down there and cashed checks for those people when they got paid off."[16]

As alcohol reformers often pointed out, this could eat up workers' earnings on paydays and squeeze family resources. On the other hand, since there were no banks in Ilasco, saloon keepers provided a valuable service. They reduced the need for workers to make the three-mile trip to Hannibal to cash their checks. Besides, as historian Madelon Powers notes, "Many workers, especially first-generation immigrants, found the stiff institutionalism of banking confusing and intimidating."[17]

The disappearance of Ilasco's saloons perhaps deprived patrons of another important service. As the result of marketing strategies by the liquor industry during this period, American saloon keepers were often provided with a plentiful, cheap supply of food that would then be offered free to regular customers who bought at least a five-cent beer. For many workers, this became a major daily source of food. Alcohol reformers like the Rev. Thomas Wallace complained about the number of children entering Ilasco's saloons each day, but many of these children may have gone there, in part, to take advantage of their father's "free lunch."[18]

In the repressive atmosphere after the United States entered World War I, users of alcohol were often seen as unpatriotic. Atlas officials also linked lower work productivity to the use of alcohol and even tobacco. They shared the views of those who put their faith in big business to reform the moral habits of employees as part of the campaign for greater efficiency and profits. In this sense, workers' loyalty to the Allied war effort went hand in hand with loyalty to the company.[19]

16. *Heinbach v. Heinbach et al.,* April term, 1918, 198–99, 252, 685; Madelon Powers, " 'The Poor Man's Friend': Saloonkeepers, Workers, and the Code of Reciprocity in U.S. Barrooms, 1870–1920," 8; Ivan Cizmic, "Yugoslav Immigrants in the U.S. Labor Movement, 1880–1920," in Dirk Hoerder, ed., *American Labor and Immigration History, 1877–1920s: Recent European Research,* 179–80.

17. " 'Poor Man's Friend,' " 8.

18. Ibid., 6–7.

19. "Talk III: A Losing Fight," *The Atlas Bulletin* (June 1917): 2–4; "Read This," *The Atlas Bulletin* (August 1917): 5.

Atlas initiated policies to ensure this and to Americanize Ilasco. Shortly after the United States entered the war, Ilasco plant Superintendent W. H. Baker sponsored a "patriotic demonstration" at a flag-raising ceremony on a Saturday morning at the plant. Even though it was Saturday, Ilasco school children, including many immigrants, were dispatched to the plant for the occasion. They sang "America" after hearing a brief speech by Baker. Several hundred workers attended the ceremony. Along with the children, they ceremonially picked up approximately six hundred small flags that dropped from a much larger flag when it unfurled.[20]

Atlas officials promoted local support for the Allied war effort. Plant Superintendent Baker played a highly visible role in the drive to sell liberty bonds, and Herbert Hoover appointed attorney George A. Mahan to spearhead food conservation efforts on behalf of the United States Food Administration. Atlas officials at the Ilasco plant devoted two acres of land to growing vegetables for use in the company restaurants. They set aside more land for raising corn and other food for horses and cattle. They also doled out 202 plots, or War Gardens, to selected workers, ninety-six of whom were immigrants who displayed undisputed company loyalty and patriotism. These plots covered fourteen acres of land. Atlas publicly touted the value of these War Gardens: "There are Austrians and Hungarians working side by side with Americans and Italians, with not an attempt to take an inch of ground from the other, nor to appropriate each other's crops . . . It is an interesting sight to see them rushing to their gardens after quitting-time at night and carrying home buckets and baskets full of vegetables with an air of accomplishment and reward."[21]

Despite Atlas's rosy description of immigrant cooperation in the drive to expand food production at the Ilasco plant, much harsher attitudes toward immigrants were gaining force. The *Ralls County Record* called for changes in immigration laws to make it harder to acquire United States citizenship. The newspaper also recommended that immigrants not be granted the right to vote before "long years of residence and ample proof of loyalty." This would curb much labor unrest, which the newspaper attributed to uneducated foreigners who did not appreciate the responsibilities that accompanied suffrage. Such restrictions, according to the newspaper's editors, were harsh but vital to the national welfare. "The time is here," warned the newspaper, "when the

20. *Hannibal Courier-Post,* May 5, 1917, and *Ralls County Record,* May 11, 1917.

21. *Hannibal Courier-Post,* June 8, 1917; Missouri Council of Defense, *Missouri On Guard* 1 (November 1917): 1; "900 Atlas Farmers," *The Atlas Circle* 3 (May 1918): 4; "More than 200 War Gardens at Hannibal Plant," *The Atlas Circle* 4 (August 1918): 6. On Hoover's appointment of Mahan, see *Hannibal Morning Journal,* October 18, 1917.

United States can no longer afford to pose as an asylum for the oppressed of all nations."[22]

At a meeting of the Missouri Council of Defense held in Hannibal, a resolution was passed instructing the Americanization Committee to draw up recommendations on how to require all prospective citizens to have a speaking knowledge of English when they take out their first naturalization papers. The Committee recommended that all immigrants who had not completed their naturalization be barred from voting. At a subsequent meeting in Jefferson City on June 8, 1918, the Missouri Council of Defense endorsed this and urged election officials to deny registration and voting to immigrants who had filed their first naturalization papers more than five years before the election or date of registration. The council recommended abolishing use of the German language in the state.[23]

Dr. Frederick B. Mumford, chairman of the Missouri Council of Defense, appointed county councils to coordinate and promote support for the Allied war effort. These councils were usually dominated by commercial interests. Mumford's appointees to the Ralls County council—C. T. Lamb (chairman), Walter Curd, Gil Richards, B. A. McElroy, E. W. Keithly, J. O. Allison, and C. R. Spalding—did not include a single representative from Ilasco. S. W. Burden, an Atlas bookkeeper, was named to head the Saverton township council. The Ralls County sheriff appointed Nelson Brown, who managed Atlas's "Family" stables, and Constable S. D. Charpentier as registrars to supervise selective service registration in Ilasco. These appointments put Atlas in a position to monitor workers' wartime attitudes and behavior.[24]

President Wilson created the War Labor Board to ensure industrial peace for the Allied war effort. Five AFL representatives and five business representatives sat on the board cochaired by Frank P. Walsh and former President William Howard Taft. The board outlawed strikes and lockouts, intervened to regulate wages and working conditions, and protected the right of workers to join trade unions. However, nonunion workers could not be compelled to join unions,

---

22. *Ralls County Record,* July 20, 1917.

23. Missouri Council of Defense, *Missouri On Guard* 2 (June 1918): 1, and *Missouri On Guard* 2 (August 1918): 1.

24. Secretary to C. T. Lamb, Chairman Ralls County Council of Defense, undated letter, and Geo. L. Elam, Secretary, to Wm. F. Saunders, Secretary, Missouri Council of Defense, July 19, 1917, Missouri Council of Defense Papers, folder 1070, WHMC–Columbia; *Ralls County Record,* May 25 and June 22, 1917. On S. W. Burden's occupation as an Atlas bookkeeper, see the U.S. Federal Manuscript Census, 1910, Saverton township, Ralls County. On the Missouri Council of Defense, see Christopher C. Gibbs, *The Great Silent Majority: Missouri's Resistance to World War I,* especially chap. 3, and Lawrence O. Christensen, "Missouri's Responses to World War I: The Missouri Council of Defense," 34–44.

and organized labor could not undertake to change the status of nonunionized plants such as Atlas's during the war. Instead, the War Labor Board supervised the implementation of employee representation plans in such plants.[25]

Atlas officials granted workers at the Ilasco plant a 12 percent pay raise in July 1917. As part of Atlas's advertising stunts in the Liberty Bond drive, plant workers posed for photos that featured them as "Atlas's Kaiser Kanners" next to a thermometer measuring campaign subscriptions. When Atlas editors included snapshots and brief biographical profiles of workers in company publications, as they often routinely did, they highlighted workers' loyalty to the company.[26]

Among Ralls County's 897 men who reported for the first draft registration on June 5, 1917, the largest number of registrants (135) from any precinct in the county came from Ilasco. During the final registration on September 12, 1918, Ilasco furnished 265 of the 1,416 registrants. According to statistics published by the *Ralls County Record,* a total of 2,419 county draft registrants had reported as of October 1, 1918. There were 349 Atlas employees from around the country who served in the military during the war. Eight of them lost their lives.[27]

It is hard to determine the level of support or opposition to the war among Ilasco's residents, but newspaper information suggests that eligible inductees were not eager to become soldiers. By August 1917, when 425 Ralls County men had been notified to report for their physical examinations, only 89 of the 214 who passed their exam did not claim an exemption. Many of those who claimed marriage or alien exemptions were from Ilasco, as were several who did not report at all. At the behest of Governor Frederick Gardner, the *Ralls County Record* soon reprinted a letter from General Enoch Crowder entitled "Concerning Deserters." The letter reminded the public that failure to appear before local draft boards constituted desertion. "Read it," warned the newspaper's editors, "as it may inform some of the people of Ralls County along some lines they had not thought of."[28]

Some of Ilasco's residents, including George R. Ragland, Rocco Arcuri, Francis Ayres, John Berghian, Frank Fontana, and Christ Politarhas, were among the first Ralls County inductees. Immigrants were under particular pressure to join

---

25. Philip S. Foner, *History of the Labor Movement in the United States,* vol. 7, *Labor and World War I, 1914–1918,* 338–45; Joseph G. Rayback, *A History of American Labor,* 273–75.

26. *Ralls County Record,* July 27, 1917; *The Atlas Bulletin* (November 1917): 13–14.

27. *Ralls County Record,* June 8, 1917, September 27 and October 4, 1918. For a list of Atlas employees who served in the military during World War I, see the back cover of *The Atlas Bulletin,* November 1917; "Atlas Honor Roll, Part I, of Men in Active Service," *The Atlas Circle* 4 (October 1918): 3–5; "Atlas Honor Roll, Part III, of Men in Active Service," *The Atlas Circle* 4 (January 1919): 17–20. A list of draft registrants at Ilasco can be found in U.S. Selective Service System, Ralls County, 1917–1918, folders 319, 320, WHMC–Columbia.

28. *Ralls County Record,* August 10 and October 5, 1917.

the military, and local authorities and wartime boosters cut them little slack if they did not. Ilasco residents like Martin Valentik, Pantaleone Genovese, Simon Radu, Antonio Arcuri, John Scampoli, Andrew Ukrop, and many others who claimed military exemptions based on their alien status drew fire from local newspapers. The *Ralls County Record* blasted them as "vipers" and "ingrates" and urged their deportation.[29]

In the face of such pressures, some of Ilasco's immigrants contributed to the Allied war effort in other ways. For example, members of the Rumanian Ardeleana Society took up a collection at a picnic in October 1917 and donated the money to the Hannibal Red Cross "to help America win the war." They did this shortly after a fire had destroyed all of the supplies of the Hannibal chapter of the Red Cross. Chapter chairman R. B. Goodson, Hannibal attorney W. T. Myers, who worked as a special agent for the Federal Bureau of Investigation during the war, and W. B. Pettibone, Hannibal chairman of the Marion County Council of Defense, feared that the fire was the result of German sabotage.[30]

When Ilasco's immigrants applied for United States citizenship during and after the war, they discovered that their wartime allegiances and behavior often determined whether they were granted citizenship. In December 1917, when a Hungarian immigrant identified by the *Ralls County Record* as Stethen Poliz applied for naturalization papers in the United States District Court at Hannibal, Judge D. P. Dyer asked him which country he would fight for if given the chance. After Poliz replied, "Hungary," Dyer immediately ejected him from the courtroom.[31]

Even into the late 1920s, immigrants seeking U.S. citizenship ran into trouble on this issue. Martin Valentik, a Slovak who filed a naturalization petition in Judge Dyer's court, could only watch in May 1926 as fellow Slovak Martin Kisel received his citizenship. Kisel had fought overseas for the United States, but Valentik's failure to provide military service during the war still stood in the way of his gaining citizenship. The same was true of Italian Antonio Arcuri in December

29. *Ralls County Record,* August 10, August 17, September 21, and October 5, 1917, and February 14, 1919.

30. *Hannibal Morning Journal,* October 21, 1917. On the suspicious nature of the fire, see Edward J. Brennan to W. T. Myers, October 12, 1917; W. T. Myers to Edward J. Brennan, October 13, 1917; and W. H. Hays to Department of Justice, October 15, 1917; all in case no. 21,700, microfilm reel 358, FBI Investigative Case Files, RG 65, NA. The list of Ilasco contributors to the Hannibal Red Cross chapter included Dan Cornea, Jacob Radu, John Manzat, Petru Limbean, John Ursu, John Bumba, Vasilie and Eva Gherman, Ispas Apostol, Dionise Blagu, John Dicu, Ignot Viorel, John Avramut, John Turcu, Daniel Todor, Michael Chinndea, Petru Stanciu, Isidor Lanka, Simon Radu, John Daian, John Moxin, Joan Moldovan, Nicolae Turcia, Luchian Negrea, John Bogdan, John Moga, Daniel Sirbu, Visaion Istrat, Josef Opripa, Sandu Gutia, Milhail David, and the Ardeleana Society.

31. *Ralls County Record,* December 14, 1917.

1921 when a naturalization officer from St. Louis notified the court of his wartime behavior. Judge Dyer denied Arcuri's application. "I will not knowingly admit to citizenship any man," he said, "who does not think that this country is worth fighting for."[32]

Postmaster T. B. Wilson, a former constable, registered aliens living in Ilasco, and like all Americans, Ilasco's residents were under enormous pressure to help finance the war by purchasing War Savings Stamps and Liberty Bonds. The Wilson administration promoted four Liberty Bond campaigns during the war and a Victory Bond drive immediately after the war. Relying on a combination of propaganda and coercion, war boosters made purchasing a government bond a test of one's patriotism and especially stressed the importance of such purchases by small subscribers. This meant that people on the local level listened to a steady drumbeat of propaganda urging them to reach deep into their pockets, even when wartime inflation and limited resources restricted their ability to contribute. An array of canvassers, including the Boy Scouts and Camp Fire Girls, combed towns and farms to sell bonds, while "Four-Minute Men" cornered moviegoers during intermissions and addressed public rallies. Local councils of defense used churches and newspapers to promote the purchase of War Savings Stamps and Liberty Bonds, and employers pressured workers to do the same.[33]

Although all Missouri counties met their subscription quotas in these drives, the fact that middle- and upper-class people and corporations were most likely to invest in war bonds makes it hard to determine how widespread the level of popular participation was.[34] In the second Liberty Bond campaign, for example, Ralls County raised $92,600, easily exceeding its quota of $53,500, but only ninety-six subscribers, or 8 percent of the population, participated. Although Ralls was one of only eleven Missouri counties to achieve a subscription rate of more than 5 percent of their population, the low rate suggests a lack of widespread enthusiasm for the government campaign. Ralls County farmers and workers were the least able to endure greater immediate deprivation in exchange for long-range investments that yielded lower interest than bank savings accounts.[35]

When the nation geared up for the Third Liberty Loan drive in the spring of 1918, the Ralls County Council of Defense set a county quota of $267,350, or twenty dollars for every man, woman, and child. Ilasco's share was $26,154, the

---

32. *Hannibal Courier-Post,* May 26, 1926; Judge Dyer quoted in *Hannibal Courier-Post,* December 5, 1921.

33. *Hannibal Morning Journal,* February 3, 1918. On the Liberty Loan campaigns in Missouri, see Gibbs, *Great Silent Majority,* chap. 4.

34. Gibbs, *Great Silent Majority,* concludes that most Missourians did not support the war. For an opposing view, see Lawrence O. Christensen, "Popular Reaction to World War I in Missouri."

35. *Ralls County Record,* April 12, 1918; Gibbs, *Great Silent Majority,* 89–91.

highest quota assessed to any school district in the county. From this formula, we can deduce that there were 1,308 people living in the Ilasco school district, still the most heavily populated in the county. New London had the next highest quota, $21,685, which was based on a school district population of 1,084. Editors of the *Ralls County Record* warned that local residents who could afford but refused to buy bonds would be required to file a yellow card with the federal government. Indexes with the names of such persons provided by neighbors were already on file in St. Louis. These cards contained names and addresses, and the amounts that these individuals could allegedly afford. "The man who dodges his financial obligations this month," warned the editors, "will be considered just as much of a slacker as the one who is an army or navy slacker."[36]

Based on newspaper assessments when the drive ended, Ilasco apparently did not meet its quota. Local officials publicly complained that some who could afford it did not contribute much to the campaign. They scheduled additional meetings in Ilasco in an effort to force it to meet its share.[37]

During the Fourth Liberty Loan drive inaugurated on September 28, 1918, Ralls County officials prepared for the biggest campaign yet. Meetings were held in all school districts and available churches in an effort to meet the county quota of $270,000. The *Ralls County Record* published a letter from county campaign chairman E. W. Keithly to the public. In this letter, Keithly tried injecting God into the bond-raising business. "The Lord loveth a cheerful giver," he prodded, "and it is our deliberate judgment that He has respect for a clean, wholesome, honest, patriotic fighter, but that of all things contemptible in His sight it must be the individual who shirks from his plain patriotic duty."[38]

Ilasco apparently failed again to meet its quota. It is unclear whether the money that Atlas officials raised directly from employees at the local plant was credited to Ralls or Marion County, or perhaps divided between the two. Plant officials, office workers, and other employees who lived in Hannibal may have had their contributions counted in Marion County. We know, for example, that plant Superintendent W. A. Baker was a leading contender for the trophy cup offered by the Liberty Loan Association in Hannibal. Atlas sold forty-five thousand dollars in bonds to approximately seven hundred local plant employees during the First Liberty Loan drive.[39]

36. *Ralls County Record,* April 5 and June 14, 1918. According to the same newspaper on April 12, 1918, Ralls County's quota for the Third Liberty Loan drive was $190,700.

37. *Ralls County Record,* July 5, 1918.

38. *Ralls County Record,* September 27 and October 4, 1918.

39. *Hannibal Courier-Post,* June 8, 1917; "Hannibal," *The Atlas Bulletin* (November 1917): 13. The *Ralls County Record,* October 4 and 11, 1918, did not note that Ilasco had failed to meet its subscription share in the Fourth Liberty Loan campaign, but it did not include Ilasco when it listed school districts that had met their quotas.

Neither is it entirely clear how much pressure Atlas applied to squeeze bond purchases out of its employees. Some employers, either directly or through implied pressure, threatened workers with loss of their jobs if they did not buy war bonds. In June 1917, about seventy-five or eighty workers at Atlas's plant in Northampton, Pennsylvania, threatened to quit if they were not released from pledges that they had made two days earlier to buy Liberty Bonds. Atlas president John R. Morron summoned the Bureau of Investigation to see if German sabotage was at work. It turned out, however, that the disgruntled workers had bought the Liberty Bonds simply out of fear of losing their jobs. Several foremen had pressured them into buying bonds which they complained that they could not afford.[40]

Atlas no doubt used a combination of carrot-and-stick incentives, including taking advantage of a contest sponsored by the Portland Cement Association to award a fifty-dollar Liberty Bond to an association member who provided the best suggestion on how to expand the association's activities during the war. This was obviously geared toward managerial and sales employees; production workers, especially immigrants, probably bought war bonds more out of a fear of losing their jobs if they refused to participate. Nationwide, 9,063 Atlas employees bought $718,600 in bonds during the first four Liberty Loan drives.[41]

The condescension that county officials, newspaper editors, and many middle-class residents expressed toward Ilasco meant that the community, despite its large population compared to other towns in the county, often did not achieve representation on local committees. When the Department of Agriculture sent demonstrators to Ralls County in July 1917 to give women lessons in the latest methods of canning vegetables and fruits, L. C. Northcutt of the county Farm Bureau scheduled demonstration meetings in Center, New London, and Perry, but not in Ilasco. In 1919, when the Young Women's Christian Association (YWCA) launched a fund-raising drive to finance in part its national campaign to "Americanize the Foreign-Born Girl," a Ralls County committee was established that included women from Saverton, New London, Center, Perry, and Spalding, but not from Ilasco. As targets of the YWCA's campaign, Ilasco women apparently deserved no place in its planning, according to those in charge.[42]

Although the war ended in November 1918, boosters foisted the Fifth Victory Loan campaign on a war-weary public still besieged by the YWCA, Red Cross, Salvation Army, Boy Scouts, and countless other organizations asking for money. To guard against a decline in the public spirit of patriotic sacrifice now that the

40. Webster Spates, Report, September 28, 1917, case no. 65,775, microfilm roll 427, FBI Investigative Case Files, RG 65, NA.
41. Gibbs, *Great Silent Majority,* 87; "Win a Liberty Bond," *The Atlas Circle* 3 (May 1918): 3; "Backing Up the Boys with Liberty Bonds," *The Atlas Circle* 4 (October 1918), inside front cover.
42. *Ralls County Record,* July 6, 1917, and April 11, 1919.

war was over, Ralls County officials brought a tank and several Four-Minute Men up from St. Louis to kick off the Victory Loan drive. Residents of New London were treated to a parade featuring the tank, which had been used in combat overseas, and numerous soldiers and speakers. About thirty Ralls County veterans joined the procession behind the tank, and afterward meetings were held to organize what became a disappointing fund-raising drive. The rate of statewide public participation fell to approximately one-half of what it had been during the Fourth Liberty Loan campaign.[43]

As the war ended, Atlas tried to impress upon workers that competition in the postwar cement industry and company loyalty required no less sacrifice than had the Allied war effort. Company publications contained poems with a clear message for employees who criticized "Old Man Atlas": "Be loyal to the boss, my son, if you would make a hit; and if you do not want his mon, be sportsmanlike and quit." The message was also clear to war veterans returning to Atlas: " . . . they're coming back to us bigger men for their experiences. They are going to jump into their work with the same vigor that carried them victorious to the banks of the Rhine, and just as they have carried their banner to victory in the greatest of wars, so will they take up the fight to keep the Atlas banner truly the standard of supremacy in commercial warfare."[44]

Opponents of alcohol had taken advantage of the patriotic atmosphere during World War I to rally public support for national prohibition by linking patriotism, prohibition, and profits. Many reformers endorsed prohibition as the antidote for America's social problems, and for many employers such as Atlas, prohibition was the culmination of a long-standing campaign against transient workers whose inefficiency and accidents on the job they blamed on alcohol. "Industrial capital required national prohibition," writes historian John J. Rumbarger, "as a solution to a major problem inherent in economic expansion; the problem of transient and undisciplined workers who, in the context of political society, were believed to be inimical to general political order."[45]

This meant that after the 18th Amendment prohibiting the manufacture and sale of alcohol was ratified in June 1919, working-class communities invited the strict surveillance of authorities. This was certainly true of Ilasco, where area law enforcement officials hounded immigrants. Attitudes in nearby Hannibal and New London toward Ilasco's immigrant prohibition violators were particularly vicious.[46]

---

43. *Ralls County Record,* April 18, 1919; Gibbs, *Great Silent Majority,* 157–58.
44. *The Atlas Circle* 4 (January 1919): 17; *The Atlas Almanac* 6 (November 1919): 12.
45. *Profits, Power,* 185.
46. For a study of how race, class, and family shaped the struggle over prohibition in two Arkansas Delta towns, see Jeannie M. Whayne, "The Significance of Race, Class, and Family in the Battle for Prohibition in Small Town Arkansas."

Atlas officials played a leading role in the local prohibition enforcement campaign. George Mahan headed a new Law and Order League formed in Hannibal in July 1919, and Ludwig Anderson also played a prominent role in the organization. After federal enforcement agents described Hannibal as "one of the wettest spots in Missouri," supporters formed a new law enforcement league at a meeting in Hannibal's Park Methodist Church on December 8, 1921. Federal officers addressed the meeting, at which Judge E. T. Cameron was elected president and W. T. Myers secretary-treasurer. The league hoped to prosecute landlords who rented buildings to convicted prohibition violators. In a move with special implications for Ilasco residents, members adopted a resolution introduced by Hannibal attorney Roy Hamlin, calling for the deportation of foreigners convicted of violating the law.[47]

Just a week later, Ludwig Anderson gave the invocation at another meeting of the league held at the courthouse in Hannibal. C. E. Miller, a justice of the peace in Ilasco, outlined the campaign for law enforcement there and pointed out that many immigrants were making moonshine liquor. He cautioned, however, against deporting violators: "A great many of them want to go back and if we deported them it might be just the thing they wanted."[48]

In the months preceding the above meetings of the Law and Order League, several moonshine raids in Ilasco had led to arrests and convictions. On June 4, 1921, Ralls County Sheriff E. S. Holt and a federal prohibition officer raided the soft-drink parlor of Eva and Vasilie Gherman, Rumanians who had lived in the United States for more than ten years. Officers confiscated a still, two barrels of raisin mash, and about a gallon of moonshine. After Eva assaulted them, they handcuffed her while they searched the premises. Vasilie told officers that he was making the stuff for his own use and for an employee. He claimed that the man who worked for them would quit unless they furnished him with whiskey.[49]

Eva, "a noted character in illicit whiskey making," was arrested in another raid less than two months later. She was fined one hundred dollars in a state court and then faced a federal grand jury indictment for having two stills in her possession. Agents caught her selling wine to a customer in her soft-drink parlor. J. O. Allison, her attorney, pleaded guilty on her behalf and tried to evoke sympathy from Judge Pat Dyer in the U.S. District Court, but Dyer fined her an additional $150.[50]

Before Dyer sentenced Gherman, the assistant district attorney told him, "We are having considerable trouble down there [Ilasco], your honor." During the

47. *Hannibal Courier-Post,* July 7, 1919, and December 9, 1921.
48. Quoted in *Hannibal Courier-Post,* December 16, 1921.
49. *Ralls County Record,* June 10, 1921.
50. *Ralls County Record,* July 29, 1921; *Hannibal Courier-Post,* December 7, 1921.

same weekend of Gherman's most recent arrest, Ilasco Constable E. M. Sanders and federal prohibition officers also conducted raids that led to the arrests of John Daian, John Ruttkur, John Lendak, George Urka, Charles Sektor, and Mary Simu, all of whom were immigrants. Mary Simu was fined two hundred dollars, and each of the men except Daian was fined one hundred dollars. Daian, arrested several times for making moonshine, was assessed fines ranging from two hundred to five hundred dollars.[51]

Earlier that spring, a raid conducted by federal agents, Constable Sanders, and other Ralls County officers led to the arrest and conviction of James Astorino, an Italian immigrant and World War I veteran, on two counts in the U.S. District Court in Hannibal. Unable to find a steady job after leaving the military, Astorino had been supported by his brother, Sam, who operated a small store in Ilasco. Jimmy could not pay his five-hundred-dollar fine, and on May 26, 1921, he was committed to jail, where he remained until July 1.[52]

As Astorino's case illustrates, making moonshine served an important economic function for residents, particularly during slack times at the cement plant. The flurry of arrests in Ilasco in 1921 occurred at a time of national economic depression. Atlas had shut down Mill Number Five on January 1, 1921, throwing approximately one thousand persons out of work, and did not restart it until March 1922. In addition, Atlas cut wages by 25 percent for the remaining workers. For unemployed workers with few resources to draw on, the manufacturing of home brew undoubtedly picked up the economic slack.[53]

For James Zugras, however, making moonshine proved especially costly. In April 1923, local officers found two copper stills, two worms, and about 450 gallons of mash hidden in a gully near his house. Zugras was convicted on three counts, fined three hundred dollars, and sentenced to thirty days in jail on each count. He appealed to the Missouri Supreme Court, which upheld his convictions. Around the same time, Zugras's wife died. Unable to take care of his two daughters, Angelina and Elsie, he put them in the Home for the Friendless, a children's home in Hannibal, and moved to Detroit.[54]

---

51. *Hannibal Courier-Post,* July 23 and December 7, 1921; *Ralls County Record,* November 9 and 23, 1923; Circuit Court Record, book 29, 559, Marion County, Office of the Circuit Clerk and Recorder, Palmyra, Mo.

52. *Ralls County Record,* May 20, 1921; *Hannibal Courier-Post,* July 1, 1921; U.S. Federal Manuscript Census, 1920, Saverton township, Ralls County.

53. *Ralls County Record,* January 21 and February 11, 1921, and March 24, 1922; *New York Times,* February 10, 1921.

54. *Ralls County Record,* November 9, 1923; *The State v. James Zugras,* December 31, 1924; *State of Missouri v. James Zugras,* February 7 and April 26, 1923, case nos. 11,627 and 11,650, Ralls County, Office of the Circuit Clerk and Recorder, New London; Angelina Zugras and Elsie Zugras, date of admission, February 6, 1926, Home for the Friendless

Against the national backdrop of intense anti-immigrant prejudice in the 1920s, Ilasco's immigrants were particularly vulnerable since they were more isolated from larger urban populations. Prohibition officers relied on Ilasco as an important source of revenue extracted from those such as Ispos Apostol, Mary Venditti, Joe Hustava, Mike Kitsock, Frank Polletti, Simon Radu, and many others caught with stills and fined in the 1920s and early 1930s. Moonshine raids were so common that members of the community learned how to anticipate them. Jim Tatman recalled what had become common knowledge in Ilasco, that if Constable Riley ("Pappy") Hill had his cane with him, it was a sure bet that revenue agents were on their way.[55]

The steady parade of Ilasco immigrants before Judge Dyer in the U.S. District Court suggested a biased policy by local officials and federal agents. Even Judge Dyer called attention to this. On one occasion, after listening to the names of those who were under indictment, he asked rhetorically if all prohibition violators were immigrants. He urged "that some of the natives who have been violating the said law be brought to the bar of justice."[56]

After the war, the Hannibal chapter of the Daughters of the American Revolution (DAR) spearheaded a drive to Americanize Ilasco and received a prize for making the largest contribution in Missouri for such efforts. Much of this work was done through Ilasco's schools and churches. In the early 1920s, the DAR donated to the schools an American flag, two hundred books, and a moving-picture machine "to show educational and patriotic films." They donated money to the mission and generally pushed patriotic education. They awarded prizes and medals to students such as Thelma McKinney in 1926 for the best patriotic essay and for exceptionally high grades maintained throughout the year by eighth-grade students in American history.[57]

Under regent Louise Hodgdon, the Hannibal chapter of the DAR also sponsored Americanization classes for foreign-born residents in Ilasco. The purpose was to prepare immigrants for the application process and test required to obtain U.S. citizenship. About twenty-five Ilasco immigrants received their citizenship

Records, 1876–1956, box 1, Hannibal Free Public Library, Hannibal. Angelina later joined her father in Detroit, but by then Elsie had died of heart trouble.

55. *Ralls County Record,* June 30 and July 11, 1924; *State of Missouri v. Simon Radu,* February 7, 1923, case no. 11,628, and *State of Missouri v. Frank Polletti,* November 5, 1923, case no. 11,719, both in Ralls County, Office of the Circuit Clerk and Recorder, New London; Jim Tatman, interview by author, June 25, 1992.

56. *Ralls County Record,* December 17, 1920.

57. Mrs. Walter Logan, "History of Hannibal Chapter D.A.R.," 4–6, and Mrs. Morris Anderson, "Hannibal Chapter Daughters of the American Revolution," undated report, 1, in Daughters of the American Revolution, Scrap Book, 1929–1936; Mrs. Frank Sayre Leach, "Missouri State History of the Daughters of the American Revolution," 301; all in Hannibal Free Public Library, Missouri Room, Hannibal; *Hannibal Courier-Post,* May 18, 1926.

papers with the aid of the Hannibal chapter, which received a commendation from the United States Circuit Court for its activities in this area.[58]

In addition, the DAR pushed its agenda in Ilasco's churches. For example, at a Christmas celebration held in the Methodist church in 1921, a regent of the Hannibal chapter incorporated patriotism into the religious program coordinated by Clarence and Katherine Nerlich of Hannibal. A large number of immigrants watched as she presented a silken flag to the Sunday school.[59]

It is clear that patriotic education was the major concern of officials in regard to Ilasco schools in the 1920s. A. F. Elsea, a rural school inspector for northeast Missouri, visited five demonstration schools in the fall of 1923, one of which was in Ilasco. He noted favorably in a report that at the other four schools he had observed numerous spelling and arithmetic contests and other intellectual activities. When it came to Ilasco, however, no such contests took place. Instead, he was treated to a short program that featured "a cantata depicting the scenes of the request for the making of the presentation and acceptance of the American flag." He praised the wonderful voice of Lucille Large, who played the part of Betsy Ross, and observed that "the scene closed with a large flag—'our flag'—displayed, each child standing at flag salute and taking the pledge of allegiance to the flag." The program closed with a singing of "America" and "The Star Spangled Banner" by pupils, patrons, and teachers.[60]

By 1930, the forces set in motion by World War I had changed the face of Ilasco somewhat. World War I had cut off the flow of immigrants, and the town had lost its boardinghouse look. Slovaks replaced Rumanians as the largest immigrant group in the community, whose total population had dropped to around eleven hundred by 1920. At the time of the 1920 census, Ilasco in fact had twice as many Slovaks as Rumanians. Approximately 31 percent of Ilasco's residents in 1920 were born outside the United States, compared with only 5.5 percent for the state of Missouri as a whole.[61]

The Americanization process and the patriotic pressures unleashed by World War I clearly put Ilasco's immigrants under the microscope of public opinion more than ever. During the war and its aftermath, the families of Mike and Susie Karabin, John and Anna Krudy, John Patrick, Severino and Carmela Fiorella, John and Susie Viglasky, John and Lena Ursu, and John and Anna Tanasse were among those from Ilasco to acquire American citizenship. They and other naturalized citizens comprised about 10.5 percent of Ilasco's immigrants in 1920. Only about

58. Leach, "Missouri State History of the Daughters of the American Revolution," 301.
59. *Hannibal Courier-Post,* December 22, 1921.
60. A copy of Elsea's report is in *Ralls County Record,* October 19, 1923.
61. U.S. Federal Manuscript Census, 1920, Saverton township, Ralls County; *Census Reports,* vol. 3, Fourteenth Census of the United States, Taken in 1920. Population, 566; Kirkendall, *History of Missouri,* 10.

7 percent of those naturalized were Slovaks. This represented by far the lowest percentage of naturalized citizens among the community's immigrants. By 1930, however, the percentage of naturalized citizens had risen sharply. Census figures for that year indicate that 58 percent of Ralls County's foreign-born whites had become naturalized.[62]

This does not mean, however, that Americanization accomplished its goal of rooting out the European cultural heritage of Ilasco's immigrants. The Slovak Lutheran community established a school to preserve the Slovak language and culture at the very time the United States joined the world war. This school directly challenged the designs of those who pushed Americanization the hardest in the 1920s.

For many Slovaks, Americanization perhaps invoked memories of efforts by the Hungarian government in the late nineteenth and early twentieth century to promote Magyarization in order to assimilate its non-Magyar subjects. Thanks, in part, to this Magyar cultural war against the Slovak language and schools, Slovaks came to the United States with a fear and contempt of public schools. Many looked instead to parochial schools to emphasize a strict moral upbringing rather than social mobility and to counter state-sponsored efforts to strip children of their Slovak heritage. This likely increased Slovak resistance to Americanization.[63]

If prohibition is a suitable yardstick for further measuring the Americanization movement's success in Ilasco, it is clear that Ilasco frustrated the middle-class Protestant culture that in the 1920s condemned what it regarded as the interrelated problems of immigration, Catholicism, and liquor. In a decade of intense racial hatred and repression in the United States, the community of Ilasco struggled to build a culture that represented a blend of the old and the new. Immigrants incorporated new features of American culture, but they often did so on their own terms.[64]

In one very important way, however, Ilasco in 1930 still looked very much like it did in 1910: it was still very white. Blacks had entered the cement plant

62. U.S. Federal Manuscript Census, 1920, Saverton township, Ralls County; *Census Reports,* vol. 3, Fifteenth Census of the United States, 1930. Pt. 1, 1335, 1344, 1383. Figures on the number of naturalized citizens in Ilasco alone are not available for the 1930 published census. Figures for the county probably skew the percentage upward somewhat, but they no doubt illustrate the general increase in the percentage of naturalized citizens in the context of 1920s Americanization pressures. Of 290 foreign-born whites in Ralls County in 1930, 177 lived in Ilasco.

63. R. W. Seton-Watson, *A History of the Czechs and Slovaks,* 267–83; M. Mark Stolarik, "Immigration, Education, and the Social Mobility of Slovaks, 1870–1930," in Randall M. Miller and Thomas D. Marzik, eds., *Immigrants and Religion in Urban America.*

64. Rudolph J. Vecoli, "Peasants and Prelates: Italian Immigrants and the Catholic Church," stresses that the Catholic Church played only a limited role as an agent of Americanization among Italian immigrants.

in growing numbers during the First World War, but most avoided Ilasco as a place to live. The small number who had moved into the community during the war faced a barrage of racial slurs, taunts, threats, and in the case of William Ward, even death. On April 24, 1917, F. H. Gregory shot Ward, a cement plant worker, in front of Ward's home just across from the Ilasco Supply Company's store. Gregory and J. R. Blanchard, both white men who worked at the cement plant, were walking by the home when one of Ward's children allegedly threw a rock at them. When they scolded the child, Ward reportedly emerged from the house with a shotgun pointed at Gregory, who quickly shot him with a revolver.[65]

Guilford Harris, coroner and co-owner of the *Ralls County Record,* conducted an inquest. A coroner's jury composed of George Douglas, William Basford, J. W. Baker, J. J. Cook, and H. Noel determined that the killing was in self-defense, but bound Gregory over for a preliminary hearing. At that hearing before a justice of the peace, the court likewise cleared Gregory on grounds of self-defense, but Angelo Venditti recalled that the killing grew out of earlier racial tensions over whether Ward and other black newcomers to the community would be allowed in Robert Purcell's barber shop. According to Venditti, this was what precipitated the shooting. He recalled gathering with other children the next morning to watch Ward's grieving widow on her hands and knees bent over her dead husband's body wrapped in a sheet.[66]

Another former resident, Perry Jones, did not remember the shooting, but he did recall a story that circulated for years about it in Ilasco. According to the story, when a black friend of Ward's came home from work soon after the killing and asked where his friend was, someone told him that Ward had been sent to the "paw paw patch." He responded that he certainly did not intend to go to the paw paw patch, and then moved out of the community, allegedly the last African American to live in Ilasco proper.[67]

In the early to mid-1920s, a rejuvenated Ku Klux Klan roamed Ralls County with impunity, flourishing in the much nastier national atmosphere after World War I. The KKK expanded its list of enemies to include immigrants, Catholics, and Jews as well as African Americans. The seeds of hate found fertile soil in Americanization programs, prohibition, restrictive immigration legislation, fears of political radicalism, and the movement of African Americans into industry as the result of wartime labor shortages. When St. Louis judge Henry S. Priest, a Democratic candidate for governor, dared to attack prohibition and the Klan

---

65. *Hannibal Courier-Post,* April 25, 1917.
66. Ibid.; *Hannibal Courier-Post,* May 8, 1917; Angelo Venditti, interview by author, July 9, 1993.
67. Perry Jones Jr., tape provided to author, December 5, 1994.

before a packed Hannibal audience in June 1924, half of the audience walked out of the courthouse in protest.[68]

Area opinion makers nurtured this racism. For example, the *Ralls County Record* regularly featured racist jokes and mean-spirited attacks on blacks. A good illustration is an article in 1925 denouncing jazz in the most vicious of terms: "Those tum-tum-tummy songs were a flareback to barbarism. It is the sort of music that is favored in the best mid-African society where the women with rings through their noses beat on drums while the men stamp the ground with the skulls of their enemies dangling around their necks."[69]

Klansmen carefully cultivated a favorable image of themselves among whites. At times, they disrupted white church services, leaving money on the altar before waving good-bye to often sympathetic congregations and ministers. The KKK donated money to Hannibal's Home for the Friendless orphanage, and had so many members and was so widely accepted in Ralls County that local newspapers often reported its activities as if it were merely another fraternal or religious organization. In August 1925 the *Ralls County Record* reported a KKK fish fry attended by fifteen hundred people on a farm near Salem. The newspaper noted in a matter-of-fact way that "a big time was had. There was plenty of fish for all present and everybody came away satisfied. There was no disorder of any kind and all present enjoyed the big picnic."[70]

The county Klan organization apparently steered clear of Ilasco, perhaps out of fear, but the bitter racism against African Americans that saturated not only the KKK but also the entire nation was deeply woven into the culture of Ilasco's native-born and immigrants alike. Harsh attitudes toward immigrants softened over time, but racism created an environment in which Ilasco residents boasted by the 1930s that they had rid their community of African Americans. For local black cement plant workers, Hannibal continued to represent the most viable place to live. In 1920, there were at least eighteen blacks in Pump House Hollow, but by 1930 there were only four in all of Saverton township. Gloria Vajda Manary, who was born in 1932 and lived in Ilasco until 1943, did not remember ever seeing an African American in the community.[71]

Later generations proudly repeated what had become a folk convention in Ilasco—that blacks were not allowed in town after dark. Such boasts, which

68. *Ralls County Record,* June 27, 1924.

69. *Ralls County Record,* October 9, 1925.

70. *Ralls County Record,* August 28, 1925; Howard, *Ralls County Missouri,* 272–77; Home for the Friendless Records, 1876–1956, box 1, Hannibal Free Public Library, Hannibal.

71. U.S. Federal Manuscript Census, 1920, Saverton township, Ralls County; *Census Reports,* vol. 3, Fifteenth Census of the United States, 1930. Population, pt. 1, 1383; Gloria Vajda Manary to Gregg Andrews, June 29, 1994.

became a central feature of the expression of white working-class identity, could still be heard when the community was dissolved in the 1960s. These boasts, along with violence, helped to erase from memory the brief history of African Americans in the community. They also overshadowed the friendly bonds and cooperative relationships that developed between some black and white neighbors in Pump House Hollow. Such racism disturbed Juanita Cross Venditti, a white woman who moved to Ilasco in 1933. She emphasized that she could never understand, in particular, how immigrants who were so exploited and despised by native-born residents could in turn exhibit such hatred for blacks.[72]

72. Juanita Cross Venditti, interview by author, July 9, 1993. See David R. Roediger, *The Wages of Whiteness: Race and the Making of the American Working Class,* for an incisive analysis of how racism shaped the construction of a white, male working-class identity in the United States.

(9)

The Culture of Cement and the Forging of an Identity

In order to know a community, one must observe the style of its funerals and know what manner of men they bury with most ceremony.
—**Mark Twain, *Roughing It***

Ilasco, a popular way station for medicine shows, hypnotists, and peddlers of magic elixirs and tonics,[1] at first resembled boom-bust mining camps on the nineteenth-century frontier. The tempo and dynamic of daily life were often geared to Atlas's production schedule. A shutdown of one or both of the mills might cause Ilasco's population to fluctuate wildly. The exodus of many immigrants and native-born workers during slack times made it hard for small stores and restaurants to survive. For those who earned income from boardinghouses, selling fish, or laundry work, the periodic shutdowns that plagued the cement plant squeezed them even more.

Labor transiency and social instability characterized Ilasco's early years. The atmosphere at first slowed the growth of cultural institutions and in many cases discouraged the development of close social relationships. Angelo Venditti recalled that workers came and went so fast and in such large numbers that they were often gone before others could even learn their names.[2] Nevertheless, Ilasco residents scratched and clawed to eke out a living, achieve respectability, and build a community. Their hardscrabble existence contained the seeds of an identity that stressed sacrifice, thrift, struggle, and hard work.

Wherever one looked in Ilasco, there were unmistakable reminders of the role of cement in daily life, from wooden dynamite boxes for school desks and early church pews to a few houses built of powder kegs. Prisoners in the local jail

1. Perry Jones, tape provided to author, December 5, 1994.
2. Angelo Venditti, interview by author, July 9, 1993.

stared at walls of Atlas cement, and plant workers from Monkey Run used an Atlas-built bridge to cross the creek on their way to and from work. At company picnics, kids used cement sacks in sack races, and Atlas donated cement for churches, schools, and playgrounds.

Enterprising women who worked in the sack house brought home cloth sacks that had been rejected for reuse, and after washing them several times to soften the material, used them to cover sleeping mattresses filled with straw. "I didn't know what it was to sleep on a cotton mattress," recalled Mildred Viglasky Martinovich, "it was straw 'til way—we were up there—but in a way it was kind of, more sanitary. Then there was children; if they wet the bed you could always throw the straw out and replenish it, where if it was a cotton mattress, they didn't have these pads and all that stuff they have nowadays."[3]

Dangerous working conditions, the need to rely on lawsuits until a workmen's compensation law was passed in 1926, and the role of lawyers in delivering much of Ilasco's property to Atlas created a climate in which tricksterism and raucous humor flourished alongside a popular hatred of lawyers. This tricksterism provided a way for Ilasco residents, like African Americans and others who lacked formal power, to gain the upper hand on the powerful and wealthy. To outsmart the elites became a badge of distinction. Corthell "Hoog" Lane, an Atlas worker who implicitly told fortunes for working people only, boasted of an alleged incident in which he got the upper hand on a lawyer during a fortune-telling session. Lane's granddaughter, Rita Mack Beaty, related the story in which a lawyer tried to fool him by dressing up like a common laborer and asking to have his fortune told. Lane, upon seeing the soft hands of the lawyer, denounced him as a fraud and told him to get out.[4]

For some who knew how to take advantage of company paternalism and the bosses' desire to be "buttered up," tricksterism at times paid important dividends, especially before Ilasco workers unionized. When Angelo Venditti once missed a week of work during the Great Depression on account of sickness, a fellow worker urged him to ask plant Superintendent Ray Hoffman for sick pay. Venditti, who recalled that Hoffman insisted that workers call him "Mister," was appropriately obsequious when he approached him about the sick pay. Venditti paid all of the necessary courtesies to "Mister" Hoffman, who reportedly enjoyed being buttered up by workers. Even though Ilasco workers were only getting about two days of work per week at the time, Hoffman wrote out a check to

3. Mildred Viglasky Martinovich, interview by Sally Polc, October 30, 1994 (copy in author's possession).

4. Rita Mack Beaty, interview by author, June 23, 1992. On the role of trickster characters in African American culture, see Lawrence W. Levine, *Black Culture and Black Consciousness: Afro-American Folk Thought from Slavery to Freedom*.

Venditti for a full week's work. With great relish, Venditti laughingly attributed this to the way he flattered Hoffman and feigned subservience: "It worked, didn't it?"[5]

Against the backdrop of job-related accidents that took a heavy toll on Ilasco, residents developed a tradition of ringing the bells of the Catholic Church when a death occurred in the community. Kenny Lawson recalled that it was John Kuzma, the village trickster as well as the butt of popular jokes, who rang the bells. The fact that it was Kuzma perhaps took some of the sting out of death, for his ability to make people laugh was legendary in the community.[6]

At times, raucous humor spilled over into solemn and sometimes tragic occasions, even mocking death itself. At one of Ilasco's elaborate wakes, tricksters substituted an intoxicated, passed-out Steve Mikula for the dead person in the casket and propped him up outside the church for viewing. As Jim Tatman recalled the story, Mikula regained consciousness and popped up just in time to frighten a woman who was coming to pay her last respects to the corpse.[7]

In 1930, Ralls County's illiteracy rate of 15.3 percent among foreign-born whites over the age of ten was the fifth highest of 115 counties in Missouri, whose overall rate for foreign-born whites was 7.5 percent. This high rate in Ralls County was due primarily to Ilasco. Only Ste. Genevieve (16.9), St. Francois (16.2), Ripley (16.0), and Benton (15.9) counties had higher rates. The illiteracy rate for native whites in Ralls County was 1.2 percent, compared to 19.9 percent for blacks over the age of ten in Ralls County. The overall illiteracy rate in Ralls County was 2.5 percent.[8]

Like other communities with high rates of illiteracy, Ilasco's popular culture celebrated the art of good storytelling. The wooded hills, dark hollows, and nocturnal sounds transported across the waters from islands in the Mississippi River provided fertile soil for ghost stories and superstitions. Frank Ayres, perhaps Ilasco's most devoted disciple of ghosts, often gathered avid listeners as he wandered around the community telling of apparitions and ghostly forms that he and sidekicks allegedly encountered. After an evening of listening to such tales in someone's home in the community, kids were often afraid to leave, and at times Ayres was so convincing that he, too, was scared to go home. For sensitive kids such as Gilbert Mack, such stories could have a traumatic impact. According to

---

5. Angelo Venditti, interview by author, July 9, 1993.

6. Kenny Lawson, interview by author, July 6, 1992; Anna Hustava Sanders, interview by author, July 2, 1992; Jim Tatman, interview by author, June 25, 1992.

7. Jim Tatman, interview by author, June 25, 1992.

8. *Census Reports,* vol. 3, Fifteenth Census of the United States, 1930. Pt. 1, 1339–46. On the eve of World War I, literacy among Slovaks in Austria-Hungary had declined as the result of the government's Magyarization campaign against Slovak schools and culture. This probably contributed to the high illiteracy rate among Ilasco's immigrants. Stolarik, "Immigration, Education," 105.

Dorothy Smith Tatman, Mack would often ask to spend the night at their house in Monkey Run rather than walk home through the hollow where a nearby house was allegedly haunted.[9]

The folk religion that many immigrants brought to Ilasco contributed to an atmosphere in which tokenism and a belief in the supernatural flourished. Southern Italian peasants, for example, believed that witches could cast spells on crops and animals, and they feared the "evil eye." A blend of Roman Catholicism and pre-Christian ingredients, this folk religion interacted with similar beliefs among Slovak and other immigrants and native-born residents to produce a parochial outlook laced with mysticism, folklore, and superstition. If, for example, cows were not producing milk, local residents might attribute this to a spell cast by a neighbor who was an alleged witch. As historian Rudolph J. Vecoli noted in regard to immigrants from southern Italy, "For the peasants, religion and magic merged into an elaborate ensemble of rituals, invocations, and charms by which they sought to invoke, placate, and thwart the supernatural. Within their 'sacred cosmos,' every moment and every event was infused with religious and magical significance."[10]

From the outset, immigrants put their distinctive mark on Ilasco's cultural landscape. Many immigrant delicacies spiced up the town's cuisine. They included a Slovak black bread made from rye flour and rolled in corn meal before it was baked and later stored, not to be eaten for several weeks. Slovaks raised dill in their gardens for use along with vinegar, salt water, and spices in making dill pickles from large cucumbers split in half. Ilasco's Italians made a special cheese and highly seasoned meats, including salami and meatballs to go with large quantities of spaghetti. In addition, they made an excellent red wine ("dago red") with which to wash down their meals.[11]

Ilasco retained a pastoral flavor of the Old World as immigrants confronted new cultural demands placed upon them by American industrial society. For those accustomed in Europe to allowing livestock to roam freely and graze on common pasturelands, Ilasco's rural setting offered temptations. In the summer of 1911, for example, county authorities fined four immigrants three dollars each after they attacked Constable T. B. Wilson in Ilasco as "he was trying to corral

9. Dorothy Tatman, interview by author, June 25, 1992.

10. Phyllis H. Williams, *South Italian Folkways in Europe and America: A Handbook for Social Workers, Visiting Nurses, School Teachers, and Physicians*, 135–59; Vecoli, "Prelates and Peasants," 227–29; Rudolph J. Vecoli, "Cult and Occult in Italian-American Culture: The Persistence of a Religious Heritage," in Randall M. Miller and Thomas D. Marzik, eds., *Immigrants and Religion in Urban America*, 26; Alexander, *Immigrant Church*, 4–6; Virginia Sanders Sudholt, interview by author, July 12, 1992; Anna Hustava Sanders, interview by author, July 2, 1992.

11. "Cuisine Peculiar to the State," 1, microfilm roll 575, folder 17505, U.S. WPA-HRS, Missouri, 1935–1942, WHMC–Columbia.

a cow that was straying on the streets of that town in violation of the county stock law."[12]

When it came to hunting, resourceful male immigrants in Ilasco did not limit themselves to squirrels, quail, rabbits, and other wild game. After Constable Wilson arrested fourteen immigrants in late October 1908 for hunting on Sunday in violation of the law, the *Ralls County Times* cheered the arrests, noting that "these foreigners have been in the habit of shooting people's chickens in that vicinity, and they are becoming tired of it."[13]

In the early 1900s, "immigrant banks" were popular among newly arrived immigrants from southern and eastern Europe who did not trust formal banking institutions. Immigrants often entrusted their savings to steamship ticket agents, labor agents, saloonkeepers, or other small merchants for safekeeping. Such practices alarmed the U.S. Immigration Commission, which pointed out that "through failure and defalcation, they have often been responsible for heavy losses on the part of the new immigration population."[14]

As an incident in Ilasco revealed, the danger of theft further threatened "immigrant banks." Mary Martin, a single nineteen-year-old Rumanian immigrant who worked in an Ilasco restaurant, stole one thousand dollars in ten-dollar bills from Rumanian Ispos Apostol in February 1911 while he was sleeping. Authorities recovered the money when they arrested Martin, who confessed to the crime. A local newspaper, pointing out that Apostol was a custodian of other immigrants' money, noted that "the foreigners that work at the cement plant do not spend much money, hoarding it up in the hope that they may be able to get a sufficient amount to take them back to the old country, where they can live like princes on a small sum. They generally have some man to take care of their savings as many of them are afraid to trust the banks."[15]

Ilasco's early immigrants retained their cultural traditions in other ways that enabled them to cope with the rigors of industrial work in a foreign land. Rumanian workers formed a fraternal society to provide burial insurance and other forms of collective support and to preserve their cultural heritage. Dionise Blagu, John Savu, Simon Stanciu, John Mafteyu, James Cazan, and Eugene Bucur were early officers in the Ardeleana Rumanian Beneficial Union, which was incorporated on November 4, 1907. During annual celebrations Rumanians typically dressed in native clothing and marched in big parades through Ilasco in the morning, carrying both American and Rumanian flags. In the afternoon they attended a

---

12. *Ralls County Times,* June 23 and July 14, 1911.
13. *Ralls County Times,* November 3, 1908.
14. U.S. Immigration Commission, *Reports,* vol. 1, 31.
15. *Ralls County Times,* February 10, 1911; U.S. Federal Manuscript Census, 1910, Saverton township, Ralls County.

banquet in Ilasco's Rumanian hall. The celebration generally ended in the evening with a play, comedy skit, or other program conducted in the Rumanian language. Dancing and other social festivities followed the program.[16]

The Ardeleana Society's celebrations not only preserved Rumanian culture but also promoted intercultural exchange in Ilasco and the Hannibal area. The galas were open to all who bought tickets. Hannibal bands often furnished the music. Many Hannibal residents attended, but Ardeleana officers warned the public in advance that these celebrations were "of a religious and patriotic nature . . . entitled to the consideration and courtesy such as would be given any American gathering of the kind."[17]

Rumanians held three-day Christmas celebrations that included eating, socializing, drinking, and dancing the waltz, the polka, and the czardas (akin to the two-step). Fiddles, accordians, and Rumanian clarinets provided the music. Rumanians also celebrated the following Monday and Tuesday after Easter. Their wedding galas and christening ceremonies typically lasted two or three days.[18]

Since no Catholic church yet existed in the early years of Ilasco's history, the marriage ceremonies of Catholic immigrants often took place in the Church of Immaculate Conception in Hannibal. These weddings introduced Hannibal residents to a cultural slice of Ilasco. On February 2, 1907, Rumanians Damitra J. Davidu (Dan David) and Anna J. Bundea were married in this church in an elaborate ceremony attended by more than forty friends who made the trek from Ilasco in carriages and surreys. They returned to Ilasco, where a big wedding feast and celebration took place the following day. All in all, the wedding entourage created "a scene seldom if ever equaled in Hannibal."[19]

Slovaks replaced Rumanians as Ilasco's dominant immigrant group after World War I. To preserve their cultural identity and cope with life in a dangerous industrial society, they, too, formed local branches of national fraternal lodges—the secular National Slovak Society, the First Catholic Slovak Union, and the Lutheran Slovak Evangelical Union. These local lodges provided life insurance, disability benefits to those crippled by work-related injuries, and sick benefits for lost work time. For those moved from community to community in search of jobs, they also provided letters of recommendation and a ready-made network

16. *Hannibal Courier-Post,* August 24, September 15, and September 22, 1908, and September 22 and 27, 1910; *John Mafteyu v. Dan Cetina,* February 15, 1908, case no. 9086, Ralls County, Office of the Circuit Clerk and Recorder, New London; "Ethnic Identity and Bilingual Community—Ilasco, Ralls County," microfilm roll 575, folder 17506, U.S. WPA-HRS, Missouri, 1935–1942, WHMC–Columbia. Circuit Court Record, book Q, 21, Ralls County, Office of the Circuit Clerk and Recorder, New London.

17. *Hannibal Courier-Post,* September 15, 1908.

18. "Ethnic Identity and Bilingual Community—Ilasco," 4, October 4, 1937; *Hannibal Courier-Post,* February 2, 1907.

19. *Hannibal Courier-Post,* February 2, 1907.

of Slovak acquaintances. They also guaranteed a proper burial with plenty of mourners.[20]

Slovak Christmas celebrations lasted three days—Christ's Day, St. Stephen's Day, and John's Day. Such celebrations featured tasty feasts of chicken, pork, and sauerkraut topped off with strudel and poppyseed and nut rolls. Whiskey flowed freely as immigrants danced the polka and czardas to the music of stringed instruments in the background. Steve Valach, an Ilasco Slovak who had immigrated in 1909, explained to Lucy Latimer in the late 1930s how celebrations typically continued after Christ's day. Latimer, who headed the Hannibal editorial office of the Federal Writers Project, in turn provided the following description of the tradition:

> The day after Christ's Day, the boys switch the girls with small trees. They dance for the girls, whose 'papas' give the dancers candy, nuts, money, and whiskey. A girl bites an apple ten days before Christmas, and eats it on Christmas—then the first boy encountered will be her future husband. Often the girl writes boys' names upon slips of paper, rolls dough around the paper, and boils the dough balls. The first to rise in the kettle contains the name of her husband to be.[21]

As the above celebration indicates, Slovak rituals during religious holidays at times had nothing to do with the official significance of the occasion. In some cases, they offered protection from bad luck, poor harvests, sickness, and alleged witches, or they predicted future marital partners. The above Christmas celebration aimed not only to reveal one's future spouse but also to ritualize and collectively contain the sexual instinct within Ilasco. In many respects, it resembled a fertility ritual. Its erotic elements suggested a symbolic recreation of the biblical Eve's sexual seduction of Adam. For fathers eager to marry off their daughters, this ritual allowed potential suitors to demonstrate their virility. In the last analysis, however, it was ritualistic fate that determined who the young woman's marriage partner would be.[22]

This suggests that so much of finding a mate was simply a matter of fate, but immigrant parents in Ilasco apparently still tried to arrange marriages into the 1930s. Their increasingly Americanized daughters rejected such matchmaking, however. Bela and Mary Nemes tried but failed to arrange for their eighteen-year-old daughter, Rosa, to marry someone ten years older. "I didn't go for that," she recalled, "and decided to go away as far as possible." Rosa left Ilasco, attended a

20. Alexander, *Immigrant Church*, 15–27; Stolarik, *Growing Up*, chap. 2.

21. "Ethnic Identity and Bilingual Community—Ilasco," 3, October 4, 1937; U.S. Federal Manuscript Census, 1920, Saverton township, Ralls County; Stolarik, *Growing Up*, 76–79. St. Stephen was Slovakia's patron saint. See Josef John Barton, *Peasants and Strangers: Italians, Rumanians, and Slovaks in an American City, 1890–1950*, 61.

22. Alexander, *Immigrant Church*, 4–6.

Missouri business college, and around 1937 accepted a secretarial position with an insurance agency in Chicago.[23]

For Anna Zivicky, perhaps influenced by less restrictive attitudes toward women in the 1920s, dating and romance were important requirements for marriage. In 1925, she and her Slovak family left Ilasco for Sugar Creek, Missouri, near Independence. Her father, George, had taken a job at a nearby plant owned by the Missouri Portland Cement Company. Anna, who was working in Atlas's sack house when she was forced to move to Sugar Creek with her family, soon developed an active social life. She and a couple of female friends went to dances regularly and at times stayed out late at night. On occasions when they came home at two or three o'clock in the morning, they took off their shoes as they walked down the sidewalks of the community so the neighbors would not awaken to the clip-clop sounds of their shoes on the cement. Her mother, Mary, was worried about neighborhood gossip. She told her daughter to stop being so picky about men, to settle down and marry before she was considered too old. She complained that Anna, about sixteen years old at the time, did not regard any man as good enough for her. Anna, however, insisted on more than just a marriage proposal: "I liked somebody that was romantic, you know, that danced and had a car and all this and that."[24]

When Anna began dating a man named Steve, the subject of marriage came up, but fireworks exploded and the relationship abruptly ended. Parked on a date one night in Steve's car, Anna listened as he insisted that he would not marry anyone unless she agreed to have the ceremony in his church, the Catholic Church. Anna, a Lutheran, replied, "You know, Steve, that's just the way I feel; that when I'm going to get married, well the man has to belong to my church, and I mean he has to be a Lutheran on top of that."[25]

Although religious differences provoked the trouble, the clash went much deeper. Anna was unwilling to assume a subservient position in the relationship. In the increasingly heated argument she in fact asserted the moral superiority of women's right to determine the religious orientation of their children. When Steve asked her what right she had to insist along these lines, the anger in her escalated. "Well, do you think I'd give my kids up?" she retorted. "Hey, who raises up the kids? The mother does. Who suffers with them? The mother does."[26]

At that point, the date went from bad to worse. "Oh boy," she recalled, "we was really going to town." Steve suddenly fired up the car and took her home on what turned out to be their last date. "He didn't even kiss me good night," she playfully remembered, "and I was looking for a last kiss. But, nah, I didn't

23. Rosa H. Nemes to author, August 2 and September 25, 1994.
24. Anna Zivicky Polc, undated tape provided to author by David and Sally Polc.
25. Ibid.
26. Ibid.

get it. So I thought to myself, 'Well to heck with you.' So I think it's always better to settle these things before the preacher or priest says 'amen.' "[27]

On the one hand, Anna's mother had chided her for being too choosy in regard to men. In this regard, her mother was simply responding to social and cultural pressures on women in that era. On the other hand, she did not want Anna to be condemned to a life of drudgery. When Anna married Ilasco's John Polc in Sugar Creek in 1927 and returned to Ilasco, her mother at first opposed the marriage because John was the only son of Steve and Mary Polc. Anna's mother worried that her daughter would become nothing more than John's maid.[28]

Elaborate Slovak wedding celebrations typically began on Sunday afternoon, although the ceremony did not take place until Monday. On occasions, they might even last a week. Two boys usually went out to make elaborate invitation speeches to guests who attended a dinner for relatives and friends following the wedding. The feast could not begin, however, until the newlyweds had " 'eaten honey.' " Afterward, the guests stayed for an all-night frolic of dancing and clowning. Around midnight, women shooed the groom out of the house or rented hall. In the groom's absence, men paid to dance with the bride in order to contribute to her dowry. As Lucy Latimer observed, "Someone holds a plate, the guests throw money at it, having the privilege of dancing with the bride if the plate is broken. The bride gets the money."[29]

Author Margaret F. Byington noted in her 1910 study of Slovak steelworkers in Homestead, Pennsylvania, that "the neighborhood considers a family under obligation to provide these festivities."[30] On other occasions, the local fraternal lodge of the National Slovak Society sponsored picnics, social activities, and children's programs supervised by John Viglasky and others. Viglasky's daughter, Mildred, later remembered that she and other children performed in these programs on a stage built with dynamite boxes.[31]

At times, the National Slovak Society hired Gypsy bands to come to Ilasco for dances. Wooden dance platforms were built for the festivities, at which young women wore native Slovak dresses. Participants danced the polka and the czardas and enjoyed liquor, homemade kielbasa sausage, and kapusta, or cabbage kraut, and other foods. "As a child," remembered Gloria Vajda Manary, "this was so exciting for me."[32]

27. Ibid.
28. Ibid.
29. "Ethnic Identity and Bilingual Community—Ilasco," 3–4, October 4, 1937; Stolarik, *Growing Up*, 82–83.
30. *Homestead: The Households of a Mill Town*, 150.
31. Mildred Viglasky Martinovich to author, October 30, 1994.
32. Gloria Vajda Manary to author, June 29, 1994; "Ethnic Identity and Bilingual Community—Ilasco," 2, October 4, 1937; Stolarik, *Growing Up*, 82. The National Slovak

During Holy Week before Easter, Slovaks joined candlelight processions, fasted, and commemorated the Last Supper. Easter celebrations usually lasted two days—Sunday and Monday—and incorporated a Slovak custom from the Old World. On Easter Mondays, boys threw perfume or water on girls they liked, and ducked those they did not like in the creek to "prevent the girls from being lazy." They exchanged colored eggs as gifts, and on Ascension Day boys planted evergreen trees for chosen girls and placed gifts on those trees. One of the most popular gifts was a bottle of soda tied to the tree by ribbons.[33]

Embedded in this ritual was the suggestion that women were valued primarily for their fertility and labor. In fact, some scenes around Ilasco in the 1930s evoked European images of peasant women as beasts of burden. When a member of the United States Immigration Commission toured a province in southern Italy between 1907 and 1910, he noted that women there were particularly industrious, that they "carry burdens up to 200 pounds on their heads without seemingly great effort." He reported that he had seen southern Italian women carrying in this manner "logs, bags of grain, fish, water, all the various kinds of crops, besides great bundles of fagots for firewood."[34]

Armenia Genovese Erlichman recalled that her mother, Rosa Raimondi Genovese, an agricultural worker from Papanice, Italy, "hoisted many a bale of hay and wore bib overalls like a man" on their farm just outside Ilasco where they grew alfalfa, corn, numerous vegetables and fruits, and raised hogs. Rosa's husband, Pantaleone, often hoisted a bushel of vegetables onto a large towel doubled several times on her head and then sent her off carrying the vegetables down the road from the garden to the house. Armenia vividly remembered that in the hot summer of 1934 her oldest sister, Angelina, would often take their baby sister, Theresa, the youngest of thirteen children, out to the field for nursing. It provided Rosa with a rare moment to rest and cool off under a shade tree while she nursed Theresa.[35]

Like many native-born as well as immigrant women of that generation, Rosa's life was one of continuous unpaid labor. Before moving to an eighty-acre farm in the early 1920s, she and Pantaleone also operated a small restaurant in Ilasco and kept boarders. Armenia emphasized that her father was not lazy, that he continued to work as a leadman for a group of track repairers at the cement plant while working during off-hours on the farm. Nevertheless, her mother's

Society was one of the three largest of the nine national Slovak federations in the United States. Barton, *Peasants and Strangers,* 61.

33. "Ethnic Identity and Bilingual Community—Ilasco," 3, October 4, 1937. For a variation of this Easter Monday ritual in Bethlehem, Pennsylvania, see Stolarik, *Growing Up,* 80–81.

34. U.S. Immigration Commission, *Reports,* vol. 4, 154.

35. Armenia Genovese Erlichman, interview by author, July 9, 1992.

particularly hard life bothered her and perhaps inflicted guilt feelings at an early age for beginning to reject that role for herself. As a child, she certainly could not protect her mother from rigorous fieldwork, but she worried that her already overworked mother would become even more so if she did not help her. "Many a time I felt ill and wanted to stay in the house," Armenia recalled, "and Mom would say 'I'll go out,' but to keep Mom in I would still go out in the field sick."[36]

The dust, smoke, dirt, and noise from the cement plant that engulfed Ilasco made women's unpaid household labor even more grueling. If the wind blew in the wrong direction, women at times scrambled to gather in clothes hanging on the line, so that coal and cement dust did not cover the wash. Dirt roads made it harder to keep clean houses in the summertime when windows were open. To make matters worse, noisy blasting at the cement plant created an even tenser atmosphere for women whose nerves were already on edge because of overwork, crying babies, and tight budgets. A local newspaper noted in December 1921 that Atlas's blasting was playing "havoc with the cisterns in its neighborhood, cracking the cemented walls—also shaking the buildings with seismic force, rattling the dishware and scaring the dogs and cats."[37]

Although Ilasco's women toiled day-in and day-out to scrape together resources for their families, they were condemned in the wider public eye for doing too much work. When World War I opened up greater opportunities for women to join the industrial labor force, the *Ralls County Record* praised their patriotic contributions but warned that heavy labor for women should not become the rule. In an article that revealed prevailing assumptions about race, gender, and class, newspaper editors invoked the Cult of True Womanhood, putting women on a pedestal and holding them responsible for producing vigorous, successful sons. "The splendid type of our American manhood could never have been evolved," they asserted, "had not this country regarded women as something to be cherished and protected and shielded from all of life's rougher and sterner experiences . . . children of over-burdened and over-worked mothers are very apt to develop in their own lives the direct results of the trials of their parents. Very few specimens of a high type of manhood comes from the homes of such people." In an appeal that had special significance for Ralls County's only immigrant town, the editors concluded, "This is most clearly seen in the countries of the old world, among the peasant classes, where over-worked mothers breed loutish and boorish sons . . . We must protect our women if we would safeguard the race."[38]

36. Ibid.

37. *Ralls County Record,* December 2, 1921.

38. *Ralls County Record,* December 14, 1917. See Barbara Welter, "The Cult of True Womanhood: 1820–1860," for a fuller discussion of the cardinal virtues contained in this middle-class definition of womanhood during the early transition to industrial society in New England. On the impact of World War I on women workers, see Maurine W.

Gender inequality and traditional notions of what properly constituted women's work limited opportunities for immigrant and native-born women alike, but women's labor in Ilasco was of vital importance to the survival of the family. They managed household budgets, learned where to find a bargain, cultivated gardens, and scavenged a bit. They also took paid jobs outside the home when they were available, and consoled each other when husbands, fathers, and sons were killed in accidents at the cement plant. Despite sexual differences, working-class men and women adopted complementary strategies to ensure their families' survival.[39]

Women's paid labor usually involved activities traditionally associated with the household. For example, keeping boarders was one of the few options available to women in Ilasco before World War I, although this stripped the home of privacy and order. Overcrowding and lack of privacy added to the tedious daily routine of cooking, washing clothes, and cleaning house. If boarders worked different shifts at the cement plant, the household routine was disrupted further as women adjusted their schedules to accommodate the flow of traffic into the home by men whose work clothes were covered with cement and coal dust.

For washerwomen, the absence of running water made their work particularly dreary. Ilasco at first contained only a single artesian well. Hattie Whitney Randolph, left to support four children after her husband apparently deserted the family for France in 1905, eked out a living for awhile as a washerwoman. Her brother, Henry Whitney, a single blacksmith at the cement plant, also moved into the household. As Hattie's daughter Velma later remembered, "She washed on a board and ironed until 11 or 12 at night, and then didn't earn much for her work. And there was no turning on a faucet for water. We carried water from the sweet well three blocks away."[40]

To contribute to the household income, seven-year-old Velma went to work in the summertime at one of Atlas's company boardinghouses. She stood on a box to wash dishes, and carried dinners to workers. Her mother later worked in the sack house at the cement plant, where she "ran the machine that printed the numbers on the sacks."[41]

Greenwald, *Women, War and Work: The Impact of World War I on Women Workers in the United States.*

39. See Ardis Cameron, "Landscapes of Subterfuge: Working-Class Neighborhoods and Immigrant Women," in Noralee Frankel and Nancy S. Dye, eds., *Gender, Class, Race, and Reform in the Progressive Era,* for a good discussion of how the consciousness of immigrant working-class women in Lawrence, Massachusetts, was shaped by their interrelated experiences in the household, workplace, and neighborhood.

40. Youell, "Renault a/k/a/ Randolph," 15–16; U.S. Federal Manuscript Census, 1910, Saverton township, Ralls County.

41. Youell, "Renault a/k/a Randolph," 17; U.S. Federal Manuscript Census, 1920, Saverton township, Ralls County. By 1920, Hattie had remarried and left the sack house. Her new husband, James Seal, worked at the cement plant.

Like Hattie Randolph, many Ilasco women took advantage of new opportunities at the cement plant that grew out of the crises of the two world wars. Earning nine dollars per week for a nine-hour day and fifty-four-hour week in the sack house during the First World War was certainly more attractive than long days of doing laundry at very low pay. During World War II, Anna Polc, Eunice Mikula, Anna Sajban, Ruth Babyak, and Omie Tatman were among those who worked on a conveyor belt as "flint pickers." They joined Local 205 of the United Cement, Lime, and Gypsum Workers Union, but after the war they left the plant as the company gave priority to hiring veterans and other men.[42]

Employment in the sack house did not represent a revolution in women's work, since sewing, cleaning, and repairing sacks mainly meant an extension of skills traditionally used in the home. The evidence suggests, nevertheless, that women embraced employment at the cement plant as a notch above the other limited options at their disposal. Such was the case of Florence "Bridgett" Lane, who as a young woman had been "loaned out," or apprenticed, as a household servant in exchange for room and board. After she married Russell Mack, she worked as a sack sewer at the cement plant. According to her daughter, Rita, she bragged that she was the fastest sewer in the department.[43]

Ilasco families used creative solutions to solve day care problems posed by single-headed households and working mothers. When Mary Tushim Hustava worked in the sack house during World War I, someone brought Anna, her baby, to the cement plant every day at noon "to take some titty." Mildred Viglasky Martinovich recalled going with one of Anna Stimel's daughters who took her baby sister to the sack house so that Mrs. Stimel could nurse the baby on her lunch hour.[44]

Others used Hannibal's Home for the Friendless as a kind of day care center instead of an orphanage. Fourteen-year-old Carl Basford was admitted to the home on November 18, 1914, and dismissed on January 21, 1915, while his mother worked at the laundry. When Mary Venditti entered a hospital in Quincy, Illinois, she and her husband, Mikel, an Atlas worker, put their children in the orphanage on November 30, 1914. Angelo, Mamie, Samuel, and Stella remained there until January 30, 1915, when their mother again was "well enough to take them."[45]

---

42. Missouri Bureau of Labor Statistics, *Missouri Red Book, 1918–1920,* 120; Stanley D. Sajban to Gregg Andrews, July 4, 1994. I would like to thank David Polc for showing me a copy of his mother's union membership book. On sex segregation on the job during World War II, see Ruth Milkman, *Gender at Work: The Dynamics of Job Segregation by Sex during World War II.*

43. Rita Mack Beaty, interview by author, June 23, 1992.

44. Anna Hustava Sanders, interview by author, July 2, 1992; Mildred Viglasky Martinovich, interview by Sally Polc, October 30, 1994; U.S. Federal Manuscript Census, 1920, Saverton township, Ralls County.

45. Home for the Friendless Records, 1876–1956, box 1, Hannibal Free Public Library, Hannibal; U.S. Federal Manuscript Census, 1910, Saverton township, Ralls County.

Parents often viewed the Home for the Friendless as a child care solution when the other parent died, particularly if poverty left no other choice. When the father of Otis, Mary, and Madaline Woodson died, their mother housed the three children there on August 5, 1930, because she could not support them. Eulah, Eunice, and Robert Schnitzler were put in the orphanage by their father, an Atlas worker, on November 19, 1920, while their mother entered a hospital. Their stay was intended to be brief, but their mother died. Although they left the orphanage eight days later, they returned on April 7, 1921, and stayed until September 21, 1924, when their father remarried.[46]

For widows and widowers, remarriage was often viewed as the only alternative to placing their children in the Home for the Friendless. When Mary Roziak Sunderlik died in 1922, her husband Julius told the kids that he would have to remarry to get them another mother. His daughter, Anna, recalled that she and her brothers and sisters protested vehemently. When Julius suggested that he would have to put them in the Hannibal orphanage, they threatened to run away. He then took a leave of absence from the cement plant for six years and purchased a farm where they lived until the kids were older. They survived by relying on garden food and livestock. Anna fondly remembered the image of her father making their clothing on a treadle sewing machine.[47]

As the case of Hattie Rodgers illustrates, for married women with much more limited access to resources and opportunities than men, the shock of divorce, separation, or desertion by their husbands sometimes left them unable to work and take care of their children at the same time. In January 1907, Rodgers's husband, Leonard, left a note telling her that he was leaving her and the children in Ilasco for parts unknown. Leonard, whose alleged womanizing had been the subject of gossip in the community, was a foreman at the cement plant who left behind numerous unpaid bills with Ilasco's merchants. Residents speculated that attachment suits by merchants against his house and furnishings would not be successful, since this would leave Hattie and her children destitute. By October 5 of that year, however, their children Byrum and Deeny were in the Home for the Friendless. Three years later, Hattie was working as a washerwoman and living as a boarder without her children in the home of Ola Gregory.[48]

In the case of Anna Balga, she had already been deserted by her husband, John, when she arrived in Ilasco. The Balgas, married on November 25, 1907, at first lived in McKeesport, Pennsylvania. Just before the birth of their son in 1911,

46. Home for the Friendless Records, 1876–1956, box 1, Hannibal Free Public Library, Hannibal.
47. Anna Sunderlik Venditti, interview by author, June 24, July 6, 1992.
48. *Ralls County Times,* January 11, 1907; Home for the Friendless Records, 1876–1956, box 1, Hannibal Free Public Library, Hannibal; U.S. Federal Manuscript Census, 1910, Saverton township, Ralls County.

John abandoned Anna for about two years, forcing her "to go out of her home and work to earn her living when to do so endangered her health, a short time before her child was born." Mrs. C. S. Knight, who employed her in McKeesport for about two years, recalled: "After the birth of her child Mrs. Balga supported herself and child by her own labor sometimes taking the child with her where she worked and at other times having it cared for at the day nursery. She did washing to support herself and babe when she was suffering from a sore hand to a degree that would disable a person ordinarily."[49]

John Balga returned to their home in a couple of years, but did not get a job. After spending most of the two hundred dollars that Anna had saved in his absence, he again deserted her and their child. He went to Chicago, where at his request Anna and their son soon joined him, only to be abandoned again. Anna and her son then went to Ilasco, where she filed for a divorce on December 30, 1914, and won legal custody of their five-year-old son.[50]

For women like Julia Horvath who felt trapped by poverty and maternal pressures, child neglect and abuse were sometimes the result. Professor F. L. Kelley, president of the Humane Society in Hannibal, went to Ilasco on March 24, 1911, to investigate reports that Horvath had neglected and abused her eighteen-month-old daughter, Eleanor. Kelley and two female members of the society who accompanied him reported that the child had been whipped cruelly and bore signs of abuse. Horvath's husband, an Atlas quarry worker, was not at home at the time of the investigation. Julia, who had two other children, reportedly said that she had no use for Eleanor and wished her dead. She then turned her over to Kelley. The child went to the Home for the Friendless until a home was found for her a few months later. According to Kelley's account, which seems a bit contrived, Horvath told him that "if the child were dead I could get a good position, one that would pay me five dollars per week, but with this undesirable charge I cannot secure any position."[51]

---

49. *Anna Balga v. John Balga,* December 30, 1914, case no. 9893, Ralls County, Office of the Circuit Clerk and Recorder, New London.

50. Ibid.; Circuit Court Record, book R, 259, Ralls County, Office of the Circuit Clerk and Recorder, New London.

51. *Hannibal Morning Journal,* March 25 and 30, 1911; Home for the Friendless Records, 1876–1956, box 1, Hannibal Free Public Library, Hannibal; U.S. Federal Manuscript Census, 1910, Saverton township, Ralls County. The newspaper did not give Horvath's first name, and there were two married women with the surname of Horvath in Ilasco, but I have concluded from other census data that the woman in this case was Julia, based on her age and the fact that she had other children in the household. Linda Gordon, "Family Violence, Feminism, and Social Control," shows that immigrant women sometimes invited intervention by social workers and agencies with regard to child neglect and abuse when it served their interests. Often there were underlying household conflicts that explain the manipulation of agencies by a family member eager

This was an era of orphanages. Poverty ripped families apart, and orphanages went hand in hand with poverty. Unless other relatives were available and willing to help raise such children, a culture of despair inflicted greater torment on families already hard-pressed to survive. Professor Kelley was well acquainted with Ilasco; in fact, only a few months after taking the Horvath child, he found a home for five other children who had been abandoned there. A local newspaper reported that these children "were not only filthy but literally covered with vermin and almost half naked."[52]

At times Kelley's intervention to take children away from their parents provoked trouble. Such was the case when he took two children away from Clarence and Mollie Lawson on May 7, 1920, and put them in the Home for the Friendless. It is not clear what led him to take the children, but the Lawsons' marriage had apparently broken up. Kelley charged that neither parent was fit to raise eight-year-old James and six-year-old Martha. Clarence, an Atlas worker, at that time had possession of James, Martha, and a thirteen-year-old daughter, Minnie.[53]

Mollie tried desperately to get her children out of the orphanage. According to the Home's records, she "caused considerable trouble two or three times," and once tried to kidnap them. In 1924, however, amid growing concern that James was "becoming a menace in the home," overseers sent him to the colony for the feeble-minded in Marshall, Missouri. He was described by overseers at the Home for the Friendless as "subnormal" and "silly."

James wrote letters to his sister, who was still in the Home, but their mother (now Mollie Lester Clark) begged the superintendent to let her kids write to her. By this time, she had moved to Cincinnati, Iowa. She apparently lost contact with James and Martha, but in 1928 was still trying to find them. She had hired an attorney in St. Louis to inquire as to their whereabouts. Jennie C. Bartlett, superintendent of "The New Home," replied that James had been sent to Marshall and that Martha had been adopted by a family who had moved west to parts unknown. Whether Bartlett was completely truthful or not, the fact is that the pain of losing her children was still driving Mollie to try to find them eight years after they had been placed in the orphanage.[54]

---

for outside intervention. In Horvath's case, we do not know enough about the context in which intervention by the Humane Society took place. We have only Professor Kelley's interpretation as expressed in the newspaper.

52. *Ralls County Record,* August 4, 1911.

53. U.S. Federal Manuscript Census, 1920, Saverton township, Ralls County; James Alexander Lawson and Martha Ellen Lawson, date of admission, May 7, 1920, Home for the Friendless Records, 1876–1956, box 1, Hannibal Free Public Library, Hannibal.

54. All letters and records that I have used in this case are in Home for the Friendless Records, 1876–1956, box 1, Hannibal Free Public Library, Hannibal.

The terrible impact of poverty can be further illustrated in the following case. In August 1903 a woman identified by a local newspaper as Mrs. Morton died of the flux in a tent just north of the LeBaume Cave where she and her three children lived. Morton, a fifty-two-year-old widow who could not afford medical attention, had earlier lived opposite Ilasco in a houseboat on the Mississippi River. Only recently had she left the houseboat for a tent. The newspaper attributed her death in part to a lack of medical attention, and described the family as "in very poor circumstances." It did not mention what happened to the children.[55]

Desperation led some Ilasco women to risk arrest, gossip, and their own lives to seek abortions. Since abortions were illegal, women were forced to rely on unsafe techniques by questionable practitioners under unsanitary conditions. Some paid for this with their lives. For example, when Lizzie Lester died in Ilasco on May 6, 1909, at the age of twenty-two, the attending physician listed the cause of death as pneumonia. According to family memory, however, the pneumonia had set in after a botched abortion.[56]

A similar fate befell Pearl Pryor on May 15, 1905. Pryor, who was from Barry, Illinois, had lived for several months in Ilasco, where she learned that Ida Clark performed abortions. At the time of her death, she was living in the home of Ilasco's Mary Perkins and allegedly dating an unidentified young man from Hannibal. Pryor became pregnant, moved back to her father's home in Barry for a couple of weeks, but then returned to Ilasco to get an abortion. Clark and her husband, Henry, met her at the train depot and took her by boat to Four-Mile Island on the Mississippi River. At a cabin there owned by Henry, they gave Pryor a drug in a fatal attempt to induce an abortion.[57]

Ida Clark, a native of Ralls County, had gone to osteopathic school and reportedly practiced for a bit before this incident. Her shadowy activities and associations, however, had alienated her from her family. A local newspaper noted that "all her relatives are highly respectable people, but none of them have anything to do with her."[58]

Ida had moved to Ilasco and apparently divorced her previous husband, Edward Duffy, while he was serving a two-year sentence in the penitentiary for horse theft. She then developed a relationship with Henry Clark, who had served two stretches in the penitentiary for burglary and grand larceny. When Duffy was released from prison early on good behavior, he went to Ilasco and found Ida and Henry living together but unmarried. After he reportedly asked

55. *Hannibal Morning Journal,* August 1, 1903.
56. Hagood and Hagood, comp., "List of Deaths"; Melvin Sanders, interview by author, July 17, 1992.
57. *Ralls County Times,* May 19 and 26, 1905; *Hannibal Courier-Post,* April 5, 1906.
58. *Ralls County Times,* May 26, 1905.

to see their marriage certificate, trouble ensued when Ida pulled a revolver on him and chased him off. Duffy threatened to have them arrested on charges of "rooming," but Constable John Wiggs put him in jail instead on a charge of peace disturbance. Nevertheless, Ida and Henry married the next day, only two months before Pryor's death. On May 3, 1906, a jury in Pike County, Illinois, returned a guilty verdict on both of them on charges of second-degree murder. Both were sentenced to fourteen years in Illinois penitentiaries.[59]

The pressures of poverty meant that many in Ilasco left school early to earn money, often to contribute to the household income. Sometimes cement plant officials simply looked the other way when young teenage boys applied for work in violation of the child labor law. Perry Jones recalled that the first time he applied for a job there, he was turned down because he was too young. The following summer, however, Jones lied about his age to Dude Hayes, who was doing the hiring. Hayes knew that Jones was too young but hired him anyway. According to Jones, Hayes hired him because he knew how desperately Jones's family needed money.[60]

In 1918, Velma Randolph went to work at the International Shoe Factory at the age of thirteen. Because of her age, she had to get a certificate from the superintendent of schools affirming that her mother was a widow and needed her income. Fortunately for Velma, she had Hannibal benefactors—Clarence F. and Katherine L. Nerlich—who knew her from the Methodist church that they had helped to establish in Ilasco. Clarence was employment manager at the shoe factory. Katherine paid for Velma's tuition, books, and tutoring, thus enabling her to attend night school while working fifty-four hours per week at the shoe factory. Velma, who graduated from Hannibal High School in 1923, later recalled the impact of Katherine Nerlich's ongoing influence upon her as she grew up: "Mrs. Nerlich would take some of us home with her on Friday evenings. She had maids and cooks and beautiful things. And oh, we were in the height of glory. I remember her fixing oranges for breakfast, quartering them and putting marmalade in the center of the plate. Oh, how that thrilled a kid who wasn't used to anything fancy."[61]

For Randolph, the money she made at the shoe factory was less important than achieving respectability. As a resident of Ilasco, she had a tremendous social handicap to overcome in the eyes of middle-class residents of Hannibal. When an office production clerk's job opened up at the shoe factory, she eagerly took

59. *Hannibal Courier-Post,* March 13, 14, and 17, 1905; *Ralls County Times,* May 11, 1906; Criminal Record, book 5, 220–21, Pike County, Office of the Circuit Clerk, Pittsfield, Illinois.

60. Perry Jones, tape provided to author, December 5, 1994.

61. Youell, "Renault a/k/a/ Randolph," 17–18; U.S. Federal Manuscript Census, 1920, Mason township, Marion County, Mo.

it, even though it did not pay as well as her previous job running a machine. The new job "had more prestige."[62]

Most Ilasco children could not count on benefactors such as the Nerlichs. Sons received priority over daughters in the allocation of scarce household resources and encouragement. Mildred Viglasky Martinovich dreamed of becoming a teacher or journalist, but found that family and social pressures to work and marry were overwhelming. "As much as I loved school," she recalled, "I was only allowed to go through the ninth grade."[63]

Virginia Sanders, one of thirteen children of Ernest and Blanche Sanders, was among Ilasco students recruited to work during the summer at the shoe factory producing army shoes during World War II. She did "man's work" on a machine that tacked insoles onto the lasts. She returned to school in the fall but continued to work nights from five to nine o'clock along with Helen Konko, Andy Krolak, her brother Gordon, and other Ilasco students. Upon graduating from the eighth grade the following year, however, she quit school and went to work full-time in another Hannibal shoe factory.[64]

The shoe industry in Hannibal represented one of the few local opportunities for women to find higher-paying factory work. This attracted Armenia Genovese, along with her sisters Angelina, Senta, and Louise. Armenia, after graduating from high school as valedictorian in the late 1940s, found work there sewing linings on the tongues of shoes. For her, part of the thrill of payday was being able to buy treats for her family and to help them financially. In particular, she enjoyed buying her mother "a real slip and dresses," since her mother and sisters customarily wore dresses made from "white and colored feed sacks."[65]

Many Ilasco women jumped at the chance to leave the area, not only because of a lack of job choices but also to escape what for many was a confining environment of endless work. Strict fathers often contributed to this discontent. Pantaleone Genovese at first refused to allow his daughters to play school basketball because it required them to wear shorts. He finally relented but refused to let them wear shorts on any other occasion. Bela Nemes would not allow his daughters to wear cosmetics, but Rosa fondly remembered an occasion on which her mother Mary helped her to violate her father's code of conduct. "I was always so pale," Rosa remembered, "so when I was graduating from high school, she secretly bought rouge to give me color. I got sick the next day and he couldn't understand it, said I looked so good the night before." When Rosa's younger sister, Magdalene, graduated from high school, an uncle from Canada suggested

62. Youell, "Renault a/k/a/ Randolph," 17.
63. Mildred Viglasky Martinovich to author, October 30, 1994; Mildred Viglasky Martinovich, interview by Sally Polc, October 30, 1994.
64. Virginia Sanders Sudholt, interview by author, July 12, 1992.
65. Armenia Genovese Erlichman, interview by author, July 9, 1992.

that Rosa talk her into joining her to work in Chicago, where Rosa had gone in 1937. Rosa recalled that "he felt she was being overworked here at home by my parents."[66]

Some men saw their wives as private property to be used and abused as they saw fit. Divorce petitions often cited the interrelationship of alcohol and violence as the source of trouble in marital relationships. In 1911, for example, Paraschiva Stoican petitioned for a divorce from Vasilie Stoican, an Atlas quarry worker, on grounds that he had beaten and kicked her repeatedly and dragged her across the floor by her hair. On one such occasion, Justice of the Peace John Northcutt had arrested Vasilie and charged him with common assault. Paraschiva charged that her husband "spends all the money he makes at the saloon and contributes nothing to support" her and their six-year-old daughter Mary.[67]

A similar case was that of Susie Betina, who had married George Betina in Austria-Hungary in December 1899. She came with her husband to Ilasco in 1901 while the cement plant was under construction. They lived together until George deserted her in July 1906 after having beaten her when he was intoxicated. She charged that on one occasion he had pulled a knife, threatening to kill her, and "would have done so had friends not come to her rescue." He had allegedly thrown their oldest child on the floor and threatened to kill her, too.[68]

In what was perhaps the most extreme case of domestic violence, George Zivicky shot his wife Ilka (Helen) in a rage of jealousy on June 26, 1921. He also fired several shots at Constable E. M. Sanders, who returned the fire and wounded Zivicky in the leg. Mrs. Zivicky suffered serious chest wounds but recovered and obtained a divorce on May 23, 1922.[69]

George Zivicky's legal fate perhaps reflected prevailing attitudes that condoned such actions on the part of husbands and legitimized views of women as property. His first trial resulted in a hung jury. According to information provided by one of the jurors, only a single juror voted to convict him on charges of assault with intent to kill. In the end, the prosecuting attorney dismissed these charges, and Zivicky pleaded guilty to a lesser charge of resisting an officer. He was fined only two hundred dollars plus court costs.[70]

Jealousy also motivated the shotgun killing of Annunziato Ciccia (Frank Sheets) by Salvatore Scalise in the latter's home in November 1925. Scalise immediately

66. Armenia Genovese Erlichman, interview by author, July 9, 1992; Rosa H. Nemes to Gregg Andrews, August 2 and September 25, 1994.

67. *Paraschiva Stoican v. Vasilie Stoican,* March 4, 1911, case no. 9432, Ralls County, Office of the Circuit Clerk and Recorder, New London; U.S. Federal Manuscript Census, 1910, Saverton township, Ralls County.

68. *Susie Bertena v. George Bertena,* February 3, 1908, case no. 9076, Ralls County, Office of the Circuit Clerk and Recorder, New London; U.S. Federal Manuscript, 1910, Saverton township, Ralls County.

69. *Ralls County Record,* July 1, 1921, and May 26, 1922.

70. *Ralls County Record,* December 2, 1921, and March 9, 1923.

reported the killing to C. E. Miller, Justice of the Peace, claiming that Sheets, a boarder in the Scalise home, "had been bothering his wife and talking about her . . . [and] had broken up several homes in Ilasco." Scalise argued that Sheets, who in 1919 had rape charges dropped against him when he pleaded guilty to a lesser charge of common assault, had fired at him first. It took a Ralls County jury only thirty minutes to acquit Scalise on March 27, 1926.[71]

Before World War I, the presence of numerous large boardinghouses that lodged single men, many of whom did not intend to put down roots in the community, created an imbalance in the ratio of women to men. In 1910, men who were age fifteen and older outnumbered women in the same age range by a margin of 4.4 to 1. This imbalance, which was even more noticeable in Ilasco's immigrant population, discouraged the growth of family life and created conditions that led many women, married or single, to drink, brawl, and carouse alongside many of Ilasco's men. In March 1917, for example, Trixie Simon shot Mollie Hooley in the eye with a .32-caliber revolver, wounding her seriously. A woman identified by a local newspaper as Mrs. Joe Stafford returned to Ilasco in July 1906 after spending sixty days in the Ralls County jail, but immediately "imbibed too freely a brand of liquid known as Old Crow, or probably of a viler degree." As a result, she became the "instigator and principal actor" in a disturbance and was rearrested and charged with peace disturbance.[72]

The unbalanced gender ratio meant that immigrant men in particular could not draw on the vital resources provided by women's paid and unpaid labor to help sustain them during plant layoffs and shutdowns. As this ratio became more balanced in the 1920s and as several immigrant families purchased farms outside Ilasco, they developed greater resources that enabled them to cope with such emergencies. For example, George Sajban bought a 140-acre farm in 1927, which he operated until 1941. He continued to work at the cement plant until he retired in 1961, while his wife, Anna, also worked at the plant's Fairmont Crusher, separating flint rock from passing limestone on a conveyor belt. Anna's gardening, canning, and paid labor, along with crops and other foodstuffs produced on the farm, provided their family with greater resources during hard times.[73]

71. *Ralls County Record*, November 21, 1919, November 13, 1925, and April 2, 1926; U.S. Federal Manuscript Census, 1920, Saverton township, Ralls County.

72. *Hannibal Courier-Post*, July 20, 1906. For the 1910 census, I have calculated the ratio of women to men by counting residents in Saverton township, Ralls County, from household number 268 to the end of the township. This encompasses Ilasco and a few farms on the outskirts.

73. Stanley D. Sajban to Gregg Andrews, July 4, 1994; Howard, *Ralls County Missouri*, 419. The Sajbans' son, Stanley, later became vice president of the Federal Land Bank in St. Louis.

Native-born workers, because of family networks, connections, and greater albeit limited resources, were better situated to withstand the ups and downs of the cement business cycle. Neil Smashey and Harrison Decker are good cases in point. Smashey, a resident of Saverton township long before Atlas built its plant there, often rotated before 1910 between working at the cement plant and farming. In addition, he cut wood and made fence posts. Decker, who came from Kinderhook, Illinois, returned there in the spring of 1911 when Atlas temporarily closed Mill Number Five. He had run a drill in Atlas's machine shop but coped with the shutdown by attending a small patch of ground owned by his mother in Kinderhook.[74]

While Ilasco's immigrants celebrated the holidays and traditions associated with the culture that they brought with them, they also quickly embraced American holidays, joining particularly boisterous public celebrations of Labor Day and the Fourth of July. They must have been somewhat confused at times, however, by an industrial regimentation that did not always recognize even the sacred holiday of Christmas. For example, the Atlas cement plant did not shut down for Christmas in 1904, but when Atlas officer and major stockholder Jose F. De Navarro died, the Ilasco plant shut down for thirty minutes on February 5, 1909, while his funeral was in progress in New York City. Workers must have wondered at the rankings within the Atlas religious pantheon, for as the *Ralls County Record* observed, "It was the first time in years at the plant that all the wheels were idle even for a few minutes."[75]

Company-sponsored baseball games and picnics, together with union-sponsored beer parties in the late 1940s and 1950s, provided opportunities for native-born and immigrant male workers at the plant to socialize and share cultural experiences. Atlas built a baseball park with grandstands that seated several hundred, and it bought uniforms for players. For many years, the park served as the center of Ilasco's recreational life for men's baseball and women's softball. In addition, it had provided a place for the Missouri National Guard to put down their guns for awhile and pick up gloves and bats during the strike of 1910.[76]

Ilasco men also bonded through common leisure activities such as hunting, fishing, gambling, and going to Hannibal for a Saturday night on the town. They also shared common work experiences. Because of cultural and family economic pressures, sons often went to work at the cement plant as soon as possible. This was true for the first, second, and even third generations. For example, not only

---

74. *Heinbach v. Heinbach et al.,* April term, 1914, 213–14, 520.

75. *Hannibal Courier-Post,* December 22, 1904; *Ralls County Record,* February 12, 1909; Rosenzweig, *Eight Hours,* 65–90. On immigrant celebrations of Labor Day and the Fourth of July in Ilasco, see *Hannibal Courier-Post,* July 2, 1907, and September 8, 1908.

76. Perry Jones Jr., tape provided to author, December 5, 1994.

did Delbert Lee work there, but so, too, did his son Leon and grandsons Gerald, Richard, George, and Merle. Like many others, Charlie, Billy, and Joe Nemes, too, followed their father, Bela, into the plant.[77]

Immigrant workers were often expected to turn their wages over to their parents, but they sometimes found ways to hold a little out for themselves without their parents' discovering it. Perry Jones remembered a Slovak worker who deliberately goofed up clocking out so that Atlas would have to cut him a second check for that one day of work. Atlas officials were often irritated with him for needlessly increasing administrative costs, but he pulled this screw-up so he could keep a day's pay for himself after he had surrendered the first check to his parents.[78]

In 1937, Lucy Latimer observed that "the cement works virtually owns the village of Ilasco, which might look more natural in a Czechoslovakian or Italian setting." She added that "the people from southern Europe like the hills among which Ilasco is built. They say it reminds them of a bit of their native country."[79]

Latimer's observations, besides calling attention to the physical setting that facilitated the adaptation of Ilasco's immigrants to their new home and workplace, revealed the vitality and persistence of immigrant culture. After consulting with V. V. Jones (Universal Atlas's quarry foreman), Walter G. Schwehn (the Lutheran minister in Hannibal), and J. A. Brown (who worked in the cement plant office), she noted that Slovaks still made up a "preponderance" of the immigrants there, and that 28 percent of those 350 cement plant workers from immigrant backgrounds were American-born. She also pointed out the impact of the Great Depression and Americanization upon ethnic celebrations and customs. "These celebrations were formerly held upon a grand scale," she observed, "but since the depression of business they have become less elaborate . . . The older people wish to continue these customs, but the younger generation are drifting away from them."[80]

Latimer's observations also suggest the continued class and cultural distance between many Hannibal residents and the people of Ilasco. In 1930, there were 89 residents of Ralls County. who were born in Czechoslovakia, compared to only 4 in Hannibal, where the largest number of foreign-born whites (144) were from Germany. Of Ralls County's 290 foreign-born whites (179 males and 111 females), the total of 89 Slovaks was the largest number from a single

77. Jim Tatman, interview by author, June 25, 1992; Rosa Nemes to Gregg Andrews, August 2, 1994; Shirley O'Keefe to Gregg Andrews, August 10, 1992.

78. Perry Jones Jr., tape provided to author, December 5, 1994.

79. "Ethnic Identity and Bilingual Community—Ilasco," topic no. 3, microfilm roll 575, folder 17506, and "Ralls County Historical Sketch," microfilm roll 574, folder 17494; both in U.S. WPA-HRS, Missouri, 1935–1942, WHMC–Columbia.

80. "Ilasco," 1.

nation. Saverton township, which had a population of 2,059 at the time, had 197 foreign-born whites, by far the greatest number of any township in the county. There were 335 white Saverton township residents of either foreign or mixed parentage.[81]

The physical layout of Ilasco suggested disorder to Latimer, who seemed a bit fearful on visits to the community. "The homes are grouped in a haphazard manner," she observed, "some on one side of a little creek, some on another. A part of the village, across the road is called 'Monkey Run.' Many of the homes are ramshackle, but each has its garden plot, which is cared for by the women of the family. The roads through the hamlet run crazily in every direction, and a stranger can easily find himself lost in the creek bottom."[82]

On Latimer's trips to Ilasco, she visited the homes of one Slovak and one Rumanian family. From her written accounts of these visits, we get a further glimpse of how Ilasco immigrants were still objects of curiosity to Hannibal residents. She described Slovaks Steve and Eva Valach as "a higher type than the average foreign immigrant," and noted that the Valach children spoke English and attended high school. There was some American furniture in the living room of their home, but Steve could speak only limited English and Eva could neither speak nor understand English. "The father ordered the children to serve wine to the visitor," wrote Latimer, "and the little boy spilled some from the jug, calling forth a flood of Slavic scolding (I suppose) from his father."[83]

Latimer also visited the home of Dan and Anesta Sirbu. She found their small home clean but cluttered with furniture, ornaments, pictures, and other knick-knacks. Anesta's limited English and attempts to communicate bewildered Latimer, who described her as "bashful and childlike." Anesta showed pictures of her family in Rumania and said to Latimer, " 'No see Papa; no see Mama; no see four sisters.' " Latimer condescendingly concluded, "Their lives do seem rather pathetic . . . A visit to this miniature 'southern Europe' at Ilasco is an experience one does not soon forget."[84]

Many of Ilasco's immigrants were slow to acquire American citizenship. Such was the case of Mary Borsos Nemes, who had immigrated in 1914. Of Ralls County's 106 foreign-born white females over the age of twenty-one in 1930, she was not among the sixty naturalized citizens or the five who had taken out their first papers. In fact, she did not become a naturalized citizen until December 6, 1943, more than fourteen years after her husband, Bela, had received his

81. *Census Reports,* vol. 3, Fifteenth Census of the United States, 1930. Pt. 1, 1335, 1359, 1383.

82. "Ethnic Identity and Bilingual Community—Ilasco," 1, October 4, 1937.

83. "Ilasco," 3; U.S. Federal Manuscript Census, 1920, Saverton township, Ralls County.

84. U.S. Federal Manuscript Census, 1920, Saverton township, Ralls County, 3; "Ethnic Identity and Bilingual Community—Ilasco," 6, October 4, 1937.

citizenship. Of Ralls County's 171 foreign-born white males over the age of twenty-one in 1930, Bela was among those 101 naturalized citizens.[85]

Harsh attitudes toward immigrants on the part of native-born residents were deeply rooted in the community. Resentments and tensions generated by the failed strike and military occupation of Ilasco in 1910 had deepened interethnic divisions and native-born hostility toward immigrants. Mildred Viglasky Martinovich remembered that children of immigrants bore the brunt of much of this hostility. Some, like David Polc and Richard Sanders, later regretted that under these pressures they had not learned the Slovak language from one or both of their parents. Such terms as "hunk," "hunkie," "dago," "garlic snapper," and "wap" were thrown about casually to downgrade Ilasco's immigrants and their children. Anna Sunderlik Venditti emphasized, however, that English Americans themselves were immigrants from an earlier period and thus had no right to suggest that she and others had a less legitimate right to call themselves Americans. She remembered that on one occasion a native-born resident had been repeatedly using ethnic slurs against someone in Ilasco who then challenged him to meet at a designated time and place to fight. With great pride, she recalled that the name-caller, a "so-called American," did not show up to fight.[86]

Not all residents agreed with the anti-immigrant prejudices. Perry Jones Jr. recalled that Nedra Miller, a former Ilasco resident and teacher, told him years later that she, in fact, considered it an honor to have been raised among so many different immigrant groups. Jim Tatman, when asked years later how he felt growing up "with all those foreigners," emphatically stated that he would gladly do it all over again in a minute if he only could.[87]

The absence of a trade union for more than forty years deprived Ilasco workers of an institution that might have at least partially bridged ethnic and racial differences by stressing the need for cooperation to further common economic interests. A union would have directed many class resentments against Atlas, whose hiring practices contributed to the widening of ethnic and racial divisions within its labor force. Instead, racism became a vehicle for scapegoating and a diversion for class anger.

85. *Census Reports,* vol. 3, Fifteenth Census of the United States, 1930. Pt. 1, 1344; U.S. Federal Manuscript Census, 1920, Saverton township, Ralls County; Mary Borsos Nemes, Certificate of Naturalization, Northern Division, Eastern Judicial District of Missouri, December 6, 1943, and Bela Nemes, Certificate of Naturalization, United States District Court, Northern Division, Eastern Judicial District of Missouri, December 4, 1929. I would like to thank Rosa Nemes for providing copies of her parents' naturalization certificates.

86. Mildred Viglasky Martinovich, interview by Sally Polc, October 30, 1994; David Polc, interview by author, October 16, 1994; Richard Sanders, interview by author, July 2, 1992; Anna Sunderlik Venditti, interview by author, June 24 and July 6, 1992.

87. Perry Jones Jr., tape provided to author, December 5, 1994; Jim Tatman, interview by author, June 25, 1992.

Ilasco workers were further isolated and fragmented between 1914 and 1933 when local option and prohibition deprived them of taverns at a time when the most vicious attitudes flourished toward immigrants and blacks. Despite some of the social problems associated with saloons, they did provide an important meeting place where cultural exchange, general socializing, and discussions of politics took place, thus promoting a degree of cohesiveness. The absence of saloons for such a long period of time further atomized members of the community who no longer had as extensive contacts with other groups in public places. This only encouraged polarization among groups who viewed each other with mutual suspicion.[88]

After the repeal of prohibition, saloons reemerged as the vibrant social and cultural institutions they had been before 1914, except, of course, they were much fewer in number since Ilasco's population had steadily declined in the meantime. Population figures are unavailable for Ilasco itself, but the population of Saverton township had declined from 2,059 in 1930 to 1,845 in 1940.[89]

World War II reduced the population even further, as many left the area to find work in defense plants and related industries. For example, Perry and Beatrice Jones moved to Long Beach, California, where Perry found a job in the shipyards. Susan and John Vajda went to Detroit, where she went to work for TRW and he acquired a welding and sheet metal fabrication job. By 1950, Saverton township's population had dropped to 1,355, a decline of 26.6 percent in ten years. This downward slide in population paralleled a similar drop in the overall population of Ralls County from 10,704 in 1930 to 10,040 in 1940. By 1950, the county's population had declined to 8,686, but this drop of 13.5 percent was much smaller than that of Saverton township.[90]

In 1939, Albert Venditti bought the building that formerly housed C. E. Miller's store and opened Al's Tavern in Ilasco. Louis Fleurdelys operated it for him while Venditti served in the military during World War II, and the tavern became a favorite hangout. Patrons gathered to play cards in the back, bowl at miniature duck pins, drink, socialize, form romances, and pull pranks. They could combine these activities with a trip to the store of Saverton's John Stevens, later owned by Rex and Omie Tatman, in half of the building occupied by Al's Tavern.[91]

88. For a positive assessment of the role of taverns in working-class lives, see Powers, " 'Poor Man's Friend,' " 1–15; Cizmic, "Yugoslav Immigrants in the U.S. Labor Movement, 1880–1920," 179–80.

89. *Census Reports,* vol. 3, Fifteenth Census of the United States, 1930. Population, pt. 1, 1335, 1383; *Census Reports,* vol. 1, 1960 Population, Characteristics of the Population. Pt. A, Number of Inhabitants, 27–21.

90. *Census Reports,* vol.1, pt. A.; Perry Jones Jr., tape provided to author, December 5, 1994; Gloria Vajda Manary to Gregg Andrews, June 29, 1994.

91. Anna Sunderlin Venditti, interview by author, June 24 and July 6, 1992.

The tavern became a center for the mingling of different ethnic groups in Ilasco. Venditti, himself the son of Italian immigrants, had married Anna Sunderlik, the daughter of Slovak immigrants. When he was not pulling pranks on customers, they were pulling pranks on him. John Kuzma, the village trickster who along with other Slovaks called Venditti "Berti," would sometimes in the morning sit and rock in an old squeaky chair outside Venditti's living quarters in the back of the building that housed the tavern. Kuzma would continue rocking until Venditti woke up, opened the tavern, and sold him a beer. One evening in the tavern, Venditti became suspicious when Kuzma and a companion made too many trips to the bathroom in the back. When Venditti went to investigate, he discovered that Kuzma, who loved warm beer and could open bottles with his teeth, along with his buddy had polished off several bottles of beer. When Venditti yelled at them, Kuzma pretended not to understand: "Ah, Berti, me no furstay."[92]

From the beginning, many Hannibal residents had feared Ilasco, at least partly because of its reputation for drinking and violence. When Paul Mojzis shot and killed Matus Gasko on August 22, 1936, however, following an argument that had prompted Gasko to leave and return with a gun threatening to kill Mojzis, this marked the last such killing in Ilasco. Nevertheless, many in Hannibal continued to exhibit a mixture of fear and condescension toward Ilasco residents, whether of native-born or immigrant families. Rita Mack was among those who had to endure class insults and ridicule. She recalled that since her family lived in a deep hollow in Monkey Run before they moved to Hannibal in the late 1950s, students at Hannibal High School at times would ask her derisively "how high the water was." They asked her this, she stressed, since floods often isolated Monkey Run and since some Hannibal students regarded her as nothing more than "poor white river trash."[93]

Ilasco's trickster culture did not include much of an interest in formal politics. This is not surprising. Since Ilasco from its inception was an unincorporated town, residents never had a voice in shaping local political institutions. To avoid higher taxes, Samuel Heinbach had refused to incorporate his tract. Atlas, once it acquired ownership of Heinbach's and Theodore Johnson's tracts, also had no interest in incorporating the town. To have incorporated Ilasco would have meant the loss of Atlas's political control over the community. Except for a constable and a justice of the peace, Ilasco lacked local officials to represent the needs of the community in county politics. Instead, a handful of corporate officials in Pennsylvania and those who did their bidding in New London, Hannibal, and Jefferson City controlled Ilasco's destiny.

92. Ibid.
93. *Ralls County Record,* August 28, 1936; Rita Mack Beaty, interview by author, June 23, 1992.

Part III

Dust to Dust

*Big Business,
the State, and
the Destruction
of Ilasco*

(10)

New Landlord on the Block

The United States Steel Corporation, "Imperfect Collusion," and Depression-Era Ilasco

So to speak, I was become a stockholder in a corporation where nine hundred and ninety-four of the members furnished all the money and did all of the work, and the other six elected themselves a permanent board of direction and took all the dividends. It seemed to me that what the nine hundred and ninety-four dupes needed was a new deal.

—**Mark Twain,** *A Connecticut Yankee in King Arthur's Court*

Shortly after the stock market crash in October 1929, conditions in the cement industry fueled a corporate merger that produced a new landlord and boss for Ilasco's workers. In December 1929, Atlas President John R. Morron notified stockholders that the United States Steel Corporation had offered to assume Atlas's assets and liabilities in exchange for 180,000 shares of stock valued at $31,320,000. This amounted to a stock swap of one share of U.S. Steel's common stock for about five shares of Atlas's common stock. Morron called a special meeting of Atlas stockholders to ratify the proposal to merge Atlas with U.S. Steel's Universal Portland Cement Company.[1]

Atlas stockholders approved the merger, which created the Universal Atlas Cement Company. In addition to Ilasco, the new company operated plants at Hudson, New York; Northampton and Universal, Pennsylvania; Buffington, Indiana; Duluth, Minnesota; Independence, Kansas; Leeds, Alabama; and Waco, Texas. The combined annual capacity of these nine plants was 35.3 million barrels. The Ilasco plant's annual capacity of 4.14 million barrels made it the new company's fourth largest plant.[2]

1. *Rock Products,* December 21, 1929, 85; *Pit and Quarry,* December 18, 1929, 112.
2. *Business Week,* January 1, 1930, 8; *Pit and Quarry,* December 18, 1929, 112; *New York Times,* December 17, 1929. For the annual capacity of Universal Atlas plants, I have

The merger strengthened monopoly within the industry. By the following year, five companies produced 40 percent of the nation's total cement output. *Business Week* praised the merger as a potentially stabilizing force in an industry that had suffered from cutthroat competition. The magazine noted that a recent tariff on cement might also benefit the industry, but emphasized that "the real significance of the purchase is rather in the lining up of the great company, with its powerful banking affiliations, on the side of order against chaos in an indispensable national industry."[3]

President Herbert Hoover hoped that voluntary cooperation by labor leaders and businessmen to determine prices, wages, and production would stabilize the economy and prevent a further deepening of the Great Depression, but his hopes were soon dashed. In Missouri, the average rate of unemployment climbed steadily from 15.9 percent in 1930 to 38.1 percent in 1932 until it reached a high of 38.6 percent in 1933. Cement companies, like others, slashed wages and resorted to layoffs and cutbacks. The nationwide production of portland cement declined by 9 percent between 1928 and 1930, and in 1932 cement plants operated at only 29 percent of capacity. Atlas's Ilasco plant had employed 1,096 men and 37 women in 1923, but by 1929 the number of male employees had dropped off to 854, largely the result of technological innovations, while the number of female employees remained the same. By May 1, 1934, only 374 employees remained at the Ilasco plant. At that time, only 437 people in Ralls County were employed in industry; only seven were women.[4]

As the depression deepened, Universal Atlas and other companies took more drastic measures. Blaine Smith, president of the Pennsylvania-Dixie Cement Corporation and head of the Cement Institute, approached officials in the Bureau

relied on a map showing the locations and annual capacities of its plants. This map, dated April 3, 1930, was among materials given to me by the USX Corporation.

Ida L. Ringler, a disgruntled Atlas stockholder, filed an injunction in an effort to prevent the merger. She denounced the stock swap, complaining that U.S. Steel was "getting the vast Atlas plant, equipment, subsidiaries, patents and good will without any actual expenditures." See *New York Times,* January 23, 1930, and *The American Contractor,* February 1, 1930, 22.

3. David Lynch, *Concentration of Economic Power,* 117; *Business Week,* January 1, 1930.

4. Fink, *Labor's Search,* 128; B. W. Bagley, "Cement," in *Mineral Resources of the United States, 1930.* Pt. 2—Nonmetals, 397; Missouri Bureau of Labor Statistics, *Annual Report* 44 (1923), 195, and *Annual Report* 50 (1929), 80; *Pit and Quarry,* February 1933, 19; Alexander Sachs and Roy Wenzlick, "Material Bearing on the Cement Industry, Prepared by the Division of Economic Research and Planning," October 27, 1933, 16, Records of the National Recovery Administration, box 1321, folder 22, record group 9, National Archives (hereafter cited as NRA Records, RG 9, NA); Missouri Relief and Reconstruction Commission, "Handbook for Community Organizers and County Social Workers in Putnam, Ralls, Randolph, Ray, Reynolds, and Ripley Counties," 101–2. On Hoover's policies, see Ellis W. Hawley, *The Great War and the Search for a Modern Order: A History of the American People and Their Institutions, 1917–1933,* chaps. 11–13.

of Mines and the Commerce Department in October 1930 for help in preventing the industry from "heading towards financial disaster." Smith complained that "a new marketing plan inaugurated by one of the leading companies" had created "a very acute competitive situation in the industry which threatens to lead to a price war." He pointed out that several companies had followed suit by cutting prices and offering discounts. In his view, a social disaster was looming on the financial horizon unless corporate leaders could agree to "practical uniformity as to terms, discounts, and other conditions of sale."[5]

Smith urgently sought a meeting with Secretary of Commerce Robert P. Lamont. He emphasized that "contending parties" in the cement industry were "very bitter." At Lamont's suggestion, he drew up a list of representatives from twenty cement companies to be invited to a conference to discuss how to stop what threatened to become a full-blown price war. Universal Atlas, the nation's largest producer, was not on Smith's list of those to receive invitations to the meeting with Lamont on December 9, 1930.[6]

Despite this conference, a price war initiated by Lehigh Portland and soon joined by other companies in the Midwest broke out in early 1931. This led to reduced production and further unemployment. Universal Atlas's share of the industry's total production dipped from 14.9 percent in 1930 to only 11.8 percent in 1931. Production at three of its plants, including the one at Ilasco, dropped in 1931 to less than half of what it had been in 1930.[7]

These developments had an important impact on the Ilasco plant. On March 1, 1931, officials discontinued the Hannibal work train to the cement plant. The Hannibal Transportation Company agreed to replace it with buses operating between Hannibal and the plant. A few months later, Universal Atlas's superintendent, Ray E. Hoffman, announced that the local plant would be put on a 35 percent operating basis, using its regular labor force on a part-time basis. This was designed to allow the company to retain its employees and avoid even more massive layoffs while reducing large supplies of cement on hand.[8]

---

5. Blaine S. Smith to Colonel W. J. Donovan, November 15, 1930, and Scott Turner, Director, Bureau of Mines, to R. P. Lamont, Secretary of Commerce, October 28, 1930; both in General Records of the Department of Commerce, General Correspondence of the Office of the Secretary of Commerce, 1929–1933 (Washington, D.C.: National Archives Microfilm Publications, 1971), microfilm roll 2, record group 40 (hereafter cited as Office of the Secretary of Commerce Records, RG 40, NA).

6. Colonel W. J. Donovan to Robert Lamont, November 18, 1930; Robert P. Lamont to Blaine Smith, November 19, 1930; Blaine Smith to Robert P. Lamont, November 24 and December 1, 1930; all in Office of the Secretary of Commerce Records, microfilm roll 2, RG 40.

7. "Cement Industry: Letter from the Chairman of the Federal Trade Commission Transmitting in Response to Senate Resolution No. 448, Seventy-First Congress, A Report Relative to Competitive Conditions in the Cement Industry," June 6, 1933, 13, 42, box 1321, folder 21, NRA Records, RG 9, NA.

8. *Hannibal Courier-Post,* February 27 and June 6, 1931.

With cement prices in a free fall as the result of bitter competition, financially strapped state governments in the Midwest took advantage of the crisis to lower the costs of highway construction. No longer willing to tolerate artificially high cement prices at a time of great social crisis, highway commissioners in Missouri, Illinois, Wisconsin, and Oklahoma began rejecting bids on cement in order to force prices down even further. The Missouri Highway Commission rejected all bids opened on January 20, 1931, and requested new bids to be opened on March 5, 1931. The lion's share of these bids ultimately went to the Missouri Portland Cement Company, prompting complaints by competitors that the company had reduced its basing-point price at Sugar Creek by twenty-five cents per barrel. The price war prompted companies to withdraw financial support for the Portland Cement Association "as profits available for such support are killed off in the fighting."[9]

The price war continued until July 1932, when the Missouri Portland Cement Company sharply raised its price on a barrel of cement by thirty cents. Other producers in Illinois and nearby states had raised prices by fifty cents per barrel. Eastern firms expressed hope that this would encourage customers to buy from them, but they, too, quickly raised prices by nineteen to twenty-nine cents per barrel. Universal Atlas shut down some of its plants, including the one at Ilasco, and used skeletal crews to fill orders from stock. Widespread rumors circulated in financial circles that U.S. Steel would sell its cement division unless conditions improved by early 1933.[10]

As anti-corporate sentiment swelled across the country, state governments battled cement companies over not only prices but also taxes. Dwight H. Brown, Missouri's secretary of state, notified the Universal Atlas Cement Company on November 27, 1933, that it had underpaid its taxes by $661.25. In response, the company's O. N. Lindahl disputed the state's method of tax computation. "We understand that this whole question is in process of litigation," he wrote to Brown, "and pending the outcome of the court action, we are paying this assessment under protest, so that in case your interpretation of arriving at our proportion is held to be in error, we will be reimbursed by the amount of this payment."[11]

9. "Big Buyers Are Winning the Cement Price War," *Business Week,* April 8, 1931, 9; "Cement Industry: Letter from the Chairman of the Federal Trade Commission . . . A Report Relative to Competitive Conditions in the Cement Industry," June 6, 1933, 42, 77–79, box 1321, folder 21, NRA Records, RG 9, NA.

10. *New York Times,* July 21, July 30, and November 2, 1932; *Hannibal Courier-Post,* January 31, 1933; *Pit and Quarry,* February 1933, 19; Loescher, *Imperfect Collusion,* 181–85.

11. The letters exchanged between Universal Atlas and Secretary of State Brown in this matter are in "Universal Atlas Cement Company," folder 6203, Corporation Division, Office of the Missouri Secretary of State, Jefferson City, Mo.

Brown replied that upon the advice of the attorney general, he would not accept Universal Atlas's payment under protest. On December 26, 1933, he threatened to revoke the company's corporate rights in Missouri "unless protest is withdrawn by wire today." Facing possible expulsion from the state, the company immediately sent a telegram to Brown withdrawing its protest.[12]

When the Ilasco plant reopened on February 1, 1933, it was the first time in more than a year that it had produced cement. At that time, Universal Atlas was preparing to convert from coal to gas in many of its operations, and the Panhandle Eastern Pipe Line Company of Kansas City was constructing a pipeline from Ilasco to intersect with its main line just south of Bear Creek near Oakwood in Ralls County. This project meant two days of work per week for about four hundred cement plant workers, but Universal Atlas permanently closed Mill Number Five in Ilasco, except for the stock and packing houses.[13]

More importantly, cement companies were about to get a big boost from the federal government. The election of Franklin D. Roosevelt in 1932 brought a more direct role for the government in attempts to prevent a deepening of the Great Depression. The centerpiece of Roosevelt's blueprint for industrial recovery was the National Recovery Administration (NRA), created in 1933 by the National Industrial Recovery Act. The NRA, headed by Hugh Johnson, promoted economic planning and cooperation to reduce bitter free-market competition. Congress empowered the NRA to establish "codes of fair competition" in each industry with regard to prices, wages, production, and working conditions. The purpose was to promote business-labor cooperation and halt strikes, wage cuts, and factory shutdowns. The government suspended antitrust laws in favor of industry self-policing in an effort to prevent further economic deterioration.[14]

This gave cement officials a dominant voice in shaping their industry's code, which they submitted to Hugh Johnson on July 19, 1933, and revised after a public hearing in Washington, D.C., on September 15. President Roosevelt signed it on November 27, 1933. The code limited the average number of hours per workweek to thirty-six in a given half-calendar period, set a ceiling of eight hours per workday, and provided that employees other than clerical and office personnel could not work more than forty-two hours per week. For workers

---

12. Ibid.

13. *Hannibal Courier-Post,* January 31 and February 1, 1933; "No. One in Series of Cities and Towns Using Panhandle Eastern Gas: Hannibal, Missouri," *Panhandle Lines* 5 (January 1948): 6–7; Fact sheets, Universal Atlas Cement Division, United States Steel Corporation, Hannibal, Missouri, Plant, enclosed in C. R. Altheide, Plant Manager, to Gregg Andrews, February 26, 1982.

14. Lynch, *Concentration of Economic Power,* 150–51. On the birth of the NIRA, see Ellis W. Hawley, *The New Deal and the Problem of Monopoly: A Study in Economic Ambivalence,* chap. 1, and Arthur Schlesinger Jr., *The Coming of the New Deal: The Age of Roosevelt,* chap. 6.

engaged in packing and shipping, the code limited the workday to ten hours and the workweek to thirty-six hours averaged over a half-calendar year. In addition, the code barred women from working after 6 P.M., and set minimum wage rates in the twelve geographical districts established for the cement industry by the U.S. Bureau of Mines.[15]

NRA officials bowed to Southern Democrats in Congress and allowed racialistic wage differentials consistent with the South's low-wage history. For workers in most districts, the code set a rate of forty cents per hour, but in two Southern districts an hourly rate of only thirty cents prevailed. Although the code established a rate of forty cents per hour for workers in district seven, it made an exception in the case of that district's workers in Ilasco. Authorities allowed Universal Atlas to set the minimum wage for Ilasco workers at only thirty-seven cents per hour.[16]

The special exemption of Universal Atlas's Ilasco workers from the prevailing wage rate in district seven illustrates the kind of ethnic and regional purgatory from which they sought deliverance. They were not black, but neither were they exactly white. Missouri was not a southern state, but neither was it Yankee. Mark Twain was a son of the South, but the company and most of the workers who had transformed his childhood terrain were not. The status of Ilasco's largely immigrant workforce, the object of ethnic and regional exploitation, resembled at best a halfway house between the world of black and white, of North and South.

In compliance with the code, Universal Atlas raised wages at the Ilasco plant from twenty-eight to thirty-seven cents per hour on July 16, 1933, and established a maximum workweek of thirty-six hours on August 1. The NRA's Labor Advisory Board, headed by Dr. Edwin Eckel, protested the discriminatory rates in Southern cement plants, and the American Federation of Labor called for a minimum wage rate of forty-five cents per hour in all districts. Despite such protests, a newly revised code adopted after a public hearing on July 11, 1934, kept the minimum wage rate for Ilasco workers at thirty-seven cents per hour.[17]

President Roosevelt's sop to organized labor in the NIRA was Section 7(a), which guaranteed workers the right to organize unions and engage in collective

---

15. National Recovery Administration, "Code of Fair Competition for the Cement Industry as Approved on November 27, 1933, by President Roosevelt" (Washington, D.C.: U.S. Government Printing Office, 1933), 326–30. A copy of the cement code is in box 1319, NRA Records, RG 9, NA.

16. Ibid.; Colin Gordon, *New Deals,* 184.

17. *Hannibal Courier-Post,* July 19, 1933; "Statement on Behalf of the Workers in the Cement Industry Affiliated with the American Federation of Labor Presented at the Public Hearing before the National Recovery Administration," July 11, 1934, box 1318, folder 12; "Brief Presented on Behalf of International Union of Mine, Mill, and Smelter Workers to Deputy Administrator of NRA," September 19, 1933, box 1319; "Code History: Code of Fair Competition for the Cement Industry," 9, 15, box 1319; Margaret S. Stabler, Secretary to Labor Advisory Board, "Memorandum," September 2, 1933, box 1320, folder 16; all in NRA Records, RG 9, NA.

bargaining. Section 7(a) breathed new life into certain unions that had been decimated by Open-Shop campaigns, hostile court decisions, company welfare plans, and the pro-business climate of the 1920s. Many unions became militant and increased their membership dramatically after the NIRA was passed. As a result, some of them, including the United Mineworkers of America, the Amalgamated Clothing Workers, and the International Ladies' Garment Workers' Union, gained a voice in shaping the NRA codes for their respective industries. In addition, the repeal of prohibition increased the strength of the Brewery Workers Union in cities such as St. Louis.[18]

The Missouri labor movement grew as the result of New Deal policies, but the NIRA undercut unionization efforts in Ilasco. In response to Section 7(a), officials in the cement industry, along with steel a bitter foe of trade unionism, organized employee representation plans, or company unions. Universal Atlas President B. F. Affleck notified workers on June 14, 1933, that the company would comply with the NIRA by forming representation plans to give workers "a voice in matters pertaining to industrial relations." Employees at the Ilasco plant elected representatives in July 1933, and under a revised plan again in June 1934 and June 1935.[19]

Cement mill workers in Tarrant City, Alabama, denounced company unions as "inimical to our rights, subversive of our best interests, and a subterfuge of the companies to defeat our efforts."[20] Missouri State Federation of Labor President R. T. Wood charged that employers such as Universal Atlas were violating Section 7(a) "with impunity by denying workers the right of organization and by employing every conceivable method of coercion and intimidation to prevent workers from becoming or remaining members of organizations of their own choosing." He complained that such employers "have discharged the workers by the wholesale and have fostered in every manner the growth and development of company-owned, company-managed and company-financed unions . . . The highway robber could be considered a gentleman as compared with many of these lawless combinations of employers."[21]

---

18. Green, *World of the Worker,* 140–41; Kirkendall, *History of Missouri,* 166.

19. Fink, ed., *Labor Unions,* 52; Kirkendall, *History of Missouri,* 166–68; B. F. Affleck, "Circular Letter to Employees of the Universal Atlas Cement Co.," June 14, 1933; Universal Atlas Cement Co., "Plan of Employee Representation: Hannibal Plant," April 30, 1936 (copies in author's possession). On the impact of the Great Depression and New Deal policies upon organized labor in Missouri, see Fink, *Labor's Search,* chap. 8.

20. "Brief of Information and Views by the Cement Plant Workers Local Union #18387, Tarrant City, Alabama (Birmingham District) to William Green, President, American Federation of Labor, To Be Used at the Hearing on the Proposed Permanent Code for the Cement Industry in Washington, D.C., on Friday September 15, 1933," box 1319, NRA Records, RG 9, NA.

21. "Report of President R. T. Wood," in MSFL *Proceedings,* 1935, 8, Missouri Historical Society, St. Louis. Missouri labor leaders at first supported the NRA and Section 7(a) but

Without a trade union to represent their interests, workers at the Ilasco plant used individualistic ways to express class resentments, protest layoffs, and get concessions from the company. Consider, for example, the case of G. A. Gaugh, a Hannibal resident who worked at the cement plant for many years before losing his job during the early stages of the depression. In July 1930 he was arrested for arson at the cement plant's rock mill. Ralls County Sheriff H. A. Adkisson told a Hannibal newspaper reporter that Gaugh "stated that he set the fire to get revenge on account of having lost his job."[22]

Ilasco workers also tried to take advantage of the growing national debate over silicosis as an industrial health hazard in the 1930s by filing lawsuits against Universal Atlas. Workmen's compensation laws generally did not cover disabilities from silicosis until the late 1930s, although concerns over dust-related job hazards had grown steadily since around the turn of the century. As explained by Secretary of Labor Frances Perkins in 1936, "Silicosis is caused by breathing very small particles of dust containing silica. The particles which are too small to be seen in the form of dust are the ones which are the most dangerous since, because of their minute size, they reach the small air cells of the lungs, penetrate the lining membranes, and cause irritation. This, in turn, causes the replacement of healthy tissue by fibrous or scar tissue."[23]

Exposure to silica dust, a mineral prevalent in sand, quartz, granite, and flint (and one of the minerals represented in Ilasco's very name), posed a special hazard for foundry workers, rock drillers, sand blasters, and metal miners. In 1915 and 1927–1928, federal studies of lead and zinc miners in Joplin, Missouri, and other towns in the tri-state region of Kansas, Oklahoma, and Missouri had revealed higher-than-normal rates of silicosis and tuberculosis. This increased public health concerns over flint dust, since the ore dug out by Joplin's miners was embedded in flint, which contained a high percentage of silica.[24]

This meant that at cement plants, quarry workers and miners were the ones most threatened, although an official of the Bureau of Mines acknowledged in

---

became critical of employers' efforts to block enforcement of the pro-labor provisions of NRA codes. Fink, *Labor's Search,* 131–32. For a more flattering view of company unions, see Daniel Nelson, "The Company Union Movement, 1900–1937: A Reexamination."

22. *Hannibal Courier-Post,* July 16, 1930.

23. Quoted in "Health and Industrial Hygiene: Committees for Prevention of Silicosis in Industry," *Monthly Labor Review* 42 (June 1936): 1546. For an excellent discussion of the evolution of political dialogue over silicosis as an occupation disease, see Rosner and Markowitz, *Deadly Dust.* Wisconsin pioneered in the inclusion of silicosis as an occupational disease covered by workmen's compensation. Max D. Kossoris and O. A. Fried, "Experience with Silicosis under Wisconsin Workmen's Compensation Act, 1920 to 1936," *Monthly Labor Review* 44 (May 1937): 1089–1101.

24. Brown, *Hard-Rock Miners,* 80–81, 93–94; Rosner and Markowitz, *Deadly Dust,* 135–45.

1933 that the danger from flint or silica may be greater than that from shale, limestone, or coal dust "if present in similar quantities." Silicosis lawsuits against cement manufacturers contributed to what became a "national social crisis" during the Great Depression. Many workers used lawsuits and workmen's compensation claims as social welfare programs to help sustain them when they lost their jobs or had wages and hours slashed.[25]

In 1934, St. Louis attorneys Otis M. Gallant and Marion J. Hannigan hired runners and agents to solicit silicosis lawsuits among former employees of Universal Atlas and the Missouri Portland Cement Company in Hannibal, Prospect Hill (just north of St. Louis), and Independence. Robert Guttman obtained most of the contracts with Missouri Portland's former employees in the Prospect Hill area. He typically showed prospective claimants a newspaper clipping reporting that the law firm of Gallant and Hannigan had earlier won twenty-five thousand dollars for Otto Horachek in a dust disease case. Guttman then suggested to other former workers that they, too, probably had a dust-related disease and should file similar suits. In contracts signed with Gallant and Hannigan, former cement workers agreed to split damages with the firm on a fifty-fifty basis.[26]

Sydney Gallant, brother of Otis, contacted individuals who formerly worked at Missouri Portland's plant at Cement City, near Sugar Creek and Independence. Workers who signed contracts with Gallant and Hannigan were brought to St. Louis for medical examinations. Since many were destitute, they were provided small sums of money to cover food, lodging, and transportation expenses. Gallant and Hannigan then filed fifty or sixty suits against the Missouri Portland Cement Company and undertook negotiations for an out-of-court settlement. Missouri Portland officials agreed to settle for a total of $55,000, half of which went to Gallant and Hannigan. About 175 claimants received individual settlements ranging from only $100 to $450, and during a later round of settlements, an additional 90 claimants received a flat sum of only $120 each.[27]

Sydney Gallant also went to Hannibal to solicit cases among former workers at the Universal Atlas plant in Ilasco. On at least five different occasions in 1934, he registered at the Mark Twain Hotel and discussed filing lawsuits with cement plant workers. Nearly one hundred workers came to his room on one day alone. Everett

---

25. Rosner and Markowitz, *Deadly Dust*, 4; "Dust Diseases of Underground Miners as an Engineering Problem," *Monthly Labor Review* 38 (January 1934): 87. A Wisconsin study of workmen's compensation claims related to silicosis showed that of a total of 154 noncompensated claims filed in 1934, only two claimants were employed and two others were on relief work at the time. Seventy-seven were unemployed due to a lack of work, twenty because they were discharged or were refused employment after failing a medical examination, and twenty due to disability. See Kossoris and Fried, "Experience with Silicosis," 1097.

26. *In RE Otis M. Gallant and Marion J. Hannigan,* June 30, 1936, 154–58.

27. Ibid., 158–60.

C. Brandon was one of about three hundred former Universal Atlas workers who signed contracts with Gallant and Hannigan. Brandon went to St. Louis for a medical examination, but the record does not show whether the law firm ever filed his or anyone else's suit against the Universal Atlas Cement Company.[28]

On September 9, 1935, the Advisory Committee to the General Chairman of Bar Committees instituted disbarment proceedings in the St. Louis Court of Appeals. The suit charged Otis Gallant and Marion J. Hannigan with unethical and unprofessional practice of law by soliciting business through paid agents and runners. On June 30, 1936, the court suspended the licenses of Gallant and Hannigan for a period of one year.[29]

Since tightfisted Missouri politicians did little for the state's unemployed during the tenure of Democratic Governor Guy B. Park, what little relief Missouri's working population did get came from President Roosevelt's programs. For unemployed young men between the ages of eighteen and twenty-five who came from needy families, the Civilian Conservation Corps (CCC), created in 1933, represented an alternative to despair and hopelessness. Designed both to provide work relief and to preserve the nation's natural resources, the CCC was quite popular, although it did little to address the needs of unemployed young women. Many southern states, including Missouri, had racially segregated camps. Participants received thirty dollars per month but had to send twenty-five dollars of that amount to their families or dependents. If enrollees had no dependents, the War Department saved twenty-five dollars per month for them. A kind of military boot-camp atmosphere prevailed in the regimented camps, which by 1937 had attracted fourteen thousand enrollees in Missouri.[30]

If Ilasco residents could pass a means test, they were eligible for meager benefits from another emergency New Deal program, the Federal Emergency Relief Administration (FERA). Congress provided direct grants to local governments and public agencies for relief payments to the unemployed, but budget-conscious Missouri legislators provided matching funds only after FERA administrator Harry Hopkins threatened to end federal payments to the state. Virginia Sanders Sudholt recalled that her family received food commodities distributed in Ilasco and sometimes picked up clothes through a relief agency. Her father, E. M. Sanders,

---

28. Ibid., 160–62; *Hannibal Courier-Post,* September 10, 1935.

29. *In RE Otis M. Gallant and Marion J. Hannigan,* 168–69. On April 11, 1935, the Hannibal Court of Common Pleas also reprimanded St. Louis attorneys William H. Corcoran Jr. and Thomas W. Carlos for similar activities. See "Court Reprimands Attorneys," *Missouri Bar Journal* 7 (May 1936): 75–76, 90.

30. Missouri Relief and Reconstruction Commission, "Emergency Relief in Missouri, September 1932 to November 1934," vol. 1, 38–40; Kirkendall, *History of Missouri,* 160–65. Otis Woodson and my father, Maurice Andrews, were among those from Ilasco who were assigned to a CCC work camp near Troy, Mo. Mr. Woodson shared this information with me at the Ilasco Reunion on May 28, 1994.

who now farmed outside Ilasco, also worked on government-funded projects in the area. Armenia Genovese Erlichmann remembered the particularly devastating impact of the Great Depression on a working-class community such as Ilasco. "It was very tough," she recalled, "all of us children had to stand in the food lines. So many unemployed."[31]

For Bela and Mary Nemes, who gardened and raised livestock, the impact of the depression was perhaps a bit less severe, but traumatic nevertheless. Their daughter Rosa remembered that although they had pigs and a cow that grazed on common pasture provided to residents by Universal Atlas, the depression quickly depleted the family savings. Rosa remembered, in particular, a period of sixteen months during which her father was out of work at the plant: "He grew a lot of onions . . . and we received staples from relief, one being 'cracked wheat' which was like oatmeal. Mom would cook it, spread it on plates and covered it with grilled onions which became our main meal for 16 months."[32]

Rosa Nemes was also a beneficiary of Roosevelt's National Youth Administration (NYA), created as part of the Second New Deal in 1935. The NYA provided jobs and educational subsidies to students and others between the ages of sixteen and twenty-five. Nemes remembered the day she was awarded two dollars by the NYA on the basis of her family's need and size: "I remember when I came home from school with it. Mom cried. It was the only money we saw in 16 months."[33]

The cement industry received a shot in the arm from the Public Works Administration (PWA), created in 1933 as part of New Deal legislation to promote capital accumulation by providing jobs and stimulating demand for goods through government spending. This had an immediate benefit for Ilasco's cement workers and unemployed alike. The PWA quickly appropriated $1.42 million for construction of the Saverton Lock and Dam on the Mississippi River just three miles south of Ilasco. This project, which used 140,840 barrels of Atlas cement, stimulated production at the plant and provided construction jobs for the unemployed in Ilasco and the surrounding area.[34]

The cement plant benefited from public works projects in other ways. The new Saverton Lock and Dam was the product of a broader campaign by the Army Corps of Engineers to promote flood control and lower the cost of commercial river transportation for companies such as Universal Atlas. This included

31. Fink, *Labor's Search*, 135; Virginia Sudholt, interview by author, July 12, 1992; Armenia Genovese Erlichmann, interview by author, July 9, 1992.

32. Rosa H. Nemes to Gregg Andrews, August 2, 1994.

33. Ibid.

34. Hagood and Hagood, *Story of Hannibal*, 179; "Safety Trophy Re-Dedication, Hannibal Plant," Universal Atlas Cement Co., June 15, 1940 (in author's possession). On the New Deal's jobs-creation programs, see Nancy E. Rose, *Put to Work: Relief Programs in the Great Depression*.

dredging, dike construction, and shoreline brush removal. In late 1938, the Works Progress Administration employed Ralls County workers to clear brush and undergrowth and shore up the west bank of the Mississippi River from Saverton to the Hannibal railroad bridge. Universal Atlas President Blaine S. Smith visited the Ilasco plant at that time to survey possibilities for making improvements, including the construction of docks for loading bulk cement onto barges. As Smith explained, "This plant was planned originally to use river transportation but only now, with development of the river channel, has there been any guarantee of proper channel stages at all seasons."[35]

PWA funding of projects in Hannibal, including construction of the Mark Twain Memorial Bridge, likewise increased demand for cement and provided jobs for the unemployed, many of whom were former cement plant workers. In 1933, Universal Atlas also received a large government contract to provide cement for the construction of locks on the Green River near Bowling Green, Kentucky. Ilasco workers produced the cement, which was shipped by rail from the cement plant to Hannibal and then by barge to the site.[36]

Partly as a result of government contracts, the number of workers in the cement industry increased in 1933 from that of the previous year. This reversed a steady downward spiral in employment over the past four years, although total production continued to fall. A study of 129 plants in the industry for the period between 1928 and 1933 revealed that at the end of 1933, employment had fallen by 38 percent while hourly labor productivity had increased 23 percent. The study, which represented about 88 percent of production in the industry, also noted a trend toward shorter hours. This, along with the introduction of the six-hour shift and thirty-six-hour workweek, accounted in part for the increased number of workers in 1933.[37]

While conservative critics mounted a growing attack on government relief and jobs programs, small businessmen and consumers complained about the price-fixing and monopolistic practices of corporate businessmen, who dominated the NRA. Clarence Darrow's National Recovery Review Board issued such complaints in a report to President Roosevelt in the summer of 1934. The cement industry was among those singled out by the board, whose report pointed out

35. Office Project No. 786–56-2–13, November 12, 1938, Works Progress Administration Central Office, Reference Card Locator Project File—Missouri: Ralls County, Saverton township, microfilm reel 8, RG 69, National Archives; Kirkendall, *History of Missouri,* 166. Smith quoted in *Hannibal Courier-Post,* October 13, 1938.

36. Hagood and Hagood, *Story of Hannibal,* 179; *Hannibal Courier-Post,* March 7 and December 26, 1933.

37. Bernard H. Topkis, "Labor Requirements in Cement Production," 577; "Productivity of Labor and Industry: Changes in Employment and Productivity in the Cement Industry," *Monthly Labor Review* 41 (October 1935): 965–66.

that the largest cement companies drew up the industry's code and included monopolistic features that benefited them at the expense of smaller firms. The board complained about the activities of the Cement Institute, which the code authorized to petition President Roosevelt to block construction or operation of a proposed new mill if that plant would worsen overproduction in the area. The institute, established on August 20, 1929, had become inactive on March 15, 1931, but was reorganized when the NRA called upon it to represent the industry in drafting the code. Darrow's board described it "as a kind of steering committee or directorate, whereby the greater units can manage, dominate and have their will over the weaker."[38]

The Cement Institute and industry pricing practices revived long-standing complaints about price-fixing and collusion. A conservative, pro-business Supreme Court had cleared the industry of similar charges in 1925, but critics renewed charges in the 1930s at a time when big business's image had become tarnished in the eyes of much of the public. The heightened demand for cement on New Deal construction projects in particular raised concern among politicians and government officials that big cement companies were gouging taxpayers by charging artificially high prices on government contracts.

Between July 1933 and December 1935, New Deal construction projects consumed more than seventy-six million barrels of cement and large sums of taxpayers' money. The high prices and bidding practices of cement companies infuriated many politicians. In January 1934, North Dakota Republican Senator Gerald Nye criticized the NRA, blasting big steelmakers as "pirates" and cement executives as "business hogs." He accused cement companies of using the NRA to protect monopolistic practices. He told fellow senators that Milwaukee's NRA administrator, for example, had received five identical bids for portland cement.[39]

That same month, Secretary of the Interior Harold Ickes, who also headed the PWA, attacked "collusive bidding" by large companies. As he explained it to the Associated General Contractors of America, "We may want to place a large order for work on Boulder Dam. Bids are asked for and then a miracle occurs which repeats itself on every similar occasion. Every bid is identical to the fraction of a cent . . . regardless of any differential in production costs as between the cement

38. NRA, "Code of Fair Competition for the Cement Industry as Approved on November 27, 1933, by President Roosevelt," 334–35, box 1319; "Summary: The Portland Cement Industry," box 1319, folder 13; both in NRA Records, RG 9, NA; *New York Times,* June 13, 1934. On the Darrow board, see Stephen J. Sniezoski, "The Darrow Board and the Downfall of the NRA," in Robert F. Himmelberg, ed., *Business and Government in America since 1870: A Twelve-Volume Anthology of Scholarly Articles,* vol. 7, *The New Deal and Corporate Power: Antitrust and Regulatory Policies during the Thirties and World War II* (New York: Garland Publishing, 1994), 351–71. For a brief discussion of the debate over work relief, see Rose, *Put to Work,* chap. 5.

39. *Congressional Record,* vol. 78, pt. 1, 73d Cong., 2d sess., January 18, 1934, 868–69.

mills. To judge from the bids alone it costs one mill exactly what it costs every mill to make the cement and it costs the material men precisely the same in freight rates whether he ships the cement a hundred miles or a thousand miles."[40]

Ickes denied that NRA codes made collusive bidding legal and warned that the public would hold cement officials responsible if the high price of cement limited construction of public works projects. He hinted that states and the federal government might set up their own cement manufacturing plants, if necessary, and that if this happened, "those who are now violating the law and cynically and unpatriotically gouging the public will have only themselves to blame."[41]

At issue was the industry's use of the NRA to revive and codify the multiple basing-point system, which had broken down temporarily during the bitter price wars in 1931. Cement officials took advantage of the Code Authority to achieve industry stabilization through this pricing formula. As historian David Lynch explains, "The system works by an automatic formula. Each producer knows the price at the buyer's basing-point and, regardless of either his location or the location of the buyer, quotes a delivered price composed of the basing-price plus the specified freight tariff from the basing-point to the customer's location." By using this formula, companies could submit identical inflated bids without having to conspire in secret.[42]

Although the Supreme Court ruled the NIRA unconstitutional in 1935, allegations continued that big cement companies were guilty of price-fixing. Ickes complained that cement firms had submitted identical bids on PWA projects no fewer than 257 times between June 1935 and March 1936. Burton K. Wheeler, a Democratic senator from Montana, notified him on April 2, 1936, that four cement companies had submitted identical bids "all the way through to the fourth decimal" on six different government projects.[43]

Industry witnesses testifying before the Interstate Commerce Committee defended the basing-point system, which was also used in the iron and steel, lime, lumber, and many other industries. In effect, they argued that because of the high cost of transporting cement, consumers without the basing-point system would buy only from local mills, thus creating many local monopolies. According to the

40. Excerpt from address by Hon. Harold L. Ickes, Secretary of the Interior and Administrator of Public Works, Washington, D.C., before the Associated General Contractors of America, January 31, 1934, in The Cement Institute, Public Relations Program, 1934 (in author's possession).

41. Ibid. For the flavor of similar criticisms by state officials, see Henry Horner, Governor of Illinois, to General Hugh S. Johnson, March 30, 1934, box 1321, folder 20, NRA Records, RG 9, NA.

42. Loescher, *Imperfect Collusion*, 181–85; Lynch, *Concentration of Economic Power,* 182–83.

43. Hawley, *The New Deal and the Problem of Monopoly*, 361; *Congressional Record,* vol. 80, pt. 5, 74th Cong., 2d sess., April 10, 1936, 5360.

industry's view, the practice of selling at delivered prices preserved rather than stifled competition, but Senator Wheeler disagreed. He dismissed the basing-point system as "nothing more or less than a juggling of freight costs so that all cement mills could arrive at an identical price to charge the Government." He complained that this pricing system provided enormous profits to cement companies while it saddled the government with increased debt and ate up funds appropriated by Congress for the jobless.[44]

John Treanor, an official of the Riverside Cement Company in California, contacted Senator Wheeler in 1934 in an effort to distance himself from other industry officials and to seek better relations with the government. Even he dismissed as "sheer bunk and hypocrisy" industry arguments that the basing-point system discouraged monopolistic practices and promoted competition: "The truth is . . . that ours is an industry above all others that cannot stand free competition, that must systematically restrain competition or be ruined."[45]

Efforts by antimonopolists against the cement and other industries languished until the economy took another sharp downturn in late 1937. Amid concerns that the monopolistic practices of American corporations were choking off the nation's economic recovery, President Roosevelt called for a Congressional Temporary National Economic Committee (TNEC) to investigate and gather information on the concentration of power in the corporate structure of the American economy. He also requested that the Federal Trade Commission investigate the links between prices and monopolistic practices. Data compiled by the Bureau of Labor Statistics revealed that 23 percent of the value of all commodities increased in price between April 1937 and February 1938, despite the fact that prices in general during this period of recession had fallen.[46]

In December 1937, the FTC opened hearings on the cement industry after charging the Cement Institute and seventy-five affiliated companies, including Universal Atlas, with price-fixing. An Interior Department official testified that only when cement officials learned of discussions to consider creating a government cement plant to finish construction on the Grand Coulee Dam and the Tennessee Valley Authority did they lower the price of a barrel of cement by seventy-five cents. Pennsylvania officials testified that they had been told by cement officials that if a company lowered the price of cement, penalties would be imposed on it by the Cement Institute.[47]

---

44. *Congressional Record,* vol. 88, pt. 5, 74th Cong., 2d sess., April 10, 1936, 5360.

45. Ibid.; Hawley, *The New Deal and the Problem of Monopoly,* 363; Loescher, *Imperfect Collusion,* 84–85.

46. Hawley, *The New Deal and the Problem of Monopoly,* 400; Lynch, *Concentration of Economic Power,* 23, 35–70.

47. *New York Times,* December 2, 3, and 4, 1937. For an example of how the Cement Institute imposed penalties against companies that sold below the delivered price, see

The Cement Institute appointed a committee to devise an ambitious public relations program to counter "misconceptions" about the industry. Mainly through personal contacts, public speeches, printed matter, and paid advertising, industry leaders set out to shape the views of the public and government officials at every level. The Cement Institute approved this public relations plan, which emphasized the following points: that prices were not too high, that uniformity in prices did not grow out of collusion, that government-owned cement plants were not a viable political or economic option, that tariff protection for cement was necessary, and that the industry's practices were fair to dealers.[48]

Nevertheless, public anger at cement companies surfaced in many states. For example, Texas highway officials began to import large amounts of foreign cement, and the state attorney general filed a suit in the district court charging the Cement Institute with price-fixing. This suit, which targeted Universal Atlas and five other cement companies in Texas, requested penalties and cancellation of these companies' charters.[49]

The TNEC urged Congress to outlaw the basing-point system, and the Federal Trade Commission, too, concluded that the Cement Institute was guilty of antitrust violations. The FTC issued a "cease and desist" order against the industry's multiple basing-point system, but a circuit court of appeals vacated the order. It was not until April 1948 that the Supreme Court upheld the FTC's order against the basing-point system, which Universal Atlas then abandoned on July 7, 1948.[50]

Universal Atlas officials had adopted a sophisticated public relations program not only to ward off antimonopoly attacks but also to keep organized labor at bay. They devised plant publications "to promote the spirit of friendliness and cooperation in the ranks of workers." Plant officials carefully screened all such publications "to prevent the insertion of matter which might be regarded political

Federal Trade Commission v. Cement Institute et al., October term, 1947, *United States Supreme Court Reports,* book 92, Lawyers ed. (Rochester, N.Y.: The Lawyers Co-operative Publishing Company, 1948), 1041.

48. See the Committee on Public Relations, "A Public Relations Plan for the Cement Institute," April 10, 1934, and "Progress Report of Committee on Public Relations," July 5, 1934; both in the Cement Institute, Public Relations Program, 1934 (in author's possession).

49. *New York Times,* March 8, 1938; Texas State Federation of Labor, *Proceedings,* 1938, 152.

50. Lynch, *Concentration of Economic Power,* 340; *Federal Trade Commission v. Cement Institute et al.,* 1010–55; *New York Times,* April 27 and 28, 1948; "Steel Industry Abandons Basing-Point Pricing," *Business Week,* July 10, 1948, 19–20; Loescher, *Imperfect Collusion,* 243–63. The American Federation of Labor supported basing-point pricing, and predicted that the Supreme Court's decision would mean massive layoffs and would create ghost towns by forcing rural cement workers to leave small towns in search of urban jobs. William Schoenberg, "The 'Basing Point' Decision: Ghost Towns Are in the Making If It Stands."

in character or otherwise provocative." President Blaine S. Smith insisted that the contents be confined to noncontroversial issues: "Labor and other questions of the moment all tend to put the corporation and its Subsidiaries under the searchlight of publicity, and for this as well as other reasons, greater caution must be exercised in the preparation of reading matter destined to reach our workers and the public."[51]

Cement companies used a drop in the frequency and severity of job-related accidents in 1935 to improve their public image and illustrate that there was no need for unions in their industry. Universal Atlas conducted highly publicized safety trophy ceremonies at the Ilasco plant to feature representatives of its company union, undercut the appeal of independent trade unions, and bolster its standing in the community. R. W. Hayden acted as the leader of a safety rally on September 6, 1935, marking the completion of one year on August 2, 1935, without a lost-time accident. E. T. Fuller, an Atlas attorney in Hannibal, presented a safety certificate to employees' representative Frank Pollard.[52]

On June 24, 1936, the company hosted a big celebration that featured orchestra music, refreshments, and free food for the hard-pressed families of workers at the Ilasco plant. Included in the celebration was the presentation of the 1935 safety trophy. For the unveiling of the trophy, plant officials chose Virginia Rose McKinney, Anna Ukrop, Edith Galluzzio, and Joan Albert, daughters of Ilasco workers. On behalf of the Portland Cement Association, A. J. R. Curtis presented the trophy to Franklin F. Webb, who accepted it as the representative of plant workers. Company president B. F. Affleck assured the audience that the company was doing everything it could to stimulate economic recovery.[53]

Cement officials particularly feared the Wagner Act, or National Labor Relations Act (NLRA) of 1935, passed shortly after the Supreme Court declared the NIRA unconstitutional. The new law, sponsored by New York Senator Robert Wagner and initially opposed but later signed by President Roosevelt, outlawed the financing of company unions and other employer activities to thwart trade

51. B. F. Affleck, Chairman, The Cement Institute, Committee on Public Relations, to Cement Manufacturers, May 3, 1934, and Blaine S. Smith to F. L. Stone and P. C. VanZandt, September 14, 1936 (both in author's possession).

52. "Accidents in the Portland Cement Industry, 1935," *Monthly Labor Review* 43 (October 1936): 890–93; *Hannibal Courier-Post,* September 6, 1935; "Safety Trophy Dedication, Hannibal Plant," Universal Atlas Cement Co., June 24, 1936 (in author's possession).

53. *Hannibal Courier-Post,* June 19 and 24, 1936; "Safety Trophy Dedication," June 24, 1936. The Ilasco plant had another perfect safety record in 1939, and similar trophy rededication ceremonies were held on June 15, 1940. Frank Pollard again accepted the trophy as the employees' representative, and H. D. Schnitzlein, L. R. Fleurdelys, James Ragan, W. C. Albert, J. L. Carter, M. E. Jones, A. C. Binns, W. L. Brady, and M. R. Simms were in charge of the reception and tours of the plant. "Safety Trophy Re-Dedication," June 15, 1940.

unionism. It guaranteed workers' rights to form unions of their own choice and engage in collective bargaining. A new National Labor Relations Board was created to supervise factory elections to determine which union would represent workers.

Cement officials put pressure on Congress to kill the Wagner bill. John B. Reynolds, head of the Information Bureau of the Cement Institute, argued that it was detrimental to "the private rights both of employers and employees." He complained that it "would unionize American industry . . . assure domination of labor boards by organized labor agents; make the labor boards star chamber bodies . . . force closed shop conditions on employers," and "provide a gag rule for industry and place a premium on strikes."[54]

Despite corporate opposition to parts of the New Deal, it is clear that the cement industry on the eve of the Japanese attack on Pearl Harbor had benefited a great deal from government-sponsored projects and contracts aimed at encouraging capital accumulation. Although many conservatives complained about alleged chiselers and others eager for a government handout, cement executives successfully defended monopolistic pricing practices that had allowed them to feast on public-funded construction projects. New Deal labor policies had enabled unions to gain a significant foothold in the industry, but the power of cement companies remained intact on the eve of World War II as executives learned to adjust to organized labor. In fact, Universal Atlas kept a union out of the Ilasco plant until well into the war.

54. John B. Reynolds to Members of the Cement Institute, March 26, 1935 (in author's possession).

(11)

Gypsies Come to Town
A Union at Last

Many a time, when I have seen a man abusing a horse, I have wished I knew that horse's language so that I could whisper in his ear, "Fool, you are master here, if you but knew it. Launch out with your heels!" The working millions, in all the ages, have been horses . . . all they needed was a capable leader to organize their strength and tell them how to use it, and they would in that moment be master.
—Mark Twain, "The New Dynasty"

Until the 1930s, organized labor had done little for workers in the portland cement industry. The small number of AFL federal labor unions organized after 1910 to represent cement workers had disintegrated. They were casualties of the AFL's stodgy craft orientation and practices, the pro-business climate of the 1920s, and the isolated rural locations of many cement plants. Not until passage of the NIRA in 1933 did cement workers begin to unionize again, and it took even another ten years for Atlas workers in Ilasco to organize under extraordinary wartime conditions.

Despite employer resistance, the AFL had taken steps to organize the cement industry in the wake of Section 7(a) of the NIRA. Between the NIRA's enactment and the AFL's annual convention in October 1934, the AFL organized about thirty federal labor unions in the cement industry, most of which were in Pennsylvania's Lehigh Valley. The AFL Executive Council authorized an organizing campaign among cement mill workers, creating the National Council of United Cement Workers in 1936 to supervise the campaign. William Schoenberg, of the International Association of Machinists, headed the unionizing drive and pushed for a greater share of federal contracts for unionized workers who produced cement for public construction projects.[1]

1. *Monthly Labor Review* 44 (January 1937): 3; AFL, *Proceedings,* 1939, 46; Fink, ed., *Labor Unions,* 52; William Schoenberg, "The National Council of United Cement Workers."

Bolstered now by the National Labor Relations Act, the AFL's growing campaign to organize cement mill workers coincided with an internal revolt against its refusal to endorse an industrial union strategy to replace its traditional practice of organizing skilled workers according to their crafts. John L. Lewis, head of the United Mineworkers of America, led a group of more militant labor leaders to form the Committee on Industrial Organization in late 1935. When the AFL later expelled them, they formed the Congress of Industrial Organizations in 1938. Millions of workers flocked to the new organization, which captured and inspired much of the militancy exhibited by American workers in the mid-1930s. The CIO put more emphasis on the recruitment of all workers, regardless of gender, race, ethnicity, or skill, and it displayed a greater willingness to include Socialists, Communists, and other radicals.[2]

In response, the AFL adopted a more flexible organizing strategy. Toney Gallo, of the National Council of United Cement Workers, praised AFL President William Green's campaign to organize cement workers into a federal labor union, and he condemned the CIO for interfering in these efforts. A cement local in Oglesby, Illinois, expressed support for Green in "the present unfortunate misunderstanding that threatens to disrupt the organized labor movement."[3]

On August 15, 1938, the National Council of United Cement Workers adopted a resolution endorsing the organization of an international union of cement, lime, and gypsum workers in the United States and Canada along industrial lines. On September 11, 1939, the AFL granted a charter to the United Cement, Lime, and Gypsum Workers International Union (CLGWU) at a convention in St. Louis, despite protests from the AFL's Building and Construction Trades Department and the International Hod Carriers, Building and Common Laborers Union of America. William Schoenberg became the first president of the CLGWU, which cement company managers later dubbed "Gypsies." By October 1939, the new union consisted of ninety-six locals with more than fourteen

---

Universal Atlas was not included on a list of AFL-approved cement companies in early 1937.

2. Fink, *Labor's Search*, 141–44, points out that although leaders of the Missouri State Federation of Labor exhibited much less idealism and had become increasingly conservative in the 1930s, they favored unity and reconciliation over the bitter approach taken by AFL leaders on the national level. A casual reading of the *Hannibal Labor Press* at that time confirms Fink's analysis. For an excellent analysis of the links between race, radicalism, civil rights, and CIO organizing in the 1930s, see Michael K. Honey, *Southern Labor and Black Civil Rights: Organizing Memphis Workers*.

3. Fink, *Labor's Search*, 144; Toney Gallo to William Green, August 21, 1937, and Wm. Neeland to William Green, January 13, 1938; both in American Federation of Labor Records, pt. 2, President's Office Files, series A, William Green Papers, 1934–1952, microfilm reel 36 (hereafter cited as AFL Records-Green Papers).

thousand members, but it still had made no attempt to organize Universal Atlas's Ilasco plant.[4]

Jurisdictional disputes plagued AFL organizing efforts. Some craft unions complained that the CLGWU would take away workers who otherwise might add to their own membership. Narrow jurisdictional jealousies contributed to the loss of plants to the CIO in Cement City, Michigan, and Des Moines, Iowa. The CIO also challenged the AFL in plants in Boston, Detroit, and New York. Schoenberg complained to AFL President Green on January 8, 1942, that "when we were unable to adjust our difficulties with the craft organizations, our members have openly deserted us and have allied themselves with the CIO." He pointed out that the CIO had successfully raided the AFL at the Lone Star Cement Company's plant in New Orleans, Louisiana, despite the fact that company officials had even worked with the CLGWU to keep the more radical CIO out of the plant.[5]

Schoenberg assured Green that he was "safeguarding" the interests of craft organizations, but pointed out that the CIO's attacks on the CLGWU were most successful in urban areas where strong AFL craft unions had opposed organizing cement workers into an industrial union. He conceded that the history of craft-based neglect of cement workers exposed the AFL to CIO criticism, but noted that "fortunately for our organization, most of our local unions are located in rural territories where the craft organizations have no local unions, and in such territories we have no difficulties with any organization."[6]

World War II had a dramatic impact on unions and labor politics and created the conditions under which Ilasco cement workers would organize. As defense production shot up, so did employment and labor's cooperation with the government to win the war. Once again, the creation of government wartime agencies such as the War Labor Board (WLB), War Production Board, Office of Price Administration, and the Office of Production Management incorporated organized labor into economic decision-making and planning. President Roosevelt persuaded business and labor leaders to accept the WLB as the ultimate arbiter of industrial disputes. To avoid interruptions in production, labor leaders pledged not to call strikes, and employers promised not to use lockouts.[7]

The shift to a war economy brought no-strike pledges, but union leaders were unable to suppress rank-and-file discontent in the face of sharp price increases in

4. AFL, *Proceedings,* 46–47, 631; Fink, ed., *Labor Unions,* 51–53; Herbert R. Northrup, "From Union Hegemony to Union Disintegration: Collective Bargaining in Cement and Related Industries."

5. William Schoenberg to William Green, January 8, 1942, microfilm reel 25, AFL Records-Green Papers.

6. See also Schoenberg to Green, May 11, 1942, in ibid.

7. Rayback, *History of American Labor,* 373–79.

1941. In fact, a series of long, bitter strikes broke out that year as the CIO stepped up its militancy. By the time of Japan's attack on Pearl Harbor on December 7, this militancy had convinced President Roosevelt to create the WLB in order to prevent work stoppages through compulsory arbitration.[8]

As inflation squeezed workers, however, the government's attempt to limit wage increases made it harder for the WLB to curb labor militancy and prevent interruptions in production. When President Roosevelt issued an executive order on April 8, 1943, to hold the line on prices and wages, Green at first objected to the freezing of wages for workers with cases pending before the WLB and arbitration panels. At Green's behest, AFL members on the WLB criticized the executive order for freezing wage inequities, but nevertheless voted with others to comply with the order.

This infuriated members of Local 309 of the CIO's International Union of Mine, Mill, and Smelter Workers at the Universal Atlas Cement Company's plant in Universal, Pennsylvania. A WLB referee had recommended that they receive a raise of five cents per hour, but President Roosevelt's order limited their raise to half of that amount. To protest the WLB's decision to honor the executive order, members of Local 309 launched a five-day wildcat strike in mid-April 1943 that ended when the WLB ordered them back to work.[9]

The organization of Ilasco workers grew out of this militancy and out of national developments in the labor movement in 1943. John L. Lewis had resigned as head of the CIO shortly after he endorsed Republican presidential candidate Wendell Willkie instead of President Roosevelt in the election of 1940. Lewis's growing hostility toward FDR because of the New Deal's conservative shift in the late 1930s contributed to divisions within the CIO and isolated him politically in the labor movement. Having failed to persuade CIO unions to repudiate FDR, he then led the United Mine Workers out of the CIO in October 1942 and stepped up efforts to organize the steel and other coal-related industries through the UMW's District 50, independent of both the AFL and the CIO.[10]

H. H. Furlow, a District 50 organizer, went to Ilasco in January 1943. Universal Atlas's workers there complained that they still had only a remnant of a company union, the Hannibal Cement Plant Employees Union. Since 1937, the company had signed collective bargaining agreements that covered only members of this organization, or what former worker Angelo Venditti dismissed as a "two-bit

8. Green, *World of the Worker,* 174–81.

9. *The Termination Report of the National War Labor Board: Industrial Disputes and Wage Stabilization in Wartime,* vol. 2, *Appendices to Volume I, Part I,* 268; Philip Taft, *The A.F. of L. from the Death of Gompers to the Merger,* 224–25. On the walkout at the Universal plant, see *Business Week,* April 17, 1943, 15, and April 24, 1943, 14.

10. Rayback, *History of American Labor,* 383–84; Nelson Lichtenstein, *Labor's War at Home: The CIO in World War II,* 26–32.

union." Furlow alleged that at that time no bona fide trade union was even trying to organize Venditti and others at the Ilasco plant.[11]

District 50 issued a temporary charter to Local No. 12,685, which elected temporary officers to represent Ilasco cement workers. Furlow and Dan Wininger, another representative of District 50, praised UMW President Lewis, and in an appeal to white ethnics and a handful of black workers at the Ilasco plant, emphasized that the union was committed to eliminating racial discrimination. They also pointed out that the union represented more than just miners. In fact, it had already negotiated contracts with the Independent Gravel and Marblehead Lime companies in the Hannibal area.[12]

In response to the competition from District 50, AFL organizers came running. On July 2, 1943, Lawrence J. Taub, a CLGWU organizer from St. Louis, held a well-attended meeting at the Knights of Pythias Hall in Hannibal. Several members of AFL locals, including Fred Mirtzwa, chairman of the organization committee of the Hannibal Trades and Labor Assembly, encouraged cement workers in the audience to join the CLGWU instead of District 50. Taub emphasized that the CLGWU at that time was the bargaining agent for 130 of the nation's 160 cement plants, including six owned by the Universal Atlas Cement Company.[13]

At a meeting on July 20, 1943, workers formed Local 205 of the CLGWU and elected officers from Ilasco and Hannibal. Carl Roberts, a former alderman from Hannibal's fifth ward, was chosen as president, and Charles Rache, a Hungarian immigrant and pastor of Ilasco's Church of the Nazarene, became vice president. W. W. Quinlan was elected as the recording secretary, Lester Gardner as the financial secretary-treasurer, and Clyde Kirgan as the guard. Steve Oslica, Lloyd Simms, and C. E. Huddelson became trustees.[14]

District 50, after presenting 140 membership cards with signatures of Universal Atlas workers, petitioned the company on July 15 to recognize it as the sole bargaining agent at the Ilasco plant. On July 24, Universal Atlas refused, instead referring District 50 to the National Labor Relations Board, which scheduled a hearing to be held in Hannibal on August 21 to arrange for an election to determine which union would be the exclusive bargaining agent. Since Local 205 of the CLGWU had since presented 130 membership cards signed by workers,

11. *Hannibal Labor Press,* August 6, 1943; Angelo Venditti, interview by author, July 9, 1993; National Labor Relations Board, *Decisions and Orders of the National Labor Relations Board,* vol. 52, 555–56.

12. *Hannibal Labor Press,* May 14, June 4, and August 6, 1943. The *Hannibal Labor Press* called District 50 "the Lewis dragnet."

13. Quoted in *Hannibal Labor Press,* July 9, 1943.

14. *Hannibal Labor Press,* July 23 and July 30, 1943. Other nominees for Local 205 offices were Earl Hicks, J. B. Love, Perry Shuck, W. E. Sampson, Joe King, Marsh Northcutt, Angelo Venditti, Cecil Pickett, Frank Herzog, L. A. Renner, Charles Kitsock, Henry Burkhead, and Frank Mueller.

the NLRB also granted it the right to participate in the hearing. Only 54 employees had refused to sign membership cards for either union.[15]

The CLGWU sent Taub and union vice president Reuben Roe, of Buffalo, Iowa, to the hearing, while Earl Suver, of St. Louis, represented District 50. C. B. Baker and G. C. Huth represented the Universal Atlas Cement Company. The NLRB had notified the Hannibal Cement Plant Employees Union of the hearing, but nobody from this organization even bothered to show up. In fact, this so-called union, whose close ties to company management were now fully exposed, quickly disbanded.[16]

The NLRB ruled that all employees, except for clerical, salaried, and supervisory workers, were eligible to vote. This included four or five watchmen and five hourly paid laboratory workers classified as composition men and samplers, whose job duties included weighing raw materials for the finished product and setting kiln controls. District 50 had sought to exclude watchmen from the list of eligible voters, and Universal Atlas had tried to exclude both watchmen and hourly paid laboratory workers.[17]

Workers had about one month to discuss which of the rival unions to choose in the upcoming NLRB election. Carson Smith, a former Ilasco resident who had helped to organize Local 5 of the CLGWU in Dewey, Oklahoma, returned to endorse the CLGWU and tell of the success of Local 5 where he now lived. Organizer Taub sent an open letter urging workers to accept the CLGWU as their bargaining agent. He touted the AFL's fight for better public schools, Social Security, and workmen's compensation, and he emphasized the CLGWU's success in winning vacations for workers in the cement industry. "Most plants now get vacation with pay," he said. "If you would have asked for a vacation with pay in the old days you were apt to be looking for a job."[18]

To counter charges of neglect made by representatives of the UMW's District 50, CLGWU officials insisted that they had been trying to organize workers at Universal Atlas's Ilasco plant since 1940. CLGWU Vice President Roe attended Local 205's meetings in Hannibal to assure workers of the union's interest in them. An organizing committee issued a statement encouraging workers to look ahead and consider how important unions would be in the postwar period: "You must look forward to the day when the worker in cement will have to be in a position to resist all attempts to lower our wages and any infringements on our seniority rights, working conditions, etc. Everyone knows that whenever there is a surplus of any commodity, the price of that commodity goes down. Each and

---

15. National Labor Relations Board, *Decisions and Orders of the National Labor Relations Board,* vol. 52, 555–56.

16. *Hannibal Labor Press,* September 17, 1943.

17. Ibid.

18. Quoted in *Hannibal Labor Press,* August 13, 1943. On Smith's return to Ilasco on behalf of the CLGWU, see *Hannibal Labor Press,* August 20, 1943.

everyone of us must face the fact that the day is coming when there will also be a surplus of labor. When that day arrives we want to be in a position to hold whatever gains we have made or will make in the near future."[19]

District 50's challenge to the AFL in Ilasco complicated efforts by Lewis to reestablish harmony with AFL leaders. While Ilasco workers were gearing up for the NLRB election, the UMW applied for readmission to the AFL. Citing District 50's activities in Ilasco as a complicating factor, Green and the Executive Council agreed to submit the UMW's reaffiliation request to the AFL's upcoming convention in October, but without recommendation.[20]

These national developments may have influenced the outcome of the NLRB election at Universal Atlas's Ilasco plant. On September 23, 1943, cement plant workers voted at two polling places, one in Ilasco and the other on South Main Street in Hannibal. Of 286 eligible voters, 236 workers cast their ballots, 152 for Local 205. Members of Local 205 were also required to join the Missouri State Federation of Labor and the Hannibal Central Labor Union. Although District 50 had signed up at least 140 members at the plant, it attracted only 84 voters. In light of the UMW's pending application for an AFL charter, this suggests that perhaps Lewis reined in District 50 organizers to avoid antagonizing AFL leaders further. It might also suggest cooperation between the company and the less radical CLGWU. Whatever the case, the CLGWU now had bargaining agreements in 132 of the nation's cement plants, and the AFL readmitted the UMW a few weeks later.[21]

Local 205 and Universal Atlas reached an impasse in their first contract negotiations. An arbitrator from the U.S. Conciliation Service arrived, and the case went before a panel representing Region 7 of the WLB. At a hearing in Hannibal in April 1944, Reuben Roe, Lawrence J. Taub, and business representative Ray Williams presented Local 205's case to a panel consisting of Andrew J. Murphy of Louisiana, Missouri, and Twyman V. Hilt and John H. Abrams, both of Hannibal. Murphy represented the public's interest on the panel, while Hilt represented industry. Abrams, editor of the *Hannibal Labor Press* and a member of the International Typographical Union, represented labor. Gordon C. Huth and P. N. Bushnell represented Universal Atlas.[22]

---

19. *Hannibal Labor Press,* August 20 and September 10, 1943.

20. Rayback, *History of American Labor,* 384; *Hannibal Labor Press,* August 20, 1943.

21. *Hannibal Labor Press,* September 24, October 1, and October 15, 1943; National Labor Relations Board, *Decisions and Orders of the National Labor Relations Board,* vol. 52, 557; Rayback, *History of American Labor,* 384. Despite success at the Ilasco plant, the CLGWU's unionizing efforts in general slowed until after 1945. This was due in large part to the closure of many cement plants regarded as nonessential to war production. Fink, ed., *Labor Unions,* 52.

22. *Hannibal Labor Press,* April 21, 1944, and January 26, 1945; Regional War Labor Board 7: Kansas City, Missouri, "Explanation of Board Action," in the Matter of Universal Atlas Cement Company, Hannibal, Missouri, and United Cement Lime and Gypsum

One of the sticking points in negotiations was the company's vacation policy, which allowed only a maximum of one week. The Hearing Panel (Abrams dissenting) had recommended continuation of the company's policy, but the Regional War Labor Board in Kansas City, which did not issue its "Interim Directive Order" until January 11, 1945, overruled the panel. The board endorsed the liberalization of vacation benefits from one week with pay after one year of service, to two weeks after five years of continuous service. This order was retroactive to February 29, 1944. At that time, the board regarded reasonable vacations as vital to securing maximum wartime production.[23]

The Regional Board did not grant a union shop but supported the panel's recommendation granting the CLGWU's demand for union security through the check-off and payment of wages to union representatives for time spent in meetings with management during working hours. The board postponed the union's request for a 10 percent wage hike but later ordered a wage increase retroactive to April 10, 1945.[24]

When the war ended in 1945, Ilasco workers had cause for both optimism and alarm as they looked to the future. On the one hand, they were among the 4.2 million workers in the United States who had joined unions since the war began. This strengthened their bargaining power and increased the nation's total union membership to 14.7 million. On the other hand, the wartime reliance on government boards and agencies bound organized labor even more tightly to the government and the Democratic Party. Workers worried, too, about the conversion to a peacetime economy. Would the return of peace bring a return to joblessness and depression?[25]

After the war, rivalries between the AFL and the CIO over the organization of cement workers continued as the CIO launched Operation Dixie, a Southern organizing initiative, in the spring of 1946. CLGWU President Schoenberg, in a speech to the annual Texas State Federation of Labor convention in June of that year, complained that the CIO had snatched away four AFL cement plants in Houston, Dallas, and New Orleans. At the Lone Star Cement Company's Houston plant, the CIO's success grew out of its strategy to appeal to black workers on

Workers International Union, Local No. 205, A.F. of L., case no. 111–6793-D, March 23, 1945, Russell S. Bauder Papers, folder 1001, WHMC–Columbia. On the CLGWU's "no-strike" pledge, see *Hannibal Labor Press*, July 16, 1943. See Howell John Harris, *The Right to Manage: Industrial Relations Policies of American Business in the 1940s*, 47–58, for a discussion of the NWLB. Just before the hearing, Universal Atlas had shut down the Ilasco plant, reportedly because of large stocks of surplus cement. The plant did not reopen until June 26, 1944. *Hannibal Labor Press*, June 16, 1944.

23. *Hannibal Labor Press*, August 11, January 26, and March 9, 1945.

24. Regional War Labor Board 7: Kansas City, Missouri, "Explanation of Board Action"; *Hannibal Labor Press*, January 26 and November 9, 1945.

25. Green, *World of the Worker*, 174.

the basis of the AFL's traditional racist policies. A similar strategy paid off among Mexican workers when the Mine, Mill and Smelter Workers Union won an NLRB election in the Southwestern Portland Cement Company's plant in El Paso.[26]

An increasingly repressive political climate contributed to the defeat of Operation Dixie, however, and restricted the American labor movement in general. In 1947, the Taft-Hartley Act banned closed shops, boycotts, and strikes by federal employees. It allowed for union decertification elections, banned the use of union funds in elections, and held union leaders individually responsible under the law for contract violations. It also granted employers the right to communicate their views on unions to workers, and allowed states to pass so-called right to work laws to prohibit the union shop.[27]

The Taft-Hartley Act also required union leaders to sign affidavits swearing that they were not Communists. Failure to comply deprived unions of a spot on NLRB election ballots. This drove a deeper wedge between Communists and non-Communists in the labor movement at a time when anti-Communist hysteria was sweeping the nation. This ideological warfare in the labor movement led to the expulsion of several left-wing unions from the CIO and robbed it of some of its most vital elements.[28]

In response to growing attacks on labor, the AFL and the now more conservative CIO merged in 1955. This gave unity to the labor movement, but at the expense of millions of members expelled from the CIO because of alleged Communist affiliations. The Cold War hysteria, along with a systematic ideological campaign by big business to win the hearts and minds of American workers after 1945, helped to shape a much more conservative labor movement.[29]

Spearheading the postwar ideological offensive by big business was the National Association of Manufacturers (NAM). From churches and schools to the airwaves and workplace, the NAM took the public-relations war against trade unions and the New Deal state into the heart of communities. Many businessmen linked the war against communism to the campaign against labor's calls for an expanded welfare state, including full-employment legislation. Although there were differences in the business community over how serious the threat from labor was, most corporations took advantage of the Cold War climate to

26. Texas State Federation of Labor, *Proceedings,* 1946, 63–67. On the postwar defeat of the CIO's Operation Dixie campaign, see Barbara S. Griffith, *The Crisis of American Labor: Operation Dixie and the Defeat of the CIO,* and Honey, *Southern Labor,* chap. 8.

27. Rayback, *History of American Labor,* 398–99. On the forces contributing to the failure of Operation Dixie's biracial organizing campaign in Memphis, see Honey, *Southern Labor,* chap. 8.

28. Honey, *Southern Labor,* chap. 8.

29. Ibid. chap. 9. For an excellent discussion of business's broad-based ideological war against unions and New Deal liberalism after World War II, see Elizabeth Fones-Wolf, *Selling Free Enterprise: The Business Assault on Labor and Liberalism, 1945–60.*

define labor's agenda as antithetical to American values. They upheld profits, individualism, and free enterprise as American core values while they steadily chipped away at the power and popularity of organized labor. In their view, patriotism required the public to grant corporations a free hand in running the country.[30]

Like many corporations, Universal Atlas bombarded workers with clip sheets and pamphlets ridiculing communism, touting free enterprise, and attacking the notion that wealth in the United States was concentrated in the hands of a few individuals. The company's Employee Information Committee distributed these clip sheets "so that fewer men need be left speechless when faced with either the glib critics of enterprise or the ardent collectivist."[31]

As Ray E. Hoffman retired after twenty-seven years as plant manager on December 1, 1946, Universal Atlas officials braced themselves for postwar labor demands. Richard D. Mayne, who had a mining engineering degree from the Carnegie Institute of Technology, replaced him. Mayne had been with the company since 1937 and had replaced Paul Kirkbride as assistant manager of the Ilasco plant in 1943. At a plant managers' meeting in 1946, Universal Atlas's G. C. Huth, manager of industrial relations, urged Mayne and others to get as much information as possible about what the unions were doing and saying in regard to time-motion studies, wage expectations, calls for a shorter workweek, and demands for a stronger union role in safety.[32]

To gear up for workers' demands, officials at the Ilasco plant stepped up distribution of literature packaged as "Employees Economic Education." Sometimes items from pamphlets attacking socialism and communism were included in the monthly plant bulletin, which otherwise emphasized safety or focused on "newsy" tidbits of information related to workers. For example, the monthly plant bulletin in August 1955 began with a brief article touting the importance of production, savings, and investment over purchasing power as the keys to economic prosperity. The rest of the bulletin was devoted to safety, the Atlas Bowling League, birthdays and vacations, jokes, and other "newsy" employee

---

30. See Fones-Wolf, *Selling Free Enterprise,* chap. 2, for the national context in which big business formulated its ideological campaign to dominate American political discourse. Also useful on the postwar attempts by companies to reestablish managerial control over the workplace is Harris, *Right to Manage.*

31. Universal Atlas Cement Company, Employee Information Committee, "July Clip Sheet," June 24, 1948 (in author's possession). On conflicts between the AFL and the CIO over the organization of cement workers after the war, see, for example, Texas State Federation of Labor, *Proceedings,* 1946, 63–67.

32. *Hannibal Courier-Post,* December 2, 1946; *Rock Products,* January 1947, 80; Universal Atlas Cement Company, "1946 Plant Managers' Meeting," June 5–6, 1946 (in author's possession).

items like a story of how Lionel Sanders recently cut his hand while cleaning a fish.[33]

Business leaders also spread their message by increasing their influence in local schools. During Business-Industry-Education days sponsored by the Chamber of Commerce, schools closed to allow teachers to tour local plants and listen to talks by company officials on the firm's contributions to the community. U.S. Steel and many corporations provided teachers with kits, filmstrips, and other materials designed to push their agenda. Some schools required teachers to adopt instructional programs developed by the NAM and the American Economic Foundation to mold the teaching of economics.[34]

Such programs and literature no doubt influenced many workers, but they could not eliminate fundamental class antagonisms over wages, benefits, working conditions, and the role of the union in shaping industrial relations. In 1949, there were about thirty-six thousand production workers in the cement industry, and all but six of the 149 plants operating that year had collective bargaining agreements. Workers in 82 percent of unionized plants chose the CLGWU as their bargaining representative. By April 1956 there were 2,567 CLGWU members from thirteen locals affiliated with the Missouri State Federation of Labor, including Local 205's 341 members.[35]

Thanks, in part, to the growing role of unions in safety campaigns and committees, the cement industry shed its earlier reputation as one of the most dangerous for workers. By 1947, the accident frequency rate had dipped 45 percent below the rate for forty industries studied by the National Safety Council. The cement industry had become one of the eight safest of the forty industries surveyed, although the number of accidents in Missouri's lime and cement industry rose sharply from 262 in 1946 to 417 in 1947.[36]

At the same time, productivity had increased significantly. Output per manhour of quarrying and manufacturing labor increased from 1.79 barrels in 1930 to

---

33. F. A. Hennigan, Plant Manager, "AIM 1955 Employees Communications Awards Program, Division C," September 1, 1955, Universal Atlas Cement Company, Hannibal. A copy of this issue of the monthly plant bulletin *Cement Plant News* is included in the above (in author's possession).

34. Organized labor tried to combat big business's growing influence in American schools but lacked the economic resources to do so effectively. Fones-Wolf, *Selling Free Enterprise,* chap. 7.

35. Anna Bercowitz, "Labor-Management Relations in the Cement Industry," *Monthly Labor Review* 72 (January 1951): 17; Northrup, "From Union Hegemony," 342; "Organizations Affiliated with the Missouri State Federation of Labor," March 31, 1956, and April 7, 1956, MSLC Records, file 106, WHMC–Columbia.

36. Bercowitz, "Labor-Management Relations," 20; Division of Industrial Inspection of the Missouri Department of Labor and Industrial Relations, *67th Annual Report,* 1946, unpaginated; Division of Industrial Inspection of the Missouri Department of Labor and Industrial Relations, *68th Annual Report,* 1947, unpaginated.

2.59 barrels in 1942 before dropping to 1.99 barrels in 1944. There were 242 male and 13 female workers at the Ilasco plant in 1944. By 1945, the number of workers had risen, along with productivity. There were now 381 male and 12 female employees at the Ilasco plant, and national output had reached 2.10 barrels per man-hour. The Bureau of Labor Statistics reported that the total production and transportation of cement in fifteen Midwest plants required 100.5 man-hours per barrel in 1945–1946, compared to 126.4 in 1934.[37]

With few exceptions, unions and companies negotiated collective bargaining contracts on a plant-by-plant basis. This, of course, favored companies, and in 1946 the CLGWU created the International Policy Committee to shape a uniform national bargaining strategy. Some companies tried but failed to ban industry-wide bargaining in the Taft-Hartley Act. Pattern bargaining would strengthen the hand of unions, helping them to overcome problems like those that developed when Universal Atlas workers at plants in Universal, Pennsylvania, Duluth, Minnesota, and Buffington, Indiana, went on strike in the summer of 1952. During that strike, the company shipped cement produced by nonstriking workers at its other plants to customers in Pittsburgh. This undercut fellow striking workers. F. T. Wiggins, vice president of Universal Atlas, singled out the Ilasco plant for praise in this regard, noting that workers there produced more cement in June and again in July than in any month since September 1925.[38]

A nationwide cement strike in 1957 moved the CLGWU closer to achieving a unified bargaining approach. The strike began soon after most of the contracts negotiated by the CLGWU expired in May. By July 3, when Ilasco's Local 205 joined, the strike had shut down more than one-third of the nation's cement plants. By the time the strike ended around the first of August, more than seventeen thousand cement workers from seventy-four locals had participated.[39]

At issue was the CLGWU's attempt to establish national pattern bargaining. The union had targeted the Penn-Dixie Cement Company when the contract expired on May 1. Other locals followed suit to block shipments by other manufacturers to Penn-Dixie's customers. After settlements were first reached

---

37. "Labor Requirements in Cement Production," *Monthly Labor Review* 63 (September 1946): 361, 363; Missouri Department of Labor and Industrial Inspection, *65th Annual Report,* 1944, 71; Missouri Department of Labor and Industrial Inspection, *66th Annual Report,* 1945, 133.

38. Bercowitz, "Labor-Management Relations," 18; Fink, ed., *Labor Unions,* 53; Northrup, "From Union Hegemony," 344–45; F. T. Wiggins, "Weekly Sales Letter," June 24, August 5, and September 2, 1952 (in author's possession). On divisions among employers over whether to include a ban on industry-wide bargaining in the Taft-Hartley Act, see Christopher L. Tomlins, *The State and the Unions: Labor Relations, Law, and the Organized Labor Movement in America, 1880–1960,* 301–4.

39. "Developments in Industrial Relations," *Monthly Labor Review* 80 (September 1957): 1106; Northrup, "From Union Hegemony," 346; *Hannibal Labor Press,* August 2, 1957.

with the Marquette Cement Manufacturing Company and other smaller firms, union officials announced that they would not settle for anything less than the hourly wage increase of sixteen cents agreed to by Marquette. Officials from other companies balked, however, insisting that talks would remain deadlocked "as long as the union insists on presenting us with a 'pattern' demand."[40]

From industry's point of view, also objectionable was a union demand for a clause to restrict subcontracting. Universal Atlas, the nation's largest cement producer, refused to budge on this issue, since such a clause would have limited its wide discretionary power to subcontract work to nonunion labor. It also opposed granting retroactive benefits in contracts, for this would encourage workers to hold out longer during strikes.[41]

On July 28, Ilasco's Local 205 accepted a compromise agreement negotiated by CLGWU President Felix Jones. The company granted a wage increase that nationwide amounted to about 16.5 cents per hour for the entire package. Included in the package were higher night-shift differentials, job classification adjustments, liberalized vacations, and increased premiums for overtime. A compromise was reached on the retroactivity of the agreement, but the CLGWU dropped its demand for a restrictive subcontractor's clause. In effect, the union conceded greater control over the production process in exchange for more money.[42]

Lone Star Cement, the nation's second-largest cement producer, quickly reached a similar agreement with the CLGWU. Other companies followed suit, accepting Universal Atlas's agreement as the basis for contract negotiations. Some cement officials warned that capitulation to national pattern bargaining meant higher prices and loss of managerial prerogatives.[43]

By 1957, then, Ilasco cement workers had overcome decades of isolation, bitter ethnic divisions, fragmentation, and powerlessness reinforced by the military occupation of the community in 1910. Long ignored by organized labor, they were no longer content to rely simply on company paternalism. Charles Rache, Steve Oslica, Angelo Venditti, Charles Kitsock, Andy Babyak, John Konko, and many others were children of immigrants who now viewed Local 205 as an important institution in their lives. To be sure, ethnic tensions still existed, but they had diminished somewhat. Inter-ethnic marriages and social contacts had created family linkages, which in turn reinforced solidarity during common struggles.

40. Quoted in *Wall Street Journal,* July 2 and 9, 1957. See also the *Hannibal Labor Press,* July 12, 1957.

41. *Wall Street Journal,* July 2 and 29, 1957; Northrup, "From Union Hegemony," 346–47.

42. *Wall Street Journal,* July 29, 1957; *Hannibal Labor Press,* July 19 and August 2, 1957; "Developments in Industrial Relations," *Monthly Labor Review* 80 (September 1957): 1106.

43. *Wall Street Journal,* July 1, 29, and 30, 1957. Northrup, "From Union Hegemony," 346–47.

Jim Tatman, Thomas Harbourn, Royce Tatman, Wilbur Whitley, and others from native-born families in the Ilasco area also assumed leadership positions in the union. Moreover, due in part to better roads and automobiles, the social, cultural, and physical distance between Ilasco and cement plant workers from Hannibal had narrowed considerably since the early 1900s. This meant that the company could no longer count as much on divisions between the communities to undercut unionism.[44]

Why had Ilasco cement plant workers taken so long to organize? After a pattern of persistent labor militancy that was squashed by the state militia in 1910, the first generation of workers abandoned collective action under the weight of state repression, ethnic antagonisms, and corporate power. For many, Atlas paternalism had been the only alternative. This does not mean that Ilasco workers preferred to rely exclusively on the company's goodwill for benefits, vacations, higher wages, and better working conditions. When the government sent a clear signal that patriotic industrial relations during World War II would include a role for unions, the moment was finally at hand for Ilasco's fragmented workers to overcome their fear of the state and organize.[45]

Post-1910 Ilasco contained elements of what author Margaret F. Byington found in her classic 1910 study of the steel mill community of Homestead, Pennsylvania. Byington found that repression and overwhelming corporate power created defeated attitudes among immigrant workers for years after the famous failed strike of 1892. She pointed out that many workers exhausted by hot mill work and cowed by the company's policy of firing anyone suspected of promoting unions lost the initiative and desire to challenge working and living conditions in the mill community. They had little energy left over for family and community life and turned instead to liquor for an outlet.[46]

As Peter Way's recent study of nineteenth-century Irish canal workers further indicates, marginalized unskilled workers who felt culturally alienated and exploited often engaged in self-destructive behavior. Brawling, heavy drinking,

---

44. Julian R. James, Delbert Lieurance, Leslie Beucke, Russell F. Harsell, Ollie Bowen, and Charles Miller were among those who became Hannibal officers of Local 205 in the 1950s. *Hannibal Labor Press,* February 13 and December 18, 1959, and June 9, 1967.

45. David Brody, *Workers in Industrial America: Essays on the Twentieth Century Struggle,* chap. 2, attributes the decline of welfare capitalism to the Great Depression and argues that corporate paternalism might not have yielded to collective bargaining were it not for the economic crisis of the 1930s. Brody argues that despite the limited achievements of welfare capitalism, American workers were generally satisfied with employer paternalism in the 1920s. The experiences of Ilasco cement workers do not support this judgment. Brandes, *American Welfare Capitalism,* chap. 14, also disputes Brody.

46. Byington, *Homestead,* 173–75. Similarly, after Bethlehem Steel used the Pennsylvania State Constabulary to crush a strike in 1910, another strike did not occur there until 1941, when workers finally obtained union recognition. Stolarik, *Growing Up,* 97–99.

theft, and crime became commonplace, straining relations between workers and impeding the formation of class consciousness. Although there is plenty of evidence of such behavior among Ilasco workers, especially in the early years, it is also true that many put a lot of energy into building cultural institutions after 1910. In fact, this absorbed much of the energy that otherwise might have gone into union organizing efforts.[47]

The slowness of Ilasco cement plant workers to organize had important implications for the brand of conservative trade unionism that ultimately emerged. The birth of Local 205 during World War II and its maturation in the context of the Cold War deprived it of more radical ideas that had shaped the philosophy of many workers during the 1930s. The absence of a militant tradition since 1910 and the pressures of Americanization on the children of immigrants in an isolated, rural area further shaped a conservative outlook. When coupled with Cold War pressures and the 1950s economic boom that allowed American cement mill workers to enjoy fatter paychecks, these factors produced a trade unionism that at times expressed militance on "bread-and-butter" issues but did not challenge corporate control over production decisions.

47. Peter Way, "Evil Humor and Ardent Spirits: The Rough Culture of Canal Construction Laborers," and idem, *Common Labour: Workers and the Digging of North American Canals, 1780–1860.*

(12)

Ilasco and the Commercial Construction of Mark Twain

Unconsciously we all have a standard by which we measure other men . . . we admire them, we envy them, for great qualities which we ourselves lack. Hero worship consists in just that. Our heroes are the men who do things which we recognize with regret and sometimes with a secret shame that we cannot do. We find not much in ourselves to admire, we are always privately wanting to be like somebody else.

—Mark Twain, *Autobiography*

I warn the reader that if he leaves out of the account an indignant sense of right and wrong, a scorn of all affectation and pretense, an ardent hate of meanness and injustice, he will come infinitely short of knowing Mark Twain.

—William Dean Howells, *Century Magazine,* 1882

When Mark Twain sank into a coma and died on the evening of April 21, 1910, he was no doubt unaware that a strike led by Hannibal's Mark Twain Machinists Lodge 537 had broken out the day before at the Ilasco cement plant. Had he lived another month, he might have seen newspaper reports that an old former Confederate soldier had commanded an expedition of Missouri National Guardsmen to Little Dixie to protect the property of Yankee cement capitalists near the cave hollow of Twain's youth. Class conflict now rocked the landscape that once featured imaginary standoffs between river pirates and Twain and his young friends in search of gold and adventure. There was nothing imaginary, however, about the cast of characters in the drama unfolding on Little Dixie's new industrial stage. Cement barons, rifle-toting militia, bugler-led columns of immigrant strikers, snipers, and ethnic brigades had turned Twain's boyhood world upside down.

For the northeastern capitalists and supporting cast of Hannibal boosters who had transformed Mark Twain's literary landscape, the strike had brought unwanted publicity. A *St. Joseph Gazette* reporter pointed out that this was the first time since the great railroad strike in 1886 that a Missouri governor had used troops to suppress a labor disturbance. What's more, the newspaper called attention to the fact that the scene of the 1910 disturbance was near the cave popularized in *The Adventures of Tom Sawyer* and *Huckleberry Finn*. The strike capped off seven years of rising anxieties among the area's "old mossbacks" in regard to labor unrest, crime, immigration, and alcohol use in Ilasco.[1]

Unfortunately, we know little about Twain's reaction to the transformation of the cave hollow area. According to Henry Sweets, director of the Mark Twain Boyhood Home and Museum, no evidence exists to suggest that Twain, on his final and emotion-laden trip to Hannibal in 1902, visited the cave hollow area or saw the construction work that was underway at the cement plant. Someone in Hannibal did invite Twain, however, to comment on the fact that "Tom Sawyer's cave was now being ground into cement." Twain, writing in March 1906, explained that several months ago he had received a telegram from someone in Hannibal whom he did not identify. That telegram requested his reaction to the conversion of one of his favorite boyhood haunts into a cement manufacturing center. "But I had nothing to say," Twain wrote. "I was sorry we had lost our cement mine but it was not worth while to talk about it at this late day and, to take it all around, it was a painful subject anyway."[2]

Soon after Twain's death, Atlas officials and their attorney, George A. Mahan, seized an opportunity to repair their public image, which had been damaged by the turmoil in Ilasco. They launched a civic campaign to tie themselves more closely to "Old Hannibal," primarily by manipulating Twain's legacy. The very elites who had transformed the Ilasco area and ushered in industrialization with all of its attendant class and cultural conflicts depicted themselves as logical caretakers of Twain's treasured boyhood playground. In an ongoing campaign to graft their legacy onto Twain's, they drew selectively upon his thought to manipulate the symbols and meaning of that legacy. This public manipulation was the product of a wider offensive designed to reinforce Atlas's cultural and political legitimacy in Little Dixie, impose order in Ilasco, and defend Mahan's legacy as one of Hannibal's leading New South advocates.[3]

This construction of Twain for the public also laid the groundwork for a campaign by Hannibal merchants to build a Mark Twain tourist industry after World War II. In the 1950s, as city, state, and national business leaders planned

---

1. *St. Joseph Gazette*, May 18, 1910.
2. Henry Sweets, interview by author, July 17, 1992; Neider, ed., *Autobiography*, 82.
3. On Missouri boosterism, see Dorsett and Dorsett, "Rhetoric versus Realism," 77–84.

regional economic development, they promoted better roads and highways to stimulate tourism. By the end of that decade, they had clearly decided that Ilasco was an obstacle in their path. Universal Atlas officials agreed, cooperating with Hannibal business leaders and state officials in a way that dovetailed with the company's own interests and future plans. The elimination of Ilasco would open the door for construction of a modernized plant with expanded quarries to combat growing competition in the cement industry.

Hannibal leaders would become the instrument of this campaign to get rid of Ilasco. They pressured the state highway commission for a new highway route that would require Ilasco's dissolution. This highway would bring tourists to sample what was rapidly becoming Hannibal's cottage industry, the commercialization of Mark Twain.

Author and media critic Ron Powers, a native of Hannibal, has pointed out that it was George Mahan who "imposed the Twain blessing and curse upon Hannibal."[4] Mahan, born on a farm outside Hannibal in 1851, attended Washington and Lee University in Lexington, Virginia, and graduated from law school at the University of Indiana in 1872. He then opened a law practice in Hannibal and was elected city attorney in 1875 and county prosecuting attorney in 1878. In 1886 he was elected as a Democratic representative to the Missouri legislature.[5]

During Mahan's distinguished legal career, he served as general counsel for several railroad companies, banks, and industries, including Atlas. A director of the Hannibal Mutual Building and Loan Association and the Hannibal National Bank, he used his close ties to financial interests in St. Louis to promote banking reform following the Panic of 1907. He was a director of the Mississippi Valley Trust Company of St. Louis, and he worked to promote a greater self-consciousness and cooperation among business organizations and banks around the state. During World War I, he promoted local food conservation in cooperation with the U.S. Food Administration. As perhaps Hannibal's most powerful and influential New South spokesman, he became a local icon whose wealth and aristocratic status were displayed through the elegant mansion in which he lived and the African American female live-in servant who cleaned it.[6]

It was Mahan who provided representatives of the Atlas Portland Cement Company with a geologist's report on the rich deposits of limestone and shale in the area. He also purchased options on the land next to the Mark Twain Cave

---

4. March, *History of Missouri,* vol. 2, 1538; Ron Powers, *White Town Drowsing: Journeys to Hannibal,* 74.

5. Shoemaker, *Missouri and Missourians,* vol. 5, 95.

6. Ibid., 95–96; Hagood and Hagood, "History of the Hannibal National Bank," 49; *Ralls County Record,* February 20, 1914; Missouri Council of Defense, *Missouri on Guard* 1 (November 1917): 1; U.S. Federal Manuscript Census, 1910, Mason township, Hannibal, Marion County.

hollow for Atlas. When Atlas officials created the Hannibal Connecting Railroad Company to serve the needs of the Ilasco plant, Mahan assumed a position on the board of directors. In short, he played a key role in facilitating, promoting, and defending Atlas's intrusion into Twain's boyhood world of robber caves and adventure.[7]

As Mahan entered his sixties, he began to take a somewhat less active role in day-to-day business transactions in order to pursue personal interests, the most significant of which was how to shape the public's understanding of Mark Twain. On September 2, 1911, he and his wife, Ida, whose father, Colonel Daniel M. Dulany, was a prominent lumber baron in Hannibal, bought Twain's boyhood home. They restored it and donated it to the city of Hannibal the following year. Mahan soon became a trustee of the State Historical Society of Missouri, and in 1925, after nine years of service as first vice president, took over the presidency of that organization. He held the presidency until his death in December 1936.[8]

During Mahan's long affiliation with the State Historical Society, he remained active in Hannibal's civic affairs, served on the Endowment Committee of the University of Missouri, and donated other Mark Twain landmarks to the city of Hannibal. These philanthropic and other significant contributions to Missouri's intellectual, economic, and political life earned him the honorary Southern title of "Colonel," officially bestowed upon him by the governor. Mahan, along with his wife and son Dulany, who joined his law firm, also commissioned a statue of Tom Sawyer and Huck Finn by Frederick C. Hibbard. At an unveiling ceremony at the foot of Cardiff Hill on May 27, 1926, they donated the bronze statue to the city of Hannibal.[9]

Mahan even tried his own hand at writing. He contributed brief historical sketches of Hannibal figures and landmarks to the *Missouri Historical Review.* It is probably true, as Ron Powers argues, that Mahan's high regard for Twain "stemmed from deeper judgments than boosterism or social *oblige,* " that in fact

---

7. *Hannibal Weekly Journal,* June 1, 1901; *Hannibal Morning Journal,* June 12, 1901; *Hannibal Courier-Post,* December 31, 1930.

8. Missouri 59th General Assembly, House Resolution #72 on the Death of George A. Mahan, February 24, 1937, 309, Typescript Collection, no. 995, vol. 11, WHMC–Columbia; Shoemaker, *Missouri and Missourians,* vol. 5, 96; Hagood and Hagood, *Story of Hannibal,* 140–41; Mark I. West, "A Hannibal Boyhood." Mahan recruited others from his social and business circles to become members of the State Historical Society. See "A Message to Members of the Society," *Missouri Historical Review* 14 (April–July 1920): 497.

9. Powers, *White Town Drowsing,* 73; Franklin Poage, "Mark Twain Memorials in Hannibal," 79–84; "Historical Notes and Comments," *Missouri Historical Review* 21 (October 1926): 112–14; *Hannibal Courier-Post,* May 27, 1926. On Mahan's efforts to increase funding for the University of Missouri, see Jay V. Holmes to Dean Wm. J. Robbins, University of Missouri, October 24, 1933, and George A. Mahan to Dr. A. Ross Hill, President, University of Missouri, January 15, 1917, both in University of Missouri, President's Office Papers, folders 2333 and 230, WHMC–Columbia.

Mahan enjoyed the acclaim that accompanied his status as an amateur historian and authority on Twain's life. Mahan wore many hats, however, and when it came to putting his own spin on the legacy of Mark Twain, the lines between amateur historian, corporate attorney, and New South promoter at times blurred. On the tablet commemorating Twain's boyhood home, for example, he added the following inscription: "Mark Twain's life teaches that poverty is an incentive rather than a bar; and that any boy, however humble his birth and surroundings, may by honesty and industry accomplish great things."[10]

This is not to suggest that Mahan did not genuinely enjoy Twain's writings, but he seemed eager to add that extra capitalist twist to Twain's literary message. Some of Twain's themes undoubtedly appealed to Mahan, who, after all, grew up in much the same cultural environment. Although they apparently never met, only sixteen years separated them in age. Nevertheless, Mahan's philosophical outlook limited his understanding of Twain. Even when assessing Twain's fundamental literary legacy, he could not resist using Wall Street language. At the ceremony unveiling the statue of Tom and Huck, Mahan observed that "Mark Twain is a man who invested lavishly in humanity's stock and made the dividends payable to the world." Thus we have Mahan's Twain, the people's capitalist![11]

Mahan was probably the driving force behind the campaign by Atlas officials to stake out their claim on Twain. "Some enterprising press agent" put articles in newspapers throughout the Southwest publicizing that when Twain described Tom Sawyer's popping up out of a hole in the ground, he probably was referring to a cave now on property owned by the Atlas Portland Cement Company. To link Atlas's activities to Twain's experiences on the Mississippi River, a company official pointed out that the steamboat and fleet of barges belonging to the Atlas Transportation Company—another subsidiary whose board of directors included Mahan—"did the Mark Twain" by hauling cement up and down the river.[12]

Not surprisingly, this public relations campaign included repeated emphasis on the well-known entrepreneurial side of Twain, who had sunk a lot of money into numerous disastrous business ventures, including the Paige typesetting machine. Atlas officials made much of the fact that their corporation was founded in 1899—at just the time that Twain was emerging from personal bankruptcy to pay off business losses, even though the law did not require him to do so. Thus, an entrepreneurial image of Twain was superimposed on the corporate

10. Powers, *White Town Drowsing*, 76. For Mahan's inscription, see "Notes," *Missouri Historical Review* 6 (October 1911–July 1912): 43. For a sample of Mahan's writing, see his "Missourians Abroad: Rear Admiral Robert E. Coontz, U.S.N."

11. *Hannibal Courier-Post*, May 27, 1926.

12. *Rock Products*, July 26, 1924, 59; Hadley, *Magic Powder*, 73; Atlas Transportation Company, "Articles of Association," April 16, 1912, Miscellaneous Deed Record, book 218, 324–25, Marion County, Office of the Circuit Clerk and Recorder, Palmyra, Mo.

merger that produced Atlas. This assigned almost sacred significance to Atlas's corporate origins.[13]

Atlas officials seemed willing to appropriate any theme even remotely connected to Twain, but perhaps their most creative attempt to legitimize themselves as heirs to the Twain tradition was a literary piece that appeared in *The Atlas Bulletin* in 1917. It took the form of a letter—perhaps written by Mahan—from Huckleberry Finn to Tom Sawyer. Designed to glorify Atlas's transformation of the Hannibal area, its publication coincided with the formation of the Hannibal Chamber of Commerce and selection of Mahan as its first president. The publication of Huck's letter to Tom also came just a year after the posthumous publication of *The Mysterious Stranger,* Twain's most pessimistic work. Although Twain had concluded *The Adventures of Huckleberry Finn* by having Huck "light out" for the West to avoid being "sivilized" by Aunt Sally, Atlas snared Huck on Aunt Sally's behalf. In the literary imagination of robber barons, Huck reemerged fully tamed and "sivilized" by the forces of industrialization and big cement.[14]

In this Atlas-constructed letter Huck informed Tom, now living in New York City, that he had recently taken a trip back to Hannibal and discovered, to his pleasant surprise, that the town had "waked up" and was now "alive." "You remember how dead it was in our early boy-hood," he wrote, "unless we played pirate or robber and thru our deviltry stirred up the town." Local banks and the chamber of commerce had increased the tempo and dynamic of Hannibal's social and economic life. No longer was Hannibal a sleepy river town mired in the financial doldrums that plagued it when Tom and Huck were boys. "Why one pay-roll of the Atlas Portland Cement Company Plant alone," Huck proudly noted, "would have bought out the town."[15]

After noting with approval the profound changes that had transformed Hannibal, including the erection of a statue honoring Mark Twain, Huck informed Tom that thanks to the supervision of one of the cement plant's engineers, a good, smooth road now led out of town south to the Cave Hollow. "I was glad enough to go down the River Road," he added, "lolling back in an easy riding car instead of floating down stream in that little skiff that we used to borrow from the absent owner. Tastes will change!"[16]

---

13. *Hannibal Courier-Post,* December 31, 1930. On Twain's account of his bankruptcy, see Neider, ed., *Autobiography,* 277–88. For an unflattering look at Twain's business failures, see Samuel Charles Webster, ed., *Mark Twain, Business Man.*

14. Mark Twain, *The Adventures of Huckleberry Finn,* 255; *The Atlas Bulletin* (September 1917): 24–26. On changing the name of Hannibal's Commercial Club to the Chamber of Commerce, see Hagood and Hagood, *Story of Hannibal,* 131, 300.

15. *The Atlas Bulletin* (September 1917): 24.

16. Ibid., 24–25.

Huck recalled how many "delightful tramps" they had taken up to Cave Hollow to explore the cave's many entrances. He told Tom that all of the entrances except one had been boarded up. He learned from a local guide, Judge E. T. Cameron, that their old entrance must have been through what is now known as the LeBaume Cave. When Huck asked to enter the LeBaume Cave, Judge Cameron warned that he would first have to secure permission from the Atlas Portland Cement Company. Judge Cameron added that it was probably too dangerous because of cave-ins, since Atlas now had a shale mine under the cave.[17]

At that point Huck expressed a desire to see "this Plant which has blown up our robber rendezvous." Cameron replied that "it is worth seeing, for it is a big plant occupying a lot of ground and doing a big business." After driving by the big plant buildings, Cameron pointed out to Huck the entrance to LeBaume Cave on Atlas's Pump House Hill. "I mourned the loss of our robber cave," Huck confided to Tom, "but so it is in this grasping age. Even robber caves are commercialized . . . I was almost consoled that our cave has fallen into such good hands."

Huck created for Tom a beautiful visual image of the cement plant. "At sunset," he said, "the huge grey buildings against the ruddy glow make a romantic picture worthy of an artist's brush." He urged Tom to visit Hannibal so they could "stir up the old town in a different way than we did years ago." In conclusion, he added, "When you build on Earth that 'Castle in the Sky' of your boyhood dreams, don't neglect to use Atlas Cement."[18]

Thus we have Atlas's Huck, a "sivilized" slick sales executive. Literary critic Roger B. Salomon has observed that "it is the rebel and outcast Huck Finn who is Twain's most complete and vivid embodiment of instinctive goodness,"[19] but Atlas officials tamed and reshaped Huck to legitimize their industrial vision and first plant west of the Mississippi River. The steady march of progress had redefined boyhood dreams and even commercialized robber caves. Hannibal was now a beehive of commercial activities; young boys no longer had to play pirates and robbers to kill the boredom. The marketplace now beckoned. Huck, awed by the transformation, had become a dedicated foot soldier in the Industrial Revolution of the New South.

Seduced by the dazzling symbols of material and cultural progress, Atlas's Huck showed none of the cynicism expressed by Twain, for example, in *The Mysterious Stranger, The Gilded Age, Letters from the Earth,* or *A Connecticut Yankee in King Arthur's Court.* Atlas's Huck did not deliver any of the biting criticism that Twain leveled against the late-nineteenth-century order that produced the robber

---

17. Ibid., 25–26. At that time the Mark Twain Cave was mistakenly thought to have had several entrances. It was later learned that the LeBaume Cave was in fact a separate cave.
18. Ibid., 26.
19. *Twain and the Image of History,* 145.

barons. Nor, in the surrealistic description of the Ilasco cement plant at sundown, did Atlas's Huck bother to note the high incidence of industrial accidents or complaints about hazardous working conditions at Atlas.[20]

Although it is not known whether members of Machinists Lodge 537 who spearheaded the Ilasco strike in 1910 named their local in honor of Twain because of his pro-labor views, Twain's defense of trade unions in *Life on the Mississippi, A Connecticut Yankee in King Arthur's Court,* and his speech "Knights of Labor—The New Dynasty" endeared him to the labor movement. Trade union publications reprinted excerpts from his writings, and he cherished the warm reception that he often received from working-class audiences. He expressed a deep sympathy for the struggles of working people at home and abroad. "Who are the oppressors?" he asked, "The few: the king, the capitalist, and a handful of other overseers and superintendents. Who are the oppressed? The many: The nations of the earth; the valuable personages; the workers; they that make the bread that the softhanded and idle eat."[21]

In effect, the letter from Huck to Tom that appeared in *The Atlas Bulletin* was a clever response to Twain's stinging social criticism. It was in *The Mysterious Stranger,* not published until 1916, that Twain launched his sharpest attack on the factory system and the social relations that condemned the industrial working class to a life of poverty and exploitation. Although he used a factory in a sixteenth-century French village as the context for his criticisms, he may well have chosen Atlas's cement plant in Ilasco. In the novel, the character of Philip Traum, or Satan, escorts Theodor Fischer through a factory "where men and women and little children were toiling in heat and dirt and a fog of dust." Satan cynically notes that "the proprietors are rich and very holy; but the wage they pay to these poor brothers and sisters of theirs is only enough to keep them from dropping dead with hunger." These workers, Satan emphasizes, "kennel together, three families in a room, in unimaginable filth and stench; and disease comes, and they die off like flies."[22]

In response to Fischer's earlier revulsion at witnessing the torture of a religious heretic in jail, Satan reminds him that this torture was less brutal than the exploitation of factory workers. "Have they committed a crime," Satan asks, "these mangy things? No. What have they done, that they are punished so? Nothing at all,

---

20. "Money-lust has always existed," Twain told Rev. J. H. Twichell on March 14, 1905, "but not in the history of the world was it ever a craze, a madness, until your time and mine. This lust has rotted these nations; it has made them hard, sordid, ungentle, dishonest, oppressive." Albert Bigelow Paine, ed., *Twain's Letters,* vol. 2, 767–68.

21. Mark Twain, "The New Dynasty," in Paul J. Carter Jr., "Mark Twain and the American Labor Movement," 384. For an excellent discussion of Twain's views on organized labor, Gilded Age corruption, and poverty, see Foner, *Mark Twain,* especially chap. 5.

22. *The Mysterious Stranger,* 52.

except getting themselves born into your foolish race." He adds that the heretic, now dead, is at last "free of your precious race; but these poor slaves here—why, they have been dying for years, and some of them will not escape from life for years to come."[23]

Twain's blistering criticism of the factory system may have hit too close to home for Mahan and Atlas officials. Reports of job-related accidents at the Ilasco cement plant appeared frequently in local newspapers, vividly reminding readers of the many industrial dangers that awaited "these ill-smelling innocents."[24] At times, local newspapers had also called attention to the squalid living conditions of Ilasco workers and their children.

Samuel Gompers, president of the American Federation of Labor, regarded Twain as an astute philosopher, but the Twain who ridiculed the "Moral Sense" of "factory proprietors" was not the "beloved humorist" of Mahan and Atlas officials. Atlas's Twain was an entrepreneur, not a trade unionist; a humorist, not a social critic. Unlike some literary critics at the time who attacked Twain's fondness for wealth, accused him of being obsequious to the rich and powerful, and dismissed him as a sell-out and mere humorist, Mahan and Atlas officials celebrated those aspects of his life and writings and ignored the social criticism that underlay his work. This, despite the fact that Twain rejected a narrow classification of himself as a mere humorist and stressed the connections between humor and social satire. On one occasion, even though mired in debt at the time, he had rejected an offer of sixteen thousand dollars per year to allow his name to be used as the editor of a humorist periodical. "I can conceive of many wild and extravagant things when my imagination is in good repair," he noted, "but I can conceive of nothing quite so wild and extravagant as the idea of my accepting the editorship of a humorous periodical . . . I could edit a serious periodical with relish and a strong interest but I have never cared enough about humor to qualify me to edit it or sit in judgment upon it."[25]

Nevertheless, the public image of Twain that Mahan perpetuated in Hannibal did not feature intellectual pessimism and social criticism. It was not that Mahan was unfamiliar with these aspects of Twain's work. According to Dr. C. J. Armstrong, pastor of Hannibal's First Christian Church, Mahan was well aware of Twain's pessimism but disagreed with "his beloved humorist in this as in other instances."[26]

---

23. Ibid., 52–53.

24. Ibid., 52.

25. Foner, *Mark Twain,* 71; Neider, ed., *Autobiography,* 290. Van Wyck Brooks's *The Ordeal of Mark Twain* (New York, 1920) set the tone for much of the literary criticism of Twain for allegedly compromising himself as a true social critic to become nothing more than a humorist. For an important corrective to this view, see Foner, *Mark Twain,* chap. 2.

26. Dr. C. J. Armstrong, "In Memoriam George A. Mahan," December 18, 1936, 2, Typescript Collection, no. 995, vol. 6, WHMC–Columbia.

Mahan's interpretation of Twain may have reflected in part a genuine, if selective, understanding of Twain's thought and writings, but the evidence suggests a degree of conscious manipulation. For example, the inscription on the tablet at Twain's boyhood home celebrating Twain's rise from poverty through honest and industrious labor tells us more about Mahan and the imperatives of the industrializing New South than it does about Twain. As Armstrong revealed in a eulogy of Mahan, Mahan's purpose in commissioning a statue of Tom and Huck "was deeper even than that of paying a tribute to Mark Twain. His genuine hope was that it might influence the boys and girls of today to an appreciation of clean, joyful, childhood that they might become finer adult citizens."[27]

Toward those ends, Mahan chose Tom Sawyer, not Huck Finn, as the enduring symbol of Twain's legacy. When he commissioned sculptor Frederick Hibbard to create the Tom and Huck statue, he insisted that Hibbard's work conform to his own vision of what the statue should symbolize. Apparently, Mahan was not easy to please, for Hibbard showed him several models before designing one that gained his approval, one that conveyed an image of two young boys embarking on an adventure to "conquer the world." Mahan insisted on a significant symbolic inversion of Tom and Huck "to show Tom Sawyer leaving his Boy Paradise and Huck Finn to engage in the more serious problems of life, while Huck, being not so intelligent and ambitious, remains among his boyhood scenes." As Hannibal's local historians J. Hurley Hagood and Roberta Roland Hagood have further observed about this inversion,

> Mahan wished Tom to be seen as a 12-year-old boy at the moment he decided to go out into the world to see what it contained. Hence Hibbard depicted Tom with a knapsack, an advanced foot, a gleam in his eye and an aggressive body posture, with a staff for protection. Huck was depicted as a friend holding Tom by the arm and a look on his face as if trying to keep Tom from being so venturesome.[28]

At Mahan's behest, Hibbard took Huck, the restless adventurer with a conscience and humanitarian instincts, and transformed him into a halting, fearful sidekick of Tom's. In contrast, he prominently featured Tom as the symbol of aggressive ambition and initiative, sculpting that entrepreneurial, or perhaps predatory, gleam in his eye. In Mahan's view, Hannibal's children should emulate Tom, not Huck—Twain the entrepreneur, not Twain the humanitarian with a conscience. Mahan's fiercely competitive world held no place for Huck, "the questing dreamer of the river current," but one for the daring Tom, "the stout lad of the land."[29]

27. Ibid.
28. *Hannibal Courier-Post*, May 27, 1926; Hagood and Hagood, *Hannibal Yesterdays*, 4, 194.
29. Powers, *White Town Drowsing*, 258.

Mahan presented the youth of Hannibal with more than the Tom and Huck statue. The Reverend Armstrong was effusive in his praise of Mahan's nurturing of children, "the future Toms and Hucks." In February 1917, for example, the Mahans had donated a new site for the Home for the Friendless, presided over for many years by Laura Hawkins Frazier (the model for Becky Thatcher). They also contributed generously to the local public schools and the University of Missouri.[30]

In Hannibal, much has been made of Mahan's largess, concern for orphans, and work as chair of the executive committee of Hannibal's Central Agency for Charity. His concern was certainly genuine. A real understanding of his philanthropic graciousness, however, requires that it be viewed in the context of his broader social philosophy and understanding of power relationships. The paternalistic Mahan who fireproofed the new Home for the Friendless because "we could not bear to think of children exposed to the danger of fire" was the same Mahan who devoted so much of his legal energy and talent to blocking damages suits against Atlas by workers or children and wives of workers who were killed or maimed in job-related accidents at the cement plant. For example, just a few months before the ceremonies dedicating Twain's boyhood home, Leroy Baxter was killed in the clinker mill at the Ilasco cement plant when he was "ground into a pulp" after his clothing caught in a belt, drawing his body into a machine. When a damages suit was initiated on behalf of little Leroy, Baxter's infant son, it was Mahan who represented Atlas in its unsuccessful effort to avoid paying damages. Mahan must have come to terms with these contradictions early in his career as a corporate attorney, but such contradictions surely troubled him on occasion and perhaps explain in part his charitable support for the orphanage.[31]

As the centennial of Twain's birth approached in 1935, the Hannibal Chamber of Commerce made plans to honor Twain, partly in hopes that an anticipated influx of tourists would help stimulate the depressed local economy. The Missouri legislature approved a bill introduced by Hannibal's Roy Hamlin to create a centennial celebration commission and appropriated ten thousand dollars for the celebration. By then, the Atlas Portland Cement Company had become the Universal Atlas Cement Company, but it had not lost its enthusiasm for exploiting Twain's legacy for commercial purposes. To prepare for the centennial celebration, Atlas officials took out an advertisement in the local newspaper that

30. Armstrong, "In Memoriam George A. Mahan"; Hagood and Hagood, *Story of Hannibal,* 141–42.

31. Armstrong, "In Memoriam George A. Mahan"; Hagood and Hagood, *Story of Hannibal,* 141–42; *Ralls County Record,* August 14 and 21, 1914; *Leroy Baxter v. Atlas Portland Cement Company,* January 23, 1914, case no. 9798, Ralls County, Office of the Circuit Clerk and Recorder, New London.

featured automobiles transporting tourists to Hannibal under a superimposed image of Twain. In the advertisement, entitled "Pilgrimage," Universal Atlas repeatedly compared Twain's literary importance and fame to the significant contributions of cement manufacturing at the local plant. "Just as Mark Twain's name remains enduringly bright in the halls of literature," the advertisement concluded, "so will portland cement made here at Hannibal continue to serve mankind permanently and efficiently."[32]

Mahan chaired the Mark Twain Centennial Committee for the state of Missouri, which kicked off the celebration when President Franklin D. Roosevelt touched a ceremonial key in the White House to turn on the beacon in Hannibal's new memorial lighthouse on Cardiff Hill. A coast-to-coast radio broadcast included speeches by Mahan, Governor Guy B. Park, Clara Clemens Gabrilowitsch (Twain's daughter), and Frank L. Russell, of the Hannibal Chamber of Commerce. Hannibal manufacturers set up a large industrial display for the activities. Later that summer an outdoor pageant was held, featuring the reenactment of scenes and incidents in Twain's life and the history of Hannibal. In a reenactment of the famous fence whitewashing episode, Governor Park sat on a barrel eating an apple while Mahan paid for the privilege of painting the fence for him.[33]

By the time of the centennial anniversary celebration, the commercialization of Twain—and the association of him with the glorification of capitalism—was well underway. But at the ceremonial unveiling of the statue of Tom and Huck at the foot of Cardiff Hill nine years earlier, the Hannibal residents who paused to honor Twain may also have paused to reflect on the sweeping changes that industrialization had brought to the area since Twain's day. They listened to several speakers, including the sculptor Frederick Hibbard; Walter Williams, dean of the University of Missouri's School of Journalism; and the mayor of Hannibal, Morris Anderson. For those in the crowd whose thoughts and recollections may have wandered to the noisy blasts and thick, hovering black smoke near the cave just south of town, Anderson put the industrial transformation of Twain's childhood world of adventure into perspective. "The cave is still a picnic ground," he said, "but it is no place for robber bands in this industrial age, for you can hear the rumble of the cement plant close at hand."[34]

32. Powers, *White Town Drowsing,* 17; *Hannibal Courier-Post,* March 6, 1935; Journal of the Senate of the State of Missouri, Fifty-Eighth General Assembly, 1935, 1131.

33. V. E. Cunningham, President, Hannibal Chamber of Commerce, to Hon. Guy B. Park, Governor of Missouri, November 12, 1934, and Geo. A. Mahan to Hon. Guy B. Park, January 23, 1935, Guy B. Park, Governor's Papers, folders 1252, 1253, WHMC–Columbia; Hannibal Chamber of Commerce, "Mark Twain Centennial, 1835–1935: Hannibal, Missouri"; *Hannibal Courier-Post,* September 9, 1935. See also Powers, *White Town Drowsing,* 16–17, and Hagood and Hagood, *Story of Hannibal,* 184–89.

34. *Hannibal Courier-Post,* May 27, 1926. On June 17, 1936, Selznick International Pictures announced plans to produce a film, *Tom Sawyer.* According to the plans, a crew

The forces of commercialization set in motion by the Mark Twain Centennial celebration in 1935 picked up steam as civic leaders and politicians urged new, upgraded highways to stimulate travel and tourism after World War II. Beginning in the 1930s, many had called for a Mississippi River Parkway, an integrated highway network running along both sides of the Mississippi River from Canada to the Gulf of Mexico. Among them were Clarence Cannon, U.S. Representative from Missouri's Ninth Congressional District, and Albert Preston Greensfelder, an engineer, St. Louis civic leader, and member of the Missouri State Planning Board. After meeting with them to discuss the Parkway vision, Missouri Governor Lloyd C. Stark invited representatives from counties along the Mississippi River to attend a special meeting on October 29, 1937. At this meeting, an association was formed to promote support for a scenic parkway through the state.[35]

Other states touched by the Mississippi River endorsed the concept and appointed members to the Mississippi River Parkway Planning Commission. This commission consisted of members appointed by the governors of Arkansas, Illinois, Iowa, Kentucky, Louisiana, Minnesota, Mississippi, Missouri, Tennessee, and Wisconsin, as well as members from the Canadian provinces of Manitoba and Ontario. They attracted the support of politicians, businessmen, and civic leaders who stressed the cultural and scenic virtues along with the economic benefits of such a route that would connect with the Trans-Canada Highway.[36]

The formation of the Missouri Recreation Commission in 1947 signaled the state's growing commitment to tourism and recreation as important components of economic planning and development. Thanks in large part to George Mahan's earlier steps to preserve the legacy of Mark Twain, an infant tourist industry had begun to take shape in Hannibal. Good roads were crucial to the development of a Mark Twain industry, and in September 1949, Hannibal business leaders held

---

would soon arrive in Hannibal to examine the landscape to determine the suitability of Hannibal for filming. After visiting the area, however, the company decided not to shoot the film there. The town's modern industrial landscape made it impossible to recreate the atmosphere of Twain's youth. In effect, as Ron Powers has observed, Hannibal had become "too modern to authentically replicate its own past." Powers, *White Town Drowsing,* 227.

35. Major Robert B. Brooks, "Albert Preston Greensfelder: First Pilot, Mississippi River Parkway Planning Commission," 2, Minutes of the Breakfast Meeting, February 3, 1959, Mississippi River Parkway Planning Commission, Mississippi Highway Department, record group 55, vol. 10, Mississippi Department of Archives and History, Jackson, Mississippi (hereafter cited as MDAH). Cannon, who later played a role in relocating Highway 79 through Ilasco, complained bitterly in 1933 when an unexpected route change in the construction of the highway threatened to slice off six trees from his large commercial orchard in Elsberry. See Clarence Cannon to George L. Clark, October 12, 1933, folder 529, Clarence Cannon Papers, 1896–1964, WHMC–Columbia.

36. Governor John M. Dalton, speech, Mississippi River Parkway Commission, September 29, 1964, folder 6130, John M. Dalton Papers, WHMC–Columbia.

a dinner honoring U.S. Congressman Cannon for promoting a bill calling for a federal survey of the proposed parkway from New Orleans to Lake Itasca Park, Minnesota. Baxter B. Bond, chair of the Good Roads Committee of the chamber of commerce, also announced that State Highway 79 would be extended into Hannibal from Louisiana, Missouri, nearly forty miles to the south.[37]

Planning for the Great River Road required cooperation between the states and the federal government. The Federal-Aid Highway Act of 1954 authorized the U.S. Bureau of Public Roads to coordinate and expedite the project. Congress appropriated $250,000 in 1954 for such purposes, and the Bureau of Public Roads provided advisory services to states involved in the planning.[38]

On November 15, 1957, after making detailed recommendations for access and scenic control, federal consultants filed a report on the proposed route through Missouri, a distance of 386.8 miles. The report noted that the location of the route between Hannibal and Saverton to the south, a distance of 6.6 miles, had been tentatively approved. The area around Hannibal posed logistical problems, but architects of the report emphasized Hannibal's importance to the parkway: "Although in an awkward location as far as being accessible by parkway is concerned, the Mark Twain site is of 'key' importance, and some means must be found of incorporating it in the parkway."[39]

The proposed route did not go through Ilasco. It ran southwest of Hannibal for about two miles on Highway 61 past the Hatch Dairy Experiment Station toward New London before cutting back due east toward the Mississippi River just south of Saverton. Here it connected with Highway 79 south along the river toward St. Louis. The report noted that care had been taken to locate the route close to the river while avoiding towns and villages where possible. For the most part, the projected route followed existing roads.[40]

37. March, *History of Missouri*, vol. 2, 1538; *Hannibal Courier-Post,* September 16, 1949.

38. U.S. Department of Commerce, Bureau of Public Roads, "Report on a Recommended Route for the Great River Road (Mississippi River Parkway) through the State of Missouri," November 15, 1917, 5; F. W. Cron, "Two Years of Progress in Planning the Mississippi River Parkway," 1, Remarks for Annual Meeting of Mississippi River Parkway Planning Commission, September 22, 1956, Mississippi Highway Department, RG 55, vol. 3, MDAH; *Congressional Record*, vol. 100, pt. 2, 83d Congress, 2d sess., 1954, 2861–62.

39. H. J. Spelman, Regional Engineer, United States Department of Commerce, Bureau of Public Roads, to Charles H. Young, Pilot, Mississippi River Parkway Planning Commission, April 10, 1957, Mississippi Highway Department, RG 55, vol. 3, MDAH; U.S. Bureau of Public Roads, "Report on a Recommended Route for the Great River Road," November 15, 1957, 9.

40. U.S. Bureau of Public Roads, "Report on a Recommended Route for the Great River Road," November 15, 1957, 10, 33; Robert W. Patten, "Mississippi River Parkway: 'The Great River Road' in Missouri," 17, Minutes of the Breakfast Meeting, Mississippi River Parkway Planning Commission, February 3, 1959, Mississippi Highway Department, RG 55, vol. 10, MDAH.

Despite progress made on the projected route, Hannibal business leaders grumbled about what they regarded as foot-dragging by the Missouri State Highway Department. Members of the Mississippi River Parkway Planning Commission, which included Hannibal's former mayor, Francis E. Kelley, blamed Rex M. Whitton, chief engineer of the Missouri State Highway Commission. Milton S. Duvall, a member of the Parkway Executive Board from Clarksville, Missouri, complained after a meeting with Whitton that he showed "very little interest in the completion of the bottleneck from Louisiana to Hannibal."[41]

Planners certainly encountered many delays and obstacles in all of the ten states for many reasons, but the chief concern of Hannibal leaders was the projected route of Highway 79 between Hannibal and Saverton. By 1958, the Hannibal Chamber of Commerce was ready to step up political pressure on the Missouri Highway Commission for a new route. Local businessmen, some of whom were directly linked to the Mark Twain tourist industry, insisted that Highway 79 be routed due south out of Hannibal past the Mark Twain Cave and cement plant to Saverton. The only obstacle was a logistical one: Ilasco stood directly in the way.

For nearly sixty years, Ilasco had been an unusual dot on the cultural landscape of Missouri's Little Dixie. The community's early volatility had aroused public fears, particularly after the state militia's arrival in 1910. Atlas officials, in an attempt to consolidate their influence, had searched for ways to tie themselves to the area ever since Twain's death during the strike. Part of that strategy included a campaign to lay claim to his childhood past. After Twain's death, they and Hannibal civic leaders had portrayed themselves as guardians of the world of Tom Sawyer, even as they busily destroyed it. By the late 1950s, they saw no further need for Ilasco and prepared to dismantle the community; it only remained for them to persuade the state of Missouri to act as their instrument.

---

41. Milton S. Duvall, Co-Pilot, District No. 3, "Missouri Report," 26, Minutes of the Breakfast Meeting, Mississippi River Parkway Planning Commission, February 11, 1958, Mississippi Highway Department, RG 55, vol. 10, MDAH.

(13)

Render unto Atlas
The War on Community and Labor

I was aware that many men who have accumulated more millions of money than they can ever use have shown a rabid hunger for more, and have not scrupled to cheat the ignorant and the helpless out of their poor servings in order to partially appease that appetite.
—Mark Twain, "The Damned Human Race"

It is hard to pinpoint exactly when Universal Atlas officials, in collusion with Hannibal leaders, decided to dissolve Ilasco. As long as the Ralls County R-1 school district used the land that the cement company had deeded to it in 1926 for educational purposes, Universal Atlas could do nothing to get rid of Ilasco's schools. The evidence suggests that by early 1959, however, a planned phase-out of Ilasco was under way as Hannibal leaders pressured the State Highway Commission for a new Highway 79 route through the heart of the community.

Frank Russell, secretary of the Hannibal Chamber of Commerce, wrote a letter to powerful U.S. Congressman Clarence Cannon on June 11, 1958, complaining about the Missouri State Highway Commission's "apparent lack of interest and certainly lack of action" in regard to the stretch of Highway 79 between Hannibal and Louisiana. Russell urged Cannon to put pressure on Rex Whitton, chief highway engineer, by writing a letter to Whitton requesting an updated timetable for completing that section of highway. According to Russell's plan, Congressman Cannon would then send him a copy of Whitton's response. Russell assured Cannon that "we will not of course ever make the fact known that we have a copy of Mr. Whitten's [*sic*] letter to you, but we could re-check the information given to you with such information as we may be able to get from Mr. Whitten." He added, "Confidentially, we hope to get our local newspaper to launch an editorial campaign which will be rather continuous on this matter believing that this may get results . . . Personally, I think they have written

305

this project off their books and do not intend to do anything unless forced to do so."[1]

Congressman Cannon complied with Russell's request. In response, Whitton assured Cannon that he supported the Great River Road project, but pointed out that Missouri's rising demand for road improvements strained the state's financial resources. He noted that survey work was underway on the gap between Louisiana and Hannibal, although he had set no timetable for completing it. He expressed interest in discussing the matter with Congressman Cannon at an early date.[2]

While the Hannibal Chamber of Commerce was pushing Whitton to revamp the projected route of Highway 79 south of Hannibal, the Ralls County R-1 school board received a petition to "annex all the territory" in the district to the Hannibal school district in Marion County. Just a year earlier, R-1 voters by a vote of 159 for and 112 against had narrowly failed to achieve the two-thirds majority necessary to approve a special bond issue of eighty-two thousand dollars for proposed additions and expansion of district facilities. R-1 board members Ernest Barr (president), Richard H. Fox (secretary), Lewis Epperson, Charles Grisham, Roger Horton, and Glenn Peikett discussed the petition and unanimously agreed to call a special election on May 12, 1959, to decide the proposed annexation to the Hannibal district.[3]

On May 6, school officials held a public meeting in the Ilasco gymnasium to discuss the proposed annexation. Barr presided over a panel discussion by Cleo White (superintendent of Ilasco schools), W. T. Crawford (R-1 superintendent), E. T. Miller (superintendent of Hannibal Schools), and Arthur L. Summers, who represented the State Board of Education. Also seated at the table were members of the R-1 school board.[4]

Hannibal Superintendent Miller assured the audience that he was not there to influence their votes during the upcoming special election. He told them, however, that the Hannibal Board of Education would probably endorse the annexation. This would require busing students from considerable distances in some cases, but he emphasized that R-1 students would have access to the same transportation facilities as did Hannibal students.[5]

1. F. T. Russell to Congressman Clarence Cannon, June 11, 1958, folder 1465, Cannon Papers, WHMC–Columbia.

2. Clarence Cannon to F. T. Russell, June 13, 1958, and Rex M. Whitton, Chief Engineer, Missouri State Highway Commission, to Congressman Clarence Cannon, June 18, 1958; both in f. 1465, Cannon Papers, WHMC–Columbia.

3. *Hannibal Courier-Post,* April 24, 1959; *Hannibal Courier-Post,* May 7, 1958. I would like to thank David Polc for providing a copy of a flier advertising the special school bond election held on May 6, 1958.

4. *Hannibal Courier-Post,* May 7, 1959.

5. Ibid.

R-1 Superintendent Crawford explained that enrollment figures had increased only slightly since 1949. In the face of rising levies, he stressed, such figures did not warrant optimism about expanding educational services in the district. The growing demand of parents for more advanced instructional facilities, coupled with rising teachers' salaries and costs of materials, had created pressures for higher taxes. Although his projected enrollment figures for the next eight years indicated a likely increase, he argued that this was not substantial enough to justify future expansion. He denied allegations that the R-1 board had already secretly discussed plans for the proposed annexation to the Hannibal district.[6]

Summers stressed that two adjoining school districts have the right to change the boundary lines between them. If R-1 voters approve the annexation on May 12, he said, it would only require an act of the Hannibal school board to accept the annexation. An audience member then asked if a district could be forced to join another district without voters' approval. In response, Summers emphasized that although voters in the R-1 system were voting according to district, since they belonged to a reorganized district they would have to abide by the election returns for the entire school system. Even if Ilasco voters opposed annexation, they would have to accept the wishes of the majority of voters in the system, which also included Saverton and Mills Creek.[7]

After Superintendent Crawford raised the specter of future higher taxes to support R-1 schools, a member of the audience shot back that annexation to the Hannibal schools would, for sure, mean higher school taxes for Ralls County residents. The tax rate in the R-1 district was $2.10, compared to $2.60 in Hannibal. Summers replied, "If you stop to think, you will buy more in the enlarged district than you could get for the same money in a smaller district. You would get a broader training in English, fine arts, vocational agriculture, and other subjects—more advanced training. The point is tremendously important. It is well worth the extra 50 cents."[8]

Voting returns for the special election held on May 12 indicate that a clear preference existed among R-1 voters for annexation to the Hannibal school district. Mills Creek voters endorsed the annexation by a vote of 161 to 18, and there were 71 votes in favor of and 18 against the proposal in the Saverton district. In Ilasco, however, only 34 supported annexation, compared to 93 voters who opposed it. Thus, voters in the Ilasco district opposed annexation by a margin of almost three to one, but R-1 voters approved it by a majority of almost two to one. The dissolution of Ilasco had begun.[9]

6. Ibid.
7. Ibid.
8. Quoted in ibid.
9. *Hannibal Courier-Post,* May 13, 1959.

Ilasco residents reacted with a combination of anger, sadness, and a sense of helplessness. Complaints surfaced that school board president Barr had conspired with others to orchestrate the merger with Hannibal schools. Anna Sunderlik Venditti recalled that Ilasco residents "cried for days" when they learned the election results. Students, families, and friends gathered less than a week after the election to hear Father Louis MacCorkle deliver the last baccalaureate address at Ilasco on May 17. At commencement ceremonies five days later, "There was not a dry eye in the house."[10]

In the meantime, Jim Tatman left the sputtering engine running in his old car while he went door-to-door gathering signatures on a petition to keep the schools in Ilasco, but to no avail. He attributed the school annexation initiative to the desire of Hannibal school officials to pull the cement plant's tax revenues into their district. Moreover, he stressed, Universal Atlas wanted the land. In fact, he recalled, the plant superintendent had told him several years earlier that the new gymnasium was a mistake, a "white elephant." This suggested to Tatman that plans to dissolve Ilasco had been in the works for several years.[11]

To ease the transition, the R-1 district kept the grade school open through the 1961–1962 school year. Ethel Lewis and Melvenah Davis then retired, but Mecky Calvert joined Lucy Moore, Jay Willows, Bob Ruth Gann, and Cleo White—teachers and administrators who earlier had been transferred to new positions in the Hannibal district.

Once plans were in place to phase out Ilasco schools, it only remained to secure the Missouri Highway Commission's cooperation in regard to Highway 79 between Hannibal and Saverton. In early 1960, the *Hannibal Courier-Post* launched editorials blasting Whitton and the highway department as "a thorn in the side of progress." These editorials urged citizens to pressure the state legislature to initiate the Highway 79 project at once.[12]

Hannibal businessmen particularly sought a better, quicker route to Saverton because of plans to convert Saverton into an industrial park. The Hannibal Realty Company, an arm of the chamber of commerce, held a two-hundred-acre tract in Saverton for this purpose. Directors of the Hannibal Industrial Development Company, organized in 1952 to entice companies to locate in the area, had become discouraged by the lack of adequate road facilities between Hannibal and Saverton. The *Hannibal Courier-Post* claimed that three companies had

---

10. Anna Sunderlik Venditti, interview by author, June 24, July 6, 1992; Ilasco High School, *The Howler,* April 1959. David Polc provided me with a copy of this edition of the Ilasco school newspaper.

11. Jim Tatman, interview by author, June 25, 1992.

12. For the flavor of these editorials, see *Hannibal Courier-Post,* January 1, January 27, and March 11, 1960.

considered but rejected Saverton as a site because of poor roads. An editorial complained that Whitton's promise to provide a better road once a company had been secured was "worth little" in the campaign to attract new investments to the area.[13]

George Wolf, district engineer for the Missouri Highway Department in Hannibal, told members of the Hannibal Chamber of Commerce on January 19, 1960, that the department had completed a survey and was planning how to secure the right-of-way in the next fiscal year. This, he noted, should encourage the construction of a Saverton industrial site. He emphasized, however, that planned construction could not begin until such right-of-way had been secured.[14]

Meyer Abelman, an urban engineer from the Missouri State Highway Commission, informed members of the Mississippi River Parkway Commission on February 9, 1960, that surveys had been completed on a fifteen-mile stretch south of Hannibal. He stressed, however, that laws governing Missouri's highway system did not authorize expenditures for acquiring right-of-way in excess of construction needs. This made it impossible at that time to comply with Parkway right-of-way standards for scenic lookout points and recreational areas. He assured members that plans for this fifteen-mile stretch would go forward, however, and that he intended to ask county courts and/or local residents to absorb the costs of securing this added right-of-way. This, he pointed out, was consistent with long-standing policies of the State Highway Commission to rely on local people to obtain the initial right-of-way. After that, the state would bear the expense of subsequent improvements or highway relocation.[15]

Abelman also pointed out that the section of Highway 79 south of Hannibal was not at that time slated for immediate construction. Since construction was based on need, only routes that sustained the greatest volume of traffic or badly needed repair received top priority. Abelman added, however, that acquisition of right-of-way would encourage early construction of at least a portion of this stretch.[16]

A week later, the Hannibal Chamber of Commerce held a session to discuss the Great River Road project. Francis E. Kelley, Hannibal's former mayor and member of the Parkway Commission, introduced G. S. Petersen, a Wisconsin field representative of the commission. Petersen complained that Missouri was

---

13. Hagood and Hagood, *Story of Hannibal,* 224, 241; *Hannibal Courier-Post,* January 1, 1960.

14. State of Missouri, *Official Manual, 1959–1960,* 781; *Hannibal Courier-Post,* January 20, 1960.

15. Meyer Abelman, "Missouri Report," 13–14, Minutes of the Breakfast Meeting, February 9, 1960, Mississippi River Parkway Commission, RG 55, vol. 10, MDAH.

16. Ibid.

the only state that had still not undertaken preparations for markings and signs along the proposed route of the Great River Road.[17]

The Hannibal Chamber of Commerce quickly undertook an initiative to generate greater publicity for the Great River Road. Clay C. Harris, Charles Clayton, James Wilson, A. B. Drescher Jr., J. Allen Eichenberger, Francis E. Kelley, Eugene Ott, M. E. Pennewell, and A. K. Cameron coordinated efforts with Petersen to drum up support for the project.[18]

Meanwhile, other developments signaled what the future held for Ilasco and the cement plant. On March 31, 1960, the Ilasco post office closed. Gizella Barbara Homolos, Ilasco's postmaster since 1944, was transferred as a senior clerk to the Hannibal post office. In addition, the U.S. Steel Corporation purchased farms on the outskirts of Ilasco. On March 8, 1960, Pantaleone and Rosa Genovese sold their farm to U.S. Steel, which also bought Walter F. Apel's farm on May 27, 1960. The company soon purchased other farms belonging to Martin Valentik, George Kristoff, and Ernest Sanders.[19]

Rex Whitton finally knuckled under to pressures, or perhaps yielded to temptations, to run Highway 79 through the middle of Ilasco. On August 9, 1960, he informed the Missouri Highway Commission of a change in the recommended route of Highway 79 that had been approved in 1957. He attributed the change to "developments since that date, coupled with discussions with civic leaders in the Hannibal area, . . . traffic needs of present and potential industrial development, also the scenic advantage of a route closer to the Mississippi River."[20]

Whitton quickly went from goat to hero in the eyes of Hannibal leaders and put himself in a position to benefit from Congressman Cannon's connections in Washington, D.C. Just four months later, President-elect John F. Kennedy appointed Whitton to head the Federal Highway Administration in the U.S. Bureau of Public Roads. Missouri Senator Stuart Symington praised Whitton's appointment, and letters of congratulation immediately poured in from the Hannibal Chamber of

17. *Hannibal Courier-Post,* February 17, 1960; Hagood and Hagood, *Story of Hannibal,* 300.

18. *Hannibal Courier-Post,* February 23, 1960.

19. *Hannibal Courier-Post,* March 17, 1960; Howard, *Ralls County Missouri,* 385. On the farm purchases, see Ponto and Rosa Genovese to U.S. Steel Corporation, March 8, 1960, Deed Record, book 162, 623; Walter F. Apel et al. to U.S. Steel Corporation, May 27, 1960, Deed Record, book 165, 460–61; Martin Valentik et al. to U.S. Steel Corporation, November 25, 1963, Deed Record, book 173, 169; George Kristoff to U.S. Steel Corporation, March 13, 1961, Deed Record, book 162, 616; Ernest M. Sanders to U.S. Steel Corporation, December 10, 1962, Deed Record, book 168, 391; all in Ralls County, Office of the Circuit Clerk and Recorder, New London.

20. Missouri Highway Commission Minutes, August 9, 1960, 3, Missouri Highway Department, Missouri Highway and Transportation Archives, Jefferson City (hereafter cited as MHTA).

Commerce. "We want to thank you for your recent cooperation in re-establishing Route 79 into our City," wrote Hannibal mayor Clyde G. Toalson, "and we hope that your advancement will not affect this project."[21]

This resolved a thorny issue that had delayed progress on the Great River Road project. Representative Cannon introduced a bill to the Committee on Public Works, calling for federal support to aid states involved in the project. Minnesota Senators Hubert Humphrey and Eugene McCarthy cosponsored a similar bill with Missouri Senator Edward Long. On January 17, 1962, 107 markers designating the route of the Great River Road through Missouri were erected.[22]

In 1963, the year after final classes met in the Ilasco grade school, cement plant officials notified tenants that their leases would not be renewed after 1969. Engineers from the U.S. Bureau of Public Roads conducted Phase II field studies in Missouri for scenic easement, land acquisition, and control of access. The Ralls County Court appointed commissioners J. Allen Eichenberger, Robert H. Coy, and Harold Flowerree to recommend the amount of compensation that should be paid to property owners on the outskirts of Ilasco whose land would be taken for highway construction. U.S. Steel quitclaimed to the State of Missouri 22.39 acres in Ilasco and granted numerous easements in exchange for guaranteed rights of access at several points along the highway.[23]

By the spring of 1964, it became clear what Universal Atlas had vested in the destruction of Ilasco: a drastic reduction of its labor force made possible by an expanded, modernized new plant that would soon be built. In April,

21. Clyde G. Toalson to Rex M. Whitton, December 28, 1960, box 2, and Baxter B. Bond to Rex M. Whitton, December 27, 1960, box 1; both in Rex M. Whitton Papers, WHMC–Columbia. See also Missouri Highway Commission, Minutes, January 10, 1961, 2–3, MHTA. Symington's remarks are in the *Congressional Record,* vol. 107, pt. 2, 87th Cong., 1st sess., 1961, 1909. Congressman Cannon, who had complained bitterly in 1933 when a sudden change in Highway 79 threatened to harm his commercial orchard, apparently did not object to the forced dislocation of Ilasco residents to accommodate a route change in 1960.

22. See S. 2968 and H. R. 13079 in *Congressional Record,* vol. 108, pts. 4, 14, 87th Cong., 2d sess., 1962, 4355, 18,924. On the road markers, see Roy M. Rucker, "Missouri Accepts the Great River Road Markers," 30, Minutes of the Breakfast Meeting, Mississippi River Parkway Planning Commission, February 6, 1962, Mississippi Highway Department, RG 55, vol. 10, MDAH.

23. Howard, *Ralls County Missouri,* 247; U.S. Bureau of Public Roads, "Report on Progress of Phase II Reports for the Great River Road," 5, Minutes of the Breakfast Meeting, February 8, 1965, Mississippi River Parkway Planning Commission, Mississippi Highway Department, RG 55, vol. 10, MDAH; United States Steel Corporation to State of Missouri, August 8, 1964, Easement Record, book 176, 1–4, and "Report of Commissioners," U.S. Steel Corporation et al. to State of Missouri, July 23, 1964, Miscellaneous Record, book 171, 578–85; both in Ralls County, Office of the Circuit Clerk and Recorder, New London. On the agreement between U.S. Steel and the State of Missouri, see also Missouri Highway Commission Minutes, November 12, 1965, 90–91, MHTA.

company president Ralph C. Moffitt confirmed that modernization and expansion of facilities in Hannibal would soon begin. Mike Henning, plant manager, told the press that this would be a multimillion-dollar project featuring the latest engineering design. The new plant would sit on an abandoned quarry just west of and overlooking the existing plant. The purchase of farms in the area would open up new quarries to ensure an abundant supply of limestone.[24]

A single-kiln, wet process would replace the current fourteen-kiln, dry process manufacturing operation. Moffitt touted the approximately 620-feet-long single kiln slated for installation as the longest cement-clinker producing unit in the United States. The new process would feature a complex of computer controls. An Atlas engineer emphasized that the new facility would practically eliminate dust.[25]

The company's automated war against labor now intensified. As construction began on the new plant, Ilasco assumed the appearance of a ghost town. Huge silos, storage tanks, and finishing and grinding mills went up, while Ilasco houses, sheds, and school buildings were torn down. Plant officials instituted layoffs and increased the psychological pressure on workers forced to play the waiting game. Atlas workers had a choice: they could accept severance pay or simply wait to see if the computerized operations would still require their labor when the new plant opened.[26]

Not all property in and around Ilasco belonged to Universal Atlas. With few exceptions, neither the highway nor the plant expansion directly threatened property in Monkey Run. Several families and property owners, however, who lived in Lendak's subdivision of Ilasco soon found themselves sandwiched between the plant and its new quarries on the other side of the highway under construction. As the center of Ilasco was gutted, the steady roar of big trucks, earth movers, and blasting made life difficult for those who tried to hang onto their homes in this section. In 1971, members of the Ilasco Slovak Lutheran Church finally decided that it was no longer practical to continue services, and voted to sell their property to Universal Atlas. Others in Lendak's subdivision who had held out finally did the same.[27]

Perhaps none more clearly expressed the emotional reaction of Ilasco residents and former residents than Mildred Viglasky Martinovich and Velma Randolph Youell. Martinovich, as she reflected on the emptiness she felt, observed: "You never get over knowing that the town you were born in is nonexisting."[28] Youell

24. *Hannibal Courier-Post,* April 3, 1964, and June 18, 1965.
25. Ibid.
26. Ibid.; Kenny Lawson, interview by author, July 6, 1992.
27. David Polc, interview by author, October 16, 1994.
28. Mildred Viglasky Martinovich to Gregg Andrews, October 30, 1994.

echoed those sentiments. "The saddest thing in my life," she recalled, "was when they started tearing down all those houses. I just didn't think I could take it. They took away part of my life. I loved that little town."[29]

The removal of Ilasco was especially tough for older residents, some of whom still spoke only limited English and whose adult children had moved to urban areas such as Detroit, Chicago, St. Louis, and Kansas City. Many had spent their entire lives in Ilasco struggling to make a living and to build a community in the face of enormous obstacles. In their day, Ilasco was teeming with perhaps as many as three thousand people, seven saloons, five churches, and numerous small businesses. They remembered when it was a dynamic town, culturally unique in Missouri's Little Dixie.

As residents watched their past being torn from them, they felt powerless to contest their fate. Most probably shared the feelings of Anna Hustava Sanders, who "hated it" but could see no way to fight it. She, too, recalled her surprise once when a power company worker told her years earlier that it was only a matter of time before Ilasco would be destroyed.[30]

For some in Hannibal who had long been afraid even to venture into Ilasco, the forced removal was only a minor inconvenience for residents, easy to justify. For those forced out, however, it was a traumatic dislocation. Kenny Lawson recalled how painful it was for his father, John, to leave their house. Julia, John's wife, had already left, but John refused, hoping that if he simply stayed there, those in charge of wrecking the house would reconsider and let him stay. When Kenny went with other family members to get John from the house, they had to pry him from the bed where they found him crying.[31]

Atlas gave residents a specified number of days in which to move. This allowed time to salvage personal items and whatever belongings they wanted before the bulldozers came, but on occasions there were mix-ups that caused tempers to flare. Pete Galluzzio remembered that there were many items in his mother's house that he wanted to get. In addition, he wanted to save the outside earth oven that his mother had used to bake bread. Believing that he still had time to get these things according to the cement plant's notice, he went to Ilasco only to find a bulldozer already leveling things. Pete, who had just returned from deer hunting, was furious. "If I would have had my 30'30 rifle with me," he recalled, "I would have shot that son of a bitch off that bulldozer."[32]

The bulldozer operator was working for Leo Riney's construction company, which Universal Atlas had hired to do the job. Pete contacted an attorney

29. Youell, "Renault a/k/a Randolph," 18.
30. Anna Hustava Sanders, interview by author, July 2, 1992.
31. Kenny Lawson, interview by author, July 6, 1992.
32. Pete Galluzzio, telephone conversation with author, June 14, 1994.

on behalf of his mother, who, he remembered, did not receive a penny of compensation. He was told to forget it. He recalled that he did call Riney at home, however, to express his anger: "These houses may not be as good as those on Country Club Drive, but, you son of a bitch, how would you like it if somebody bulldozed your house?"[33]

For some Hannibal businessmen who were in a position to influence Ilasco's fate, the community's dissolution and the construction of a new highway and cement plant furthered their own interests. Riney, owner of a ready-mix concrete business, certainly figured prominently in these interrelated developments. He was a member of the Hannibal school board and the Hannibal Industrial Development Company, which sought to create the much-touted industrial park in Saverton. When Universal Atlas began construction on its new plant in 1964, Riney's company filled the orders, using local portland cement. His firm also played a major role in the construction of Highway 79, a lucrative project for contractor and portland cement manufacturers alike. Membership in the Chamber of Commerce put him in close touch with cement plant officials and gave him access to state and federal officials.[34]

Other Hannibal businessmen linked to the growing Mark Twain tourist industry had lobbied for the highway through Ilasco. Such was the case of John A. Winkler, whose wife, Ida Estelle Winkler, was the granddaughter of George A. Mahan. In keeping with Mahan's legacy, John Winkler did much to preserve Twain landmarks in Hannibal. As president of the Mark Twain Home Board between 1945 and 1977, he supervised numerous restoration projects, including that of the Becky Thatcher Home and bookstore. In 1958 the National Trust for Historical Preservation honored him with a silver cup in St. Louis for his role in preserving buildings connected to Twain's life and writings. Like Mahan, he fused civic, historical, and private economic interests. He became a vice president of the State Historical Society of Missouri, owner of the Becky Thatcher Book Shop, and member of the Mississippi River Parkway Planning Commission. He also headed the Hannibal Chamber of Commerce's Committee on Tourist Development.[35]

As residents searched for new places to live and as many former employees looked for new jobs, Universal Atlas officials and Hannibal leaders planned

---

33. Ibid.

34. March, *History of Missouri,* vol. 3, 335; Hagood and Hagood, *Story of Hannibal,* 224. On efforts by the Portland Cement Association to persuade state highway officials to use portland cement on state roads, see Missouri Highway Commission Minutes, July 14, 1959, 92, MHTA.

35. Powers, *White Town Drowsing,* 22, 78, 214–15; Shoemaker, *Missouri and Missourians,* vol. 5, 96–97; *Hannibal Labor Press,* April 19, 1957. On Winkler's civic activities, see Hagood and Hagood, *Story of Hannibal,* 237, 239, 261, 271, and Hagood and Hagood, *Hannibal Yesterdays,* 196.

dedication ceremonies for their new plant. On June 2, 1967, Missouri politicians and dignitaries, Miss Hannibal, business leaders from several states, and about one thousand invited guests gathered to praise and showcase the computerized plant. Because of traffic rerouting due to construction on Highway 79, many dignitaries climbed aboard the chartered *Lady M* excursion boat in Hannibal for the trip down to the cement plant. Others took smaller boats or chartered buses.[36]

The plant's new wet process of manufacturing featured closed-circuit television cameras that provided a computer operator with a constant look inside the 620-feet-long kiln. Pulverized coal burned a limestone and shale slurry mixture into clinker at around 2,600 degrees fahrenheit. Universal Atlas had added new distribution stations at Bettendorf, Iowa, and Summit, Illinois. In addition, the company showcased two new self-unloading cement barges, the *Huck Finn* and *Tom Sawyer*.[37]

Picket lines went up the very next night as the result of a dispute over wages, benefits, and job reclassifications at the fully automated plant. Although Local 205 of the Cement, Lime and Gypsum Workers' Union, led by its president, Wilbur Whitley, approved a new agreement seven weeks later, Universal Atlas's new plant was a sign of coming troubles for labor. The modernization and expansion at Ilasco took place against the backdrop of what was becoming increasingly bitter competition among industry giants. About five months after the dedication ceremonies, the Dundee Cement Company dedicated a new plant about forty-five miles down the Mississippi at Clarksville. Whereas Universal Atlas's facility could now produce three million barrels per year, Dundee's new plant contained the world's largest kiln with an annual production capacity of seven million barrels. An unnamed executive of a rival company in the region complained to *Business Week* that "Dundee's been nothing but bad news to the industry."[38]

At the time both of these plants were built, the rate of profit in the cement industry had begun to decline, largely the result of too much investment in production capacity. By 1975, the average return on investments had dipped to 6.5 percent, far below the 15 percent return necessary in the eyes of analysts to attract enough capital for capacity modernization and other important undertakings. This, coupled with skyrocketing oil prices, had created serious problems for the energy-intensive industry by the end of the 1970s. To promote energy conservation, industry analysts urged companies to convert from the wet to dry manufacturing process, but Universal Atlas was saddled with its new,

36. *Hannibal Courier-Post,* June 2, 1967.
37. Ibid.
38. "Dundee Solves a Weighty Problem," *Business Week,* November 25, 1967, 150–52; Joseph C. Arundale and James A. Martin, "The Mineral Industry of Missouri," in *Minerals Yearbook 1967,* vol. 3, Area Reports: Domestic, 471–72. On the strike, see *Hannibal Labor Press,* June 9 and 16, 1967, and *Hannibal Courier-Post,* July 24 and 26, 1967.

more energy-consuming wet kiln at the Ilasco plant, built in the mid-1960s when energy costs were much lower.[39]

What has happened at the Ilasco plant since then is indicative of larger nation-wide trends. In 1980, U.S. Steel sold its cement division to the Lehigh Portland Cement Company, a wholly owned subsidiary of Heidelberger Zement, a German company. The Federal Trade Commission blocked the sale of the Ilasco plant on grounds that it violated the Clayton Act by encouraging a monopoly in the Midwest. Lehigh then sold it to the predominantly Swedish-owned Continental Cement Company.[40]

Foreign companies increased their control of the American cement industry throughout the 1980s. By the end of 1981, foreign investors controlled three of Missouri's five cement plants. Six years later, 55 percent of cement production capacity in the United States had fallen into the hands of foreign owners. By the end of 1991, that percentage had increased to 65 percent. What was true of the Ilasco plant, therefore, was true of many in the United States. No longer did cement plants feature mainly immigrants working for American-owned companies; instead, American workers now produced profits for foreign firms.[41]

The merger mania of the early 1980s contributed to the growing concentration of ownership in the cement industry. As cement production and consumption in the recession-ridden United States hit a twenty-year low in 1982, the five largest cement manufacturers produced 37 percent of the industry's output. The ten largest companies accounted for 58 percent of production.[42]

The history of Ilasco parallels the rise and decline of American manufacturing power. The local plant once employed more than two thousand workers, but by the time Universal Atlas dedicated the new automated plant in 1967, the number of employees had dropped from 250 before automation to 135. This was consistent with trends in the industry as a whole. In 1974, the average number of workers in cement plants around the nation was 180. Although output had

---

39. Ronald F. Smith and James E. Levin, "Multimedia Assessment and Research Needs of the Cement Industry," 12–13, 28–30.

40. "In the Matter of Lehigh Portland Cement Company, et al.," *Federal Trade Commission Decisions,* vol. 98, October 30, 1981, 856–63; *Minerals Yearbook 1981,* centennial ed., vol. 1, Metals and Minerals, 183; *Hannibal Courier-Post,* February 16, 1980. On January 15, 1969, the Missouri secretary of state had revoked Lehigh's corporate authority to do business in the state because of the company's failure to file an annual registration report and antitrust affidavit for the preceding year. "Lehigh Portland Cement Company," folder 2962, Office of the Missouri Secretary of State, Corporation Division, Jefferson City, Mo.

41. Jane P. Ohl, Heyward M. Wharton, and Ardel W. Rueff, "The Mineral Industry in Missouri," in *Minerals Yearbook 1981,* centennial ed., vol. 2, Area Reports: Domestic, 296; *Minerals Yearbook 1987,* vol. 1, Metals and Minerals, 187; Cheryl Solomon, "Cement," *Minerals Yearbook 1991,* vol. 1, Metals and Minerals, 327.

42. *Minerals Yearbook 1982,* vol. 1, Metals and Minerals, 175–76. On mergers in the cement industry, see *Minerals Yearbook 1980,* vol. 1, Metals and Minerals, 164.

risen by 31 percent between 1958 and 1971, total employment for the same period dropped by 30 percent, mainly the result of capital investment in plant modernization. The number of production workers during this thirteen-year span declined from 34,800 to 23,200.[43]

Heightened competition between giant cement firms has encouraged a shift to production overseas and rising cement imports. In 1985, clinker imports shot up 109 percent as some plants idled clinker production capacity. Lone Star Industries reported that year that it had become the leading cement importer in the United States. It had become more profitable to import cement than to manufacture it at home. In 1986, domestic cement producers accounted for 70 percent of all U.S. cement imports. This dependency on foreign cement, coupled with declining domestic capacity, raised government concerns in the late 1980s that these trends might jeopardize future U.S. access to adequate supplies of cement at affordable prices.[44]

Like other trade unions in the declining manufacturing sector, the United Cement, Lime and Gypsum Workers' Union took a beating in the 1980s. Plant closures, wage concessions, the hiring of replacement workers during strikes, the exodus of companies in search of cheap labor abroad, and aggressive corporate union-busting encouraged by Ronald Reagan's antilabor policies shaped the new climate of industrial relations. By 1984, national pattern bargaining coordinated by the CLGWU had collapsed. CLGWU membership entered a state of free fall, dropping off sharply from thirty thousand in 1979 to twenty-four thousand in 1983. The union, no longer able to negotiate many contracts, lost its clout and merged with the International Brotherhood of Boilermakers, Iron Shipbuilders, Blacksmiths, Forgers, and Helpers (IBB). The merger provoked much bitterness among cement workers, however, and a group of former CLGWU staff members bolted from the IBB and created the Independent Workers of North America (IWNA). These divisions further weakened a financially strapped and demoralized labor movement.[45]

---

43. *Hannibal Labor Press,* June 9, 1967; Smith and Levin, "Multimedia Assessment," 11.

44. Ohl, Wharton, and Rueff, "Mineral Industry of Missouri," 339; Wilton Johnson, "Cement," *Minerals Yearbook 1985,* vol. 1, Metals and Minerals, 230–31; C. B. Pitcher, "The U.S. Cement Industry: Trade and Trends," *Construction Review* 36 (September/October 1990): iii-xiii.

45. In 1981, the AFL-CIO Executive Council approved a CLGWU request to change its name to "United Cement, Lime, Gypsum and Allied Workers International Union." *Proceedings of the Fourteenth Constitutional Convention of the AFL-CIO,* vol. 2, Report of the Executive Council, 1981, 58; *Proceedings of the Fifteenth Constitutional Convention of the AFL-CIO,* vol. 2, Report of the Executive Council, 1983, 42. Some nonunion employees at the Ilasco plant lost their pensions as the result of corporate takeovers in the 1980s. Richard Sanders, interview by author, July 2, 1992. On the disintegration of the union and the creation of the IWNA, see Northrup, "From Union Hegemony," 366–75.

The crisis of American labor has deepened even further in the 1980s. By 1990, only 12 percent of the private sector's labor force belonged to unions, down from 20 percent when the "Reagan Revolution" began in 1980. This represents a dramatic departure from the mid-1950s when CLGWU leaders geared up for a nationwide strike to bring pattern bargaining to the cement industry. At that time, approximately one of every three nonfarm workers in the United States enjoyed union membership, and the CLGWU had thirty-five thousand members.[46]

Much of this crisis is rooted in the recent repressive political climate and in structural changes in the world economy, but it is partly the product of the AFL-CIO's own policies and ideology, including its reliance on government for growth and survival. Since the Wagner Act, for example, unions have become increasingly dependent on legal mechanisms set up by the federal government to resolve industrial relations disputes. During World War II, special boards encouraged this dependence by promoting several items on labor's pre-war social agenda. It was President Reagan's appointment of corporation lawyers and anti-union advocates to the National Labor Relations Board, however, that dramatically underscores the limits of relying on the good graces of the government to safeguard labor's rights. A sharp increase in the number of unfair labor practices in the 1980s, including the firing of union leaders, and the NLRB's willingness to uphold anti-union tactics have punctuated the recent trend toward a more repressive legal climate for labor. Few could quarrel with historian Christopher L. Tomlins's conclusion that "a counterfeit liberty is the most that American workers and their organizations have been able to gain through the state."[47]

Labor embraced the job-conscious politics of productivity and anticommunism after World War II, but this has been of little help in the post–Cold War era. Not even the AFL-CIO's collaboration in Cold War foreign policy initiatives has spared it from the "leaner and meaner" strategies employed by American companies in the more competitive global economic environment of recent years. Coupled with organized labor's continuing internal problems of racism and sexism, this has left American workers poorly armed against a powerful capitalist class, its allies in government, and a bloated pool of professional "gentrified union busters."[48]

Intertwined with labor's social crisis is an environmental crisis involving the cement industry. Dust, toxic wastes, and particulates have long damaged the

46. Brody, *Workers in Industrial America,* 242; Tomlins, *The State and the Unions,* 317; *Proceedings of the Fifteenth Constitutional Convention of the AFL-CIO,* vol. 2, Report of the Executive Council, 1983, 42.

47. Tomlins, *The State and the Unions,* 328; Nelson Lichtenstein, "From Corporatism to Collective Bargaining: Organized Labor and the Eclipse of Social Democracy in the Postwar Era," 123–25; Patricia Cayo Sexton, *The War on Labor and the Left: Understanding America's Unique Conservatism* (Boulder, 1991), 218–26.

48. Colin Gordon, *New Deals,* chap. 8; Sexton, *War on Labor,* 224–26.

quality of air and created health hazards for those who live near factories, but by the fall of 1994, the Continental Cement Company's Ilasco plant and the industry in general were embroiled in a new environmental controversy. In 1985, the Continental Cement Company was sold to Scancem, a Norwegian firm, and to Material Services Corporation of Chicago. Since 1986, the Ilasco plant, like many others, has burned hazardous wastes in its large kiln. The growing use of kilns for such purposes has provided companies with a cheap fuel supply and boosted profits. Cement firms often receive as much as eight hundred dollars per ton from other industries to dispose of hazardous waste in their kilns.[49]

In the late 1970s, the U.S. Environmental Protection Agency (EPA) had initiated studies to determine the feasibility of using cement kilns to burn hazardous organic wastes such as waste oils, PCBs, and pesticide wastes. An agency report published in 1979 called for additional such projects, and in 1981 the EPA funded a project to monitor the burning of hazardous chemical wastes in a kiln owned by the San Juan Cement Company in Puerto Rico. In effect, the government chose Puerto Ricans as guinea pigs, but from the perspective of government and industry leaders, such burning would enhance the profitability of American cement companies. At the same time, it would partially solve the growing problem of waste disposal in the United States.[50]

Industry officials, in bitter competition with commercial waste incinerators, defend the burning of hazardous wastes in kilns at temperatures around 3,000 degrees as an environmentally sound, efficient way to dispose of hazardous materials. Ron Powell, vice president and general manager of Continental's Ilasco plant, emphasizes that PCBs and pesticides are not burned, only liquid solvents such as paint thinner and dry-cleaning fluids, as well as solid wastes such as oil-contaminated soil from refineries. He also stresses that stack emissions are strictly monitored. According to Powell, more than 99 percent of emissions from the plant's kiln consist of carbon dioxide and water vapor. "We believe it is recycling at its best," he asserts. "We are conserving fossil fuels—taking matter we can't take to landfills and getting the heating benefits from it and disposing of it in high-temperature gases."[51]

49. Bev Darr, "Continental Cement: Recycling on Grand Scale," in *Hannibal Courier-Post,* February 9, 1993; Betsy Carpenter and David Bowermaster, "The Cement Makers' Long, Sweet Ride: And Washington's New Environmental War," *U.S. News & World Report* 115 (July 19, 1993): 52. Andrew Hurley, *Environmental Inequalities: Class, Race, and Industrial Pollution in Gary, Indiana, 1945–1980,* is an excellent study of the connections between industrial pollution, class, and race in the steel community of Gary, Indiana, where the Universal Atlas Cement Company's Buffington plant was among the polluters.

50. Smith and Levin, "Multimedia Assessment," 62–63; *Minerals Yearbook 1981,* centennial ed., vol. 1, Metals and Minerals, 206.

51. Quoted in Darr, "Continental Cement."

Despite such assurances, public concern has mounted over the use of kilns to burn hazardous wastes. In January 1994 several environmental groups joined the Hazardous Waste Treatment Council, which represents commercial waste companies, in a petition requesting that the EPA ban waste burning at several cement plants, including those in Missouri. This has added fuel to the conflict between cement officials and the federal government over environmental regulations. The industry had no trouble with the more lax environmental policies of Presidents Reagan and Bush, but a recent EPA internal memorandum in the administration of President Bill Clinton called attention to numerous problems and spotty enforcement. According to this memorandum, 20 percent of plants inspected by the EPA failed to provide adequate training to personnel; 56 percent did not properly analyze burned waste; and 62 percent did not feed waste into kilns in compliance with established guidelines. In 1993 the EPA slapped a $3.4 million fine on the River City Cement Company's plant near St. Louis for such violations. "It seems to me," noted Roger Pryor, executive director of the Missouri Coalition for the Environment, "the last thing they need is any break from regulation."[52]

At a time when the U.S. Justice Department has launched a nationwide investigation into alleged price-fixing in the cement industry, the EPA's proposal to tighten regulatory guidelines for stack emissions of dioxins from cement kilns has particularly angered the Continental Cement Company and its subsidiary, Missouri Fuel Recycler, which handles the waste materials. This, along with the publication of a letter from a former discharged employee warning of regulatory violations at the Ilasco plant, produced an ambitious public relations program by Continental to ease public fears. In September 1994 the company held an open house so that the public could tour the Ilasco plant's laboratory and computerized monitoring equipment. Henry Winders, director of environmental affairs at the plant, acknowledged that a few "records-keeping" violations had occurred, but emphasized that there had been "no spills, no fires, no major violations."[53]

---

52. *Wall Street Journal,* January 31, 1994; Jeanne Zelten and Ardel Rueff, "The Mineral Industry of Missouri," *Minerals Yearbook 1992,* vol. 2, Area Reports: Domestic, 306; Carpenter and Bowermaster, "The Cement Makers' Long, Sweet Ride"; Jock Ferguson, "Burning Question: Cement Companies Go Toxic," 306–8. Pryor quoted in *St. Louis Post-Dispatch,* July 14, 1995.

53. Quoted in Susan Denkler, "Continental Shows Off Fuels Lab," *Hannibal Courier-Post,* September 14, 1994. At the open house, the Continental Cement Company distributed a brochure, "Taking the Resources of Nature and Giving Them Back," which explains plant operations and touts the company's commitment to the environment. On the allegations by a former Continental employee and denials by other company employees and officials, see the "Letters to the Editor" section of the *Ralls County Herald-Record-Enterprise,* July 21 and August 4, 1994. On the Justice Department's price-fixing investigation, see *New York Times,* March 11, 1994. By February 1995, the price of cement

A few weeks after the open house, Ron Powell publicly warned that tougher regulations under consideration by the EPA might force a shutdown of the plant. In a letter to plant employees, he dismissed the EPA's proposal to lower allowable dioxin emissions as nothing more than an attempt to carry out "a political agenda set by the Clinton White House." He urged them to flood Congress with letters of protest to save their jobs.[54]

Powell did not have to worry about the Republican-dominated Congress elected in 1994 or Missouri Senators John Ashcroft and Christopher Bond, who have stood guard over the cement industry's interests. Through the budget process and a new regulatory overhaul bill in late 1995, Missouri's Republican senators have sought to curtail the EPA's regulatory power over cement kilns. Missouri's four cement plants that burn waste in their kilns do a sizable business taking in wastes from other states and countries. They account for about 25 percent of disposal capacity in the cement industry.[55]

As this simmering environmental controversy further suggests, the history of Ilasco and workers at the cement plant illustrates the overwhelming power of the twentieth-century alliance between big business and the State. Atlas and the state militia had snuffed out growing labor unrest in 1910; afterward, ethnic and racial divisions, company paternalism, and the desperate plight of Ilasco workers further delayed the unionization of cement plant workers until 1943. Unable to make much headway against the political and economic power of Atlas in the meantime, workers devoted their energies to building schools, churches, and a stable community life. In the end, however, the State and private capital gutted their union and destroyed the community, too. Many former residents no doubt share Juanita Cross Venditti's frustration that just as they were beginning to build good schools and other institutions, outside forces tore down everything they had built.[56]

The extinction of Ilasco wiped out more than sixty years of community building. An eyesore and nuisance in the eyes of many in the area, Ilasco from the beginning had posed problems for Atlas officials. The need to control not only the land but also the people themselves had led Atlas to maneuver to acquire the Heinbach and Johnson tracts in order to convert the community

---

had reached as high as sixty-six dollars per ton in some areas, an increase of more than ten dollars per ton since July 1994. See Robert Lenzner, "Set in Concrete: Cement Industry Thrives," *Forbes,* July 18, 1994, 42–43, and *Wall Street Journal,* February 2, 1995.

54. Quoted in Gil Stuenkel, "EPA Regulations: Plausible or Politics?" *Hannibal Courier-Post,* October 6, 1994.

55. "Cement Makers Get Fired Up over EPA Waste-Burning Rules," *St. Louis Post-Dispatch,* July 14, 1995; "House Conservatives Step Up Assault on Regulations," *Washington Post,* July 19, 1995.

56. Juanita Cross Venditti, interview by author, July 9, 1993.

into a company town and stabilize labor relations. When Hannibal commercial interests and plans for regional highway construction intersected with Universal Atlas's need to become more competitive in Mississippi River Valley markets by modernizing and expanding production facilities, Ilasco's fate was sealed. The search for ever greater corporate profits and the commercialization of Mark Twain required destruction of the "city of dust."

In most respects, Ralls County has yet to experience a New South transformation. By 1960, its population had steadily dropped to 8,078, a 37.4 percent decline since 1910. New London, the county seat and largest town, had a population of only 875 in 1960.[57] Racism, public fears and ethnic hatred of Ilasco's immigrants, Atlas's overwhelming power, and the subservience of Ralls County politicians to Atlas officials cut short Ilasco's growth on any terms other than those dictated by the company. Because of Ilasco's location so near to Hannibal and Marion County, Hannibal businesses reaped the lion's share of economic benefits brought by the cement plant. The Saverton industrial park concept, so touted by those who pressured the highway commission to reroute Highway 79 through Ilasco, never got off the ground.

Despite a rich legacy of struggle and resistance, Ilasco is a symbol of the broader political defeat of the American working class in the twentieth century. The increasing globalization of capital has shredded American workers, their institutions, and in the case of Ilasco, even their community. Former residents and workers at the present time can only express their sense of loss through their private thoughts, anger, and cultural tenacity as they try to hang on to their past and perhaps consider alternative strategies of resistance.

---

57. *Census Reports,* vol. 1, 1960 Census of Population, Characteristics of the Population, pt. A, Number of Inhabitants, 27–21; *Census Reports,* vol. 1, 1960 Census of Population, Characteristics of the Population, pt. 27, Missouri, 21.

(EPILOGUE)

Whose History? Whose Mark Twain?

Life does not consist mainly—or even largely—of facts and happenings. It consists mainly of the storm of thoughts that is forever blowing through one's head.
—Mark Twain, *Autobiography*

My first time home after the farm was sold was hard for me, when I saw how the Cement plant had drilled and blasted away all the farmland. It was nothing but big holes instead of fields.
—Armenia Genovese Erlichman, July 9, 1992

On May 28, 1994, a few hundred people gathered at the Holiday Inn in Hannibal, Missouri, to attend the Ilasco–Marble Creek–Stillwell School Reunion. Attendance had dropped since the last reunion on May 23, 1987, but thanks in large part to the Ilasco Committee, enthusiasm was still high. Anita Altheide, Andy Babyak Jr., Virginia Beckett, Doris Benz, Mary Rita Brothers, Pete Galluzzio, Mary Alice Hamilton, Mildred Mozis, Loraine Robb, and Jim and Dorothy Tatman had worked hard to arrange the special weekend festivities for former residents, who now lived all over the country. Throughout the dinner that evening and picnic the following day, attendees shared food, drinks, memories of Ilasco, and a lot of old stories.

As the invited speaker that evening, I went not just to fulfill an obligation, but also to find a piece of myself that I had somehow lost since the days when I used to ride with my mother from Monkey Run through Ilasco to the cement plant quarry to pick up my dad after work. Here was a chance to reconnect with the kid who used to rummage through his father's lunch bucket for a piece of pie or cupcake generously left there at the end of a hard workday. A chance to remember Al's Tavern after little league baseball games, when Al Venditti smiled and handed me free sodas for every home run I hit. A chance to reconnect with tricksters and the art of storytelling.

In most respects, all of us from Ilasco came from "the wrong side of the tracks," or in the case of my mother's maternal boat dwellers, from the wrong side of Hannibal's river levee. The reunion would provide an opportunity to observe how we had coped with that stigma in our own individual ways. Here was a chance to reflect on common struggles that had shaped our identities and destinies. In some cases, such reflection risked reopening old wounds. Why, thirty years after my father's death, could I still see that unmistakable look of age in the eyes of a young bent-over man when the cement plant's four o'clock whistle sent him home exhausted at the end of a day? Why did emphysema rob him of life at the early age of forty-eight after years of suffering and disability?

But this would also be a time of renewal, a time of appreciation. A time to look into the proud eyes of my mother in the audience, to give her back something. A time to thank her for those strong working hands, for teaching me to embrace struggle, sacrifice, and hard work as a way of life. For being two parents, for her love of community and Ilasco. For the humor she finds in people and storytelling, for emphasizing education.

I remembered how surprised and excited I was when Andy Babyak called in the fall of 1993 to invite me to speak at the reunion. Over the years, I had written a few songs about the community, but this was different. In May 1994, I felt a deep sense of responsibility as I grabbed notecards and guitar and loaded the car for the trip home from San Marcos, Texas.

I became apprehensive as the evening approached. I had been home many times to see my family over the years, but this trip unsettled my emotions more than others. Perhaps I had read Ron Powers's *White Town Drowsing* too many times for my own good. Which Mark Twain would I invoke that evening? Since Hannibal businessmen and cement plant officials had long appropriated Tom Sawyer, could I then claim Huck Finn for Ilasco? Which side of himself would Twain display if he were there? What would he say? Would he restrict himself to "corn-pone opinions" so as not to ruffle anyone's feathers, or would he unleash his humanitarian side—that "pen warmed-up in hell"?[1]

Maybe I should not have read Twain's biting analysis of industrial capitalism in *The Mysterious Stranger.* Had I read too many grisly descriptions of accidents at the cement plant before the 1930s? Too many court cases in which crippled and dead victims of accidents seemed less important than the "Moral Sense" of property rights and corporate quarterly earnings? Perhaps I had spent too much time in the basement of dusty courthouses puzzling out the history of legal battles over land ownership in Ilasco? Too much time figuring out why the county committed Euphemia Koller to the state insane asylum in Fulton in

---

1. Quoted in Frederick Anderson, ed., *A Pen Warmed-Up in Hell: Mark Twain in Protest,* x, xiii.

1927? Did other former residents of Ilasco share my view that we had as much right to own the history of our community as did those in corporate boardrooms and high commercial chambers who destroyed it? Or was it that old tombstones, unmarked graves, and buried communities weighed too heavily on my mind as I entered Hannibal's city limits for the reunion?

I wondered how the audience would react to a critical interpretation of Ilasco's history. With few exceptions, many knew nothing about the occupation of the town by the state militia in 1910. Many assumed that the cement plant had always owned the town site, and few understood exactly why Ilasco was destroyed. So with a bit of trepidation on a weekend devoted to sharing old memories, visiting, and funny stories, I chose to focus my talk on the politics of the history of our community.

After sharing my thoughts and a few community-related songs that I had written, I was overwhelmed by the approving eyes of people in the audience eager for their history to be told at last. Afterward, many told me privately of their long-standing anger at the way the company had handled the community's dissolution and treated their families. Others chose to remember Atlas in a more favorable light, emphasizing company paternalism and the new job opportunities created in Ilasco. For better or worse, their families' lives had been connected to the cement plant. The struggle was especially hard for the first and second generations, and many in the community and Europe had lost loved ones in accidents at the plant. On the other hand, many took advantage of the cement plant's comparatively high wages in an otherwise low-wage area to do well. No matter how successful they had become or how far away they had moved, however, Ilasco was still at the core of their identity. Ilasco was still home.

Before leaving Hannibal a couple of weeks later, I had many opportunities to reflect on the meaning and significance of the Ilasco experience. Each time I drove to Hannibal and back from my mother's home just south of Ilasco, I contemplated the changes in the landscape since the mid-1960s. Beautiful new homes and subdivisions now dot the countryside along Highway 79 south of Ilasco. Ilasco was a casualty of the relocated route, but the highway has stimulated Hannibal's tourist industry and provided a beautiful scenic route along the Mississippi River. Passengers on the Twainland Express now catch an impressive view of the river as they top a hill south of Hannibal before dropping down to visit the Mark Twain Cave picnic area. On the east side of the highway across from the cave area, Sawyer's Creek features dining, miniature golf, and other amusements and gift shops, as well as a good view of the river.

Thanks to the Mark Twain Home Foundation and its director, Henry Sweets, an impressive restoration of the Mark Twain Boyhood Home has taken place in recent years. Beyond that, however, routine commercialization has left Twain, his thought, and his writings devoid of meaning in most quarters of Hannibal. In the mid-1980s, author Ron Powers observed how meaningless Twain's name has become to most Hannibal residents bombarded daily by commercial exploitation of their town's most famous citizen. The appropriation of Twain by local restaurants, hotels, stores, and even the community mental health center has created among residents "a weariness bordering on contempt" for his very name. Hannibal, as Powers noted, has chosen Tom, not Huck, as its "defining symbol . . . Tom the entrepreneur, the slick swapper, the get-ahead politician of the white-washed fence—the embracer, in the end, of the adult burgher values."[2]

On this trip, however, I was not looking for slick swappers, gift shops, or get-ahead politicians. I parked the car at Al's Tavern and walked through the brush and weeds to find the floor of the old gymnasium, sidewalks, and other remains of what had once been school buildings. These were the souvenirs that I was after. If only Melvenah Cattle Davis, my fifth- and sixth-grade teacher, were still alive, I could share so much with her. I could thank her for encouraging intellectual curiosity, for later buying me a Hannibal library card, and for introducing pupils to classical music. Most importantly, I could thank her for devoting her life to educating Ilasco's working-class children.

As I carefully picked my way through thickets and kept an eye out for snakes, I could not help but note how quickly brush, trees, dynamite, and bulldozers can bury the history of a community. Frustrated, I stepped back and tried to recall visually where each house and building once stood, but the highway and cement plant expansion made it impossible to do so. I closed my eyes and strained to hear joyous singing coming from the brush where I once sat in pews of the small Church of the Nazarene, but noise from nearby highway traffic interfered. At least the abandoned old jail was still there for me to look inside of once again before getting back into the car and heading south on Highway 79.

I noticed that new landscaping between the highway and the plant has gotten rid of some of the residual ugliness left by the flattening of Ilasco. In part, this beautification is a product of the Continental Cement Company's recent public relations campaign to calm public fears of dioxin emissions from kiln stacks. On both sides of the highway, however, the plant's seemingly insatiable appetite for limestone has led to the dramatic expansion of quarries into what was once productive farmland. The cement plant's tract now consists of about thirty-five hundred acres.[3]

Since it was Memorial Day weekend, I stopped at the Marble Creek Cemetery to visit my father's grave. I recalled how the community had done so much to help us when he was sick. During the early stages of his illness, when he often could not perform his job duties in the quarry but was not yet eligible for disability benefits,

---

2. *White Town Drowsing,* 68, 258.

3. Bev Darr, "Continental Cement: Recycling on Grand Scale," *Hannibal Courier-Post,* February 9, 1993.

fellow workers pulled his load as well as their own. I recalled a Christmas when women from the Nazarene Church brought groceries to our house when he was bedridden and we were strapped for money. I also remembered when Denny Kolarik packed heavy oxygen tanks over a steep hill to our house when flood waters had cut off access to Monkey Run by road. These were memories of a working-class community pulling together for survival.

As I walked past Old World tombstones to the back of the small cemetery and stared off in the distance at Continental's quarries, I wondered what we had gained and lost in the last thirty years since the destruction of Ilasco. How would I answer that question if it were put to me? What would I say if my history students ask why we have become an atomized society that seems to have lost a sense of community? Would I tell them about Dorothy and Jim Tatman's "ILASCO" license plates and photo collection? Al's Tavern? John Wojcik's continued care of the Ilasco Holy Cross Catholic Church? David and Sally Polc's collection of Ilasco postcards and memorabilia? My mother's putting flowers on the unmarked grave of Euphemia Koller? Or, like Mark Twain when he was asked for his reaction to the fact that "Tom Sawyer's cave was now being ground into cement," would I say that "it was not worth while to talk about it at this late day and, to take it all around, it was a painful subject anyway"?[4]

All around me were visible signs that Atlas's definition of twentieth-century progress has triumphed, but at what price? I locked the gate to the cemetery and backed the car down to the highway without taking a final look back. I had done this too many times. I told myself to let go of the issue, but somehow could not push these thoughts out of my mind as I pulled onto the highway for the trip back to Texas. As I drove away, I was haunted by a remark that Anna Hustava Sanders had made to me about Atlas's version of progress that led to the destruction of Ilasco. "You know, Gregg," she said, "you can't just measure progress by the amount of concrete you pour."[5]

4. Neider, ed., *Autobiography*, 82.
5. Anna Hustava Sanders, interview by author, July 2, 1992.

(BIBLIOGRAPHY)

Manuscripts and Archival Sources

Center for American History, University of Texas, Austin: Texas State Federation of Labor. *Proceedings of the Annual Conventions 1935–1950.*

Western Historical Manuscript Collection, University of Missouri, Columbia:

Russell S. Bauder Papers, 1910–1971

James T. Blair Jr. Papers, 1957–1961

Clarence A. Cannon Papers, 1896–1964

John M. Dalton Papers, 1921–1965

Richard Dalton Papers, 1859–1922

James A. Davis Papers, 1937–1975

Herbert S. Hadley Papers, 1830–1943

Guy D. Helmick Manuscript, collection no. 995

Missouri Council of Defense Papers, 1917–1919

Missouri Council of Defense Papers, 1940–1945

Missouri Reports to North Central Association of Colleges and Secondary Schools, 1892–1962

Missouri State Labor Council, AFL-CIO Records, 1891–1975

Guy B. Park, Governors Papers, 1932–1936

George N. Peek Papers, 1911–1947

Typescript Collection, no. 995, vols. 6, 11

United States Selective Service System, Missouri, 1917–1918

University of Missouri, President's Office Papers, 1892–1966

U.S. Work Projects Administration, Historical Records Survey, Missouri, 1935–1942

Rex M. Whitton Papers

Hannibal Free Public Library:

Hannibal Chapter, Daughters of the American Revolution, Scrap Book, 1929–1936

Hannibal Chapter, Daughters of the American Revolution, Yearbooks, 1915–1941

Home for the Friendless, Records, 1876–1956

Mississippi Department of Archives and History, Jackson, Miss.:

Mississippi Highway Department, record group 55

Missouri Highway and Transportation Archives, Jefferson City, Mo.:

Missouri Highway Commission, Minutes

Missouri Office of the Secretary of State, Corporation Division, Jefferson City, Mo.:

Folders on Corporations Registered in Missouri

Missouri State Archives, Jefferson City, Mo.:

Missouri Supreme Court Files

State Historical Society of Wisconsin, Madison:
> American Federation of Labor Records, pt. 2, President's Office Files, series A, William Green Papers, 1934–1952 (Frederick, Md.: Microfilm, University Publications of America, Inc., 1986)

Missouri Historical Society, St. Louis:
> David Francis Papers
> Missouri State Federation of Labor, Proceedings 1935

Western Historical Manuscript Collection, University of Missouri, St. Louis:
> International Association of Machinists and Aerospace Workers, District No. 9, 1901–1965

National Archives, Washington, D.C.:
> Record group 1, Records of the War Labor Policies Board
> Record group 9, Records of the National Recovery Administration
> Record group 28, Records of the U.S. Postal Service
> Record group 40, General Records of the Department of Commerce. General Correspondence of the Office of the Secretary of Commerce, 1929–1933.
> Record group 61, Minutes of War Industries Board Meetings, 1917–1918
> Record group 65, Records of the Federal Bureau of Investigation. Investigative Case Files of the Bureau of Investigation, 1908–1922.
> Record group 69, Work Projects Administration Central Files: State, 1935–1944

Local Court Records

Hannibal Court of Common Pleas, Hannibal, Mo.
Lewis County, Office of the Circuit Clerk and Recorder, Monticello, Mo.
Marion County, Office of the Circuit Clerk and Recorder, Palymra, Mo.
Pike County, Office of the Circuit Clerk, Bowling Green, Mo.
Pike County, Office of the Circuit Clerk, Pittsfield, Ill.
Pike County, Office of the County Clerk, Pittsfield, Ill.
Ralls County, Office of the Circuit Clerk and Recorder, New London, Mo.
Ralls County, Office of the County Clerk, New London, Mo.
Ralls County, Office of the Probate Clerk, New London, Mo.

Published Court Proceedings

Mary Goucan, Appellant v. Atlas Portland Cement Company and L. J. Boucher, July 30, 1927. *Missouri Reports: Reports of Cases Determined by the Supreme Court of the State of Missouri.* Columbia: E. W. Stephens Publishing Company, 1928. Vol. 317, 919–33.

Mary Alice Heinbach, Appellant v. Jesse Heinbach et al., November 24, 1914. *Missouri Reports: Reports of Cases Determined by the Supreme Court of the State of Missouri.* Columbia: E. W. Stephens Publishing Company, 1915. Vol. 262, 69–91.

In RE Otis M. Gallant and Marion J. Hannigan, June 30, 1936. *Missouri Appeal Reports: Cases Determined by the St. Louis, Kansas City and Springfield Courts of Appeals of the State of Missouri.* Columbia: E. W. Stephens, 1937. Vol. 231, 150–69.

State v. James Zugras, December 31, 1924. *Missouri Reports: Reports of Cases Determined by the Supreme Court of the State of Missouri.* Columbia: E. W. Stephens Company, 1925. Vol. 306, 492–99.

Joseph C. Thomas, Respondent v. Atlas Portland Cement Company, Appellant, December 5, 1922. *Missouri Appeal Reports: Cases Determined by the St. Louis, Kansas City and Springfield Courts of Appeals of the State of Missouri.* Columbia: E. W. Stephens Publishing Company, 1923. Vol. 211, 141–49.

George E. Yost, Respondent v. Atlas Portland Cement Company, Appellant, June 8, 1915. *Missouri Appeal Reports: Cases Determined by the St. Louis, Kansas City and Springfield Courts of Appeals of the State of Missouri.* Columbia: E. W. Stephens Publishing Company, 1915. Vol. 191, 422–34.

Bulletins, Reports, Proceedings, and Official Publications

American Federation of Labor (AFL-CIO). *Report of Proceedings of the Annual Conventions* 1903–1987.

The Atlas Almanac (Atlas Portland Cement Company)

The Atlas Bulletin (Atlas Portland Cement Company)

The Atlas Circle (Atlas Portland Cement Company)

Biennial Report of the Adjutant General of the State of Missouri for the Years 1909–10 (Jefferson City, Mo.: Hugh Stephens, 1910)

Cement Record

Congressional Record

Federal Trade Commission Decisions

Missouri Air News (monthly newsletter of the Missouri Air Conservation Commission)

Missouri Anti-Saloon League. *The Missouri Issue The American Issue.*

Missouri Bar Association. *Report of the Proceedings of the Annual Meeting 1880–1930.*

Missouri Bar Journal

Missouri Bureau of Labor Statistics. *Annual Reports.*

Missouri Council of Defense. *Missouri on Guard.*

Missouri Department of Labor and Industrial Inspection. *Annual Reports.*

Missouri Department of Natural Resources, Air Pollution Control Program. *Missouri Air Resources: 1982 Air Quality Report.*

Missouri Department of Natural Resources, Division of Environmental Quality Waste Management Program. *Annual Report.*

Missouri General Assembly, House of Representatives. "Report of the Committee to Investigate the Feasibility and Practicability of the State Acquiring Raw Materials for the Purpose of Manufacturing Portland Cement to the Fifty-First General Assembly." Jefferson City, Mo., 1921.

Missouri Red Book 1918–1920

Missouri Relief Commission. "Work Relief in Missouri, 1934–35." Compiled by William Gammon. Jefferson City, Mo., 1935.

Missouri Relief and Reconstruction Commission. "Emergency Relief in Missouri, September 1932 to November 1934." Vol. 1.

———. "Handbook for Community Organizers and County Social Workers in Putnam, Ralls, Randolph, Ray, Reynolds, and Ripley Counties." Columbia, Mo., The Commission, 1934.

Missouri Secretary of State. *Official Manual.*

Missouri State Board of Health. *Annual Report 1914–1917.*

Missouri State Board of Immigration. *First Annual Report* 1910.

Missouri State Federation of Labor. *Proceedings* 1906, 1909–1912, 1914, 1935.

Missouri State Highway Commission. *Annual Report.*

Missouri Workmen's Compensation Commission. "Third Annual Report for the Period from January 1, 1929, through December 31, 1929." Jefferson City, Mo.

Missouri. "Biennial Report of the State Tax Commission."

Missouri. *Journal of the House of Representatives.*

Missouri. *Journal of the Senate.*

Monthly Labor Review

National Labor Relations Board. *Decisions and Orders of the National Labor Relations Board.* Vols. 52, 292. Washington, D.C.: U.S. Government Printing Office, 1944, 1991.

"Parkway for the Mississippi: A Report to the Congress by the Bureau of Public Roads and the National Park Service." Washington, D.C.: U.S. Government Printing Office, 1951.

Portland Cement Association (Association of American Portland Cement Manufacturers). *Bulletin.* Philadelphia: Portland Cement Association, 1905–1911.

Rock Products

Smith, Ronald F., and James E. Levin. "Multimedia Assessment and Environmental Research Needs of the Cement Industry." Cincinnati: U.S. Environmental Protection Agency, 1979.

Stone

United States Bureau of Public Roads. "Report on a Recommended Route for the Great River Road (Mississippi River Parkway) through the State of Missouri." November 15, 1957.

United States Bureau of Public Roads. "Report on Recommendations for Land Acquisition, Scenic Easement, and Control of Access for the Great River Road in the State of Missouri." December 21, 1965.

United States Department of the Interior, Bureau of Mines. *Minerals Yearbook.*

United States Geological Survey. *Mineral Resources of the United States.*

United States Immigration Commission. *Reports of the Immigration Commission, 1907–1910.* Washington, D.C.: U.S. Government Printing Office, 1911.

United States Supreme Court. *Reports.*

Women's Christian Temperance Union, Missouri. *Proceedings of the Annual Convention* 1900–1917.

World Cement

Published and Unpublished United States Censuses

United States Bureau of the Census. Federal Manuscript Censuses, 1850–1960. Lehigh County, Pa.; Marion County, Ralls County, Mo.; Pike County, Ill.

United States Census. *Census Reports.* Twelfth Census of the United States Taken in the Year 1900. Vol. 1: Population, pt. 1. Washington, D.C.: United States Census Office, 1901.

———. *Census Reports.* Thirteenth Census of the United States Taken in the Year 1910. Vol. 2: Population. Washington, D.C.: U.S. Government Printing Office, 1911.

———. *Census Reports*. Fourteenth Census of the United States Taken in the Year 1920. Vol. 1: Population. Washington, D.C.: U.S. Government Printing Office, 1921.

———. *Census Reports*. Fifteenth Census of the United States, 1930. Vol. 3, pt. 1. Washington, D.C.: U.S. Government Printing Office, 1932.

———. *Census Reports*. Sixteenth Census of the United States, 1940. Vol. 2: Population, pt. 4. Washington, D.C.: U.S. Government Printing Office, 1943.

———. *Census Reports*. 1960 Census of Population. Vol. 1: Characteristics of the Population, pt. A. Number of Inhabitants. Washington, D.C.: U.S. Government Printing Office, 1961.

Interviews and Correspondence

Interviews by Author

Rita Mack Beaty, June 23, 1992, Ilasco, Mo.
Armenia Genovese Erlichman, July 9, 1992, Hannibal, Mo.
Charles Glascock, July 10, 1992, Hannibal, Mo.
Kenny Lawson, July 6, 1992, Ilasco, Mo.
David Polc, October 16, 1994, Ilasco, Mo.
Anna Hustava Sanders, July 2, 1992, Monkey Run, Mo.
Richard Sanders, July 2, 1992, Monkey Run, Mo.
Virginia Sanders Sudholt, July 12, 1992, Ilasco, Mo.
Henry Sweets, July 17, 1992, Hannibal, Mo.
Dorothy Smith Tatman, June 25, 1992, July 26, 1993, New London, Mo.
Jim Tatman, June 25, 1992, July 26, 1993, New London, Mo.
Angelo Venditti, July 9, 1993, Hannibal, Mo.
Anna Sunderlik Venditti, June 24 and July 6, 1992, July 27, 1993, Ilasco, Mo.
Juanita Cross Venditti, July 9, 1993, Hannibal, Mo.

Other Interviews and Tapes Provided to Author

Perry Jones Jr., tape, December 5, 1994
Mildred Viglasky Martinovich, interview by Sally Polc, October 30, 1994
Ruby Douglas Northcutt, undated video interview by Jim Tatman, c. 1990
Ruby Douglas Northcutt, interview by Virginia Sudholt, March 25, 1993
Anna Zivicky Polc, tape, March 9, 1989
Bryan Sigler, interview by Roberta Roland Hagood and J. Hurley Hagood, January 24, 1983.

Correspondence

C. R. Altheide, Plant Manager, Continental Cement Company, to author, March 4, 1982
Jane Hemeyer to author, October 29, 1994
Charles C. Huntbach, International Representative, Cement, Lime, Gypsum and Allied Workers Division, to author, October 13, 1993
Perry Jones Jr. to author, September 6, 1994
Mildred Kitsock King to author, March 10 and 20, 1993
John Konko to author, June 16, 1994

Gloria Vajda Manary to author, June 29, 1994
Mildred Viglasky Martinovich to author, October 30, 1994
Rosa H. Nemes to author, August 2 and September 25, 1994
Shirley Lee O'Keefe to author, October 17, 1992
David J. Polc to author, September 5, 1994
Stanley D. Sajban to author, July 4 and August 28, 1994
Henry Sweets to author, August 26, 1991

Telephone Interviews

Pete Galluzzio, June 14, 1994
Jane Hemeyer, October 30, 1994

Books

Alexander, June Granatir. *The Immigrant Church and Community: Pittsburgh's Slovak Catholics and Lutherans, 1880–1915.* Pittsburgh: University of Pittsburgh Press, 1987.

Allen, Barbara, and Thomas J. Schlereth, eds. *Sense of Place: American Regional Cultures.* Lexington: University Press of Kentucky, 1990.

American Social History Project. *Who Built America? Working People and the Nation's Economy, Politics, Culture, and Society.* Vol. 2, *From the Gilded Age to the Present.* New York: Pantheon Books, 1992.

Anderson, Frederick, ed. *A Pen Warmed-Up in Hell: Mark Twain in Protest.* New York: Harper and Row, 1972.

Arlacchi, Pino. *Mafia, Peasants and Great Estates: Society in Traditional Calabria,* translated by Jonathan Steinberg. Cambridge: Cambridge University Press, 1983.

Asher, Robert. "Industrial Safety and Labor Relations in the United States, 1865–1917." In *Life and Labor: Dimensions of American Working-Class History,* edited by Charles Stephenson and Robert Asher, 115–30. Albany: State University of New York Press, 1986.

———. "The Limits of Big Business Paternalism: Relief for Injured Workers in the Years before Workmen's Compensation." In *Dying for Work: Workers' Safety and Health in Twentieth-Century America,* edited by David Rosner and Gerald Markowitz, 19–33. Bloomington: Indiana University Press, 1987.

Asher, Robert, and Charles Stephenson, eds. *Labor Divided: Race and Ethnicity in United States Labor Struggles, 1835–1960.* Albany: State University of New York Press, 1990.

Ayers, Edward L. *The Promise of the New South: Life after Reconstruction.* New York: Oxford University Press, 1992.

Ayres, Alex, ed. *The Wit and Wisdom of Mark Twain.* New York: Meridian, 1989.

Bacon, Thomas H. *A Mirror of Hannibal.* Hannibal, Mo.: C. P. Greene, 1905.

Baron, Ava, ed. *Work Engendered: Toward a New History of American Labor.* Ithaca: Cornell University Press, 1991.

Barton, Josef John. *Peasants and Strangers: Italians, Rumanians, and Slovaks in an American City, 1890–1950.* Cambridge, Mass.: Harvard University Press, 1975.

Bernstein, Irving. *Turbulent Years: A History of the American Worker, 1933–1941.* Boston: Houghton Mifflin, 1970.

Blackford, Mansel K., and K. Austin Kerr. *Business Enterprise in American History.* 2d ed. Boston: Houghton Mifflin Company, 1990.

Blair, Walter, ed., with an introduction. *Mark Twain's Hannibal, Huck and Tom.* Berkeley: University of California Press, 1969.

Bluestone, Barry, and Bennett Harrison. *The Deindustrialization of America.* New York: Basic Books, 1982.

Blunt, Roy D. *Historical Listing of the Missouri Legislature.* Jefferson City, Mo.: Missouri State Archives, 1988.

Boan, Fern. *A History of Poor Relief Legislation and Administration in Missouri.* Chicago: University of Chicago Press, 1941.

Bodnar, John. *Immigration and Industrialization: Ethnicity in an American Mill Town, 1870–1940.* Pittsburgh: University of Pittsburgh Press, 1977.

————. *Workers' World: Kinship, Community, and Protest in an Industrial Society, 1900–1940.* Baltimore: Johns Hopkins University Press, 1982.

Bodnar, John E., Roger Simon, and Michael P. Weber. *Lives of Their Own: Blacks, Italians, and Poles in Pittsburgh, 1900–1960.* Urbana: University of Illinois Press, 1982.

Bordin, Ruth. *Women and Temperance: The Quest for Power and Liberty, 1873–1900.* Philadelphia: Temple University Press, 1981.

Boris, Eileen. "Reconstructing the 'Family': Women, Progressive Reform, and the Problem of Social Control." In *Gender, Class, Race, and Reform in the Progressive Era,* edited by Noralee Frankel and Nancy S. Dye, 73–86. Lexington: University of Kentucky Press, 1991.

Borsody, Stephen, ed. *The Hungarians: A Divided Nation.* New Haven: Yale Center for International and Area Studies, 1988.

Brandes, Stuart D. *American Welfare Capitalism, 1880–1940.* Chicago: University of Chicago Press, 1970.

Brecher, Jeremy. *Strike.* San Francisco: Straight Arrow Books, 1972.

Brody, David. *In Labor's Cause: Main Themes on the History of the American Worker.* New York: Oxford University Press, 1993.

————. *Steelworkers in America: The Nonunion Era.* New York: Harper and Row, 1969.

————. *Workers in Industrial America: Essays on the Twentieth Century Struggle.* 2d ed. New York: Oxford University Press, 1993.

Brown, Ronald C. *Hard-Rock Miners: The Intermountain Years, 1860–1920.* College Station: Texas A&M University Press, 1979.

Bucke, Emory Stevens, ed. *The History of American Methodism.* 3 vols. New York: Abingdon Press, 1964.

Buehler, Henry Andrew. *The Lime and Cement Resources of Missouri.* Jefferson City, Mo.: Hugh Stephens, 1907.

Burchard, Ernest F. *The Cement Industry in the United States in 1909, 1910, 1911, 1914.* Washington, D.C.: Department of the Interior, U.S. Geological Survey.

Burnett, Joe, et al. "A Brief History of Ralls County." n.p., 1936.

Byington, Margaret F. *Homestead: The Households of a Mill Town.* With a new introduction by Samuel P. Hays. Pittsburgh: University of Pittsburgh Press, 1974. Originally published in 1910.

Bynum, Victoria E. *Unruly Women: The Politics of Social and Sexual Control in the Old South*. Chapel Hill: University of North Carolina Press, 1992.

Cameron, Ardis. "Landscapes of Subterfuge: Working-Class Neighborhoods and Immigrant Women." In *Gender, Class, Race, and Reform in the Progressive Era*, edited by Noralee Frankel and Nancy S. Dye, 56–72. Lexington: University of Kentucky Press, 1991.

Carlton, David L. *Mill and Town in South Carolina, 1880–1920*. Baton Rouge: Louisiana State University Press, 1982.

Carroll, S. S., et al. *Atlas of Ralls County Missouri*. Des Moines, Iowa: Kenyon Printing and Manufacturing, 1904.

The Cement Industry: Descriptions of Portland and Natural Cement Plants in the United States and Europe, with Notes on Materials and Processes in Portland Cement Manufacture. New York: reprinted from *The Engineering Record 1900*.

Clinton, Catherine. *The Other Civil War: American Women in the Nineteenth Century*. New York: Hill and Wang, 1984.

Conroy, Jack. *The Disinherited: A Novel of the 1930s*. Introduction by Douglas Wixson. Columbia: University of Missouri Press, 1991. Originally published in 1933.

Corbin, David Alan. *Life, Work, and Rebellion in the Coal Fields: The Southern West Virginia Miners, 1880–1922*. Urbana: University of Illinois Press, 1981.

Crow, Hiawatha. "I Remember." In *2 good 2 be 4 gotten*, compiled by Hannibal Writers Club, 40–42. 2d ed. Hannibal, Mo.: Hannibal Writers Club, 1982.

Cuff, Robert D. *The War Industries Board: Business-Government Relations during World War I*. Baltimore: Johns Hopkins University Press, 1973.

Marianne Debouzy, ed. *In the Shadow of the Statue of Liberty: Immigrants, Workers, and Citizens in the American Republic, 1880–1920*. Urbana: University of Illinois Press, 1992.

De Navarro, Jose F. *Sixty-Years' Business Record*. New York: H. Bigelow and Company, 1904.

Douglas, Mary. *Purity and Danger: An Analysis of Concepts of Pollution and Taboo*. Baltimore: Penguin Books, 1970.

Dublin, Thomas, ed. *Immigrant Voices: New Lives in America, 1773–1986*. Urbana: University of Illinois Press, 1993.

Eckel, Edwin C. *The Cement Industry in the United States, in 1906, 1907, 1908*. Washington, D.C.: Department of the Interior, U.S. Geological Survey.

Ehrlich, Richard L., ed. *Immigrants in Industrial America, 1850–1920*. Charlottesville: University Press of Virginia, 1977.

Eller, Ronald D. *Miners, Millhands, and Mountaineers: Industrialization of the Appalachian South, 1880–1930*. Knoxville: University of Tennessee Press, 1982.

Epstein, Barbara Leslie. *The Politics of Domesticity: Women, Evangelism and Temperance in Nineteenth-Century America*. Middletown, Conn.: Wesleyan University Press, 1981.

Erlichman, Armenia Genovese, comp. "Genovese Family History, 1907–1994." Peoria, Ill.: n.p., 1994.

Faragher, John Mack. *Sugar Creek: Life on the Illinois Prairie*. New Haven: Yale University Press, 1986.

Faue, Elizabeth. *Community of Suffering and Struggle: Women, Men, and the Labor*

Movement in Minneapolis, 1915–1945. Chapel Hill: University of North Carolina Press, 1991.

Fellman, Michael. *Inside War: The Guerrilla Conflict in Missouri during the American Civil War.* New York: Oxford University Press, 1989.

Fenton, Edwin. *Immigrants and Unions, A Case Study: Italians and American Labor, 1870–1920.* New York: Arno Press, 1975.

Fink, Gary M. *Labor's Search for Political Order: The Political Behavior of the Missouri Labor Movement, 1890–1940.* Columbia: University of Missouri Press, 1973.

Fink, Gary M., ed. *Labor Unions.* Westport, Conn.: Greenwood Press, 1977.

Fink, Gary M., and Merl E. Reed, eds. *Race, Class, and Community in Southern Labor History.* Tuscaloosa: University of Alabama Press, 1994.

Foner, Philip S. *History of the Labor Movement in the United States.* Vol. 2, *From the Founding of the A.F. of L. to the Emergence of American Imperialism.* New York: International Publishers, 1980.

———. *History of the Labor Movement in the United States.* Vol. 3, *The Policies and Practices of the American Federation of Labor, 1900–1909.* New York: International Publishers, 1981.

———. *History of the Labor Movement in the United States.* Vol. 7, *Labor and World War I, 1914–1918.* New York: International Publishers, 1987.

———. *Mark Twain: Social Critic.* New York: International Publishers, 1958.

Fones-Wolf, Elizabeth A. *Selling Free Enterprise: The Business Assault on Labor and Liberalism, 1945–60.* Urbana and Chicago: University of Illinois Press, 1994.

Frankel, Noralee, and Nancy S. Dye, eds. *Gender, Class, Race, and Reform in the Progressive Era.* Lexington: University Press of Kentucky, 1991.

Fraser, Steve, and Gary Gerstle, eds. *The Rise and Fall of the New Deal Order, 1930–1980.* Princeton: Princeton University Press, 1989.

Gabaccia, Donna. *Militants and Migrants: Rural Sicilians Become American Workers.* New Brunswick: Rutgers University Press, 1988.

Galambos, Louis. *Competition and Cooperation: The Emergence of a National Trade Association.* Baltimore: Johns Hopkins University Press, 1966.

———. *The Public Image of Big Business in America, 1880–1940: A Quantitative Study in Social Change.* With the Assistance of Barbara Barrow Spence. Baltimore: Johns Hopkins University Press, 1975.

Georgescu, Vlad. *The Romanians: A History.* Edited by Matei Calinescu. Translated by Alexandra Bley-Vroman. Columbus: Ohio State University Press, 1991.

Gerlach, Russel L. *Settlement Patterns in Missouri: A Case Study of Population Origins.* Columbia: University of Missouri Press, 1986.

Gerstle, Gary. *Working-Class Americanism: The Politics of Labor in a Textile City, 1914–1960.* Cambridge: Cambridge University Press, 1989.

Gibbs, Christopher C. *The Great Silent Majority: Missouri's Resistance to World War I.* Columbia: University of Missouri Press, 1988.

Gordon, Colin. *New Deals: Business, Labor, and Politics in America, 1920–1935.* Cambridge: Cambridge University Press, 1994.

Gordon, Linda. *Heroes of Their Own Lives: The Politics and History of Family Violence.* New York: Penguin, 1988.

————. *Woman's Body, Woman's Right: A Social History of Birth Control in America.* New York: Penguin Books, 1977.

Graff, Gerald, and James Phelan, eds. *Mark Twain Adventures of Huckleberry Finn: A Case Study in Critical Controversy.* Boston: Bedford Books, 1995.

Green, James R. *The World of the Worker: Labor in Twentieth-Century America.* New York: Hill and Wang, 1980.

Green, Marguerite. *The National Civic Federation and the American Labor Movement, 1900–1925.* Washington, D.C.: Catholic University of America Press, 1956.

Greene, Victor R. *The Slavic Community on Strike: Immigrant Labor in Pennsylvania Anthracite.* Notre Dame: University of Notre Dame Press, 1968.

Greenwald, Maurine W. *Women, War and Work: The Impact of World War I on Women Workers in the United States.* Westport, Conn.: Greenwood Press, 1980.

Griffith, Barbara S. *The Crisis of American Labor: Operation Dixie and the Defeat of the CIO.* Philadelphia: Temple University Press, 1988.

Gross, James A. *The Reshaping of the National Labor Relations Board: National Labor Policy in Transition, 1937–1947.* Albany: State University of New York Press, 1981.

Gusfield, Joseph R. *Symbolic Crusade: Status Politics and the American Temperance Movement.* 2d ed. Urbana: University of Illinois Press, 1986.

Gutman, Herbert G. *Work, Culture, and Society in Industrializing America: Essays in American Working-Class History.* New York: Alfred A. Knopf, 1976.

Hadley, Earl J. *The Magic Powder: History of the Universal Atlas Cement Company and the Cement Industry.* New York: G. P. Putnam's Sons, 1945.

Hagood, J. Hurley, and Roberta Roland Hagood, *Hannibal: Mark Twain's Town.* Marceline, Mo.: Jostens, 1987.

————. *Hannibal Yesterdays: Historic Stories of Events, People, Landmarks and Happenings in and near Hannibal.* Marceline, Mo.: Jostens, 1992.

————. "History of the Hannibal National Bank, 1888–1988." Hannibal, Mo.: n.p., 1988.

————. "A List of Deaths in Hannibal, Missouri, 1880–1910." Rev. ed. Hannibal: n.p., 1990.

————. *The Story of Hannibal.* Hannibal, Mo.: Standard Printing, 1976.

Hall, Jacquelyn Dowd, James Leloudis, Robert Korstad, Mary Murphy, Lu Ann Jones, and Christopher P. Daly. *Like a Family: The Making of a Southern Cotton Mill World.* Chapel Hill: University of North Carolina Press, 1987.

Hannibal Chamber of Commerce. "Hannibal, Missouri: The Boyhood Home of Mark Twain, Where the Traditions of Huckleberry Finn and Tom Sawyer Still Live." Hannibal, Mo.: Hannibal Chamber of Commerce, n.d.

————. "Mark Twain Centennial, 1835–1935: Hannibal, Missouri." Hannibal, Mo.: n.p., 1935.

Hannibal Writers Club, comp. *2 good 2 be 4 gotten.* 2d ed. Hannibal, Mo.: Hannibal Writers Club, 1982.

Harris, Howell John. *The Right to Manage: Industrial Relations Policies of American Business in the 1940s.* Madison: University of Wisconsin Press, 1982.

Harrison, Bennett, and Barry Bluestone. *The Great U-Turn: Corporate Restructuring and the Polarizing of America.* New York: Basic Books, 1988.

Hawley, Ellis W. *The Great War and the Search for a Modern Order: A History of the American People and Their Institutions, 1917–1933.* 2d ed. New York: St. Martin's Press, 1992.

———. *The New Deal and the Problem of Monopoly: A Study in Economic Ambivalence.* Princeton: Princeton University Press, 1966.

Himmelberg, Robert F. *The Origins of the National Recovery Administration: Business, Government, and the Trade Association Issue, 1921–1933.* New York: Fordham University Press, 1976.

Himmelberg, Robert F., ed., with introductions. *Business and Government in America since 1870.* Vol. 7, *The New Deal and Corporate Power: Antitrust and Regulatory Policies during the Thirties and World War II.* New York and London: Garland, 1994.

Hine, Darlene Clark. "Rape and the Inner Lives of Southern Black Women: Thoughts on the Culture of Dissemblance." In *Southern Women: Histories and Identities,* edited by Virginia Bernhard, Betty Brandon, Elizabeth Fox-Genovese, and Theda Purdue, 177–89. Columbia: University of Missouri Press, 1992.

Hoerder, Dirk, ed. *American Labor and Immigration History, 1877–1920s: Recent European Research.* Urbana: University of Illinois Press, 1983.

———. *"Struggle a Hard Battle": Essays on Working-Class Immigrants.* DeKalb: Northern Illinois University Press, 1986.

Honey, Michael K. *Southern Labor and Black Civil Rights: Organizing Memphis Workers.* Urbana: University of Illinois Press, 1993.

Howard, Goldena. *Ralls County Missouri.* Marceline, Mo.: Walsworth, 1980.

Hoy, Suellen. *Chasing Dirt: The American Pursuit of Cleanliness.* New York and Oxford: Oxford University Press, 1995.

Hurley, Andrew. *Environmental Inequalities: Class, Race, and Industrial Pollution in Gary, Indiana, 1945–1980.* Chapel Hill: University of North Carolina Press, 1995.

Hurt, R. Douglas. *Agriculture and Slavery in Missouri's Little Dixie.* Columbia: University of Missouri Press, 1992.

Huthmacher, J. Joseph, and Warren I. Sussman, eds. *Herbert Hoover and the Crisis of American Capitalism.* Cambridge, Mass.: Schenkman, 1973.

Janiewski, Dolores E. *Sisterhood Denied: Race, Gender, and Class in a New South Community.* Philadelphia: Temple University Press, 1985.

Kirkendall, Richard S. *A History of Missouri, Volume V: 1919 to 1953.* Columbia: University of Missouri Press, 1986.

Land Atlas and Plat Book: Ralls County, Missouri. Rockford, Ill.: Rockford Map Publishers, 1981.

Leach, Mrs. Frank Sayre. *Missouri State History of the Daughters of the American Revolution.* Sedalia, Mo.: n.p., 1929.

Lesley, Robert W., John B. Lober, and George S. Bartlett. *History of the Portland Cement Industry in the United States.* New York: Arno Press, 1972. Originally published in 1924.

Levine, Lawrence W. *Black Culture and Black Consciousness: Afro-American Folk Thought from Slavery to Freedom.* New York: Oxford University Press, 1977.

Lichtenstein, Nelson. "From Corporatism to Collective Bargaining: Organized Labor and the Eclipse of Social Democracy in the Postwar Era." In *The Rise and Fall of the New Deal Order, 1930–1980,* edited by Steve Fraser and Gary Gerstle, 122–52. Princeton: Princeton University Press, 1989.

———. *Labor's War at Home: The CIO in World War II.* Cambridge: Cambridge University Press, 1982.

Loescher, Samuel M. *Imperfect Collusion in the Cement Industry.* Cambridge, Mass.: Harvard University Press, 1959.

Lynch, David. *The Concentration of Economic Power.* New York: Johnson Reprint Corporation, 1970. Originally published in 1946.

McCandliss, Edgar S., and Henry H. Armsby. *An Investigation of Blended Portland Cement.* Rolla, Mo.: School of Mines and Metallurgy, University of Missouri, 1918.

McElvaine, Robert S. With a New Introduction. *The Great Depression: America, 1929–1941.* New York: Times Books, 1993.

McKiven, Henry M. Jr. *Iron and Steel: Class, Race, and Community in Birmingham, Alabama, 1875–1920.* Chapel Hill: University of North Carolina Press, 1995.

McReynolds, Edwin C. *Missouri: A History of the Crossroads State.* Norman: University of Oklahoma Press, 1962.

March, David D. *The History of Missouri.* 4 vols. New York and West Palm Beach: Lewis Historical Publishing, 1967.

Meade, George. *Portland Cement.* 2d ed. Baltimore: Chemical Publishing, 1911.

Milkman, Ruth. *Gender at Work: The Dynamics of Job Segregation by Sex during World War II.* Urbana: University of Illinois Press, 1987.

Miller, Randall M., and Thomas D. Marzik, eds. *Immigrants and Religion in Urban America.* Philadelphia: Temple University Press, 1977.

Miller, Sally M. *From Prairie to Prison: The Life of Social Activist Kate Richards O'Hare.* Columbia: University of Missouri Press, 1993.

Mitchell, Franklin D. *Embattled Democracy: Missouri Democratic Politics, 1919–1932.* Columbia: University of Missouri Press, 1968.

Mixon, Wayne. *Southern Writers and the New South Movement, 1865–1913.* Chapel Hill: University of North Carolina Press, 1980.

Montgomery, David. *The Fall of the House of Labor: The Workplace, the State, and American Labor Activism, 1865–1925.* Cambridge: Cambridge University Press, 1987.

———. *Workers' Control in America: Studies in the History of Work, Technology, and Labor Struggles.* Cambridge: Cambridge University Press, 1979.

Moody, J. Carroll, and Alice Kessler-Harris, eds. *Perspectives on American Labor History: The Problems of Synthesis.* DeKalb: Northern Illinois University Press, 1990.

Morawska, Ewa. *For Bread with Butter: The Life-Worlds of East Central Europeans in Johnstown, Pennsylvania, 1890–1940.* Cambridge: Cambridge University Press, 1985.

Mormino, Gary Ross. *Immigrants on the Hill: Italian-Americans in St. Louis, 1882–1982.* Urbana: University of Illinois Press, 1986.

National Guard, Missouri. *History of the Missouri National Guard.* n.p., 1934.

Neider, Charles, ed. *The Autobiography of Mark Twain.* New York: Harper and Row, first Perennial Library Edition, 1975.

Nelli, Humbert S. *From Immigrants to Ethnics: The Italian Americans.* New York: Oxford University Press, 1983.

Nelson, Daniel. *Managers and Workers: Origins of the New Factory System in the United States, 1880–1920.* Madison: University of Wisconsin Press, 1975.

Paine, Albert Bigelow, ed. *Mark Twain's Letters.* 2 vols. New York: Harper and Brothers, 1917.

———. *Mark Twain's Notebook.* New York: Harper and Brothers, 1935.

Painter, Nell Irvin. *Standing at Armageddon: The United States, 1877–1919.* New York: W. W. Norton and Company, 1987.

Parrish, William E., Charles T. Jones Jr., and Lawrence O. Christensen. *Missouri: The Heart of the Nation.* 2d ed. Arlington Heights, Ill.: Harlan Davidson, 1992.

Pettit, Arthur G. *Mark Twain and the South.* Lexington: University of Kentucky Press, 1974.

Portrait and Biographical Record of Marion, Ralls, Pike Counties Missouri 1895. Rev. ed. New London, Mo.: Ralls County Book Co., 1982. Originally published in 1895.

Powers, Marion. "Today Is Better." In *2 good 2 be 4 gotten,* compiled by Hannibal Writers Club, 19–21. 2d ed. Hannibal, Mo.: Hannibal Writers Club, 1982.

Powers, Ron. *White Town Drowsing: Journeys to Hannibal.* Boston: Atlantic Monthly Press, 1986.

Primm, James Neal. *Lion of the Valley: St. Louis, Missouri.* 2d ed. Boulder, Colo.: Pruett, 1990.

Prpic, George J. *South Slavic Immigration in America.* Boston: Twayne, 1978.

Rafter, Nicole Hahn, ed. *White Trash: The Eugenic Family Studies, 1877–1919.* Boston: Northeastern University Press, 1988.

Ravage, M. E. *An American in the Making.* New York: Harper and Brothers, 1917.

Rayback, Joseph G. *A History of American Labor.* Expanded and updated ed. New York: Free Press, 1966.

Reid, Loren. *Hurry Home Wednesday: Growing Up in a Small Missouri Town, 1905–1921.* Columbia: University of Missouri Press, 1978.

Roberts, Charles Rhoads, Rev. John Baer Stoudt, Rev. Thomas H. Krick, and William J. Dietrich. *History of Lehigh County Pennsylvania and a Genealogical and Biographical Record of Its Families.* Allentown, Pa.: Lehigh Valley Publishing, 1914.

Roediger, David R. *The Wages of Whiteness: Race and the Making of the American Working Class.* London: Verso, 1991.

———. *Towards the Abolition of Whiteness: Essays on Race, Politics, and Working-Class History.* London and New York: Verso, 1994.

Rose, Nancy E. *Put to Work: Relief Programs in the Great Depression.* New York: Monthly Review Press, 1994.

Rosenblum, Gerald. *Immigrant Workers: Their Impact on American Labor Radicalism.* New York: Basic Books, 1973.

Rosenzweig, Roy. *Eight Hours for What We Will: Workers and Leisure in an Industrial City, 1870–1920.* Cambridge: Cambridge University Press, 1983.

Rosner, David, and Gerald Markowitz. *Deadly Dust: Silicosis and the Politics of Occupational Disease in Twentieth-Century America.* Princeton: Princeton University Press, 1991.

Rosswurm, Steve, ed. *The CIO's Left-Led Unions.* New Brunswick: Rutgers University Press, 1992.

Rumbarger, John J. *Profits, Power, and Prohibition: Alcohol Reform and the Industrializing of America, 1800–1930.* Albany: State University of New York Press, 1989.

Salomon, Roger B. *Twain and the Image of History.* New Haven: Yale University Press, 1961.

Scarpino, Philip V. *Great River: An Environmental History of the Upper Mississippi, 1890–1950.* Columbia: University of Missouri Press, 1985.

Schiavo, Giovanni. *The Italians in Missouri.* New York: Arno Press, 1975. Originally published in 1929.

Schlesinger, Arthur Jr. *The Coming of the New Deal: The Age of Roosevelt.* With a New Foreword. Boston: Houghton Mifflin, 1988. Originally published in 1958.

Schwehn, Rev. W. G. "A Brief Historical Sketch of Saint John's Evangelical Lutheran Church, Hannibal, Missouri." Hannibal, Mo.: n.p., 1935.

Seton-Watson, R. W. *A History of the Czechs and Slovaks.* Hamden, Conn.: Archon Books, 1965. Originally published in 1943.

Settle, William A. Jr. *Jesse James Was His Name; or, Fact and Fiction Concerning the Careers of the Notorious James Brothers of Missouri.* Columbia: University of Missouri Press, 1966.

Sexton, Patricia Cayo. *The War on Labor and the Left: Understanding America's Unique Conservatism.* Boulder, Colo.: Westview Press, 1991.

Shepherd, Fred C., and Associates. *The New 1968 Atlas of Ralls County, Missouri.* Webster Groves, Mo.: Fred C. Shepherd and Associates, 1968.

Shifflett, Crandall A. *Coal Towns: Life, Work, and Culture in Company Towns of Southern Appalachia, 1880–1960.* Knoxville: University of Tennessee Press, 1991.

Shoemaker, Floyd Calvin. *Missouri and Missourians: Land of Contrasts and People of Achievements.* 5 vols. Chicago: Lewis, 1943.

Smashey, Philip C., comp. "History of the Smasheys, 1770–1992." Osprey, Fla.: n.p., 1972.

Smith, Timothy L. *Called Unto Holiness. The Story of the Nazarenes: The Formative Years.* Kansas City: Nazarene Publishing House, 1962.

Stolarik, M. Mark. *Growing Up on the South Side: Three Generations of Slovaks in Bethlehem, Pennsylvania, 1880–1976.* Lewisburg: Bucknell University Press, 1985.

———. "Immigration, Education, and the Social Mobility of Slovaks, 1870–1930." In *Immigrants and Religion in Urban America,* edited by Randall M. Miller and Thomas D. Marzik, 103–16. Philadelphia: Temple University Press, 1977.

———. "Immigration and Urbanization: The Slovak Experience, 1870–1918." Ph.D. diss., University of Minnesota, 1974.

Synan, Vinson. *The Holiness-Pentecostal Movement in the United States.* Grand Rapids, Mich.: William B. Eerdmans, 1971.

Taft, Philip. *The A.F. of L. from the Death of Gompers to the Merger.* New York: Harper and Brothers, 1959.

Teller, Michael E. *The Tuberculosis Movement: A Public Health Campaign in the Progressive Era.* Westport, Conn.: Greenwood Press, 1988.

The Termination Report of the National War Labor Board: Industrial Disputes and Wage Stabilization in Wartime. Vol. 2, Appendices to vol. 1, pt. 1. Washington, D.C.: U.S. Government Printing Office, 1947.

Thelen, David. *Paths of Resistance: Tradition and Democracy in Industrializing Missouri.* Columbia: University of Missouri Press, paperback ed., 1991.

Tomlins, Christopher L. *The State and the Unions: Labor Relations, Law, and the Organized Labor Movement in America, 1880–1960.* Cambridge: Cambridge University Press, 1985.

Towne, Ruth W. "The Movement for Workmen's Compensation Legislation in Missouri, 1910–1925." Master's thesis, University of Missouri, 1940.

Twain, Mark. *A Connecticut Yankee in King Arthur's Court*. New York: Signet, n.d. Originally published in 1889.

———. *Letters from the Earth*. Edited by Bernard DeVoto with a Preface by Henry Nash Smith. New York: Harper and Row, Perennial Library Edition, 1974.

———. *Life on the Mississippi*. New York: Harper and Brothers, 1903.

———. *Roughing It*. With a Foreword by Leonard Kriegel. New York: Signet Classic, 1962. Originally published in 1872.

———. *The Adventures of Huckleberry Finn*. New York: Airmont Books, 1962.

———. *The Adventures of Tom Sawyer*. New York: Airmont Books, 1962. Originally published in 1876.

———. *The Innocents Abroad*. With an Afterword by Leslie A. Fiedler. New York: Signet Classic, 1966.

———. *The Mysterious Stranger*. New York, 1916.

Universal Atlas Cement Company. "Safety Trophy Dedication Hannibal Plant." N.p., June 24, 1936.

Vecoli, Rudolph J. "Cult and Occult in Italian-American Culture: The Persistence of a Religious Heritage." In *Immigrants and Religion in Urban America,* edited by Randall M. Miller and Thomas D. Marzik, 25–47. Philadelphia: Temple University Press, 1977.

———. *Italian American Radicalism: Old World Origins and New World Developments*. Staten Island, N.Y.: American Italian Historical Association, 1973.

Vecoli, Rudolph J., ed. *Italian Immigrants in Rural and Small Town America*. Staten Island, N.Y.: American Italian Historical Association, 1987.

Way, Peter. *Common Labour: Workers and the Digging of North American Canals, 1780–1860*. Cambridge: Cambridge University Press, 1993.

Webster, Samuel Charles, ed. *Mark Twain, Business Man*. Boston: Little Brown, 1946.

West, Percy C. H. *The Modern Manufacture of Portland Cement: A Handbook for Manufacturers, Users, and All Interested in Portland Cement*. Vol. 1, *Machinery and Kilns*. London: Crosby Lockwood and Son, 1910.

White, Ronald C. Jr., and C. Howard Hopkins. *The Social Gospel: Religion and Reform in Changing America*. Philadelphia: Temple University Press, 1976.

Williams, Phyllis H. *South Italian Folkways in Europe and America: A Handbook for Social Workers, Visiting Nurses, School Teachers, and Physicians*. New Haven: Yale University Press, 1938.

Williams, Walter, ed. *The State of Missouri: An Autobiography*. Columbia, Mo.: E. W. Stephens, 1904.

Williamson, Joel. *The Crucible of Race: Black-White Relations in the American South since Emancipation*. New York: Oxford University Press, 1984.

Woodward, C. Vann. *Origins of the New South, 1877–1913*. Baton Rouge: Louisiana State University Press, 1951.

Youell, Velma. "Renault a/k/a Randolph." In *2 good 2 be 4 gotten,* compiled by Hannibal Writers Club, 14–18. 2d ed. Hannibal, Mo.: Hannibal Writers Club, 1982.

Zieger, Robert, ed. *Organized Labor in the Twentieth-Century South*. Knoxville: University of Tennessee Press, 1991.

Articles

Andrews, Gregg. "From Robber Caves to Robber Barons: New South Missouri and the Social Construction of Mark Twain, 1910–1935." *Gateway Heritage* 15 (fall 1994): 4–15.

———. "Ilasco Cement Workers and the War on Booze in Ralls County, Missouri, 1903–1914." *Gateway Heritage* 16 (spring 1996): 2–13.

———. "Immigrant Cement Workers: The Strike of 1910 in Ilasco, Missouri." *Missouri Historical Review* 89 (January 1995): 162–83.

Baily, Samuel L. "The Italians and the Development of Organized Labor in Argentina, Brazil, and the United States, 1880–1914." *Journal of Social History* 3 (winter 1969–1970): 123–34.

Barrett, James R. "Americanization from the Bottom Up: Immigration and the Remaking of the Working Class in the United States, 1880–1930." *Journal of American History* 79 (December 1992): 996–1020.

———. "Unity and Fragmentation: Class, Race, and Ethnicity on Chicago's South Side, 1900–1922." *Journal of Social History* 18 (1985): 37–55.

Bodnar, John, Michael Weber, and Roger Simon. "Migration, Kinship, and Urban Adjustment: Blacks and Poles in Pittsburgh, 1900–1930." *Journal of American History* 66 (December 1979): 548–65.

Brownlee, Richard S., James W. Goodrich, and Mary K. Dains, "The State Historical Society of Missouri, 1898–1973." *Missouri Historical Review* 68 (1973): 1–27.

Bucki, Cecelia F. "Workers and Politics in the Immigrant City in the Early Twentieth-Century United States." *International Labor and Working-Class History* 48 (fall 1995): 28–48.

Buhle, Paul. "Italian-American Radicals and Labor in Rhode Island, 1905–1930." *Radical History Review* 17 (1978): 121–51.

Cantor, Milton. "Work, Industry, and Community: A Review Essay on Labor and Ethnicity." *Journal of American Ethnic History* 3 (spring 1984): 74–81.

Carpenter, Betsy, and David Bowermaster. "The Cement Makers' Long, Sweet Ride: And Washington's New Environmental War." *U.S. News and World Report* 115 (July 19, 1993): 51–53.

Carter, Paul Jr. "Mark Twain and the American Labor Movement." *New England Quarterly* 30 (September 1957): 382–88.

Castiglione, G. E. DiPalma. "Italian Immigration into the United States, 1901–1904." *American Journal of Sociology* 11 (1905): 183–206.

"Cement Company Paves a Route for Waste Disposal." *The Oil Daily,* November 20, 1990, 4.

Christensen, Lawrence O. "Missouri's Responses to World War I: The Missouri Council of Defense." *Midwest Review* 12 (1990): 34–44.

———. "Popular Reaction to World War I in Missouri." *Missouri Historical Review* 86 (July 1992): 386–95.

Crisler, Robert M. "Missouri's 'Little Dixie.'" *Missouri Historical Review* 42 (October 1947–July 1948): 130–39.

"Demand Grows for Cement Plants to Burn Waste." *The Oil Daily,* July 16, 1991, 5.

Dorsett, Lyle, and Mary Dorsett. "Rhetoric versus Realism: 150 Years of Missouri Booster-ism." *Bulletin of the Missouri Historical Society* 28 (January 1972): 77–84.

Fatima, S. K., P. A. Prabhavathi, M. H. Prasad, P. Padmavathi, and P. P. Reddy. "Frequencies of Sister Chromatid Exchanges in Lymphocytes of Portland Cement Factory Workers." *Bulletin of Environmental Contamination and Toxicology* 55 (November 1995): 704–8.

Fenton, Edwin. "Italians in the Labor Movement." *Pennsylvania History* 26 (April 1959): 113–48.

Ferguson, Jock. "Toxic Cement." *The Nation,* March 8, 1993, 306–8.

Fink, Gary. "The Unwanted Conflict: Missouri Labor and the CIO." *Missouri Historical Review* 64 (July 1970): 432–47.

Gabaccia, Donna R. "Worker Internationalism and Italian Labor Migration, 1870–1914." *International Labor and Working-Class History* 45 (spring 1994): 63–79.

Gerstle, Gary. "The Politics of Patriotism: Americanization and the Formation of the CIO." *Dissent* 33 (winter 1986): 84–92.

Gobel, Thomas. "Becoming American: Ethnic Workers and the Rise of the CIO." *Labor History* 29 (spring 1988): 173–98.

Gordon, Linda. "Family Violence, Feminism, and Social Control." *Feminist Studies* 12 (fall 1986): 453–78.

Gutman, Herbert G. "Work, Culture, and Society in Industrializing America, 1815–1919." *American Historical Review* 78 (June 1973): 531–88.

Hall, Jacquelyn Dowd. " 'The Mind That Burns in Each Body': Women, Rape, and Racial Violence." *Southern Exposure* 12 (November/December 1984): 61–71.

Hiles, Bradley S., and Robert F. Wilkinson, "Bevill Amendment: Burning Hazardous Waste in Cement Kilns." *Missouri Law Review* 55 (spring 1990): 391–409.

Himmelberg, Robert F. "Business, Antitrust Policy, and the Industrial Board of the Depart-ment of Commerce, 1919." *Business History Review* 42 (spring 1968): 1–23.

Holt, John B. "Holiness Religion: Cultural Shock and Social Reorganization." *American Sociological Review* 5 (October 1940): 740–77.

Howenstine, E. Jay Jr. "The Industrial Board, Precursor of the N.R.A.: The Price-Reduction Movement after World War I." *Journal of Political Economy* 51 (June 1943): 235–50.

Jones, Charles Edwin. "Disinherited or Rural? A Historical Case Study in Urban Holiness Religion." *Missouri Historical Review* 66 (April 1972): 395–412.

Kossoris, Max D., and O. A. Fried. "Experience with Silicosis under Wisconsin Workmen's Compensation Act, 1920 to 1936." *Monthly Labor Review* 44 (May 1937): 1089–1101.

Lorch, Fred W. "Mark Twain in Iowa." *Iowa Journal of History and Politics* 27 (July 1929): 408–56.

Mahan, George A. "Missourians Abroad: Rear Admiral Robert E. Coontz, U.S.N." *Missouri Historical Review* 13 (July 1919): 372–76.

Mormino, Gary Ross. "Over Here: St. Louis Italo-Americans and the First World War." *Bulletin of the Missouri Historical Society* 30 (October 1973): 44–53.

Nelson, Daniel. "The Company Union Movement, 1900–1937: A Reexamination." *Business History Review* 56 (autumn 1982): 335–57.

Nichols, Alfred. "The Cement Case." *American Economic Review* 39 (May 1949): 297–310.

Norrell, Robert J. "Caste in Steel: Jim Crow Careers in Birmingham, Alabama." *Journal of American History* 73 (December 1986): 669–94.

Northrup, Herbert R. "From Union Hegemony to Union Disintegration: Collective Bargaining in Cement and Related Industries." *Journal of Labor Research* 10 (fall 1989): 337–76.

Pitcher, C. B. "The U.S. Cement Industry: Trade and Trends." *Construction Review* 36 (September/October 1990): iii–xiii.

Poage, Franklin. "Mark Twain Memorials in Hannibal." *Missouri Historical Review* 20 (October 1925): 79–84.

Powers, Madelon. "'The Poor Man's Friend': Saloonkeepers, Workers, and the Code of Reciprocity in U.S. Barrooms, 1870–1920." *International Labor and Working-Class History* 45 (spring 1994): 1–15.

Powers, Mary Buckner. "Toxics in Cement Kilns Fuel Industry Dispute." *ENR,* September 27, 1990, 80.

Pozzetta, George E. "Immigrants and Ethnics: The State of Italian-American Historiography." *Journal of American Ethnic History* 9 (fall 1989): 67–95.

Raiche, Stephen J. "The World's Fair and the New St. Louis, 1896–1904." *Missouri Historical Review* 67 (October 1972): 98–121.

Renner, G. K. "Prohibition Comes to Missouri, 1910–1919." *Missouri Historical Review* 62 (July 1968): 363–97.

Schoenberg, William. "The 'Basing Point' Decision: Ghost Towns Are in the Making If It Stands." *American Federationist* 56 (January 1949): 30–32.

———. "The National Council of United Cement Workers." *American Federationist* 44 (April 1937): 396–99.

Scott, Joan. "On Language, Gender, and Working-Class History," *International Labor and Working-Class History* 31 (spring 1987): 1–13.

Sheridan, Frank. "Italian, Slavic, and Hungarian Unskilled Immigrant Laborers in the United States." *U.S. Bureau of Labor Bulletin* 15 (September 1907): 403–86.

Smith, Henry Nash. "Mark Twain's Images of Hannibal: From St. Petersburg to Eseldorf." *Texas Studies in English* 37 (1958): 3–23.

Thompson, E. P. "Time, Work-Discipline, and Industrial Capitalism." *Past and Present* 38 (December 1967): 56–97.

Topkis, Bernard H. "Labor Requirements in Cement Production." *Monthly Labor Review* 42 (January 1936): 564–77.

Vecoli, Rudolph J. "Peasants and Prelates: Italian Immigrants and the Catholic Church." *Journal of Social History* 2 (spring 1969): 217–68.

Way, Peter. "Evil Humor and Ardent Spirits: The Rough Culture of Canal Construction Laborers." *Journal of American History* 79 (March 1993): 1397–1428.

Welter, Barbara. "The Cult of True Womanhood: 1820–1860." *American Quarterly* 18 (summer 1966): 151–74.

West, Mark I. "A Hannibal Boyhood." *Americana* 20 (October 1992): 34–42.

Whayne, Jeannie M. "The Significance of Race, Class, and Family in the Battle for Prohibition in Small Town Arkansas." *Locus* 7 (spring 1995): 129–49.

(INDEX)